Psychoanalysis and Management

Contributions to Management Science

Ulrich A. W. Tetzlaff
Optimal Design of Flexible Manufacturing Systems
1990. 190 pages. Softcover DM 69,-
ISBN 3-7908-0516-5

Fred von Gunten
Competition in the Swiss Plastics Manufacturing Industry
1991. 408 pages. Softcover DM 120,-
ISBN 3-7908-0541-6

Harald Dyckhoff/Ute Finke
Cutting and Packing in Production and Distribution
1992. 248 pages. Hardcover DM 120,-
ISBN 3-7908-0630-7

Hagen K. C. Pfeiffer
The Diffusion of Electronic Data Interchange
1992. 257 pages. Softcover DM 85,-
ISBN 3-7908-0631-5

Evert Jan Stokking / Giovanni Zambruno (Eds.)
Recent Research in Financial Modelling
1993. 174 pages. Softcover DM 90,-
ISBN 3-7908-0683-8

Richard Flavell (Ed.)
Modelling Reality and Personal Modelling
1993. 407 pages. Softcover DM 120,-
ISBN 3-7908-0682-X

Lorenzo Peccati / Matti Virén (Eds.)
Financial Modelling
1994. 364 pages. Softcover DM 98,-
ISBN 3-7908-0765-6

Michael Hofmann · Monika List (Eds.)

Psychoanalysis and Management

With Contributions by
S. Allcorn, G. Amado, H. S. Baum, M. A. Diamond, L. Gruenfeld
L. Hirschhorn, M. F. R. Kets de Vries, J. Krantz, J.-P. Larçon
H. Levinson, M. List, R. Reitter, H. S. Schwartz, H. F. Stein
A. Zaleznik

With 4 Figures

Springer-Verlag Berlin Heidelberg GmbH

Series Editor
Werner A. Müller
Peter Schuster

Editors
Professor Dr. Michael Hofmann
Mag. Monika List
Wirtschaftsuniversität Wien
Augasse 2-6
A-1090 Wien, Austria

ISBN 978-3-7908-0795-0

CIP-Kurztitelaufnahme der Deutschen Bibliothek

Psychoanalysis and management / Michael Hofmann; Monika List (eds.). With contributions by S. Allcorn ...

(Contributions to management science)
ISBN 978-3-7908-0795-0 ISBN 978-3-662-12847-3 (eBook)
DOI 10.1007/978-3-662-12847-3

NE: Hofmann, Michael [Hrsg.]; Allcorn, Seth

Ursprünglich erschienen bei Physica-Verlag Heidelberg 1994

2201/2202-543210 - Printed on acid-free paper

Preface

In the last years Europe was dominated by rapid changes in economic life. Increasing international competition and the opening of new markets were the basis for economic alliances. Many organizations were forced to merge with others in order to survive during a time of steady changes in technology. Due to the recession of today, insolvencies become more and more on this continent. The consequences are: restructuring of organizations, changes of organizational hierarchies and reduction of costs and personnel. This leads to different forms of anxiety of managers and subordinates, as well as to greater difficulties in cooperation, which is of specific importance in times of crisis. Workers and employees are afraid of losing their place of work. Distrust and competition between colleagues lead to the wish for a strong leader who guarantees order and security. Due to this fact leaders are confronted with many difficult demands which are still unknown to them. Changes in organizations lead to many fears: rivalry between parts of organizations, processes of defense and regression in groups of workers may have the consequence that a charismatic leader is asked. Managers who are not in the position to deal with this new situation and to understand the unconscious basis of this behavior will not be able to stand this stress. Due to such a change it becomes more and more important to draw attention to those unconscious and irrational ways of behavior which deteriorate a productive cooperation between the members of organizations.

Gaining a better knowledge for unconscious ways of behavior and their motivations is absolutely not new. There are already many interesting and important contributions such as papers which deal with psychodynamic aspects in organizations. Psychoanalytical concepts and ideas are extremely helpful for the analysis of organizations and the behavior of their members. As this fact has been accepted a small group of pioneers started in 1980 a symposium which was organized by Professor *Michael Hofmann* (University of Economics, Vienna) and took place for the first time in Austria.

This symposium was followed up by annual conferences, held by Professor *Leopold Gruenfeld* under the auspices of Cornell University. The foundation of ISPSO (International Society for the Psychoanalytic Study of Organizations) in 1986 led to an important forum of discussion which until today is including a great number of members and professionally interested persons. Each year their contributions are presented in a symposium. Due to discussions of case studies and their scientific results the development of this research work with the aim to understand not only conscious but also unconscious contents (imaginations, fantasies) makes it possible to recognize people and organizations much better. Working with fantasy turned out to be more effective than a mere positivistic approach.

This book has the intention to introduce this research work also to readers in Europe by specially chosen contributions from leading psychoanalytically oriented management theorists and clinicians. These papers which have been published between 1980 and 1992 in diverse journals, newspapers and books appear in a collection in order to demonstrate the development of this specific approach to the reader. The authors deal with different topics such as leadership, corporate culture, family business, organizational stress, career dynamics and so on. All of them try to win an understanding and insight into conscious, unconscious, rational and irrational behavior. This book has the intention to show to scientists, students, managers, consultants but also to the interested layman the possibility to gain new perspectives towards human behavior. The purpose of this book is fulfilled if this knowledge can be practiced in order to achieve improvements for the cooperation between people in general.

Overview of the Contents

The first contribution "Leadership Styles: The Psychological Picture" of *Seth Allcorn* demonstrates a psychodynamic model of leadership styles which are based on unconscious processes. The model is useful for understanding the motivations and actions of managers who experience stress originating from both internal and external sources.

"Psychoanalysis and Organization: A Cross-Cultural Approach" was presented by *Gilles Amado* at the 1st Interational Symposium on Applied Psychoanalysis in 1980. In this paper *G. Amado* develops the idea that the relations between psychoanalysis and organizations have been shaped by the cultural context in which they took place. In his second paper "A Clinical Approach to Meetings" *G. Amado* explains why meetings may become dysfunctional. The author describes different symptoms of such meetings and what can be done to avoid conflicts.

Modern service work in bureaucratic organizations requires possibilities for acting aggressively in intimate relationships without anxiety. *Howell S. Baum* describes in the article "Creating a Family in the Workplace" a local planning agency where staff created a "family" to solve these problems. This case offers lessons for modern, bureaucratic service work. In his second contribution "Mentoring: Narcissistic Fantasies and Oedipal Realities" *H. S. Baum* examines the literature on mentoring from a psychoanalytic perspective. He describes two common contrasting experiences of mentoring, harmony between a protege and a perfect mentor and sexuality and aggressive conflict between the protege and mentor, which are typically successive stages in mentoring relationships.

Michael Diamond focuses in his paper "The Social Character of Bureaucracy: Anxiety and Ritualistic Defense" on the analysis of the social character of bureaucracy. He describes the deeper connections between the psychodynamics of obsessional neurosis in the individual and ritualistic practices in bureaucracy. In his second contribution to this book "Organizational Identity - A Psychoanalytic Exploration of Organizational Meaning" *M. Diamond* examines the phenomenon of organizational identity and its underlying unconscious processes.

The essay of *Leopold Gruenfeld* "Field Independence/Dependence Reconsidered" calls for a reassessment of the polarized unidimensional construction of the field independent/dependent cognitive style. His paper consists of four parts. In the first part, a conceptual overview of the global-articulated style is presented with special emphasis on the domain of social behavior. In the second part, the application of the field independent/dependent framework to the study of leadership and teaching style is described. In the third part, a modified typology of stressed and composed cognitive styles is delineated and buttressed by findings from Bales' (1970, 1979) research on individual behavior in groups. In the fourth part, several methodological issues which appear to retard research on the field independent/dependent cognitive style are explored.

Larry Hirschhorn explains in his paper "Leaders and Followers in a Postindustrial Age: A Psychodynamic View" how important it is that leaders and followers recognize their dependence on one another and their need to collaborate. The author presents a typology of authority and illustrates his thoughts by means of case studies.

Manfred Kets de Vries discusses in his contribution "The Impostor Syndrome: Developmental and Societal Issues" the role of impostors in society. He shows psychodynamic inferences about the origin and characteristics of this particular character type and presents the case of Refaat El-Sayed, a recent example of an impostor in business. Alexithymia is a clinical construct which refers to individuals with an extreme reality-based cognitive style, an impoverished fantasy life, a paucity of inner emotional experiences, a tendency to engage in stereotypical interpersonal behavior, and a speech pattern characterized by endless, trivial, repetitive details. *M. Kets de Vries* hypothesizes that there is an interesting parallel between the organization man and those people with an alexithymic disposition. He discusses this in his paper "Alexithymia in Organizational Life: The Organization Man Revisited."

James Krantz analyses in his contribution "The Managerial Couple: Superior-Subordinate Relationships as a Unit of Analysis" effective and ineffective superior-subordinate relationships. His conclusion is that managers and subordinates must confront their feelings of dependency and vulnerability in order to work together successfully.

Larçon and Reitter view the man - organization relationship in the context of corporate imagery and corporate identity. The authors examine the foundations of this imagery and examine how it changes in time and how its identity can be created or altered. Their thoughts are illustrated by a study of a french furniture company in the article "Corporate Imagery and Corporate Identity".

In "Counseling with Top Management" *Harry Levinson* demonstrates that consultation with top management is a wide-ranging and varied task. He shows how important it is that the consultant makes use of developmental, clinical, child, family, organizational and industrial psychology, as well as management theory. In the paper "Leadership Anyone?" *H. Levinson* illustrates his opinion that leaders and leadership are cultivated by established leaders and other cultivators and are not "born" as suggested by many. Numerous examples of political, intellectual, artistic and business leadership are presented to support this view.

Howard Schwartz explains in his first paper anti-social actions of organizationally committed individuals on the basis of the "ontological" function of organizations. The author shows how the development of the potentiality for such anti-social action is built into the process of socialization for organizational commitment. *H.Schwartz* analyses in his second contribution "Narcissism Project and Corporate Decay" the case of General Motors and describes how dangerous it can be if an organization loses touch with reality.

By means of a case study of a medical corporation *Howard F. Stein* analyses and interpretes the group psychology of response to the threat of organization dissolution. The dynamics of catastrophic reaction are explored, and the writer's role as facilitator of verbalization and expression of group anxiety is described in the paper "Adapting to Doom: The Group Psychology of Organization Threatened with Cultural Extinction".

"Power and Politics in Organizations: Pragmatics and Pathologies" is the title of the paper in which *Abraham Zaleznik* examines the differences in the meaning of the concept of power in literature.

As *Zaleznik* is one of the founders of the ISPSO and an important pioneer in this movement, the last contribution is dedicated to his person and research work. "Human Dilemmas of Leadership" is one of the books which introduced this totally new scientific development concerning the problem of how to combine applied psychoanalysis and management discourse. Therefore I want to indicate in my paper how important these basic studies and ideas are still today.

By this collection of papers of different authors it is only possible to give to the reader an insight into this interesting research work. The application of psychoanalytical concepts on management is of great variety and of great hope for the future. Many more interesting contributions can be expected.

Monika List

Vienna, March 25th, 1994

Contents

Leadership Styles: The Psychological Picture

Seth Allcorn

Why do some managers give orders every step of the way while others leave employees almost entirely on their own? Why do some managers invite questions and suggestions while others decree the "right way" to do a job and discourage input from employees? Managers are effective not only because they demonstrate good administrative skills and technical know-how; an appropriate leadership style is equally important. Managerial leadership styles so profoundly affect employee morale and productivity that successful leadership can ultimately mean a successful organization. Understanding how and why organizations succeed thus includes understanding how various leadership styles develop. And learning to deal with the difficult manager can make life in the workplace easier for employees, colleagues, and supervisors.

Classification

Leadership styles, like many other types of human behavior, are often outcomes of coping mechanisms unconsciously developed in response to anxiety and stress. Figure 1, a psychodynamic model of leadership styles, illustrates how responses to stress lead to six basic leadership styles.

FIGURE 1: Psychodynamic Model of Leadership Styles

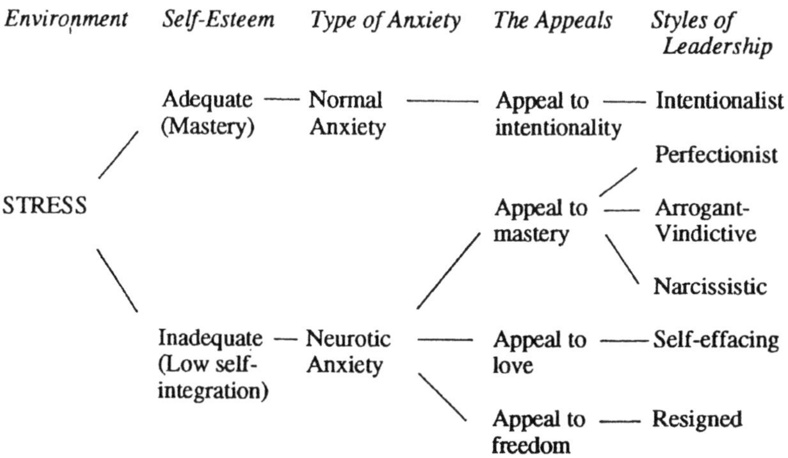

Academics, researchers, and theorists have identified and classified many other leadership styles according to various criteria. All of these leadership styles are reflections of the managers' psychological makeups. All have some elements in common with those shown in the model. After becoming familiar with some of these other leadership styles, we will study the model and learn more about how leadership styles develop.

Gordon L. Lippitt classifies leadership styles according to how decisions are made in an organization. His decision-making styles include:
- The autocratic style, in which decisions are made by the leader.
- The laissez-faire style, in which decisions are made by individuals.
- The democratic style, in which decisions are made by groups.
- The benevolently autocratic style, in which decisions are made by the leader (although some aspects of the democratic style are present).

In another system of classification, George R. Terry and R. H. Hermanson characterize leadership styles according to the type of communication and interaction that occur in the organization. They identify:
- Personal leadership, in which close interpersonal relationships develop and communication is usually face-to-face.
- Nonpersonal leadership, in which either (1) others communicate instructions from the leader or (2) oaths, creeds, and pledges are relied upon to elicit conforming behavior.
- Democratic leadership, in which group members participate in discussion and analysis of proposed management actions.
- Paternalistic leadership, in which the leader promotes dependence by protecting and taking care of group employees.
- Authoritarian leadership, in which a person in a position of authority makes decisions on the basis of that authority.
- Indigenous leadership, in which informal leadership is provided by different individuals at different times despite the presence of a formal leader.

Glenn A. Bassett discusses leadership styles with a view toward their long-term implications for the organization's culture. In this system:
- The authoritarian leadership style is a formal, bureaucratic style in which the leader makes all decisions and provides all organizational values. The style encourages dependency and reduces initiative among employees.
- The permissive leadership style provides employees with high levels of personal responsibility for organizational operations. The leader does not take an active part in directing work or setting values. The

style promotes employee independence, initiative, and self-development.
• The integrative style combines elements of the above two styles. Here, the leader is neither authoritarian nor permissive. Instead, he or she encourages a team effort in which everyone participates - under the direction of the leader.

Stephen J. Knezevich notes that some of the terms he uses to categorize leadership styles - anarchic, democratic, and autocratic - may have positive or negative connotations for readers.
• In the autocratic style, all decisions are made by the leader.
• In the democratic style, group participation occurs when appropriate to help the leader make decisions.
• In the anarchic style, a leader is present but provides no direction. Employees make all decisions.
• In the manipulative or pseudodemocratic style, the leader makes a decision but then appoints a committee to approve it, thus giving the appearance that he or she shares power.

J. W. Getzels and E. G. Guba describe three styles of leadership. The first two represent opposite poles on a continuum and the third is at the midpoint or compromise position:
• The nomothetic leader seeks employees' unthinking compliance with impersonal rules and formal organizational roles.
• The idiographic leader delegates authority and stresses the meeting of individual employee needs over the accomplishment of organizational objectives.
• The transactional leader tries to balance employees' personal needs with organizational objectives, usually by finding areas of compatibility. This leader may, however, adopt one of the other two styles under certain circumstances.

William J. Reddin identifies leadership styles and groups them according to their levels of effectiveness - effectiveness measured in terms of task-oriented and relationship-oriented behavior. It is important to note that in this system each manager's effectiveness depends not only on his or her orientation, but also on the appropriateness of that orientation to a particular situation. For example, the "missionary" and the "developer" both have low task and high interpersonal orientations. But because for the missionary this orientation is inappropriate to the situation, he or she is ineffective - while the developer, who has a similar orientation, is effective because the orientation is appropriate to a different situation. Less effective leadership styles include the compromiser, the autocrat, the missionary, and the deserter. These managers' styles do not fit their situations, and employees lack confidence in them.

- The compromiser has both a high task and a high interpersonal orientation when only one or neither of these is appropriate. This leader appears ineffective and easily influenced by others and by events. The results for the organization are short-term compromises that sacrifice long-term effectiveness.
- The autocrat has a high task and a low interpersonal orientation in situations where this is inappropriate. This leader is perceived to have little confidence in others and is generally disliked by employees.
- The missionary has a low task and a high interpersonal orientation in situations where this is inappropriate. This leader is seen as sacrificing organizational objectives in the pursuit of interpersonal harmony.
- The deserter has a low task and a low interpersonal orientation in situations were this is inappropriate. He or she is perceived as uninvolved and passive and unable to provide needed leadership and direction.

By contrast, the executive, the benevolent dictator, the developer, and the bureaucrat have more effective leadership styles. These managers' orientations are appropriate to their situations and their employees trust and respect them.

- The executive has a high task and a high interpersonal orientation in situations where this is appropriate. Thus this leader is perceived as setting standards and treating employees according to their individual needs. He or she is a good motivator.
- The benevolent dictator has a high task and a low interpersonal orientation in situations where this is appropriate. This leader is perceived as having clearly defined goals and being able to achieve them without alienating others.
- The developer has a low task and a high interpersonal orientation in situations where this is appropriate. He or she is perceived as trusting others and being interested in their personal development.
- The bureaucrat has a low task and a low interpersonal orientation in situations where this is appropriate. This leader is perceived as effectively using rules and procedures to control the actions of employees for the benefit of the organization.

Alexander W. Astin and Rita A. Scherrei identify five major styles of administrative behavior on the basis of an analysis of 60 different measures of college administrators. According to their findings:

- Hierarchical administrators tend not to communicate with employees. They reward competitiveness, discourage openness and frankness, and generally frustrate employees' needs for recognition and security.
- Humanistic administrators communicate freely with others. They reward openness and good interpersonal skills, discourage competitiveness and "apple polishing" to gain influence, and

generally create a setting where employees are comfortable and productive.

• Entrepreneurial administrators are aggressive, risk-taking, competitive, and frank. They reward these traits in others.

• Insecure administrators reward "apple polishing," influence peddling, and cronyism in their departments. They discourage their employees from demonstrating creativity, taking the initiative, and supporting others. They create an atmosphere of distrust where gossip and manipulative behavior abound.

• Task-oriented administrators reward employees for taking the initiative, cooperating, demonstrating professional and technical competence, and supporting others. They generally develop a work setting where employees feel secure and have a healthy sense of personal importance.

Motivation

The above leadership style classifications are based on observations of how managers behave and how their behavior affects the organization. But these classifications fail to explain the causes for this behavior. A conceptual framework for the psychological motivations of managers can help explain these causes.

As mentioned earlier, Figure 1 depicts a psychodynamic model of human behavior under stress. (This model was adapted from a 1985 model by Michael Diamond and Seth Allcorn.) The model is useful for understanding the motivations and actions of managers who experience stress originating from both internal and external sources - and how various leadership styles develop.

Stress

Stress consists of environmental events, very often interpersonal in nature, that are experienced as threatening. Punishment and disapproval, for example, are usually experienced as stressful. Driving home on icy streets is stressful. Encountering the resistance or rejection of others is stressful. Stress is not a feeling. Individuals who feel anxious in stressful situations are responding to stress in a particular way. The way an individual responds to stress is one of the factors that determine his or her leadership style.

Self-Esteem

Self-esteem is the ability to cope with environmental stress without (1) losing one's self-confidence or (2) feeling unable to cope with the situation (loss of self-integration). Depending on the individual's level of self-esteem, stress leads either to feelings of normal anxiety (where self-integration is sustained) or to neurotic anxiety, where self-fragmentation occurs. Self-esteem originates in interpersonal experiences starting at birth. An infant that experiences its mother and other caregivers as insensitive and unpredictable feels insecure. Because of this insecurity, the individual may develop a fragile (vulnerable) sense of self. He or she has difficulty coping with the environment and establishing successful interpersonal relationships. For such an individual, life may become filled with events and relationships that are experienced as distressing. As a result, the individual develops defensive coping mechanisms and compulsively relies upon them to feel safe in distressing situations.

Anxiety Levels

The model illustrates how individuals with adequate and inadequate self-esteem experience and handle stress. The individual with adequate self-esteem handles stress with self-confidence. He or she experiences normal anxiety and is not overly threatened by the stressor. The individual with inadequate self-esteem, however, experiences the stressful situation as unmanageable and threatening to the sense of self and personal security. These feelings lead to the more distressful experience of neurotic anxiety. The attempt to dispose of this neurotic anxiety, as depicted in the model, results in one of three self-defensive tendencies or appeals. For the individual in a leadership role, these tendencies, in turn, motivate certain leadership styles.

Responses to Anxiety: The Appeals

As the model illustrates, every individual responds to anxiety with an appeal: a tendency to approach people and problems in a particular way. When the individual experiences normal anxiety, the response is the nondefensive appeal to intentionality. Neurotic anxiety, however, brings about one of the three self-defensive appeals: the appeal to mastery, the appeal to love, or the appeal to freedom. As Karen Horney has explained in "Neurosis and Human Growth" (Norton, 1950), these three self-defensive tendencies are responses loaded with compulsive needs to control the distressing experience of neurotic anxiety.

APPEAL TO INTENTIONALITY

The appeal to intentionality arises from a secure sense of self. The individual experiences anxiety but does not respond defensively; he or she continues to feel and act competently despite feeling anxious. The individual can accept criticism and remain confident about his or her abilities and self-worth. Characteristics of the appeal to intentionality are nondefensive acceptance of criticism and feedback, self-reflection, sensitivity to the thoughts and feelings of others, flexible and critical thinking, innovation, willingness to change, rational decision making, and accurate perception of the environment. The appeal to intentionality leads to the intentionalist leadership style. He or she treats employees fairly and professionally and is not overly influenced by personal feelings. The individual adapts easily to organizational change and is generally liked and respected by employees and colleagues. Of the leadership classifications mentioned earlier, the appeal to intentionality is associated with the integrative, democratic, transactional, and executive styles.

APPEAL TO MASTERY

The appeal to mastery is a defensive response to neurotic anxiety. It is characterized by an attempt to dominate and control others. The individual believes that if he or she is energetic, smart, manipulative, aggressive, and persistent enough, anything can be accomplished. This appeal has its origins in the individual's contempt for his or her own feelings of weakness and dependence. He or she is determined to maintain a powerful, infallible self-image and makes every effort - through denial, rationalization, or other psychological defenses - to overcome any threat to this image. The appeal to mastery implies contempt for others - whose sole role is to bend to the leader's will.

The appeal to mastery leads to three possible leadership styles: perfectionistic, arrogant-vindictive, and narcissistic.

In the perfectionistic style, the individual sets nearly perfect standards for him- or herself and for the employees. Meeting these standards gives the individual a sense of superiority over others, and seeing others fail to meet them is taken as further proof that these people are inferior. Those who do not perform satisfactorily are judged as falling short of the leader's high standards. Perfectionistic leaders have clearly identifiable behavioral patterns. They pay obsessive attention to detail and order, punctuality, and dress. They have very strict moral and ethical standards governing most behavior and take an excessively critical view of the behavior and work of others.

The arrogant-vindictive manager, who also appeals to mastery, is arrogant and proud, and places high value on competitiveness and winning. Weakness, self-doubt, and dependence are abhorred. Anyone who injures this individual's arrogant pride or appearance of mastery is vindictively defeated. The leader is capable of destructive rages directed toward himself or herself and others, which are limited only by the need for self-preservation. The arrogant-vindictive leader also has a number of easily identifiable characteristics. He or she strives to dominate, humiliate, and exploit others. Executive positions are sought as a source of power. The individual may regularly make excessive demands of employees and otherwise violate accepted behavioral norms in the belief that he or she is above rules and conventions.

The narcissistic manager also appeals to mastery. He or she wishes to appear competent and in control at all times and to be viewed as a great leader. The individual surrounds himself or herself with people willing to express their trust and admiration. The narcissistic manager behaves lovingly, caringly, and generously toward others - but only in anticipation of receiving their love and admiration in return. This individual often fails to recognize his or her personal limitations. In the quest for attention and praise, he or she often makes grandiose plans but neglects to take care of the details necessary for carrying them out.

The manager who appeals to mastery may exhibit elements of the perfectionistic, arrogant-vindictive, and narcissistic leadership styles - but one of the three will usually dominate. All three of these managers relish the leadership role for the opportunity it affords them to master and subjugate others. Their compulsiveness and poor interpersonal skills make them unpopular with employees, however, and this undermines their effectiveness. In cases where the manager is extremely compulsive, the organization may suffer severe disruptions as a result. Some colleagues and employees may become passive and compliant, while those few who resist the manager may be fired or choose to resign.

APPEAL TO LOVE

The appeal to love is the opposite of the appeal to mastery. It is characterized by a longing for help and protection and a need to surrender to others in love. The individual who appeals to love feels incapable of mastery and has no wish to feel superior; in fact, feelings of pride and self-worth are avoided.

The individual willingly subordinates him- or herself in order to assume a dependent role and to appease others, even at considerable personal cost. The appeal to love has a number of recognizable behavioral patterns. The person avoids acting competent or feeling confident. He or she behaves in ways that bring about failure and, as a result, often feels guilty, inferior, contemptible, and unlovable. The individual does not speak up for him- or herself to request a raise or deny an unjust accusation. He or she is noncompetitive, preferring to let others have their way; avoids attracting attention to him- or herself; values lovable qualities such as unselfishness, goodness, generosity, humility, vulnerability, and sympathy; and hopes only to be cared for and loved by others.

The appeal to love is realized in the self-effacing leadership style. This leader is uncomfortable in the leadership role and is perceived as ineffective by others in the organization. He or she finds taking decisive action, dealing with employees, and assigning tasks difficult and unpleasant. Employees in this manager's span of control must assume responsibility in place of the leader, who they feel has left them bereft of guidance.

APPEAL TO FREEDOM

In the appeal to freedom, the individual feels unable to cope with conflicts and tries instead to withdraw from problems. Life without pain, problems, and frictions is sought - but a life lacking in love, anger, challenge, and zest results. The person may function normally but in the search for inner peace sacrifices active participation in life.

This appeal is characterized by a lack of drive toward achievement or accomplishment. The individual wants only to be left alone, and becomes detached both from his or her own sense of self and from people and events. He or she may generate good ideas in the workplace but lack the initiative to follow them through. The individual avoids or limits goal setting and longterm planning. He or she has low personal expectations and does not wish for or aspire to anything beyond easy reach. By not making commitments to goals or people, the individual hopes to avoid stress and suffering. The appeal to freedom from obligations and stress leads to the resigned leadership style.

The resigned leader makes few demands on him- or herself or employees. The status quo, as a result, is seldom challenged. Change and motivation are avoided, as is "making waves." The individual resolves problems in the least confrontational way possible. His or her low expectations and detachment may lead to low morale in the department. Employees are not only left without direction - they are discouraged from offering direction of their own.

Leadership Styles - Not Leaders

The behavioral tendencies and patterns of leadership described by the model are a key to understanding most leadership behavior. It is important to note that the appeals are mutually exclusive categories for classifying behavior; it is not possible to realize or act out more than one appeal at a time. A person cannot appeal to mastery while simultaneously appealing to love (its opposite) or freedom. Keep in mind, however, that conflicting thoughts and feelings may be held simultaneously, and that defensive behavior may change rapidly. Compulsive behavior is, in fact, motivated by psychic conflict. It is also important to appreciate that the three defensive tendencies and the nondefensive intentional tendency are the bases of most leadership behavior in the workplace. A person may deal with a stressful situation directly, seek to control or dominate it, flee from it, or look to someone else to take care of it.

Most important, the appeals and the patterns of leadership behavior are not classifications of people. People are much too complex to categorize. Instead, the appeals and leadership styles are guides for the analysis of behavior which changes over time. A person may appeal to mastery at one moment to reduce the experience of neurotic anxiety and, if that fails, shift to the appeal to freedom.

Managerial Characteristics

All the leadership styles identified above are observed at some time in the workplace - but some are more common than others. It is not surprising that many managers rely on the same appeals, since individuals generally must have had certain characteristics in order to have become managers in the first place. First, while they have experienced the same developmental problems as everyone else during infancy and childhood, managers usually have high expectations for their own performance. Further, managers are generally committed to high achievement and have little patience with obstacles that stand in the way of their success. In addition, if they are to succeed, managers cannot be overly dependent on other people for assistance and cannot shrink from difficult problems.

These common personal attributes play a role in determining who becomes a manager. Thus managers are frequently individuals who appeal to mastery when they experience stress in the leadership role - and, as a result, behave in the perfectionist, arrogant-vindictive, or narcissistic leadership style. By virtue of their position, managers are expected to make decisions, influence others, and exercise a certain degree of control over employees - but all managers are inevitably confronted by responsibilities that make them feel anxious about their role of leadership. When this occurs, their response is most often the appeal to mastery.

Depending on the classification system being used, the behavior resulting from this appeal is labeled autocratic, benevolently autocratic, manipulative, pseudodemocratic, authoritarian, paternalistic, nomothetic, bureaucratic, hierarchical, entrepreneurial, or task-oriented.

Managers appeal to love or freedom less frequently. These behavioral patterns are not compatible with the managerial role. However, a manager who feels under attack may crave love from employees or wish to withdraw and be free of the painful, unfulfilling situation. The appeal to love leads to a helpless and, of necessity, a more participative leadership style than that resulting from the appeal to mastery. Some of the previously mentioned leadership styles that may arise from this appeal are laissez-faire, democratic, personal, permissive, anarchic, compromiser, missionary, developer, humanistic, and insecure. Of the classifications mentioned earlier, the appeal to freedom is associated with the non-personal and deserter leadership styles.

Recognizing managers' leadership styles and understanding their psychological motivations can help employees, colleagues, and the supervisors who work with them. For these "others," some suggestions are given below for intervening in situations in which a manager is consistently anxious and defensive and when interaction with him or her is unrewarding and unproductive.

Intervention Strategies

As the psychological model illustrates, managers may act out behavior in the unconscious pursuit of relief from neurotic anxiety. Directly challenging this behavior simply creates more anxiety. In some cases, a challenge provokes a vindictive response; in others, the manager may mobilize a group specially developed to meet his or her needs (a "kitchen cabinet"); these people rally around the manager and fend off detractors.

Attempts to defend oneself against, resist, or change a distressed leader will suceed only if they do not heighten the manager' s anxiety and thereby increase his or her reliance on the defensive appeal. Holding low-key discussions in the manager' s office, for example, is less threatening than are public confrontations. Approval, when merited, should be offered. Recommending readings and workshops on leadership and management styles to the manager may promote self-reflection and can lead the way to discussions of the manager' s style. Those who can win the manager's respect may be able to influence his or her leadership style at key moments. Before the leader makes a characteristically autocratic decision without involving others, for example, they may suggest that a task group be formed to gather more information. By contrast, if the manager typically avoids decision making, it's possible to encourage him or her to make a particular decision by providing a thoughtful analysis of the advantages and disadvantages of each alternative and a recommendation for action.

Many complex factors contribute to the development of a leadership style. But recognizing the defensive leadership styles and understanding their motivations can give us insights into managers' behavior. This, in turn, can lead to better working relationships with managers - and to a more complete knowledge of how organizations succeed.

Psychoanalysis and Organization: A Cross-Cultural Approach

Gilles Amado

In this paper I would like to develop the idea that the relations between psychoanalysis and organizations (mostly the world of enterprises) have been shaped by the cultural context in which they took place. In support of this position, I shall use the writings produced mostly in the U.S.A., Great Britain and France which refer explicitely to an application of psychoanalytic knowledge to the understanding of organization. I shall characterize the specific contributions of the specialists in the field as symptomatic-adaptive in the U.S., mediative in Great Britain and dialectic in France.

The Symptomatic Adaptive Mode

Even if the books and articles about organization psychoanalysis in the U.S. have been written mostly by former Europeans (Zaleznik, Levinson, De Vries) it seems to me that they have been influenced by a trend, very strong in the U.S. (even if it comes once more from Europeans), I mean the ego psychology of Hartmann, Kris and Loewenstein. We know that this approach is based on a quasi biological view of psychoanalysis. It suggests that there is an autonomy (with primary and secondary functions) of the ego which aims at a psychic adaptation to reality. According to this theory, the ego is not in conflict with the instinctual drives; it is basically in harmony with the sociocultural environment of the person. Most of the papers written by psychoanalysts about work and relationships within organizations show that they give credit to this theory. On the other hand, at an organizational level, the basic implicit assumptions seem to be: that a consensus is possible among the various participants; and that the conflicts can be solved by better communication and better understanding of human relations at a psychological level. Entrepreneurship and the capitalistic model are valid ideals in most companies. Accordingly, the problems to be faced are those of superior-subordinate relationships (cf. the dynamics of subordinacy, the human dilemmas of leadership, folie à deux), leadership and exercise of power, psychology of managers, consistency with strategy, stress and psychosomatic reactions - in short, the intrapsychic and interpersonal dysfunctions that can be interpreted along the lines of the "human relations movement".

Reprinted, by permission of publisher, from Sigmund Freud House Bulletin, Vol. 4, No. 2, Winter 1980. Sigmund Freud Society, 1090 Wien, Berggasse 19.

Normality (or abnormality) is defined mostly in terms of coping with reality which is considered as a stable basis. Therefore, the ways of change are mostly individual. They use the techniques of psychotherapy within the firm or from without in order to adapt individuals to their tasks within the organization. They can also follow the lines of action of the movement and practicioners of "organization development", such as interpersonal confrontations, career development etc. Let us mention also some other cultural factors that may help define this symptomatic adaptive mode:

- the psychiatric attitude is highly dominant within many psychoanalytic societies,
- the relationships between universities and business corporations are generally good,
- historically, there has been a close relationship between psychologists and managers of companies (the National Training Laboratory in Bethel is a good example for such a collaboration),
- the impact of sociologists inspired by psychoanalysis, of those who tackle the organization from outside, is very limited in the work of psychoanalysis applied to business corporations.

I think that for example, the theories of Marcuse and Erich Fromm have not been taken into account in Business Schools. To summarize, applied psychoanalysis in the United States impresses us as resembling the total system to which it belongs and as reflecting the dominant culture there. "Adaptation" and "development" are the keywords both for individuals and organizations in a world of "potential harmony".

To be in good health appears as an aim. Thus it is not surprising if consulting psychoanalysts appear as experts of psychology, psychopathology and psychiatry rather than psychoanalytic theory. They prefer to get in touch with individual psychic processes, mostly those of top managers considered to be the potential agents of change. They do not pay much attention to people's involvement in other social contexts nor do they examine the sociocultural reality outside the organization. As experts of management theory they are mainly concerned with the inside of the organizations.

The Mediative Mode

The growth of applied psychoanalysis in organizations in Great Britain is obviously influenced by the Tavistock Institute of Human Relations and the work of W.R. Bion, E. Jaques and H. Bridger. Here, the basic theory and influence is that of Melanie Klein. Two main aspects of her theory have been used in the application to organizations: the anxieties (paranoid and depressive) against which the social structures would be built and the realm of fantasy that she discovered through her work with children. In a way one might say that the picture is less uniformily "positive" than that of ego psychology. The "bad" inner object, the destructive drives, and ambivalence are basic unconscious phenomena which drive behavior. There is nothing here like an autonomous ego sphere dealing with adaptation to an external reality but a basic intrapsychic life driven by conflicting originary fantasies. Social structures and organizations are not considered so much as vital places for interpersonal relationships but rather as control systems against basic anxieties.

A specifity of the Tavistock approach has been the central light put on the consultant's role: his independency, his analysis of the transference (and countertransference) process, his willingness to work in the broader context, not through an exclusive relationship with management but rather in a collaborative style of intervention (interacting with all social categories of organization). Let us not forget at this level the influence of Winnicott (pediatrist and psychoanalyst), mostly in the work of H. Bridger who uses the concepts of "transitional object" in his consulting and theoretical work.

Compared with American psychoanalysis one should also note that the focus is placed upon group processes rather than individual ones and on unconscious fantasies that prevent from acting with "rationality". The influence of the engineers right after the end of the war, in a rebuilding period, allowed, with the Glacier Metal Company project, an exemplary experience which remains unique and helped develop the sociotechnical approach. No doubt that this double influence in U.K. of engineers and psychoanalysts displaced the action from the top management to the shop floor and put more emphasis on the relationship between the individuals and the structures. Like in other countries of Northern Europe, the Scandinavian, the dialogue between government and unions reflects a system where face-to-face negotiation is accepted as the necessary way of acknowledging the legitimacy of adversary viewpoints. The sociopolitical tradition is a liberal one without such implicit values as a "preexisting harmony".

Let us remember that the collaborative approach of E. Jaques led him to be part of the organization in the same time as he developed the model of the independent consultant. The problem of the "in" and "out" was already put into question. Neither M. Klein nor Winnicott were psychiatrists, and Great Britain has been one of the most important places in the world for the fight against traditional psychiatry (R.D. Laing and D. Cooper). In a way we might say that the application of psychoanalysis to organizations in Great Britain are rather inspired by a "motherly imago".

The Dialectic Mode

The Kleinian approach has been the point of reference for most of the French psychologists since the end of the War. But is has been a reference only at the psychoanalytic level which was considered insufficient for work with organizations.

One of the first groups of psychoanalysts working with organizations, the CEFFRAP, after limited interventions, stopped working with them, preferring to develop a group analytic approach (inspired by Menzies and Bion) outside the companies for individuals wanting to understand unconscious phenomena. One of the reasons for this withdrawal was the diagnosis that the paranoid potential of French organizations was too heavy to carry out real work. We immediately recognize the key variable of the investigations of organizations men and clinicians: the power relationships.

Between a type of management often considered to be one of the most authoritarian in Europe, and unions known for their "political" outlook on society and work, the French clinicians can be defined as people who:

- were interested more in organizations basically as places where social contradictions are produced and reproduced, i.e., organizations as "intermediary" places,
- at that time were not very interested in organization theory per se (as it developed in the U.S.)
- but rather in social philosophies (above all since May 1968), not only in Marx but also Reich, Marcuse, Lukacs, and the philosophers of the Frankfurt School.
- have been trained in psychology, philosophy and sociology more than in management and psychiatry,
- are more accepted in Universities than in Management Schools or business firms,
- are distant from the establishment of the psychoanalytic societies whether they belong to them (Mendel) or not (Enriquez, Pagès), or, like some others, have been analysed but did not choose to practice psychoanalysis,
- are ready to accept that reality is not given but constructed (the non-positivist approach, cf. Viderman).

To give a schematic view of the French productions on psychoanalysis applied to organizations, I might say that they try to mix the Kleinian ideas of fantasies and social structures as defense mechanisms with social philosophies. The alienation of the individual from the organization is then a key issue of the literature, a fact not so surprising in a country where bureaucratic organizations and phenomena are pervasive. One should also mention the influence of a typical French movement in the social sciences not very well known in Anglosaxon countries, more appreciated in Latin countries and even Germany and Belgium: the institutional intervention to discover the unconscious phenomena and, above all, to take off the masks of power within organizations. Psychoanalysis, social philosophies and institutional analysis have characterized even the most recent and impressive French books and papers whose titles illustrate the tendency described above: "Social anaesthesia within the corporation" (L. Loue), "Sociopsychoanalysis" (books and papers by Mendel), "Social imaginary `refoulement´ and repression within organizations" (E. Enriquez), as well as "The grasp of the organization" (M. Pagès).

Describing the new techniques of management (MBO, performance appraisal, etc.) or the functioning of multinational firms as sophisticated ways of controlling and manipulating individuals, these action-researchers seem to withdraw from the firms when they are not pushed out. It is as if the phenomena they helped to discover were too dangerous for the managers of the companies. This might explain why French clinicians who apply psychoanalyis to organizations:

1. work less in large industrial organizations which they consider as machineries for the perpetuation of an oppressive system, and as centers of resistance against macrosocial change and innovation,

2. work more and more with what they call "real social movements supporting cultural change" (ecological movements, unions, etc.) or more socially acceptable institutions (schools, hospitals, etc.),

3. tend to abandon the concept of the neutrality of the consultant in favour of a specific focus in their work (e.g., development of the social power of a group for Mendel, psychocultural conditioning of the individual and demystification, increase of the areas of freedom for people in organizations, etc.)

4. invent new methodologies to discover the latent, underlying functioning of the organizations (Group SP for Mendel, dialectic analysis, drawings, body expression for Pagès, transitional groups for Kaes and Rouchy).

Some Tentative Conclusions

I have tried to exemplify through these three modes that there are differences and there can even be conflicts between the various approaches of applied psychoanalysis. If they are mostly reflections of the cultural environment in which they were developed, they also represent in a way the preferences of the organizational psychoanalysts who know more or less about what has been done elsewhere. Let us focus here for a moment on a key issue: the question of leadership. Do we tackle it as a necessary function of management (as Zaleznik and other U.S. psychoanalysts do) or as a defense mechanism against basic anxieties (as Bejarano sees it)? Is there, within a group, a vital need for a leader or an unconscious need for collective self-management (as Pagès explained it)? One can easily see the implications of the answers given to such questions. If the consultant applying psychoanalysis must be clear about his theoretical orientation, he is probably (or should be) more sensitive than others to some basic questions in any intervention or action research: who is the psychoanalyst's or consultant's "patient" within the organization? Must he remain aloof or participate in its functioning? Must he tackle personal problems? Group problems? Organizational problems? Is psychoanalysis really relevant to the understanding of organizations if the corporation is interpreted as a moving platform of strategies and power fights rather than a place for authentic personal growth? "If psychoanalysis can teach us about all we know of psychic life as an experienced subjectivity, fantasmatic production or expression of the unconscious, let us not forget that it teaches us nothing about external reality", as Mendel said.

This means that psychoanalysis, as soon as it leaves the specific situation of the couch, needs an explicit theory of the social context in which it operates. Otherwise there is the risk of "psychologization" of social relations.

If one follows this line of thought, personal growth (toward better knowledge/mastery of oneself) within the organization might be enhanced by a session explaining the functioning of the organization (taught by managers, unions, jointly or separately, and by outside specialists) much more than by a group analytic session. At least this might be a good question to be discussed.

Are psychoanalysts the kind of people who can apply psychoanalysis to organizations? The answer might appear obvious to them. Actually, it is far from being so simple; we might indeed be saying that they are no more able to understand organizations than managers would be able to understand the unconscious. The functioning of societies of psychoanalysis is a "good" example of this idea. Therefore, one of the means which seems to me most appropriate for coping with external reality would be to associate all people skilled in understanding parts of reality: psychoanalysts, organization men, workers, technicians, sociologists, engineers, etc. in multidisciplinary groups.

But again we would have this question: as soon as the psychoanalyst deals with the outside world, is he still practicing psychoanalysis? It is not the role of psychoanalysis to remain outside of a certain reality, out of the organization and the institution, in order to cope with human problems apart from pressures of all kinds?

References

U.S.

BION, W.R. Experiences in groups. London: Tavistock Publications, 1961.
FÜRSTENAU, P. La psychologie du moi et le problème de l'adaption. Connexions, nr. 8, 1973, 59-78, (traduit et extrait de Jahrbuch der Psychoanalyse III, Bern und Stuttgart, 1964).
HARTMANN, H. Die Grundlagen der Psychoanalyse. Leipzig, 1927
HARTMANN, H. La psychologie du moi et le problème de l'adaptation. Paris: P.U.F., 1968.
JAQUES, E. The changing culture of the factory. Tavistock Publications, 1951.
KERNBERG, O.F. Leadership and organizational functioning: organizational regression. International Journal of Group Psychotherapy, 28, 1978, 3-25.
KERNBERG, O.F. Regression in organizational leadership. Psychiatry, vol. 42, February 1979, 24-39.
KETS DE VRIES, M.F.R. Crisis leadership and the paranoid potential, an organizational perspective. Bulletin of the Menninger Clinic, vol. 41, nr. 4, July 1977, 349-365.
KETS DE VRIES, M.F.R. Defective adaptation to work. Bulletin of the Menninger Clinic, 42, 1978, 35-51.
KETS DE VRIES, M.F.R. Folie à deux: acting out your superior's fantasies. Human Relations, vol. 31, nr. 10, 1978, 905-924.
KETS DE VRIES, M.F.R. Leadership in a narcissistic age. February 1980, working paper nr. 8002, Mc. Gill University, Montreal.
KETS DE VRIES, M.F.R. Managers can drive their subordinates mad. Harvard Busines Review, vol. 57, nr. 4, July-August 1979, 125-134.
KETS DE VRIES, M.F.R. Power and helplessness. In: Organizational paradoxes: clinical approaches to management. London: Tavistock Publications, 1980.
KETS DE VRIES, M.F.R. Stress and the entrepreneur. In: Current Concerns in Occupational Stress by C.L. Cooper and R. Payne. John Wiley & Sons Ltd., 1980, 43-59.
KETS DE VRIES, M.F.R. Superior-subordinates entanglements. Winter 1980, working paper nr. 8001, Mc. Gill University, Montreal, 21 p.

KETS DE VRIES, M.F.R. The entrepreneurial personality: a person at the crossroads. Journal of Management Studies, 14, 1977, 34-58.

KETS DE VRIES, M.F.R. The Midcareer Conundrum. In: Organizational Dynamics. Autumn 1978, Amacom, 45-62.

LEVINSON, H. Executive stress. New York: Harper & Row, 1970, 289 p.

LEVINSON, H. Les cadres sous tension. Les Editions d'Organisation, Paris, 1973.

MACCOBY, M. The games man. New York: Simon & Schuster, 1976.

ZALEZNIK, A., & KETS DE VRIES, M.F.R. Stress reactions in organizations: syndromes, causes and consequences. Behavioral Science, 22, 1977, 151-162.

ZALEZNIK, A. Friends, lovers and enemies: reflections on coalition politics. Journal of the Philadelphia Association for Psychoanalysis, vol. 11, nr. 1, Spring 1975, 79-94.

ZALEZNIK, A. Human dilemmas of leaderrship. New York: Harper & Row, 1966, 273 p.

ZALEZNIK, A. The dynamics of subordinacy. Harvard Business Review, vol. 43, nr. 3, May-June 1965, 119-131.

ZALEZNIK, A., & KETS DE VRIES, M.F.R. Power and the corporate mind. Boston: Houghton Mifflin, 1975, 288 p.

GREAT-BRITAIN

BION, W.R. Experiences in groups. London: Tavistock Publications, 1961.

BION, W.R. The leaderless group project. Bulletin of the Menninger Clinic, 10, 1946, 77-81.

BRIDGER, H. The increasing relevance of group processes and changing values for understanding and coping with stress at work. In: Stress at Work, eds. C.L. Cooper & R. Payne. Wiley, 1978, 241-256.

BRIDGER, H. The Northfield experiment. Bulletin of the Menninger Clinic, 10, 1946, 71-77.

BRIDGER, H., & COLES, R.B. The consultant and his roles. British Journal of Medical Psychology, 42, 1969, 231-241.

DE BOARD, R. The psychoanalysis of organization. Tavistock Publications, 1978.

DICKS, H.V. Fifty years of the Tavistock Clinic. London: Routledge & Kegan Paul Ltd., 1970.

EMERY, F.E. The next thirty years: concepts, methods and anticipations. Human Relations, 20, 1967, 199-237.

EMERY, F.E., & TRIST, E.L. The causal texture of organizational environments. Human Relations, 18, 1965, p. 21.

EZRIEL, H. The role of transference in psychoanalytic and other approaches to group treatment. Acta Psychother., 7, Suppl., 1959, 101-116.

FOSTER, M. Work involvement and alienation. Manpower and Applied Psychology, 2, nr. 1, 1968, 35-48.

GRAY, J.L., ed. The Glacier Project: concepts and critiques. London: Heinemann Educational Books Ltd., 1976.

HIGGIN, G.W., & BRIDGER, H. The psychodynamics of an intergroup experience. Human Relations, 1964, 391-446.

JAQUES, E. Disturbances in the capacity to work. International Journal of Psychoanalysis, 41, 1960, 357-67.
JAQUES, E. Interpretative group discussions as a method of facilitating social change. Human Relations, 1, 1947-48, 533-549.
JAQUES, E. On the dynamics of social structure. Human Relations, 6, nr. 1, 3-23.
JAQUES, E. Social diagnosis and social therapy. Journal of social issues, 3, nr. 2, 1947.
JAQUES, E. Social therapy: technocracy or collaboration. Journal of social issues, 3, nr. 2, 1947, 59-66.
JAQUES, E. The changing culture of the factory. Tavistock Publications, 1951.
JAQUES, E. Work, creativity and social structure. London: Heinemann Eductional Books, 1970.
MENZIES, I.E.P. A case-study in the functioning of social systems as a defence against anxiety: a report on a study of the nursing service of a general hospital. Human Relations, 13, 1960, 95-121.
MENZIES, I.E.P. Some mutual interactions between organizations and their members. Psychother.-Psychosom., 13, 1965, 194-200.
RICE, A.K. Learning for leadership. Tavistock Publications, 1965.
SANDLER, J., DE MONCHAUX, C., & DIXON, J.J. Patterns of anxiety: the correlates of social anxieties. British Journal of Medical Psychology, 31, 1958, 24-31.
SOFER, C. The assesment of organizational change. Journal of Management Studies, 1, 1964, 128-142.
SOFER, C. The organization from within: a comparative study of social institutions based on a sociotherapeutic approach. Tavistock Publications, 1961.
SUTHERLAND, J.D., & MENZIES, I.E.P. Two industrial projects. Journal of social issues, 3, nr.. 2, 1947, 51-58.
TRIST, E.L. Social structure and psychological stress. In: C. Walker & al. (eds.) Modern Technology and Civilization. New York, 1962.

FRANCE

ALTHABE, G. Oppression et libération dans l' imaginaire. Maspéro, 1969.
AMADO, G. Imaginaire groupal et résistance au changement. Etudes Psychothérapiques, nr. 2, Juin 1975, 89-93.
AMADO, G., & GUITTET, A. Psychologie et conduite des réunions de travail. C.E.S.A., E.R, nr. 126, 1979.
AMADO, G., & GUITTET, A. Psychologie et conduite des réunions de travail. C.E.S.A., E.R. nr 126, 1979.
ANDSHA, L' intervention dans les organisations et les institutions. Epi, 1974.
ANZIEU, D. Le groupe et l' inconscient. Dunod, 1975.
ANZIEU, D., & coll. Le travail psychoanlytique dans les groupes. Dunod, 1972.
BASAGLIA, F. L' institution en négation. Seuil, 1970.
BEJARANO, A. Résistance et transfert dans les groupes. In: Le travail Psychanalytique dans les Groupes, op. cité, 65-140.
CASTEL, R. L' inconscient social de la psychanalyse. Topique, nr. 1, Oct. 1969, 129-141.

CASTORIADIS, C. L' institution imaginaire de la société. Seuil, 1975.
C.E.R.F.I. Analyse institutionelle à la FNAC. Education permanente, nr. 9, 1971.
CLEMENT, C. Les fils de Freud sont fatiqués. Grasset, ed. Figures, 1978.
DESGENETTES (GROUPE) La sociopsychanalyse institutionelle. Connexions, nr. 29, 1980, 69-80.
ENRIQUEZ, E. Imaginaire social, refoulement et répression dans les organisations. Connexions, nr. 3, 1972.
ENRIQUEZ, E. Probèmatique du changement. Connexions, nr. 4, 1972.
ENRIQUEZ, M. et E. Le psychoanalyste et son institution. Topique, nr. 6, Mai 1971, 29-64.
FERENCZI, S. Sur l' ontogenèse de l' ìntérêt pour l' argent. In: E. Borneman, op. cité.
FOUCHARD, R. Le piège de l' intervention interne. Epi, 1975.
FREUD, S. Caractère et èrotisme anal. In: E. Borneman, Psychanalyse de l' argent, P.U.F., 1978.
GUIGOU, J. Critique des systèmes de formation. Anthropos, 1972.
HESS, R. La socianalyse. Editions Universitaires, 1975
KAES, R. et coll. Crise, rupture et dépassement. L' analyse transitionelle en psychanalyse individuelle et groupale. Dunod, 1980.
LAPASSADE, G. Groupes, organisations et institutions. Gauthier Villars, 1967.
LAPASSADE, G. L' analyseur et l' analyste. Gauthier Villars, 1971.
LAPASSADE, G. Socioanalyse et potential humain. Gauthier Villars, 1975.
LOUE, L. L' anesthésie sociale dans l' entreprise. Payot, 1973.
LOURAU, R. L' analyse institutionnelle, Ed. de Minuit, 1970.
LOURAU, R. L' analyseur LIP, U.G.E., coll. 10/18, 1974.
LOURAU, R. L' instituant contre l' institué, Ed. Anthropos, 1969.
MENDEL, G. De la régression du politique au psychique. Sociopsychanalyse 1. Payot, 1972.
MENDEL, G. Pour décoloniser l' enfant. Payot, 1968.
MENDEL, G. Psychanalyse et sociopsychanalyse. In: Sociopsychanalyse 3. Payot, 1973.

A Clinical Approach to Meetings

Gilles Amado

Monday 9 o'clock: The manager of a sales staff has called up his seven subordinates to check the functioning of the department and try to set up new targets for the coming year. He relies on the "natural" competitive feelings between salesmen to make this meeting creative, and solve as best as he can the unavoidable minor problems of temperament. Unfortunately, the meeting rapidly takes on a demanding nature: bonuses are deemed too low, quotas hard to keep up; arguments set salesmen against each other, some of them being accused of encroaching into fields which are not theirs. In this atmosphere, the manager tries to bring back order, to remind everyone of the purpose of the meeting and to appeal to the group spirit. But in vain. After an hour, he stops the meeting, strengthened in his opinion that participation means anarchy and that problems are more quickly solved through individual consultation.

A foreman comes more or less to the same conclusion, after calling in all his mechanics. Here, the claims of some customers, the pressures of the past week concerning the organization of the work did not result in stimulating them or providing the expected answers. On the contrary, it was the mechanics' passiveness and dependency which, in the end, dampened the foreman's spirits.

There are plenty of examples of dissatisfactions related to meetings which may show both the best and the worst. Indeed, it all depends on the way they have been conceived, planned and conducted (by the manager). We shall focus our attention here on meetings of already existing small teams (services, shops, committees, etc.). We shall first try a psychological approach, noticing reasons for frequent dysfunctioning, before showing what kind of steps have to be taken in order to facilitate this kind of group work. Therefore, we shall not directly deal here with purely informative meetings (e.g. the dissimination of a policy) or meetings about negotiation, or those of an essentially strategic character (e.g. employers - union negotiations). Instead, we will focus our attention on groups at work within which cooperation is a functional necessity recognized by all the participants from the start.

I. ANXIETIES AND STRATEGIES

A current study of meetings in various types of organizations brings out the preeminence of wishful thinking over analytical approaches. "Play the game", "be spontaneous", "don't be afraid", "we are all in the same boat", are injunctions meant to increase participation and cohesion. The lack of realism and the ineffectiveness of such encouragements proceed from a fact that is sometimes forgotten in the heat of the action: the groups at work are themselves a source of anxiety, a place of narcissistic expression and a crossroad of strategies.

A source of anxieties: Each participant at meetings finds himself exposed to the others, their judgments and, possibly, their criticisms. The status of the participant and his competence, are particularly put on trial even if his own self is not questioned through or beyond the solving of technical or organizational problems. Personal or individual anxieties are often increased by anxiety related "splitting" processes (Anzieu, 1975) which can be found in any group; in the course of debates, every one can feel himself torn between the different ideas and propositions expressed, as if he more or less agreed with each of them. This identification with each and all creates a feeling of undifferentiation, confirmed by false recollections. Many participants will get mixed up and claim later in good faith as their own words or deeds which, in fact, are those of other participants. Thus, the internal coherence of each individual, his self-image, his personal influence are particularly vulnerable at meetings.

A place for narcissistic expression: It is the "positive" aspect of being able to influence what is so important in groups. Those who establish their authority in such instances know it better than others. If one can lose face, one can also try to win other people's recognition of his own technical and human capacity. This more or less conscious aim may get the better of the purely operational purpose of the meeting: thus, up to a point, one may become the witness of oratorlike contests, monologues or arguments, which are meant to strengthen the identity and authority of a particular participant whatever the task at hand might be.

A crossroad of strategies: As a rule, the relations within a group, the positions of each participant, are seldom as they appear to be at first sight. Each individual's behavior consequently is the result of several determining factors: the personal history of the individual (bio-psycho-social), his status in the organization and his role (accepted or recognized) in the group at work. Attitudes are also determined by more or less transient wishes and fears in relation to the task or identity of each man within the organization and the group. Consequently, we can say that behavior, at least in the beginning stage of a group, has a specific logic, a more or less unconscious strategy: thus, for example, each one will aim at:

1) the realization of satisfactions in relation to his own fantasies (capturing the audience, preserving his power, etc.)

2) the rehearsing of parts accepted or recognized by the group (the role of the moderator, the heckler, the organizer, etc.)

Thus, the reality of daily work shows that, beyond its obvious outlines, a task often deeply involves individuals, leading them to adopt a strategy of gain or no-loss. Rather than avoiding these phenomena, they should be acknowledged, in order to overcome their possible negative consequences. We shall now try to point out some directly observable processes which aim is to cope with the side effects of group behavior but which may in fact, actually increase the problems faced by these groups.

II. DEPENDENCE AND CONFORMITY

There are two general sorts of psychological responses to reduce these anxieties and the occurrence of these strategies:
- identification with a strong personality who will suggest the most appealing way of dealing with the problem.
- an attempt towards fusion within the group through minimizing or refusing to accept differences between participants.

A. Search for a leader

To turn a participant into a leader, to identify one-self with a member of the group or with the person in charge, it is necessary to invest this person somehow with magic and exaggerated qualities, creating savior imagery. Of course, these qualities are not without their pitfalls. If, for a while, the leader solves the problems he has encountered, it means he probably has the qualities or psychic structures which are most needed at the time. However, he may then implicitly wipe out the autonomy of judgement of the participants who run the risk of falling into a noted state of dependency.

Besides, it is not sure that the leader will be able to carry out all the tasks he has been given. (A technical expert may find himself organizing a task for which he has not been prepared). If he complies with such orders (i.e. "you should know", "it's up to you to decide") he will find himself called upon as soon as a difficulty arises. In the end, the group will leave it to the omnipotent authority figure and gradually stray away from taking a more autonomous position. Depending upon the leader turns into the best way of avoiding any attempt at analyzing the differences between individuals.

This defensive process within groups is certainly a very powerful one which especially can be found in Latin countries characterized by a great preoccupation with authority issues. Many participants as well as managers resort to this kind of action since it satisfies both. They do not fully grasp, however, the negative implications which such a relationship of dependency can cause over time.

B. The "fusion" group

A way for participants to preserve their identity and to avoid splitting up is to regress, to fuse. While forgetting about their arguments and differences, they identify with the same idea and even cherish similar illusions. Thus, the internal reality of the group is lived in a very positive manner; all questions liable to threaten such a harmony are discarded. The pressure in favour of conforming to the norms of the group are obvious in every sect, clique, party, or in every association where faithful adherence to a doctrine is demanded. To a lesser degree, one can notice the same sort of process at meetings.

1. The quest for consensus at all cost: this is most often attempted in case of conflicts. It aims at eliminating conflicts through a formal and illusive agreement. Those who do so (participants, managers, leaders) cannot accept divisions and often keep in mind that to accomplish something necessarily means an agreement. When reality does not fit this vision, they attempt, through whatever means, to get a consensus "on the cheap", on points so trivial that, in the end, the outcome of the meeting has little or no value to the participants. The caricature of such an attitude is quite well illustrated by some specially refined syntheses. For example, after an hour's work the manager's conclusion might be that "in spite of all, we have succeeded in coming to an agreement on one point", in the meantime leaving aside all the other points which might have been controversial and actually were the really important ones.

2. The pressure on deviants: This is exerted on those who defend a position or do not comply with the temporary or stable norms established within the group. In that case the participants tend to communicate with these nonconformists in a privileged and even concerted way, with a view to bring them back to normal standards and to talk some "reason" into them. In some groups - run as closed systems - the deviant is often resented as an intruder and an obstacle; if he is the only one who sticks to his position, he must be wrong.

3. The scapegoat: This well-known political and psychological phenomenon can specifically be observed in groups at work. It is used to focus the discontent of some of the participants on a particular

person or thing. For instance, failure in work will be laid upon the man who "monopolizes the debate" or upon another who "has sabotaged it" or "upon the agenda that has listed the important questions at the end", upon the "too noisy and confined conference room", upon the "heterogeneous" composition of the group, etc. It all happens as if the participants were refusing to deal with the deep and diverse causes of their discontent. In such a case, they either focus on one symptom, or withdraw. By rejecting a participant as the only one responsible for the evils of the group, they fail to see that the reactions of this individual may be shared by some others who dare not speak out. The same problem is likely to crop up again at a later stage in a different shape.

We can see that through a consensus at all cost, pressure on deviants and looking for a scapegoat, the group preserves its atmosphere, jeopardizing effective execution of the task. Apart from the search for a leader and the emergence of the merged group, we can identify certain procedures in groups which are meant to deal with the same anxieties. Avoidance of the risks attached to confrontation leads to a re-enforcement of the control process.

III. THE CONTROL OF SPACE, TIME AND INFORMATION

Excessive formal control is certainly the most frequently observed process of protection (against socio-affective divergence) in meetings. It can assume different aspects:

<u>Spatial formalism in two forms:</u> The participants' seating arrangement can be settled beforehand. In such a case questions may be raised about the reasons for the choice ("why did they sit me between X and Y?") creating the impression of manipulation. Such planned actions are often meant to avoid cliques or asides between people who know each other. The exception is then dealt with by the rule, and groups will form at another level (in debates for instance).

The participants remain sitting all through the session; in this they resemble schools; their energy level may drop as time passes. Depending on the nature of the meeting, it may be advisable to allow the participants to stand up, to walk around within reasonable limits. The type of body language will reflect the atmosphere within the group.

<u>The formal aspect of agenda and work schedule:</u> If the agenda and work schedule are an important starting point, they often turn out to be sclerotic shackles. Indeed, the debates may go at such a pace that one item in the agenda may be dealt with more or less explicitly, at an

unexpected time. Likewise, an unforeseen problem may turn out to be the essential one while it has not been put down on the agenda. The manager and the group must consider that they are facing a choice: either preserve the rigor of the schedule (which may result in neglecting to study a question, on the spur of the moment, while every one is motivated to do so) or stray from the plan (which may result in a waste of time and efficiency). The manager's flexibility should be tied into the consequences of the adopted choices.

Going around the table: In fact, this process - known as the safest and quickest to find out where every participant stands - proves to be not only an inadequate way to disseminate but also to be costly with respect to attention and atmosphere in the group. The most valuable information is, indeed, the one spontaneously provided by the individual given in his own language and free from all constraints. A piece of information wrenched by an authoritarian procedure is less credible. It lacks the hesitations, the type of phrasing, the reticences which show how an idea really progresses. Moreover:

Going around the table tends to rigidify people's behavior and, often artificially will widen the potential gaps between the members of a group. The statements made in this process are often used later as references by those who will try to show their authors that they are contradicting themselves. ("You should know better, a moment ago you were pretending just the reverse").

Going around the table also entails an implicit competition in language. A sword-play of explanations (or "rationalizations") of the subtleties of words will emerge to prove one's position. The participants will give a point of view close to the ones expressed (therefore redundant) rather than merely joining in.

In actuality, at meetings, going around the table may have a screening effect making it difficult to assess the positions revealed in the course of the debate. To avoid this pitfall, the manager needs frequent bearings and summing ups.

The fear of silences: Quite often silent spells occur during meetings. When they do not, one can be sure there must be "a flight" somewhere. When silences are "pregnant", they are indeed a sign of common questions, unavoidable if engaged in real group work. Still, observation shows that silences cause anxiety. The participants may be caught unaware and may wonder what is going on. Since the implicit standard for the "good" progress of a group is that "where there's talk, there's result", silence is often perceived as an idle period, a blank, or even a failure. Fairly often, then, some participants are tempted to fill it up by re-starting an idea suggested by one of them, or making signs to the person in charge. If the latter is anxious, he will feel responsible for this idle period and take some kind of action.

In fact, silences hold important information and are often the moments when collective feelings are the most real. For example,take a meeting set up with the purpose of looking into the causes of a decline in the sales of a company manufacturing consumer goods. After being called upon by their manager, the members of this group were keeping silent, making it seem that they were short of ideas. The manager was astute enough to realize that in reality the participants were reluctant to commit themselves, afraid to question one another about their statements: What this example suggests is that each silence leads to questions about causation. It is not a reason to re-start a doubtful debate which would certainly not have stopped if there had been no problems.

The secretary reporter: It sometimes happens that the person who takes notes sits next to the leader of a group at work. It is often a secretary who writes down the essential parts or even the whole discussion. This function may prove useful when the subject is a very technical one, for which a careful and exhaustive account is needed. Sometimes the manager will ask a participant to fulfill this task; the price to be paid is that the group will lose one of its discussants. Such a practice seems to us objectionable also for a deeper reason: if the manager carries out his mission well, he is, in fact, the person best qualified to give this account. Owing to the different concrete aids at his disposal (board, notes, etc.), owing to the check-lists, the reformulations and partial syntheses already done, he must be able to give this account orally at the end of the session, making sure that the group agrees with his statements. At that time, this account can be noted down. In acting in this way, he avoids at once the misunderstandings and even controversies that sometimes arise during the reading of a report which has not been ratified by the participants. In complying with both the climate and the contents of the meeting, he will be able to make an impression at both levels which includes all the nuances and accents that an outsider would not be able to describe as accurately (or refrain from describing). This apparent loss of time is in reality a considerable gain from everyone's point of view; it will lead to transparence, an instant understanding, and a common language. In the light of the above, we begin to understand that the commitment or the exclusion of a participant depends on the climate of confidence and the feeling of security experienced by each of them. In an ill-defined situation where the objectives are vague and where the participants feel danger instinctively, the quality of exchange runs the risk of being shallow, bringing out only publicly known information. In contrast, in a group where the objectives are well defined and well perceived, where everyone's position is clear and can be questioned, the information which each will contribute will reflect the preferences of each individual. The contrast between a statement of facts and the expression of opinions and intimate feelings needed to solve a problem, will create the indispensable dynamics necessary for effective group work. (See Figure 1).

FIGURE 1

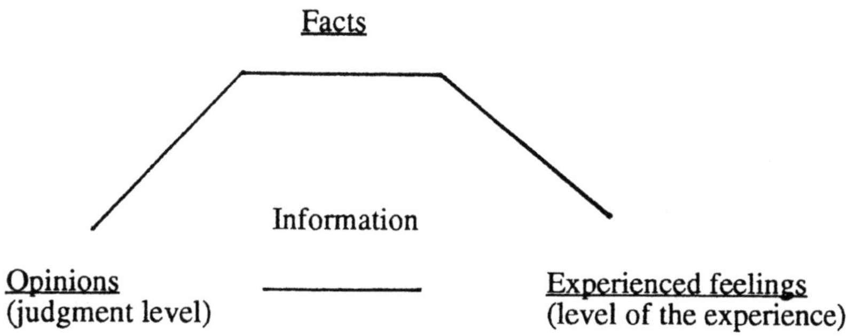

IV. BORDERLINE FUNCTIONING

Groups at work often show special recurrent attitudes; eventually a balance will occur between communications and relations. To understand these modes of functioning, it is necessary to observe methodically the habits of the group, and ask the following key-questions:

- what are the dominant affective tones?
- how does the group use its energy?
- how does the group cope with anxiety, uncertainty, danger?

Even if it often looks difficult to unravel what belongs to the manager's style and what to the behavior of the members of the group, some clinical observations will lead us to sort out several varieties of what can be called borderline functioning.

Perverted meetings

These are the ones where the "unspoken", the hidden gets the better of the explicit and where the attitudes, the problems and the choices made are consciously or unconsciously biased. Several symptoms help to identify such meetings.

1. A certain haziness exists and may remain, concerning the type of meeting, its objectives, the reason for the presence of some of the participants, the persons entrusted with the decisions, and the rewards for solving a specific problem.

2. The preliminary information needed to solve the problem is unevenly distributed, without anyone really knowing the reasons for it. In the course of the discussion, this information might emerge gradually. Dispensing information at times deemed favorable to the manager will enable the latter to establish his power over a group that lives in a state of confusion not realizing that it has been manipulated.

3. The manager's behavior is questionable: The manager seems to be playing with the participants rather than managing the meeting on the basis of a precise, well understood role. His style may range from seduction to authoritarianism; he may persuade, challenge, stir up some antagonisms, call back to order, or make the group feel guilty. The manager under the pretense of adjusting himself to every participant - in order to win everyone to his cause, will change his role. Unfortunately, his attitude will get entangled in more or less inconsistent strategies which makes him, in the end, lose sight of his own self.

Perverted meetings are the prime examples of manipulation, and may have the following consequences:

- Their managers cause such a sense of distrust that the participants are scared to express themselves freely or contribute effectively to the execution of the task. Some members of the group who feel themselves on the firing line will be guarded, while others just play the game.
- Some more dependent participants who are organizationally (hierarchical) or affectively more dependent (relation to authority) run the risk of imitating such a model.
- Discord arises openly between the members of the group. But in front of the manager this will be disguised resulting in the latter's continuation of his dysfunctional style.

In perverted meetings, one hardly ever asks himself the question "why". The energy is invested in the "how", the logic of means is the winner. The world with its rules and laws can be transgressed: no more chance, no more contingencies, everything goes. Reality is re-built through plans and programs by means of which one attempts to subject the others to his will. It is in this way that change is mastered, planned and manipulated. The meetings of technocrats often give us a good example of this phenomenon.

Obsessive meetings

In such meetings, rule and ritual take precedence over substance. Formalism and ponderousness prevail. Some proceedings which can be subtly used elsewhere, become here overpowering and smother spontaneity and affectivity. The agenda becomes like an iron collar, the going around the table a disembodied ritual, the language polished and lifeless and the attitudes rigid. Apparent rationality and logic opposes substance. Digressions and contestations are brought to order under pretense of efficiency, whereby the compulsive exertion of authority remains hardly hidden. The reality of the group appears codified and bureaucratic, similar to bureaucratic organizations ruled by impersonality and regulations. One ignores the essential at the expense of details. In such situations, reflection becomes isolated from reality. The energy shifts to the idea, the discourse on action takes the place of action. One avoids anguish through a methodical but sterile quest for the conditions of action. Often obsessive meetings repeat at a microscale, in bureaucratic organizations, the type of behavior expected from their members. Consequently, one ends up in a bureaucratic vicious circle.

A paranoid tendency is sometimes inserted in such meetings; an outside threat is perceived, which would endanger the equilibrium of the group. Whether it has to do with competition, a neighboring department or new rules, the magnified fear gets the better of reason and, accentuated by the manager or an anxious participant, it contaminates the rest of the group. Only the deflation of such fantasies (which sometimes requires calling in an outside consultant) allows a return to reality.

The personality of an individual may also strongly influence the atmosphere of the group. A meeting managed by a man with a paranoid tendency will show characteristics related to the features of the leader's personality. The paranoiac is a fighter, he wants truth, his right to triumph. For him there is no possible doubt, everything follows a very specific kind of logic. Any criticism, any observation become offensive. Rigid, self-centered, the paranoiac wants to be objective and independent in his relations, because the others mean potential threats. No doubt this attitude generates an atmosphere of distrust and pseudo-submissiveness. People prefer to be lost in apparent dependency rather than be submitted to the leader's aggression. Very often, paranoiacs and the perverted find themselves in the same boat. The former thinks about and suggests great fights or grandiose ideas while the latter carries out, plans, controls and fulfills somewhat delirious schemes.

Hysterical meetings

Contrary to the previous meetings, the emotions are here freely expressed. Excess will determine pathology symptomized by the following:

1. Dramatization: a scheme or an order becomes invested with quite a magical "aura". It is a "unique bargain", an "opportunity not to be missed".
2. A sportsmanlike need to excel emerges: the call for mobilization is the major message of the manager who stimulates and musters all he has, tries to communicate his faith, insists upon the potential results and seduces the group.
3. The forward escape is often the result of a question of choice. A specific alternative becomes favoured with respect to means and resources. A rational analysis of the situation and of the pressure involved by its realization is repudiated under pretense of opportunity and efficiency. Immediate action (often confused) does not allow for the appearance of differences. Action is the name of the game and will consume all available energy.

This theatrical climate is often preferred in business meetings where external stimuli from the market demand quick decisions. But it also lends color to all the meetings, gathering the more extrovert personalities for whom action is the key word.

Depressive meetings

The depressive strain can be found on occasion in every meeting. Depressive meetings, however, are those conferences where this tendency is persistent:

1. The over-estimation of external pressures: The ability to take action seems to be paralyzed, blocked as it were, by perceived boundaries and expected negative consequences. The external world seems omnipotent in contrast to the perceived power of the group. The

feeling of being merely powerless pawns invades the participants leading to fatalism.
2. The "rationalization" of failure: In meetings one is preoccupied with explaining previous failures at the price of action.

This contagious depressiveness runs the risk of spreading, given the existence of real constraints. It is as if fantasy takes over from reality; most energy seemed to be devoted to rationalization, to the demonstration of constraints and the passive contemplation of helplessness rather than at an attempt of mastery. It is obvious that, if the manager is the cause of such an atmosphere, he, in the end, will become its accomplice. If he lets such a situation prevail, he may then be held responsible for the "failure syndrome" which pervades the group.

However, this depressive "balance" of the group runs a high risk of being endangered by some more active participants. Refusing to take the situation for granted, they will question the set of explanations offered, the attitude of the members of the team and of the manager (if they can) or quit (if it seems a more expedient solution). A breach of this kind alone can cause the group to question its own progress, provided its defensive system is not too much rigidified.

V. ABOUT FUNCTIONAL PRINCIPLES

The majority of meetings that have been thought satisfactory are those in which there exists a positive balance between the fulfillment of the task and a persistently pleasant work atmosphere. Although efficiency in production, economy of time and of means may be the managers' major concerns, he must keep in mind that a negative climate, a lack of approval of decisions arrived at by the group may thoroughly destroy those other benefits. Other effects of engaging in group processes should be kept in mind. What may be gained in information at meetings may be negated by the conflicts which may arise during these sessions. The emphasis on the need to create or maintain a good climate may actually lead to inefficiency and even manipulation. To avoid such dangers, it will be necessary to observe four essential functions: the way the group process is organized, active and objective listening, conflict integration and clarification.

1. The function of organizing the group process

Elements important in the organization of the work of the group will be classified in chronological order. We shall briefly mention these aspects (Amado and Guittet, 1975):

Preparation: on this level, it is essential to be sure about the purpose of the meeting, its aims, the composition of the group (the participants' qualifications, their interests in the problem, the type of relationships), the number of the participants (optimal from 6 to 10), and the initial differences (hierarchy, levels of information). The text of the memo concerning the meeting must enable the participants to be informed about the problems in advance. An oval table, a blackboard, a flip chart, sufficient ventilation and light, a quiet room, will put the finishing touch to the more material organization of the task at hand.

Presentation should theoretically only be a reminder of the agenda: purpose, constraints, aims and decision criteria. But in fact, a mere reminder, without checking the participants' perceptions, interpretations or even reserves from the beginning, may be risky, allowing the meeting to start on an uncertain basis. Consequently, everything must be done from the beginning to clear up these points.

Suggestion and choice of working methods: the leader of the conference has to draw out the different propositions and compare their respective advantages and drawbacks: check lists, a go "around the table", brainstorm, the use of sub-groups, etc. If the group cannot arrive at a reasonable agreement, it is the task of the manager to make that decision, keeping the arguments which have been brought up in mind. In addition, taking regular stock of the efficiency of the methods used often proves useful.

Redistribution of roles and tasks: To avoid wasting people's time, to facilitate the best use of resources, it may be important, at certain times, to assign individual responsibility for the work to be done. Such an intervention is often important at the end of the meeting to bring out the adopted propositions and maintain the people's commitment.

Control of the progress and of time: throughout the meeting, one must keep an eye on the original purpose and the time. Indeed, both these elements condition the available choice of working methods. Reminding the participants of such constraints (not defensively) can only help them take responsibility.

2. Active and objective listening

This crucial function often sets the tone of the meeting. When one says "listening" one sometimes thinks of passive listening and the inevitability of selecting among what has been heard. This conception is then reflected in the attitude of the benevolent but hardly dynamic manager, often interrupting at the wrong time, having distorted perceptions. These difficulties can and must be avoided through an effort towards empathy at an individual, interpersonal and group level. This capacity of understanding the group from the inside and of grasping the reality experienced within a group can be learned by practicing. Useful techniques are:

Reformulations: their purpose is to check with a participant whether we have understood what he meant, by trying to be attentive to the essence of his statements and non-verbal signals.

Stock-taking and summaries: they must be done regularly. They are designed to give an account of the discussion at a given time, thus reflecting not only the contents of the different interventions but also the various positions taken. They represent some form of "group" reformulation.

Controlling subjective biases: such a control is indispensable to make reformulation and stock-taking a relatively unbiased process. The more one behaves as a mere participant, instead of a leader, the less one risks, but at the cost of group progress. Moreover, when reformulations and stocktaking are not ratified by the participants (guardedness, silent show of dissatisfaction, silent spells) it becomes a sign for the individual in charge of the meeting that he has not been perfectly understood, that his personal opinions color his perceptions.

The use of the board: when done wisely, it allows the identification of important elements and to provide common and unique landmarks while the meeting is in progress. In this way, a blackboard is preferable to just making private notes. Acting in this manner has many advantages:

- first, it assures that all participants are at the same level
- it allows for a progressive and collective memory
- it demonstrates that the manager is helpful and capable of being objective or at least of understanding and transcending his subjectivity
- it helps "bring out" everyone's preferences
- it shows what has been gained and how it has been achieved.

3. The function of conflictual integrations

There is no real integration between people or positions without a study of their differences. Integration and conflict seem to be the two poles of an axis. It is the alternation of the two which leads to a balance. To attain it, several missions must be accomplished:

Make everyone's participation easy: which means that participation must not be forced on the participants. If they do not participate, there are reasons for this which are not necessarily of their own making. It is therefore the manager's role to create the kind of climate, or to behave in such a way as to make everyone feel free to step in. For that purpose, he must understand what kind of relationships exist between the participants, their concerns with the problem, the kind of risks they see and the difficulty they have in expressing themselves.

Adopt a positive approach: with regard to the work of the group, it means that the elements obtained must be strengthened when necessary (especially when in a depressive phase), so that the available energy does not disappear.

It also means that apparent digressions are tolerated. A manager confronted with a participant who drifts from the topic must always suppose (or even give proof) that this divergence may be of some help in clarifying the problem in question, before restoring order. Such an attitude often has a pedagogical effect on the members of the group who will perhaps try to focus their attention to the positive side of the discussion rather than on criticism.

Go deep into the arguments and differences: this task is an essential condition to prevent overlooking fundamental oppositions. The progress and dynamics of the discussion are partly a result of the examination of the divergence and contradictions in the group given different backgrounds. It is an important task indeed, to help the participants go further into their analyses, to understand the motives of their arguments, and to be not content with mere opinions or feelings. Therefore, it is useful to recognize the differences and conflicts, to present and deal with it, thus preventing the possibility of overlooking the essential elements.

Alternate the levels of expression: true thinking rests on logic, opinions, information, intuition and fantasies. To discard one of these elements or merely singling out only one restricts creativity which can have serious consequences. Alternation of expression will favor interpersonal dynamics and will allow for the study of the same problem from different points of view. Taking those different levels into account is important for creative group development.

4. The role of clarification

A manager may have carried out with ease the three tasks previously mentioned and yet be surprised with the unsatisfactory progress of the group. He must then keep in mind that many psychological phenomena may counteract the progress of a group at any time. When confronted with a lull, a clash, an cluded problem, an anomalous attitude, the manager must begin to question himself. First, he could try another way of tackling the problem and appraise its consequences. If he thinks that an obstacle will be too much of an impairment to the work which has to be done and to the group, a talk is needed with the participants to find a way out. On this level, the manager's intuition and insight are of great importance. It will help him in dealing with this more pedagogical and formative phase. It will lead to an explanation of the dynamics of the discussion leading to a better grasp of the associations of ideas and sequences that have led to the slow down. Clarification is bringing up the unspoken, creating awareness about the sometimes unconscious elements which make up the essence of the discussion. Such a task is certainly a most delicate one and is not easy to do. The existence of "corridor conversation" indicates how difficult this role is. Often only at these moments all that remains unsaid, all the inhibitions are set free. We can argue that the role of clarification has really been performed when the essential of what is expressed in the corridor has actually already been dealt with in the course of the meeting.

VI. FURTHER REMARKS

The issues we have dealt with in this paper must not keep us from dealing with three other problems:

- the respective roles of the manager and the group in team work,
- the cultural context in which it takes place,
- the role which psycho-analysis plays.

The manager and the group

With respect to the above, a remark could be made: does the proposed model after all not confer a very specific or even too important a role to the manager vis à vis the participants in the meeting?

Ideally, in fact, all the roles described should be fulfilled by members of the group, whether they organize themselves for that purpose, or step in spontaneously at the different levels which have been mentioned. It would prove that the importance of those numerous roles has been understood by the members of the group. We could say that such a group has attained "maturity"; its members having become free from too much dependence on authority and have agreed to move towards the same objective. In reality, however, it is very difficult for a participant to free himself from his subjectiveness, to intervene neutrally on those different levels. Paradoxically, perhaps, it seems that the hierarchical manager is the person best qualified to assume these different roles. But our model will put up neither with aloofness nor machiavellianism. The manager who conforms to it must be ready to:

- make the goals, procedures, responsibilities and positions of each one (including himself) clearer, in relation to the problems tackled
- assume his responsibilities as a decision-maker if a general agreement is impossible. If he has performed in his roles correctly, he has indeed at his disposal all the ingredients to make the decision.

The cultural context

With respect to the second remark, it is necessary to put the universality of such an approach to groups at work into perspective. Any group and its management not only has to be viewed in a certain organizational context with all its specifications (types of technology, market, management) but it also belongs to a given culture. For such a model to be workable in North America, a manager should act cautiously as soon as he crosses the ocean. Two short examples will illustrate what we are referring to:

In France, our approach meets with several obstacles (Amado and Guittet, 1979):

- The lack of an early acquaintance with group work, through insufficient training at school.
- Cartesian rationalism which leads to oratory contests based more on superficial logic which hides the underlying assumptions or emotions.
- Since the ideology of conflict rules the universe of firms, the dimension of power creeps into meetings. The struggle of opinions, of influences, the craving for leadership, for control, often gives the impression that the essential is not the task or the goal to be attained. Instead the critical elements seem to be gains or losses in terms of status or social power.
- The authority-dependency dynamics connotes many attitudes and makes it often difficult to arrive at real participation, be it only a division of responsibilities.

If we turn to Africa, we find:

- The great importance given to the group as such and to the consensus which results in pressure on deviants to join the majority.
- The weight of authority, when status (social and even magical) wins over competence or personal qualities.

- A relation with time which makes the future seem less hazardous than in European countries, but also less predictable leading to more risky decision making.

We could, of course, give many more examples showing the impact of culture on the attitudes observed in group situations. What is important is to understand this dimension for anyone interested in team work.

Once a manager spots the various determinants bearing on collective decision making, he finds himself faced with a choice: to adjust to the perceived reality or to take a course which he thinks is more satisfactory. Realism and what is really wanted do not necessarily conflict at that level, but they eventually will put the manager face to face with his own objectives.

The role of psychoanalysis

All things considered given the complexity of the phenomena to be found in a group at work one may wonder how much of a help psychoanalysis is to the manager. In our opinion, two essential points must be emphasized:

- First, psychoanalytic research of groups will enable a better understanding and an improved diagnosis of the many individual and collective unconscious phenomena which take place in groups.
- Secondly, psychoanalysis teaches us to question ourselves, that is to find out to what extent our personal positions, our values, our emotions, our affectivity have an influence on our behavior and actions.

The managers who achieve this understanding both of others and of themselves:

- on one hand, will lessen their anxiety or even stress reactions when faced with sometimes disturbing phenomena which occur during meetings,
- on the other hand, they develop a more analytic approach, that is to say a less moral and more empathic one.

Being able to alternate between intense observation and free floating attention, they know better what is going on in the socio-affective substratum of groups at work. Consequently, they can more efficiently conduct their actions and decisions.

At the close of this set of reflexions, we have come full circle: meetings are not only crossroads of anxieties and strategies, they are also the chosen place for social learning and collective action. These last characteristics probably explain why, in spite of scepticism (which is often nothing more than the expression of personal frustration), the members of organizations are in fact more or less unconsciously attracted to meetings. The amount and complexity of the phenomena which occur at meetings underline better than anywhere else the real (if not clear) entanglement of technical and human problems. In this way, these are, to some extent, the reflection or the elongation of everyday life events with all the implicit games. Thus, managers find in meetings unique opportunities putting to test those two qualities for once coexisting: analysis and action.

REFERENCES

AMADO, G., & GUITTET, A. La dynamique des communications dans les groupes. Paris: Armand Colin, coll. "U", 1991.

AMADO, G., FAUCHEUX, C., & LAURENT, A. Ethonomanagement, a latin provocation. International Studies of Management and Organization, vol. 21, nr. 3, Fall 1991.

AMADO, G. Identité psychique, crise et organisation pour une théorie de la résonance. Psychologie Clinique, nr. 3, 1990, 115-128.

ANCELIN-SCHUTZENBERGER, A. L'observation dans les groupes de formation et de thérapie. Paris: Epi, 1972.

ANZIEU, A. Le groupe et l'inconscient. Paris: Dunod, 1975.

BEAUDOT, X. La créativité. Paris: Dunod, 1973.

BEJARANO, A. Résistance et transfert dans les groupes. In D. Anzieu, Le travail psychanalytique dans les groupes. Paris: Dunod, 1972, 65-140.

BION, W.R. Recherches sur les petits groupes. Paris: P.U.F., 1965.

CROZIER, M. L'acteur et le système. Paris: Seuil, 1978.

ENRIQUEZ, E. De la horde à l'Etat. Paris: Gallimard, 1983.

FAUCHEUX, C., & MOSCOVICI, S. Le style de comportement d'une minorité et son influence sur les réponses d'une majorité. Bulletin du C.E.R.P., XVI nr. 4, 1967, 337-360.

FREUD, A. Le moi et les mécanismes de défense. Paris: P.U.F., 1967.

FREUD, S. Psychologie collective et analyse du moi. In Essais de Psychoanalyse. Paris: Payot, 1923.

KETS DE VRIES, M.F.R. Prisoners of leadership. New York: John Willy and sons, 1989.

LAPIERRE, C. Mourning, potency and power in management. Human Resource Management, vol. 28, nr. 2, Summer 1989, 177-189.

Creating a Family in the Workplace

Howell S. Baum

INTRODUCTION

Work requires acting both aggressively and lovingly - assertively enough to transform objects but caringly enough not to break them. This challenge, and the dangers of miscalculating a balance, are multiplied many times with modern service work. The objects of work are people, who often resist being transformed and fight back before being broken.

In addition, much service work involves special challenges regarding aggression and intimacy. Intellectual activity which "attacks a problem" intrudes into people's lives. It entails applying a particular rationality to the circumstances of people who do not readily accept it. For example, professionals often oppose a collectively-oriented rationality to privately rationalized interests. In so doing, they provoke, and need to defend themselves against, others who will resist and fight back.

Much of this intellectual work entails close collaboration. People work closely for long periods of time in loosely bounded creative effort. This closeness encourages intimacy. Depending on the amount of time people spend together, as well as the intensity of their collaboration, work relationships may displace other intimate relationships, such as those of family. This cohesiveness may provide strength needed to promote intellectual positions, but it also requires regulation. People do not want to feel uncomfortably close, anxious about losing themselves in intimacy with others.

Bureaucracy, the organizational setting for much of this service work, does not help with these challenges. Set up to keep workers at regulated distances, it does not contribute to closeness. Moreover, its structure adds anxiety about aggression to anxiety about intimacy. In hierarchical situations where responsibility exceeds authority and both are ambiguous, people worry about being blamed for mistakes. Shame anxiety makes them hesitate to assert themselves. When the person in authority is several hierarchical levels away from subordinates, when subordinates rarely see or have access to him or her and cannot understand his or her motives for exercising authority, they worry about offending authority. Anxiety about being punished makes them

---

Reprinted, by permission of publisher, from Human Relations, 44, 11 (1991).

hold back on acting aggressively, either to assert a position or to work hard generally (Baum, 1987).

Hence many service workers face the challenge of finding safe ways to work that allow them to act aggressively in intimate relationships (Hirschhorn, 1989; Hodgson, Levinson and Zaleznik, 1965; Jaques, 1990; Kets de Vries and Miller, 1984; Levinson, 1968; and Neff, 1985). To do so, they must defend themselves against anxiety aroused by the work or its context and develop alternative procedures or settings. This design effort entails reacting to both real work conditions and unconscious fears and wishes associated with them.

Meeting this challenge involves what Cooper and Gustafson identify as unconscious planning (Cooper and Gustafson, 1981; Gustafson and Cooper, 1979; also Hirschhorn and Krantz, 1982). In defining problems, setting goals, and devising and implementing strategies, some activity can be conscious, but much of it, especially that concerned with unconscious fantasies, anxieties, and needs, can only be unconscious.

This paper describes a city planning department where staff members responded to these work dilemmas by trying to transform their organization into what they called a "family." Consciously and unconsciously, they organized "family" activities and interpreted events in "family" terms. This "family" solved the basic problems of work in a number of ways but floundered when new staff members changed organizational realities and fantasies.

STORIES OF THE FAMILY

The planning department, in an eastern United States city, has 70 staff members, including secretaries and administrators. Professionals conduct studies, prepare plans, and make recommendations related to land use, economic development, transportation, coastal resources and the environment, capital improvements, and urban design. Work is intense, relationships are informal and often quite unbureaucratically intimate, and people socialize a great deal. These conditions, while unusual, often characterize cliques or small organizations of creative professionals. What distinguishes this agency is that many staff members insist on seeing their relationships and activities as unique expressions of an organizational "family."

I first heard staff members talk about the organization as a "family" in the course of earlier research, and I returned two years later to find out what people meant by this unexpected term. Now, however, I heard people say that the family no longer existed or else was not as robust as it had been. Estimates of past and present family membership varied considerably. Moreover, people told two distinct family histories. Both concluded with strained relations between black and white staff centered on equity in promotions, but they accounted for this situation differently.

Some people said that all, or nearly all, of the staff, including administrators and secretaries, were part of an organizational family. These people were particularly likely to recount a history going back to a "golden era," or "heyday," when everyone - blacks and whites, men and women - got along well. This time was heralded in "lore" carefully conveyed to newcomers. It was recorded in photographs of staff basketball and softball games, picnics, and other events. Then something happened, and the organization became racially divided.

Others estimated family size between about 5 and 25. They were likely to tell a different history, in which there had always been some racial conflict, mostly expressed in periodic grievances about promotions. Present racial tensions continued from the past and perhaps were not even as intense as earlier. In this account, family activities, with fluctuating participation over time, mainly involved a minority of whites.

As histories, both versions refer to actual events; they differ in emphasis but do not conflict. However, as stories about the organization and the organizational family, they are distinct. One describes the demise of a large, all-inclusive organizational family, while the other portrays the family as a relatively small group, often affecting, but never comprising, the whole staff. The accounts refer to different families, or different aspects of family.

Those who describe the smaller family present an account of a social family. They define a family in terms of relationships and activities that members participate in. For example, people eat together, go out together, play sports together, and help one another renovate houses. In addition, at which times the core family becomes an extended family, they voluntarily assist others with their work and do things to boost spirits or morale. These activities include organizing parties to mark personal landmarks and, centrally, participating in skits in the annual Christmas party. This family has an identifiable membership, a social structure, and clear boundaries.

Those who include nearly everyone in the family emphasize a sentimental family. They consider people members of the family when they share certain sentiments. Most commonly, they care about one another, feel close, are concerned about others' triumphs and problems, and feel others protect them. This family has no distinct membership or social boundaries. Indeed, people who do not volunteer for social activities and may not consider themselves family members may be identified as such by those who emphasize periodic swellings of close, caring feelings. This family is defined by an emotional structure.

Only a minority characterize the organization as a family, and only a minority actively participate in the family; nevertheless, they affect others and make the department distinctly unbureaucratic. Socially, many are drawn into voluntary activities, and nearly everyone has attended the Christmas party. Sentimentally, most find working relations informal and often caring, at least partly the result of efforts by family members. The recently retired director encouraged familyness in both aspects.

ORIGINS: THE FAMILY AS A MEANS OF DEVELOPING INTIMATE RELATIONSHIPS

The family began as a variety of social activities that allowed staff members who worked long hours together to enjoy close relationships with one another. In the early and middle 1970's, several community activists joined the department. They had worked in poverty programs, the anti-war movement, progressive, usually Democratic politics, and neighborhood organizations. They were not planners by training, but they had grown up in the city, and they wanted to build and shape a city they cared deeply for. They developed together as planners during the heyday of planning in the city, when infusions of federal money swelled the staff and the city became nationally famous for its "renaissance."

They liked being part of community organizations, and they almost intuitively tried to create a community for themselves in the planning department. They did not clearly distinguish their personal and professional lives. Some of their projects involved neighborhoods where they were leaders. They worked long hours, and they thought nothing of working evenings or weekends on their own or others' projects. They were young, most were single, and none had children. Thus, it seemed natural that staff members should eat together, celebrate birthdays and other events together, date one another, organize athletic teams, put out a staff newspaper, and support one another in myriad ways.

By the early and middle 1980's, several of these people had become administrators. They used their positions to foster community and closeness in the department. They hired others whom they considered good potential family members. These newcomers differed mainly in that they had professional planning degrees and came from out of town. Most were away from home for the first time, except possibly school years. In a new city, they knew no one, and the first people they met were co-workers. Like the family founders, they were young and single. They were middle class, mostly white, well educated, starting work careers, and beginning to think about starting their own families. They were creative, they shared professional goals, most held politically left and/or counter-cultural views, they were idealistic, and they shared a growing love for the city, itself an object of national adoration as a place which had redeemed itself through planning.

At a time when people form intimate relationships, working long hours, they turned to co-workers for the satisfactions of closeness. These friendships and occasional romances both substituted for attenuated ties to families of origin and satisfied needs for intimacy while also simply orienting people to a new city and workplace.

In discussing their activities, these people emphasize their creativity and special personal qualities. When creative people work together intensely, they say, they stimulate one another to new creativity. Some of this they can express in their work; some must find other outlets. When people work long hours together, these other expressions may turn up on the job, as in elaborate Christmas party skits, a satirical newspaper (The Daily Planet), and outings.

The departmental family had various relations to the families that staff members came from. For many, the organizational family was a compensation for at least the geographic distance of their families. For some, it was clearly a compensation for the failures of their families, which they described as "dysfunctional," "evil," conflict ridden, or split by divorce. In other cases, the departmental family was apparently a continuation or reenactment of family satisfactions.

This social family served staff members' developmental wishes to become mature, integrated members of a community. It also helped defend them from political attacks on unpopular positions. Nevertheless, personal distinctiveness and intimacy are not natural to a work organization. Family members recognized this, and they devised activities to negotiate room for aggression and caring, as well as to initiate newcomers into the family.

THE FAMILY AS AN INITIATORY DEFENSE AGAINST THE DANGERS OF ORGANIZATIONAL MEMBERSHIP

Organizational membership poses dilemmas for both newcomers and veterans. A new worker wants to know whether it is possible to have the rewards of belonging, such as competence, a recognized professional identity, and affiliation with colleagues, without giving up uniqueness and autonomy (see Anzieu, 1984; Bion, 1961; Colman and Geller, 1985; Freud, 1962 [1930]; and Slater, 1966). Veterans want to increase their numbers but fear new members will bring dangerous influences in from the outside, and they set up initiations to "neutralize" newcomers (Baum, 1990; Graen, 1976; Schein, 1968; Van Gennep, 1960 [1908]; and Van Maanen, 1976).

As veterans, the family members established their own initiation rituals, both to win newcomers over to the social family and to change the organization to allow social family activities and sentimental family feelings.

Family members actively recruit newcomers. Routinely, when a new hire starts out, someone from the family invites him or her to lunch with other family members. The meal and subsequent discussions comprise what some family members call an "indoctrination," in which newcomers are told the family history. They hear about softball, basketball, and volleyball games, the Christmas and other parties, and ways in which people have volunteered to help others at work or at home. They are told about extensive staff socializing. Often veterans note that dating among staff members is acceptable, even approved of. Sometimes they explain who is dating whom, who has previously gone with whom, and which staff members are presently married to each other. All this encourages new arrivals to become intimately involved in the organization.

The family character of staff relations is reinforced by routine wedding showers, baby showers, and going-away parties. Even though not everyone participates in all parties, they mean that the department is a family, where anyone's marriage or parenthood increases everyone, and anyone's departure diminishes them. Staff often send cards or flowers to those who are sick or disabled. Birthdays are celebrated by groups of varying size. The message is that personal transitions affect the organization, that it changes as its members change.

The most elaborate, complex, and explicit initiation ritual has been the Christmas party. (1) Family members boasted it was the year's ultimate event. The hallmark of the party was the skits and songs.

Begun in the early 1980's as parodies of the year's events, they became satires on the director, staff members, politicians, and community activists. The skit included costumes and props, participants rehearsed for days or weeks, and the events were videotaped for repeated viewing. These parties became models for smaller-scale showers and going-away parties.

Each year, about two weeks before the party, veterans approached staff members who had come on during the year and told them they had to take responsibility for some skits. Anyone who refused was looked down on. What resulted was a sophisticated accomplishment of conscious and unconscious planning. The events momentarily made explicit the conflicts between individuality and organizational membership and provided a combination of real and symbolic resolutions. Three aspects of the party helped both to initiate the newcomers and to re-initiate the veterans.

First, the performers did outrageous, embarrassing things. They might dress in drag. Some wore bizarre costumes, did parodies of themselves, or sang silly songs. Thus, the newcomers, like others who participated, had to make fools of themselves for instance, by showing they couldn't really sing, saying inane things about administrators or themselves, or putting on outlandish costumes.

Once they had exposed their most embarrassing facets, as a veteran explained, there was nothing they could do to be a bigger fool at work. Everyone had seen them at their worst - everyone had shown everyone their worst - and now they could get down to work without fear of shaming themselves. (2) The skits showed people at the outset that what they feared most was tolerable and then allowed them to get down to work more securely. The mistakes one inevitably makes on the job, one staff member observed, could be nothing in comparison with the (harmless) embarrassment of the Christmas performance.

Second, the skits and songs were aggressively humorous. People openly made fun of co-workers, particularly, though with his seeming enjoyment, the director. (Indeed, he began asking people about skits in early December, to be sure they were produced.) Explaining the aggression, several staff members observed that intense work, often under pressure from a demanding mayor, often in the face of attack from politicians or community groups, created tensions, even among the best meaning colleagues.

The Christmas party allowed, even required people to vent their anger, resentment, and envy. People could present grievances they had not worked out during the year. The director was a frequent target. One party featured a photograph of him with a dunce cap drawn on his head. His acquiescence shaped the spirit of an event where newcomers, as everyone, were expected to act aggressively toward others, including those in authority, and then saw no dangerous consequences. The lesson was that normal resentment could be expressed without danger, that conflicts could somehow be addressed and resolved. (3)

The third important aspect of the skits, implicit in the first two, is that all was forgiven. After embarrassing themselves and attacking others, everyone was caringly accepted (back) into the departmental family. (A few staff members, however, felt that some skits, perhaps an increasing number, crossed the bounds from good-natured joking to hostility in poor taste. By and large, these people did not think of themselves as family members, and, if anything, the performance only distanced them from those who did.)

The party had the structure and effects of initiation rituals in traditional societies (Turner, 1969; and Van Gennep, 1960 [1908]). In a first stage, it stripped newcomers (and re-stripped veterans) of the status and dignity of their formal roles. In a transitional stage, it forced them to confront one another as persons, more or less spontaneously and honestly, with their weaknesses exposed. In a third stage, at the end of the party, they could (re-)enter organizational identities empowered but also permanently humbled by the confrontation. It would be hard to pull rank on co-workers after having embarrassed oneself at the Christmas party.

The Christmas ritual transformed the organization as well. Skits and songs defined the department as a place where aggression was limited and ultimately safe, where people would not be punished or shamed for their work. Participation in the party, either actively as performer or passively as audience, (re-)affirmed the unity of the department as more than a mere workplace.

THE FAMILY AS A MEANS OF TRANSFORMING ORGANIZATIONAL AUTHORITY

The annual Christmas party by itself cannot make over the organization. In fact, the friendly attack on the director in skits and songs is only the most explicit act in a general conscious and unconscious campaign to contain aggression by softening and leveling hierarchical authority. The clearest sign of this is linguistic. Staff members who do not consider the department a family speak of "management," "bosses," "employers," and "employees." Those who think of it as a family never use these terms: instead of conflict, they speak of loyalty.

In a Weberian bureaucracy, authority is hierarchical, and lines of authority are definite (Weber, 1967). Beginning with the director, each administrator has authority to assign responsibilities to specific subordinates. Administrators evaluate work and decide on promotions. Formality keeps personal loyalties from interfering with accountability. However, subordinates want to know how those with authority will use their power, so that decisions will be comprehensible and predictable. When formality conceals superiors' personalities, subordinates make assumptions about their boss. Typically, they unconsciously attribute to him or her great power and a readiness to shame them for inadequacy and punish them for assertiveness (Baum, 1987). Thus, formality arouses anxiety about aggression.

If staff members recast the workplace in family terms, bureaucratic administrators become parents, and irrational commitments supplant rational relations. For example, a number of planning staff seriously or jokingly talked about the recently retired director as a father or like a father; some, considering his age, likened him to a grandfather; others criticized him as a poor father figure.

Few people identify any maternal figure in the organization, but a woman who had a mother role in the past commented on the consequences of turning managers into parents. In her case, she and some of her supervisees at least half seriously talked of her as their mother. She closely oversaw their work and watchfully made sure they were prepared for meetings (even, in winter, asking whether they had their gloves). She took a caring interest in their private lives. Everyone, she said, enjoyed this relationship. It recaptured the moment when she was their equal, before she became an administrator. At the same time, it modulated the impact of her assignments, which she insistently tried to enforce.

Regarding her as a mother, she observed, was a way of taking away some of her power. You can tell a mother off. You cannot take her seriously. You can avoid respecting her. You can question her reasons. At least for women, she felt, considering bosses parents is a way of diminishing their authority. Whenever a female administrator is cast as a parent, subordinates, who become her children, may insist that she care for them, not punish them.

Not all mothers are the same, and fathers are not the same as mothers, but hierarchical authority seems to be softened when an administrator is considered a parent. For example, when staff characterized the director as fatherly, they emphasized that he personally cared about their work and was accessible to them.

This reconceptualization of relations has both advantages and hazards for administrators. Several people observed that an administrator may ask subordinates for extraordinary efforts in the name of family loyalty. On the other hand, once managers invoke family obligations, they open themselves to refusals from "children," who expect "parents" to be caring and tolerant of personal feelings and circumstances.

The fluidity of authority in a family offers subordinates new benefits. They may negotiate assignments or evaluations with their bosses. They may also get assistance from others by appealing to family loyalty. On the other hand, there is a danger of exploitation: it is difficult to say no to a boss or anyone else who is a friend and like a family member. One person said he sometimes wants to appeal to a shop steward, and there isn't one.

Transformation of Work Relations

Hierarchical authority is the cornerstone of bureaucracy. When that authority is turned into parental authority, work is transformed. Staff members disagree about the effects of the changes. Most simply, some who are not in the family, including some administrators, argue that caring and socializing take up time and break down needed discipline. In contrast, family members argue that close relationships help get work done.

One person said that, although nobody likes to work, his family feelings toward others get him to work. Beyond that, because he cares about his boss and people in his section, he works hard, to reflect well on them. Moreover, because people like each other, they willingly work late. Another planner added that close relations contribute to work not simply because people care about each other, but also because people understand one another's idiosyncrasies. They can distinguish when someone is really angry about work from when he is just letting off steam in his own peculiar way. Repeatedly, staff members said they feel cared for, appreciated, and respected as mature professionals and work harder as a result.

What family members say is consistent with psychological views of work. In psychoanalytic terms, work requires a partly conscious, partly unconscious compromise between two basic drives: aggression, which expresses itself in physical and emotional force against objects and persons, and which tends to push an actor apart from those objects or persons; and libido, which expresses itself in sexuality and caring, and which draws people toward others. Getting work done requires acting sufficiently aggressively toward physical materials or other people to change them in appropriate ways. At the same time, a worker must care sufficiently for the objects of work to preserve them and help and allow them to change in desired ways (Erikson, 1963 and 1968; and Neff, 1985).

Planning is typical of collaborative services, where the work involves creating and maintaining relationships. For example, people must work aggressively enough to initiate and complete studies; they must work caringly enough to get along with team members and to come to agreement on how to conduct the studies and what to conclude from them. Nevertheless, in any work, it is easy for aggressive impulses to displace libidinal or caring ones. Encouragement to "work hard" emphasizes aggression. Hierarchy, where people are assigned, evaluated, and promoted individually, emphasizes aggressive separation of workers from one another. Concerns about "productivity" tend to reward aggression and penalize caring.

When workers find such conditions unpleasant, they may try to introduce ways of allowing themselves to act libidinally, caringly, and intimately. They may organize luncheons, parties, or picnics. They may create side-games. Making the organization familylike is another way to do this. It legitimates a more caring compromise with aggression. For people who work 60 hours a week, including time they might be with friends or family, treating the workplace as a family allows, and encourages, them to satisfy libidinal needs in variously intimate relations with co-workers.

In general, calling the organization a family replaces bureaucratic individualism, self-interest, and autonomy with caring, social cohesion, and collective loyalty. Whereas a hierarchy is defined in terms of regulated distances between numerous levels of workers, a family is defined in terms of loyalty between two or, at most, three generations. In contrast with the competitive politics of normal organizations, the family aims at consensus.

The acceptance of libidinal interests into the organization has two effects in everyday relationships. First, it legitimates lengthy close collaboration without anxiety about intimacy or sexuality. After all, it is simply a matter of family members caring for one another. Some of these relations become the basis for deep friendships, while others end at work. If relationships become romantic, they are acceptable. (4) Moreover, if office romances break up, people can continue working together. In addition, crucially, this emphasis permits the expression of greater aggression, since there is now more caring to balance it. Thus, staff talk about not only the special support they feel, but also the freedom to be ironic, irreverent, and profane.

As noted, when administrators become parents, they have difficulty enforcing assignments. In addition, this effort to tame aggression with caring makes evaluating subordinates more complicated. Instead of rendering clear, specific judgments on promotions or raises, administrators may write or act ambiguously, to soften their blow and to avoid protest. The results, as we will see later, leave few people happy.

Transformation of the Individual Experience of the Organization

In making it acceptable to act on both libidinal and aggressive wishes, family members create a setting which generally allows and encourages freer emotional expression. One manifestation of this is what several staff call acceptance of "immaturity." Within broad limits, people may act spontaneously, without considering professional demeanor or etiquette. For example, they may rudely interrupt one another at staff meetings. A literal meaning of acting immaturely is acting like a child, which is explicitly authorized by the terms of family. Thus, staff members may at least tacitly ask of others, including administrators, what children want from parents and other family members - including nurturance, recognition, and childlike autonomy.

For an adult, being immature is regressive. One unconscious concomitant of this regression is to encourage, or at least allow, people to engage in what psychoanalysts call primary process thinking. Out of consciousness and free from everyday reality, connecting phenomena on the basis of convenient analogies rather than formal or explicit logic, people see what brings them pleasure, what they would like to be true (Freud, 1965 [1930] and Holt, 1967). Dreams are the most visible products of primary process thinking, but it occurs all the time, simultaneous with conscious, logical thinking.

In the planning department, Christmas party skits, for instance, portray a world in which administrators and staff, father and children, are equal and where people can act aggressively without reprisal. Another example of this merging of unconscious and conscious thought is an experience of timelessness that some members describe. The recently retired director headed the department for 24 years and during the expansive 1960's and 1970's hired many young people. Several of them talk about how, though years have passed, as they stayed together under the same director, they don't seem to have gotten older. They made time stand still.

There is another aspect to what one person described as "a strong acceptance of personalities." On the one hand, people tolerate irritating behavior, such as "hangups," smoking, alcoholism, and uncontrolled outbursts. On the positive side, everyone can be special - in the family metaphor, a special child. One person began his discussion of family characteristics of the organization with a 15-minute description of his unique personal history, culminating in the story of his initial interview, where he was hired as much for his interests in softball and music as for his professional qualifications. Another staff member related how support from other musicians enabled him to build on his classical training to learn to play jazz.

By containing aggression and encouraging personal expression and caring, staff make room for the activities of the social family and create the possibility of a sentimental family.

SAFEGUARDING THE FAMILY: AVOIDING FAMILY CONFLICTS

The departmental family is a happy one, but there is no reason why a family must be happy, nor need a father be good. Indeed, unconscious associations between bureaucratic bosses and fathers often make the boss appear threatening because the father seemed dangerous. And yet the departmental family does not suffer certain basic family conflicts. Those who made the organization a family seem unconsciously to have recognized the hazards that accompany childhood and to have designed the family so as to exclude them.

In both everyday talk and psychoanalytic theory, two fundamental features of families are the Oedipus complex and sibling rivalry. Most simply, the Oedipus complex is a relationship between two parents and a child, where the child seeks to overthrow the parent of the same sex and form a liaison with the parent of the opposite sex. In attempting to carry out this project, the child must think about acting aggressively against the same-sex parent, including the possibility of being destroyed or injured retributively or pre-emptively. In the child's mind, the Oedipus complex is resolved when he (or she) agrees to accept the parents' relationship with each other and decides, instead of attacking the same-sex parent, to identify with that parent, drawing strength from thinking of himself as somehow having the loving parent "inside" him. The child experiences that internal representation as conscience. In return for abiding by parents' rules, the child becomes part of their moral community (Fenichel, 1945; Freud, 1977

[1920], 1989 [1924], and 1965 [1933]; Grunberger, 1979; Klein, 1948 [1928 and 1945]; and Rangell, 1972).

When parents have a second child, they set the conditions for sibling rivalry. The first child, finding parents' love and attention are not infinite, discovers hate, for the intruding brother or sister (as well as for the parents). The second child eventually understands that he or she could have more of the parents' love and power if the firstborn were not present, and the two actively compete for the parents' affection. Sibling rivalry may become implicated in the Oedipus complex, where, for example, two sisters may struggle for the father. Sibling rivalry is resolved when a child can accept the apparent finitude of love and balance hatred for a brother or sister with a way of loving him or her (Colonna and Newman, 1983; and Provence and Solnit 1983). The Oedipal and sibling dramas require struggling to learn to exercise aggression realistically in a world of finite love so as to maintain the love of others who matter.

Significantly, these features are absent from the departmental family. To begin with, the former director was not exactly a father. On the one hand, seriously or half-seriously, staff members often spoke of him as "paternal," "fatherly," "a father figure," "like a father," or "the departmental father." Some, because of his age, referred to him in grandfatherly terms. He had hired virtually everyone, and he was at least a generation older than most. He took a personal interest in people's work, and he had helped several young staff members get college degrees and training they needed to get ahead. He gave helpful advice on projects, and he defended the department against critics.

On the other hand, being "like a father," "a father figure," or grandfatherly is not the same as being a father. A grandfather is old and weak, perhaps once a strong father but no longer so. He is caring without being threatening. Staff members, whether they described the director as fatherly or not, debated whether he was a strong leader, or whether he had been more forceful when he was younger. He was not directive; he was interested more in ideas than administration. Several years ago, in response to complaints, he brought in a consultant, who helped create a structure to manage the department.

The resultant split between intellectual leadership and personnel and fiscal management encouraged a split between the emotional images of the director and the deputy for administration. The director was seen as largely caring, and the deputy, as largely aggressive and punitive. (5) Staff explicitly took pleasure in calling the director by his first name. This was in keeping with the informality he encouraged, but it helped to make the father a pal - more like the children than a parent.

A second way the departmental family differed from normal families is that, as most people quickly said, it had no mother. The easiest explanation is that no woman has held high administrative position, able to draw the transferred feelings that made the director seem like a father. However, a couple of women section chiefs did become like mothers for their staffs. They desired the role, and most of their subordinates wanted or accepted it. Thus, the wish to be motherly affects whether someone is considered maternal. At the same time, a few women occupied positions in the departmental managerial structure, and none was seen as parental like the director. Perhaps none desired the role. In addition, the emotional split between intellectual leadership and personnel management defined the director as caring and the others as controlling.

There are hints that, for at least some family members, the director combined both fatherly and motherly attributes. One person, for example, began to describe the department as a "matriarchy" before correcting himself to call it a "patriarchy." Another, commenting "there is no dominant feminine figure," added "but the feminine figure may not be a woman." Significantly, many of the words of both praise and criticism characterized the director in ways conventionally associated with women: soft, not a strong disciplinarian, permissive, personal, caring, nurturant, interested, and weak. Even many who said they would have preferred him to be more forceful appreciated his softness.

One family member said he didn't "think anyone would take too kindly to anyone who took a mother role [because staff were] too collegial for that." At its simplest, such a statement suggests that a hierarchical differentiation like that between a mother and children would dissolve the equality of staff members. But he seems to mean, further, that a mother would break up collegial cooperation. This would happen if childlike subordinates each had separate relationships with the mother. Competition for special status would reproduce sibling rivalry in the workplace.

A more complex, speculative interpretation is possible: competition for someone in a mother role in the presence of a fatherly director would create an intricate organizational Oedipus complex. By unconsciously reminding individuals of their own Oedipal conflicts, such a situation would arouse anxiety. In addition, unconsciously triggered efforts to compete for the mother figure by challenging the fatherly director and sibling-like co-workers could split the organization and damage work. Two alternatives, if the department is to be a family, are to insist that there can be no mother or, if that is not plausible, to assume that the director can be both father and mother.

At the same time, it is possible that this configuration of the organizational family is symbolically parricidal. In the end, the director is a father but not a (real, strong) father. He is enough of a father to reassure the "children" that identifying with him secures them from engulfment by the mother, but he does not present any danger to them (see Chasseguet-Smirgel, 1986). He is a father, but perhaps he is also a mother. The symbolic combination of father and mother in him would allow the "children" unconsciously not only to identify with the father without risk but also to take possession of the mother without harm. In this process, the father is killed and castrated.

In reality, the director was not father to anyone on the staff, and no one there was anyone's mother. The observation that a mother role would destroy collegiality invokes this reality. A number of people who considered themselves part of the departmental family did not identify either an organizational father or mother. In saying this, they point to a third distinctive characteristic of the departmental family: it is child centered. It is a family of children without parents.

Not only is "immaturity" acceptable, but the "irreverence," "profanity," and "irony" that family members enjoy aiming at the director, elected officials, and community leaders are reminiscent of children's aggressive ridicule of parents. When parents make statements or attempt to enforce rules that make no sense to children, the children make fun of them, openly if possible, covertly, as in games, if necessary. They mean to say that what makes sense to them is the only sense there is. Another expression of childlike egocentrism is the long-time staff member's comment, already noted, that because so many people had entered the department at a young age and had stayed together, they were "forever young."

In this context, it is particularly significant that dating among staff members is acceptable and even encouraged. In a workplace where people spend long hours together, this is certainly reassuring. At the same time, unconsciously, it suggests that children can reproduce themselves. Because there aren't really any parents (meaning: adults) in the family, children can and should mate without becoming grown-ups. This fantasy is similar to groups members' occasional unconscious assumption that pairings between members magically reproduce and save the group (Bion, 1961). The staff is actually reproduced through recruitment of new workers, and, when members of the departmental family are involved, they try to select people like themselves. A symbolic meaning of this reasonable practice is that the offspring of children are other similar children. When children reproduce themselves, when there are no generational differences, there is no sibling rivalry and no Oedipal conflict.

These speculations suggest some of the different meanings of the social and sentimental families. The social family is a more literal family: it involves specific persons acting toward one another in tangible ways. It has membership criteria and boundaries. Although entry is easy, it depends on someone's taking the initiative to help out others. In contrast, the sentimental family is less specific. It does not so much have members as people who participate in it by feeling joined to others. Its boundaries are amorphous. It is hard to be certain who is part of it at any time, though, because of its nature, people who feel part of it feel that others are part of it.

Although the two families may co-exist and reinforce one another, and although they both emphasize cooperating and caring, they are different in an important way. The social family involves separate persons choosing to be together, thus creating and re-creating the family. In contrast, the sentimental family is based on a collective feeling, which subsumes individuals. This sentiment exists apart from, and, in an important way, prior to any separate persons.

The data relevant to the histories of these two families would be different. A social history would focus on the actions of individuals, whereas a sentimental history would focus on general feelings. In these terms, people's confusion about the departmental family history is understandable.

At the same time, the confusion between the two families serves a useful, largely unconscious purpose. In the social family, because it is made up of individuals who may enter and exit, conflict, as well as decline, is possible. In the sentimental family, because it consists of only idealized caring feelings, only harmony and life are possible. Thus, merging the two images makes it possible to save the family when the department encounters conflicts.

One special meaning of this confusion pertains to the unconscious dangers of Oedipal conflict and sibling rivalry. The social family, because it consists of specific individuals, includes a number of discernible roles. Some mentioned were "the yente," "the class clown," and "the coffee commissioner." Consistently, it is possible for someone to become "the mother" or "the father." For example, although the director was not an active participant in the social family (more an approving outsider), insofar as he was even occasionally considered a member (at the Christmas party, for example), then he might take a defined role, such as father. And this would lead to all the dangers of Oedipal conflict and sibling rivalry.

By moving to think of everyone, including the director, as people whose feelings make up one harmonious sentimental family, people could avoid the unconscious and real dangers of family competition and conflict. However, to be successful at this unconscious maneuver, people would have to hide from themselves and confuse themselves about what they were doing by substituting one image of family for another.

REALITY RESISTS AND CHANGES: TRYING TO OVERCOME DIFFERENCES AND CONFLICTS

In the end, these efforts to create an inclusive sentimental family encountered stubborn realities. The social family was small, homogeneous, and harmonious. However, the department was not only larger, but it distinguished people hierarchically, it contained groups, including racial groups, who insisted that they differed in important ways, and its members fought over promotions and raises.

Attempts to soften organizational authority were an effort to eliminate one basic difference between categories of people. If relations are personal, rather than hierarchical, then no one is much higher, and no one is much lower, than anyone else. This vertical difference evokes the second difference an infant encounters - the generational distinction from the seemingly omnipotent parents. This difference is an elaboration of an earlier one, where the infant recognizes a growing psychological and physical separation from the mother. In short, the first experience of difference is separateness itself (Chasseguet-Smirgel, 1985; Mahler, Pine, and Bergman, 1975; and Winnicott, 1965).

The discovery of separateness is the discovery of dependence on others, whether the parents of childhood or the co-workers of adulthood. It is an encounter with a world where obstacles block one's aims and one must make an effort to get from others what one wants. This is a world where love is conditional. In contrast with the fantasy world of infancy, where wishes for power and love seem magically to lead to their satisfaction, later reality entails strategic relationships.

And yet infants, and children and adults, yearn to re-experience the power and love of the first narcissistic moments of life. One way they do this is by identifying with persons they imagine can give them this power and love. (6) Glorification of parents and hero worship are common examples. Adults may idealize and identify with a work organization. They may fantasize that it is a place where all are united and that, by joining it, they absorb the collective power and love (Schwartz, 1990). In this imaginary organization, they are not separate or different, and only fantasy is necessary to satisfy their wishes (Chasseguet-Smirgel, 1986).

In the real workplace, hierarchical authority constitutes a basic separation, difference, and obstacle to individual satisfaction. To some degree, as in the planning department, formal authority differences can be reduced. Still, people bring into an organization other differences, such as age, gender, and race, that cannot easily be regulated. In fantasy, however, they can be removed. Group members, for example, sometimes fantasize there are no differences among them: all seem sexless, raceless, and ageless (Bion, 1961; and Slater, 1966).

Although it is difficult to know the motives of planning department staff, the softening of hierarchical authority seems linked with interests in eliminating or ignoring other basic differences. The sentimental family depends on the fantasy that everyone is in important ways the same. An example is the way people equate racial differences with the demise of the family.

When some white staff members try to reconcile current racial tensions with the "family" history, they seem confused. Was the "family" a myth? Did they delude themselves into believing the organization was like a family? Some puzzlement comes from real complexities in the departmental history. But some also reflects the dual consciousness required to make a family from people who are different. Motivation for believing that everyone is the same stems from the (simultaneous) recognition that people are different. Consistently, several white staff members said they are aware of racial issues but don't want to know anything specific and want someone else to resolve them.

One history of departmental race relations highlights cooperation at work and in social and athletic activities. The other acknowledges differences and conflicts. The accounts converge in recognizing that new young black staff with planning degrees want more than blacks have traditionally gotten in the department.

The department has had few black professionals until recent years. Most administrators have been white. As a series of complaints raised questions about prejudice and as the proportion of blacks on the staff grew, people looked at each successive promotion increasingly in terms of race.

Even if there were no discrimination, a paucity of opportunities could be expected to produce conflict. The organization is small, it has few hierarchical levels, and people rarely leave for other jobs. Consequently, promotions are scarce, and an opening can produce intense competition. Administrators say they have tried to handle promotions so as to minimize conflict. However, the reality of a growing number of increasingly senior people seeking promotions into a few positions makes this harder and harder to do. Both black and white staff complain that managerial efforts to maintain harmony have led to ambiguous promotion standards and seemingly arbitrary decisions. The result, often is anger.

Tensions between black and white staff present two problems. Relations become acrimonious and unpleasant. In addition, these conflicts jeopardize the belief that the organization is like a family. In this respect, racial differences represent every difference that separates people. These problems are related.

Psychodynamically, differences are the product of aggression, by which someone asserts himself and sets himself apart from others. Staff members who insist on differences and distance resist the libidinal merging of colleagues in an organizational family. In addition, by introducing new aggression into the organization, blacks or others who insist on their individuality raise the risks of uncontrolled aggression. Unconsciously, people may imagine that the measure of aggression a group take to assert their separateness can become totally destructive, setting off an endless chain of reprisals.

People who consider themselves part of the organizational family are uneasy about various divisions among staff. Clerical and professional workers have different responsibilities, schedules, and interests. Secretaries sometimes resent planners' autonomy, as well as their requests, and some planners feel guilty about their seemingly unwarranted position.

Some staff members who do not identify with the family think of it as one of several departmental cliques, but family members resist this term. A clique, they say, is exclusive, based on differences, whereas the family is open to everyone. Some family members recognize cliques in the department but insist the family includes people from each.

New procedures or greater friendliness might reduce some of these divisions, with the unconscious dangers they represent, but complaints about promotions remind everyone of two basic, persistent organizational divisions. Promotion involves hierarchical advancement, and any opening recalls fundamental differences in authority. When people compete for openings, managers, as well as anyone else who cares, must value some people more than others.

Demands for new promotional procedures entail new psychological negotiations over the balance of aggression and affection in an organization. Implicitly, blacks argue that they want to be appreciated and cared for even while they compete for promotions. This request requires people to figure out anew how much aggression is necessary and acceptable not just in trying to get promoted, but on the job generally.

For those who want to think of the organization as a loving family, this is an unsettling project. Talking practically about promotion procedures violates fantasies about being part of a unified, powerful, caring organization. The wish (to advance) is not equivalent to the act. Loving the administrators is not enough to evoke their love and the gift of promotion. Other people are obstacles, one must aggressively strategize against them, and they may react in kind.

CONCLUSION

Some of the "family planning" described here was conscious and deliberate. Family founders and members responded explicitly and realistically to needs for friendship and support. In addition, many activities and assumptions involved unconscious planning. Without saying so, and apparently without consciously knowing it, people recognized and designed an intricate solution for the dilemmas of service work in a bureaucracy. They created a "family" that allowed them to work aggressively and intimately without great anxiety. Particularly impressively, they seem to have recognized that, if they created a family to manage problems of aggression and libido, they would have to give this family special features that would avoid introducing new aggressive and libidinal problems of Oedipal conflict and sibling rivalry.

This planning was an effort to resolve largely unconscious problems that stood in the way of work, and for some time it succeeded. The current failures of the original family solution reflect changing realities. More blacks joined the staff at the same time that competition for promotions intensified. Not only did many blacks have different professional and social interests from many whites, but few blacks wished to join a family with a white father. At the same time, crucially, the long-standing white director was approaching retirement and finally left, to be succeeded by a black director.

These changes have altered the organization's unconscious life in ways that elude the original family design. Fundamentally, there is no longer a father. There can be no family without a parent. The department has lost the affectionate center that guides the family and nurtures caring responses to aggression. The director's departure let staff members surface conflicts they might have suppressed when the family was more cohesive.

When a father dies, children need to mourn his death, confronting both guilt about any patricidal wishes and anger at being abandoned. Yet nobody in the planning department speaks angrily about the director's retirement. Perhaps the racial conflict has become a focus for this feeling. The arrival of a new black director symbolically slays the old father, and the changing racial composition of the staff both encourages and provides a vehicle for splitting and polarization. It may be easier for white staff to resent blacks for breaking up the family by displacing the father than to be angry at the father who left them, who thus wasn't infinitely loving and betrayed their love and illusions. Whereas family members earlier saw themselves united against politicians, developers, and local leaders, now whites identify an adversary in the organization.

Whether staff members revive the family depends on whether and how they deal with these changes in reality and fantasy. Whether the department becomes again a workplace of unusually good feeling turns on how staff members think about differences among themselves and whether they again accept the challenge of finding safe ways to act aggressively in close working relations.

This story describes an effort to find a solution for dilemmas confronting modern service workers in bureaucratic organizations. For a time, these planners found a solution; there are others. Crucial to their success was that they trusted one another enough to be able collectively to recognize and deal with unconscious obstacles to work. Such unconscious planning cannot be consciously planned, but it can be, as it was here, allowed and encouraged.

NOTES

(1) The most recent Christmas party was not like the parties described here.

(2) Bureaucratic structures tend to make workers anxious about being shamed for inadequacy (Baum, 1987). This self-mortification might be considered a

homeopathic inoculation against this danger. In psychoanalytic terms, it can be seen as an effort to manage anticipated passive embarrasment by actively inflicting it on oneself (Freud, 1977 [1920]; Klein, 1976; Peller, 1954; Waelder, 1933).

(3) This is in contrast with common organizational norms not to express feelings or surface conflict, on the tacit premise that they would lead to chaos (see, for example, Argyris & Schon, 1978; Rafaeli & Sutton, 1989; Van Maanen & Kunda, 1989; Zaleznik, 1989).

(4) If the family methaphor were interpreted literally, romance and attendant sexual relations would be incestuous. In this respect, staff members are practical enough to distinguish metaphorical siblings from actual family members. Perhaps they tacitly agree with one person who suggested the department seemed more like a tribe than a family.

(5) This distinction was based on real personality differences. Nevertheless, members of an organization often split their views of management, separately attributing positive and negative characteristics to different administrators (see Hodgson, Levinson & Zaleznik, 1965; Kets de Vries & Miller, 1984).

(6) In psychoanalytic terms, they unconsciously project an image of their ego ideal (an image of their perfect, powerful, completely loved self) onto someone or something, identify themselves with that person or thing, and in this way recapture some of these powerful feelings (Chasseguet- Smirgel, 1985).

REFERENCES

ANZIEU, D. The group and the unconscious. Translated by B. Kilborne. London: Routledge and Kegan Paul, 1984.

ARGYRIS, C., & SCHON, D.A. Organizational learning. Reading: Addison-Wesley, 1978.

BAUM, H.S. The invisible bureaucracy: The unconscious in organizational problem solving. New York: Oxford University Press, 1987.

BAUM, H.S. Organizational membership: Personal development in the workplace. Albany: State University of New York Press, 1990.

BION, W.R. Experiences in groups. New York: Basic Books, 1961.

CHASSEGUET-SMIRGEL, J. The ego ideal: A psychoanalytic essay on the malady of the ideal. Translated by P. Burrows. New York: W. W. Norton and Company, 1985.

CHASSEGUET-SMIRGEL, J. Sexuality and mind. New York: New York University Press, 1986.

COLMAN, A.D., & GELLER, M.H., editors. Group relations reader 2. Washington: A. K. Rice Institute, 1985.

COLONNA, A.B., & NEWMAN, L.M. The psychoanalytic literature on siblings. Psychoanalytic Study of the Child, 38, 1983, 285-309.

COOPER, L., & GUSTAFSON, J.P. Family-group development: Planning in organizations. Human Relations, 34, 1981, 705-730.

ERIKSON, E.H. Childhood and society. Second edition. New York: W.W. Norton and Company, 1963.

ERIKSON, E.H. Identity: Youth and crisis. New York: W.W. Norton and Company, 1968.

FENICHEL, O. The psychoanalytic theory of neurosis. New York: W.W. Norton and Company, 1945.
FREUD, S. Introductory lectures on psychoanalysis. 1920. Translated by J. Strachey. New York: W.W. Norton and Company, 1977.
FREUD, S. The dissolution of the Oedipus complex. 1924. In The Freud Reader, edited by P. Gay. New York: W.W. Norton and Company, 1989.
FREUD, S. Civilization and its discontents. 1930. Translated by J. Strachey. New York: W.W. Norton and Company, 1962.
FREUD, S. The interpretation of dreams. 1930. Translated by J. Strachey. New York: Avon Books, 1965.
FREUD, S. New introductory lectures on psychoanalysis. 1933. Translated by J. Strachey. New York: W.W. Norton and Company, 1965.
GRAEN, G. Role-making processes within complex organizations. In Handbook of industrial and organizational psychology, edited by M.P. Dunnette. Chicago: Rand McNally, 1976.
GRUNBERGER, B. Narcissism: Psychoanalytic essays. Translated by J.S. Diamanti. New York: International Universities Press, 1979.
GUSTAFSON, J.P., & COOPER, L. Unconscious planning in small groups. Human Relations, 32, 1979, 1039-1064.
HIRSCHHORN, L. The workplace within. Cambridge: M.I.T. Press, 1989.
HIRSCHHORN, L., & KRANTZ, J. Unconscious planning in a natural work group: A case study in process consultation. Human Relations, 35, 1982, 805-844.
HODGSON, R. C., LEVINSON, D. J., & ZALEZNIK, A. The executive role constellation. Boston: Harvard University, The Graduate School of Business Administration, 1965.
HOLT, R. R. The development of the primary process: A structural view. In Motives and thought, edited by R. R. Holt. Psychological Issues, Volume 5, Monograph 18/19. New York: International Universities Press, 1967.
JAQUES, E. Creativity and work. New York: International Universities Press, 1990.
KETS DE VRIES, M. F. R., & MILLER, D. The neurotic organization. San Francisco: Jossey-Bass, 1984.
KLEIN, G.S. Psychoanalytic theory: An exploration in essentials. New York: International Universities Press, 1976.
KLEIN, M. Early stages of the Oedipus complex. 1928. In Contributions to psychoanalysis, 1921-1945. London: the Hogarth Press and the Institute of Psychoanalysis, 1948.
KLEIN, M. The Oedipus complex in the light of early anxieties. 1945. In Contributions to psychoanalysis, 1921-1945. London: the Hogarth Press and the Institute of Psychoanalysis, 1948.
LEVINSON, H. The exceptional executive: A psychological conception. Cambridge: Harvard University Press, 1968.
MAHLER, M.S., PINE, F., & BERGMAN, A. The psychological birth of the infant. New York: Basic Books, 1975.
NEFF, W.S. Work and human behavior. Third edition. New York: Aldine, 1985.
PELLER, L.E. Libidinal phases, ego development, and play. Psychoanalytic Study of the Child, 9, 1954, 178-198.
PROVENCE, S., & SOLNIT, A.J. Development-promoting aspects of the sibling experience. Psychoanalytic Study of the Child, 38, 1983, 337-351.
RAFAELI, A., & SUTTON, R.I. The expression of emotion in organizational life. Research in Organizational Behavior, 11, 1989, 1-42.

RANGELL, L. Aggression, Oedipus, and historical perspective. International Journal of Psycho-Analysis, 53, 1972, 3-11.

SCHEIN, E.H. Career dynamics: Matching individual and organizational needs. Reading: Addison-Wesley, 1968.

SCHWARTZ, H.S. Narcissistic process and corporate decay: The theory of the organization ideal. New York: New York University Press, 1990.

SLATER, P.E. Microcosm: Structural, psychological, and religious evolution in groups. New York: John Wiley and Sons, 1966.

TURNER, V. The ritual process: Structure and anti-structure. Ithaca: Cornell University Press, 1969.

VAN GENNEP, A. The rites of passage. 1908. Translated by M. B. Vizedom & G. L. Caffee. Chicago: University of Chicago Press, 1960.

VAN MAANEN, J. Breaking in: Socialization to work. In Handbook of work, organization, and society, edited by R. Dubin. Chicago: Rand McNally and Company, 1976.

VAN MAANEN, J., & KUNDA, G. "Real feelings": Emotional expression and organizational culture. Research in Organizational Behavior, 11, 1989, 43-103.

WAELDER, R. The psychoanalytic theory of play. Psychoanalytic Quarterly, 2, 1933, 208-224.

WEBER, M. From Max Weber. Edited and translated by H. H. Gerth & C. W. Mills. New York: Oxford University Press, 1967.

WINNICOTT, D.W. The maturational processes and the facilitating environment. New York: International Universities Press, 1965.

ZALEZNIK, A. The managerial mystique. New York: Harper and Row, 1989.

Mentoring: Narcissistic Fantasies and Oedipal Realities

Howell S. Baum

INTRODUCTION

The literature on mentoring is growing. Some of this interest reflects changes in work. Professional and managerial positions, in contrast with blue-collar work, are ambiguous. Instead of finding well-organized roles, workers must negotiate their own boundaries and relationships. In addition, career patterns are uncertain; for many jobs there is no clear or specific line of advancement. Under these conditions, a new worker can benefit from personal guidance by someone who knows an organization and can offer advice, protection, and entree.

Demographic and economic trends make this need especially acute. The baby boom brings a growing crowd of applicants to the corporate world, each looking for the special advantage that will ensure success. Moreover, women make up an increasing proportion of workers seeking professional and managerial careers, and many are concerned about breaking into what has been largely a male organizational world. At the same time, corporate mergers have reduced the number of top positions available.

Thus, getting ahead in an organization is uncertain and risky. Those who enter together often compete for the same positions, and rivals may do whatever they can to eliminate one another. Someone who moves up may displace someone higher up, and those at the top may try to ruin anyone who threatens them. Realistically, a mentor's tutelage can be an important, if not essential way to facilitate organizational and career advancement. Roche typically describes mentoring's benefits in a study of executives:

> Executives who have had a mentor earn more money at a younger age, are better educated, are more likely to follow a career plan, and, in turn, sponsor more proteges than executives who have not had a mentor. (1979, p.15) (1)

Writers often describe the personal relationship between mentor and protege in strikingly instrumental terms. Zey (1984), for example, refers to mentoring as a way of dealing with "politics in the modern corporation". Hunt and Michael characterize mentorship as "a career

---

Reprinted, by permission of publisher, from Human Relations, 45, 3 (1992).

training and development tool" (1983, p. 475; emphasis added). Phillips-Jones calls mentoring "a strategy that successful people have known about for centuries" (1982, p. 16; emphasis added). Collins' (1983) book "Professional Women and Their Mentors" has the subtitle "A Practical Guide to Mentoring for the Woman Who Wants to Get Ahead." The title of a Harvard Business Review (1978) article declares that "Everyone who makes it has a mentor."

Even with a mentor, can making it be a peaceful process? The literature offers two distinct answers, each depending on a different image of mentoring. Optimistic tales of mentoring, most often found in books of advice, tell an encouraging story: the neophyte who finds a mentor can be tutored by someone knowledgeable and powerful, protected from conflicts, and, finally, placed in a deserved top position. Advancement is possible without conflict, and a newcomer need not be anxious about not knowing how to do a job, whether any workers will be collegial, or whether those he or she might pass by in the hierarchy will yield gracefully or fight. Virtue will be rewarded.

One common variant portrays mentoring as purely instrumental, whereby a senior staff member tutors a promising newcomer in work and organizations skills, receives valuable assistance from the junior partner on projects enhancing the mentor's prestige, and in appreciation helps the protege find a high-level position of his or her own. This relationship is focused on work, and it is shaped around the requirements of cognitive teaching and learning. Its premise is that advancement depends on esoteric knowledge which only a few people can and choose to impart.

Yet there is a second view of mentoring, which more often comes from reports on actual experiences. Here the relationship appears ambiguous, tempestuous, conflictual, and often disappointing. In this view, mentoring is not only instrumental, but also developmental. Advancement depends on more than cognitive learning: it requires a basic transformation of the newcomer's expectations, hopes, assumptions, and identity (Baum, 1990). Effective mentoring requires an intense, emotional relationship, in which the protege is not only interested in learning about work but also willing to become a new person. The mentor will engage a younger person so intimately because the mentor, too, can and wants to develop, by passing on some of him- or herself to the next generation.

The first model is a neater, more controlled, certainly more controllable relationship, whereas the second, by encouraging emotional spontaneity, may run an uncertain course. The second model is risky to its participants, who cannot be sure of emerging safely. It is also organizationally dangerous. When two workers become intensely attached to each other, they exclude others and may find the pleasures of their intimacy more satisfying than organizational rewards. This is a potentially subversive relationship. Understandably, formal organizational mentoring programs generally are presented in terms of the first model (for example, Klauss, 1981; Zey, 1984).

Both types of relationships may be observed in organizations, and both are called "mentoring." However, can both be equally effective in helping newcomers advance in organizations? Can cognitive learning alone be sufficient for developing the competence that mentors and managers reward? Perhaps the models respond to different aptitudes and needs, or they may suite different personalities. But it is also possible that the second model represents a more complete description of mentoring relationships than the first. Any human relationship inevitably has emotional components, and even the most instrumental of mentors has feelings about a protege. In addition to referring to more narrowly and carefully bounded relationships, the first model may represent a description of only the conscious aspects of mentoring relationships. Are belief in and promotion of the first model perhaps a defense against the risks in the second? Does the first model express a fantasy about getting important career assistance from someone without any emotional entanglements or dangers?

Existing research does not provide clear answers to these questions. However, the high expectations placed on mentoring in the face of real organizational conflict encourage us to explore these relationships for defensive as well as developmental aims, fantastic as well as realistic assumptions, and unconscious as well as conscious dynamics. The contrast between the peaceful and the conflictual images of mentoring is a good place to start. Reports on actual mentoring relationships indicate that both may be part of mentoring, that, further, the first is often succeeded by the second. In other words, there may be a developmental logic to mentoring that requires an amicable relationship to give way to passion and conflict in order for the protege to grow.

This article examines this possibility from a psychoanalytic point of view and offers the following interpretation: In the successful mentoring relationship a protege unconsciously goes through stages analogous to earlier life stages, including narcissism, the Oedipus complex, and the formation of an identity. Mentoring is a rebirth.

THE IDEALIZED MENTORING RELATIONSHIP

Both the promises of many advice books and the reports of many studies portray the mentoring relationship as wonderful. Missirian, reporting on a study of women managers, says:

> ...mentors were perceived to be larger-than-life. They were seen as brilliant, charismatic, physically attractive, boundlessly energetic, innovative, and totally inspiring human beings. (1982, p.39) (2)

Proteges see their mentors as very successful, very knowledgeable, and very powerful, able to support and guide (Kram, 1985). Proteges like, admire, respect, and look up to their mentors; they hold them in awe, and they love them. Proteges feel gratitude, excitation by the association with power, and a feeling of being somehow special, worthy of attention, and valued (Burke, 1984; Collins, 1983; Kram, 1985; Levinson, et al., 1978; Missirian, 1982).

Proteges and mentors come to trust, take care of, and feel loyal to each other (Burke, 1984; Collins, 1983; Dalton, Thompson, and Price, 1977; Kram, 1985; Missirian, 1982; Reich, 1985 and 1986). Their relations become close, intimate, friendly, and affectionate (Bowen, 1985; Burke, 1984; Clawson and Kram, 1984; Collins, 1983; Hunt and Michael, 1983; Missirian, 1982; Reich, 1985 and 1986).

And yet, Kram concludes after interviewing people who have had mentors, many such initial impressions of mentors represent at least as much fantasy as reality, an opinion offered retrospectively by many proteges. In general, these qualifications mean that proteges exaggerate their mentors' abilities and the intimacy and caring of their relationship.

The fantasies have two aspects, one involving organizational reality and the other involving the protege. One possible motivation for such idealization is to defend new workers against the dangers of organizational life and to transform the organization into a place where work and advancement are safe. Instead of confronting a hierarchical organization where many are competing for power and position, a new worker finds an exclusive two-person relationship where a wise and powerful older person cares for him or her and helps him or her advance (and implicitly takes responsibility for any aggressive actions along the way).

In this vision, the aggression expressed in competition and embodied in hierarchical distinctions is balanced, even replaced by libidinal caring. In work where boundaries are fuzzy and continually susceptible to negotiation, it is affection, rather than aggression, that will fill in relationships. This is a reassuring organizational portrait for workers who feel anxious about the consequences of aggressively working hard (see Baum, 1989). Thinking of an organization in these terms transforms it from an economic enterprise into a family, where appeals to trust and loyalty supplant concerns about the fairness of the division of labor and profit. This image encourages workers to believe they can advance in the organization without obstacles or conflict (see Baum, 1991). The language and emotions of mentoring are not those of industrial conflict or class struggle.

In fantasizing about their relationships with mentors, proteges also transform themselves. Mentoring relations are not simply intimate and caring, but they resemble two specific other relationships. Phillips-Jones writes that they have "many of the characteristics of parenting or of falling in love" (1982, p. 111). Similarly, Collins says, "Losing a mentor can be almost as emotionally devastating as the loss of a parent, spouse, or other member of the family" (1983, p.85).

Repeatedly, accounts of mentoring characterize the relationship as like that between parent and child (for example, Collins, 1983; Hennig and Jardim, 1977; Levinson et al., 1978; "The Mentors," 1979; Missirian, 1982; Phillips-Jones, 1982; Shapiro, Haseltine, and Rowe, 1978). The mentor has the strength and concern of a father or mother who wants his or her child to grow up strong and safely. Such an analogy rests on some realities. The mentor is older than the protege, often by a number of years that might separate a parent and child. The mentor is, indeed, more competent, more knowledgeable, more powerful, more privy to organizational secrets than is the protege. It is easy for mentor and protege to cast their relationship in these familiar terms. It is also reassuring to do so. Defining an intimate relationship in terms of parentlike tutoring avoids considering, alternatively, that the relationship is somehow romantic.

And yet many mentoring relationships between men and women do become romanticized (Bowen, 1985; Clawson and Kram, 1984; Collins, 1983; Fitt and Newton, 1981; Lean, 1983; Missirian, 1982; Phillips-Jones, 1982; Ragins, 1989; Shapiro et al., 1978). Discussions of male-female mentoring repeatedly characterize the relationship in terms of falling in love and being in love. Guidebooks to women seeking mentors caution them against confusing mentor and lover or husband (for example, Collins, 1983). Even when mentor and protege do not become romantically involved, they often find themselves forced to define their intimacy in terms besides parent and child.

The mentoring literature does not discuss romance between mentor and protege of the same sex. (3) This absence is probably due to taboos which make it difficult both for protege and mentor to recognize or make sense of homosexual wishes and for writers to mention them. There is no reason to doubt that similar emotions and aims motivate and become part of all mentoring relationships. However, while male-female mentoring relationships can be acceptably interpreted in terms of romantic attraction, members of same-sex relationships are probably more likely to interpret them exclusively in parent-child terms.

Thinking of the mentoring relationship as a romance has a more realistic basis than the parent-child analogy. And yet, when mentor and protege are in love, their relationship has all the unconscious origins and meanings of any being-in-love. And these meanings, finally, include a wish to merge with a parent. A woman interviewed by Missirian refers to both aspects in describing her fantasy about her relationship with her mentor: "He had sort of a proprietary interest in the precocious little girl he'd discovered. After all, he had invented me" (1982, p. 41). A lover is discovered; a child is invented, although lovers are always convinced they are reborn in their relationship.

The ambiguously parental and romantic fantasies apparently express a single wish, to restore feelings of omnipotence and omnipresence associated with the narcissism of life's earliest moments. Originally a child imagines himself to be the center of a good and loving universe, or, perhaps more accurately, the self-sufficient entirety of the universe. The child has no sense of being separate from anyone or anything. When he discovers that there are separate persons in the world, that these persons set limits on him and do not always love him, and thus that he is not omnipotent, he attempts to recreate his earlier experience by projective identification with an ego ideal (Chasseguet-Smirgel, 1985).

The ego ideal begins as the infant's mental image of the experience of lost omnipotence. When he attributes the qualities of this image to another person or object and then identifies with that object, he can recapture the feeling of being loved and powerful. The first specific object to which a child ascribes such perfection is a parent. If the child imagines himself to satisfy all this parent's expectations, and can identify with the parent, he feels perfect and thus loved. Later in life, people associate their ego ideals with teachers, bosses, and even organizations. (4) If an adult creates an ego ideal which seems realistically demanding, he may feel moved to be ambitious, to work and be creative. If, in contrast, the ego ideal calls for apparently unachievable results or perfection, he may either become a workaholic or retreat from practical activity and substitute fantasy for instrumentality.

One way that people unconsciously attempt to identify with the ego ideal in fantasy is by falling in love. Being-in-love involves projecting one's ego ideal onto another person and then feeling merged with the other, becoming perfect in the union. Being-in-love is not really experienced as a relationship so much as like the oneness of the early period before the discovery of separateness and limits. Normally, the ego ideal associated with a parent serves as the model for the love object. Thus, being-in-love is a way of unconsciously regaining a powerful, loving relationship with the parent of childhood.

Chasseguet-Smirgel (1986) describes narcissistic fantasies as an effort to escape from a world unconsciously associated with the appearance of the father (as a separate person) into a world associated with the mother ('s body, which is a place before separateness). Unconsciously, Chasseguet-Smirgel argues, people think of the world of the father in contrast with the world of the mother. The father's world is a world, first, of differences: in it there are separate objects. Moreover, it is a world of roughness and human and other obstacles. Consequently, it is also a world of cause and effect; instrumental action is necessary to achieve anything. While accomplishment is possible in this world, imperfection is inevitable. In contrast, the mother's world is a unity; there are no separate objects, no differences. It is a smooth world, where there are no obstacles. Here, instrumentality is irrelevant, because the wish, including the wish to become perfect, is equal to the action.

Striving for accomplishment in the real world, associated with the father, can bring some of the pleasures identified with the perfect world of union with the mother's body. However, those whose ego ideals do not make reasonable demands of them, or who cannot accept their imperfection, may turn to fantasy to join with the mother. Falling in love is one fantasy. Falling in love with a mentor at work is a particularly compelling fantasy. (5)

Explicitly and implicitly, many proteges speak of feeling intimately, intensely in love with a perfect mentor. Not only does this experience make the protege feel powerful in a workplace that is probably overwhelming, but it also "solves" the problem of advancement. Not simply is the organization transformed into a domain of libido, rather than aggression, where efforts to move ahead are safe, but the organization becomes a place where advancement is effortless.

If a protege is merged with a powerful, caring mentor, the relationship itself seems to move the protege to the mentor's high position. Levinson et al. describe these fantasies about the mentor:

> The little boy desperately wants the mentor to be a good father in the most childish sense - a father who will make him special, will endow him with magical powers and will not require him to compete or prove himself in relation to would-be rivals. (1978, p. 147)

Regardless of whether the mentor is a man or a woman, the relationship unconsciously leads into the world of the mother, in which there are no differences, no obstacles, and no need for instrumental action. In this world, advancement is really unnecessary, because the union with the mentor means it has already taken place.

These fantasies, by their nature, are regressive, in leading away from organizational reality. But they serve clear aims in defending the protege from dangers. Idealizing the mentor's powers makes the organization a safe place. Seeing the mentor as purely benevolent, further, protects against fears that the mentor might use these powers to punish a neophyte who grows too quickly. And yet, by pointing out a line of advancement, these fantasies also aid and encourage development. They are regressive but might, depending on how they are used, serve the ego in moving ahead in the organization (Kris, 1952).

Here it is germane to look at the entry of sexual attraction and conflict, envy, and intimidation into mentoring relationships.

SEXUALITY AND AGGRESSION IN MENTORING RELATIONSHIPS

Sexuality

Collins' (1983) admonition to women not to confuse mentors with lovers or husbands is a warning not simply against emotional attachment but also against sexual involvement. Many mentoring relationships between men and women lead to sexual relations (Clawson and Kram, 1984; Collins, 1983; Fitt and Newton, 1981; Lean, 1983; Ragins, 1989; Shapiro et al., 1978). (6)

Psychoanalytic theorists (for example, Chasseguet-Smirgel, 1985) distinguish being-in-love from loving. Being-in-love, as already described, is a state of identification with another person to whom ideal characteristics are attributed. It is a form of self-love, admiring another person who is unconsciously seen as simply the perfect version of oneself. In an important way, being-in-love, despite the physical presence of two identifiable persons, is a one-person "relationship" for each participant: each adores an idealized image of him- or herself.

Loving, in contrast, is a two-person relationship. Each person recognizes the other as separate, and also as imperfect. Each appreciates certain strengths or characteristics of the other while accepting shortcomings or distasteful aspects as relatively unimportant. Although a love relationship may not be devoid of idealization, its affection rests on a more or less realistic appraisal of the other person.

Sexual activity has different unconscious meanings depending on whether it expresses being-in-love or loving. As an act of being-in-love, sexual activity with another is a way of rediscovering an early condition of union with existence. It represents an effort to retreat from the world of real persons and objects to a place where there are no separate objects. It is an effort to recapture the remembered experience of oneness with the mother's body. If successful, it brings the narcissistic feelings of omnipotence and omnipresence.

Sexual activity which expresses loving may include some of these aspects but also recognizes the sexual partner as a distinct person. The partner may be unconsciously identified in part with the parent of the Oedipal period of childhood, so that the relationship and sexuality include an effort to gain that imagined earlier partner. However, just as the Oedipal parent was a separate person, so, too, is the contemporary sexual partner.

The implication of this distinction is that, insofar as the reported sexual relations between mentors and proteges express being-in-love aims, then they are consistent with either partner's idealization of the other. Theoretically, at least, however problematic the sexual activity becomes at work and at home, it is consistent with the ideal mentoring relationship. In contrast, sexuality which expresses loving for a mentor or protege is quite different. It recognizes the other as a distinct person. It is a departure from idealization into reality. Thus, theoretically, the puzzle about sexual activity in mentoring concerns those relations in which mentor and protege - or at least one of the partners - has moved from one-person narcissism to a two-person relationship. (7)

The mentoring literature, on the whole, is not psychoanalytic. Authors do not distinguish being-in-love and loving with any precision, nor do those they interview. Thus, it is impossible to know the balance of meanings for the sexual relations which evolve from mentoring. However, it seems likely that many of the sexual relationships start as or become more or less realistic two-person relationships. For example, writers describe women who marry their mentors. Some of these women report that their husbands remain their mentors, whereas more say that their husbands have ceased to be their mentors, that their relationship has changed from the early idealization (for example, Collins, 1983; Missirian, 1982; Phillips-Jones, 1982).

These latter sexual relationships, among couples who do or do not get married, represent an important change from the ideal mentoring relationship. They rest on a new, realistic recognition of the partner as a separate, imperfect person. Unconsciously, this change involves another. It recapitulates an earlier developmental progression from the one-person world of infantile narcissism, through the discovery of the mother as a separate person, to the encounter with still a third person, the father whose entry creates the Oedipus complex.

In allowing a protege to encounter a symbolic equivalent of one of the parents and to try to resolve the Oedipus conflict more successfully in childhood, the mentoring relationship is regressive. In themselves, fantasies that bosses and supervisors are parental lovers only serve to avoid organizational realities and career interests. However, the Oedipus complex represents an important developmental advance over narcissism: It accepts the inevitability of becoming a separate person and requires giving up the idealization of the parent-mentor and coming to terms with him or her more realistically.

This progression is encouraged by unconscious memories of past development, which presents a model for subsequent transitions. In addition, working conditions themselves impose on the idealized mentoring relationship. As a protege learns more about a job and an organization, gains more self-confidence, becomes intellectually and professionally more the mentor's equal, and works more closely with the mentor, the protege has the ability, opportunity, and necessity to appraise the mentor more realistically.

This new realism brings professional benefits, but it bears unconscious costs. Missirian captures much of this ambiguity: "When a child is ready to be born, it must leave the safety of the mother's womb, or both parent and child will surely perish" (1982, p. 71). Accepting the separateness and imperfection of a mentor means giving up illusions of being perfect. It feels like losing a good part of oneself. This narcissistic loss leads to rage against whoever, such as the mentor, who now shows him- or herself to be imperfect, has caused the protege to feel separate and imperfect (Kohut, 1972). To the degree that the protege can accept his or her own responsibility for having created the no longer tenable illusions, then he or she feels angry toward himself, and these losses bring grief and depression (Klein, 1935/1948 and 1940/1948). Phillips-Jones observes, "Just as in romantic relationships, when you realize you're both only human, feelings of disappointment can be very strong" (1982, p.107).

Thus the emergence of loving sexual relations suggests two unconscious departures from the idealized mentoring relationship: the redefinition of the mentoring relationship at least partly in Oedipal terms and inwardly and/or outwardly directed rage about the loss of the ideal relationship. In constructing an Oedipal fantasy, the protege retreats from organizational dangers but also unconsciously can begin to move closer to differentiated and conflictual reality.

Aggression

These descriptions of mentoring relationships emphasize the merging impulses of libido. Quite differently, other reports refer to the dividing impulses of aggression. The contrast between these experiences has led researchers to postulate stages in the development of mentoring relations. Typically, idealization appears at the beginning, and sexuality in its various expressions shows up at many stages, but aggression and division arrive later on. Phillips-Jones (1982) speaks of "disillusionment" and "parting", Kram (1983) writes of "separation", Levinson et al. (1978) describe intense conflict and separation, Hunt and Michael (1983) point to "breakup", and Missirian (1982) refers to "termination."

These terms refer to tension and conflict that often arise when a protege has learned many of the mentor's skills, has developed strategic relationships of his own, and is ready to move ahead by himself. The mentor may envy the fresh opportunities that the protege's new abilities and youth allow, in addition to resenting the protege's wish to become independent. The mentor may feel disappointed and angry at what he considers the protege's lack of gratitude. Mentors are particularly likely to feel resentful if they are stuck themselves, if they see little opportunity for their own advancement. It looks to them as if they have simply prepared someone to displace them. Some mentors may begin to make more demands on their proteges while insisting they are not ready to go out on their own. Some may even take steps to block their proteges from leaving or finding new positions elsewhere.

Proteges, in turn, may simply feel constrained or may also feel disillusioned and disappointed with their mentors. They have seen their mentors turn from nurturers to stiflers. They resent what they interprete as deliberate efforts to keep them from moving on. In response to mentors' charges of ingratitude, they rail against duplicity: their mentors agreed to teach them, they served loyally, and now their mentors block their advancement (Collins, 1983; Hunt and Michael, 1983; Kram, 1983 and 1985; Levinson et al., 1978; Missirian, 1982; Phillips-Jones, 1982; Reich, 1986).

Reich quotes two women leveling such charges at their mentors. The first complains,

> As I outpaced and outgrew the relationship my mentor grew defensive and fearful that I would make him look bad. Now instead of making me look good he calls me a know-it-all.

Pointedly, the second accuses, "My supervisor wanted a clone, not a protege" (1986, p. 53). A woman interviewed by Phillips-Jones says,

> Ultimately, you get caught up in the feeling that you've got to be yourself, because I get so angry at people who are unable to differentiate me from her. (1982, p. 118)

Some proteges are realistically angry at mentors who stifle their development. However, it is difficult to be certain about all the meanings of conflict between mentors and proteges because the mentoring literature is not psychoanalytic. For example, neither writers nor their interviewees carefully distinguish or connect proteges' anger toward their mentors and proteges' anger toward themselves. Nevertheless, proteges' comments suggest two themes consistent with earlier analysis of the meanings of sexual relationship between mentors and proteges.

First, many proteges are both angry and disillusioned. The obvious fact that they are angry toward another person is not trivial. The protege is angry against a mentor whom he or she regards as a separate person. The mentor, in contrast, apparently wants to maintain the ideal one-person "relationship" in which the protege is simply a clone. Not only has the protege himself lost the ideal relationship in which he was merged with a wonderful parentlike mentor, but the now separate mentor is not even good enough to help the protege advance. (8)

At the same time, Phillips-Jones' interviewee suggests a protege's own conflicts about this transition. When she says she is "caught up in the feeling" she must be independent, she hints that the "people" at whom she is "angry" include herself. It is necessary but painful to be separate. She may experience anger against herself as depression, and the anger toward "people," including, undoubtedly, her mentor, probably expresses rage against her for depriving her of the narcissism of the ideal mentoring relationship.

Envy and jealousy introduce a second theme. Klein (1975) associates envy with a two-part relationship, where one person attributes some good quality to another, sees him- or herself lacking it, admires but also resents the other for having it, and wishes to rob or harm the other. One example of such a two-part relationship is the idealizing one-person pseudo-relationship described earlier. In contrast, jealousy is part of a three-person relationship, in which one person loves another and fears loss of that person to a third (see also Joffe, 1969; Kets de Vries, 1988; Spielman, 1971).

Unfortunately, the mentoring literature makes no such distinction between envy and jealousy. Although writers do not associate envy with the idealized mentoring relationship, there is no reason to doubt that proteges envy the mentors whom they also idolize. Thus, the idealization that defends against organizational dangers may have this cost, and proteges who resent their seemingly perfect mentors may unconsciously try to debase them and bring on the "realistic" disillusionment that follows idealization (Klein, 1975).

Yet, much of the "envy" reported in the literature has all the characteristics of three-person jealousy. In the background of the relationship between a mentor and his protege lies the mentor's own relationship with someone powerful higher up. Just as the mentor may begin to worry that his protege will leave him and displace him with his own superior partner, the protege may start to wish and plan to establish his own relationship with an organizational superior.

Levinson et al. (1978) observe that men who have men for mentors may unconsciously formulate and re-enact the relationship in terms of an Oedipal conflict with their father. Along these lines, some writers argue that conflict is more likely in male-male mentoring relationships than in male-female relationships (for example, Collins, 1983; Reich, 1986). Thus, a male protege may be jealous of his mentor's access to organizational bounty (unconsciously associated with the father's possession of the mother) and think of learning his skills and knowledge as the means to displacing him.

Two aspects of this account are important. First, although the Oedipus complex is joined by and raises issues of both sexuality and aggression (Rangell, 1972), only the aggression is apparent in male-male mentoring relationships. Not only is the homosexual aspect of the relationship unacknowledged, but little is said about the protege's attraction to others in the organization to whom the mentor apparently blocks access. Second, as is clear, the sex of mentor and protege matters. Unlike in the idealized one-person "relationship," where both male and female mentors seem like mothers, in the real three-person relationship, males seem like fathers, and females seem like mothers. Proteges seem distinctly like sons or daughters, rather than genderless infants.

Differences Between Male and Female Proteges

Thus, a common view of male-male mentoring is that initial attractions give way to rivalries that rend the relationship. Male-female relationships (usually male mentors and female protegees) are described in contrasting terms. In general, conflict is less common (for example, Collins, 1983; Reich, 1986). But, even when jealousy emerges, conflict is often succeeded by resolution that continues the relationship. Several writers report that a reconciliatory stage is "often" part of a "complete" mentoring relationship. Kram (1983 and 1985) finds "separation" succeeded by "redefinition"; Phillips-Jones (1982) sees "parting" followed by "transformation"; and Hunt and Michael (1983) report that "breakup" often ends in "lasting friendship." Hunt and Michael write,

> The final phase of the complete mentor-protege relationship is one of redefinition. After a period of separation, mentors and proteges who reestablish contact go through a period in which their relationship is significantly changed. It may become a more peer-like friendship....Now a mutual or perhaps equal status and reciprocal relationship exists between mentor and protege. (1983, p. 483)

Although these writers portray this final stage as part of a general mentoring model, their, and others', examples often involve women with male mentors. (9) Missirian, studying businesswomen, observes that for them "the [mentoring] relation never ends" (1982, p. 69). Reich (1986), surveying executives, found significant differences in the course of men's and women's mentoring relationships. Sixty-seven percent of women protegees, in contrast with 42% of men, reported their mentoring relationship developed into a close friendship, and 69% of women, in contrast with 59% of men, continued to have a close relationship with their mentor. Collins (1983), after interviewing women executives, concluded that, when their relationships with mentors do end, the reasons are different from those in male-male relationships, where conflict is the primary cause of breakup. Of the four-fifths no longer involved with their mentor, 57% say the reason is that he moved away geographically, 26% say he moved away within the company, 8% say he died, and only 9% say conflict was the cause of the separation. In short, these women might have continued the relationship if their mentor had not left them. Consistently, Missirian found the relationship changed largely as a result of changes in the organizational positions of mentor and protegee.

Thus, jealousy and conflict are more likely in male-male mentoring than in male-female relationships. The presence of these conditions in the former relationships can be interpreted as a transference of Oedipal conflicts to mentoring. (10) Their absence in the latter may have a similar root. Significantly, Collins observes,

> Men seem to understand more than women that the relationship is temporary, shorter-lived, and will come to an end. Women hold on to their mentors longer than men do, and, according to my survey, often longer than is good for their careers. (1983, p. 97)

Somehow, men "understand" that the mentoring relationship must end, and this knowledge seems to be based on something other than a simple realistic appraisal of their career requirements. At the least, women develop expectations that conflict with their career realities.

Men's "understanding" is consistent with what they would unconsciously remember about the course of their relationship with the Oedipal father. Rivalry led to conflict which was resolved only by the son's agreement to give up jealous competition and accept the parents' moral values in return for peace and their love. Women would lack such an "understanding" from their relationship with the Oedipal father. What they would unconsciously understand, and anticipate of mentoring, instead, is that the relationship would be affectionate and that, indeed, it need have no definite ending in crisis. It might continue for a long time until succeeded by another with someone in many ways similar.

Descriptions of the course of women's relations with male mentors following the initial idealization support the view that these relations are shaped by Oedipal memories. As with men, women experience the relations as three-person relationships, including the mentor, the organizational resources to which he is attached, and the protegee.

Also as with men, the real sex of the mentor matters. However, protegees' and researchers' accounts emphasize the affectionate or sexual aspect of the relationship and say relatively little about aggression. Not only are there fewer jealous conflicts with mentors, but there is also little rivalry with anyone else for the mentor's affection. The absence of rivalry is consistent with the female Oedipal relationship, in which daughter-mother rivalry is normally less intense than son-father rivalry. (11) It also fits organizational reality: it makes little sense for a protegee to spurn the possibility of her own attachments to higher-ups, though memories of the Oedipus complex may, as Collins suggests, unconsciously encourage her to resist those higher up and to stay longer with her mentor than reasonable.

Thus, the appearance of aggression in mentoring relationships is significant in two respects. First, it marks a break with narcissistic idealization of the mentor and recognition of the mentor as a separate person. In addition, the association of aggression with male-male relationships and its lower incidence in male-female relationships signals a transference of Oedipal assumptions to the mentoring relationship. The protege's unconscious regressions are progressing closer to reality. In particular, the willingness to act aggressively prepares the protege to assert him- or herself instrumentally in the organization.

THE END OF THE MENTORING RELATIONSHIP

Some mentoring relationships, perhaps particularly those between men and men, end decisively. Others, perhaps especially those between men and women, continue for a while, gradually diminishing in force. In either case, at some point, the relationship moves from active reality to memory. "The excitement," as Kram puts it, "is replaced [for many] with gratitude and realism" (1983, p. 620).

Descriptions of subsequent relations between mentor and protege emphasize three developments. First, most noticeably, the structure of the relationship changes. Childlike relations to a parentlike mentor give way to relative equality in adulthood. Hunt and Michael's observation quoted earlier records typical impressions: "It may become a more peer-like friendship" (1983, p. 483). Kram says, "the relationship becomes, primarily, a friendship," with "more equal footing" and "peer status" (1983, p. 620). While former proteges feel "gratitude" for past help from a more experienced senior, now they "realistically" recognize they can move out and up on their own.

A second development involves a source of this equality: the protege has learned what the mentor could teach. The protege has gained the experience and contacts to make independent judgments and take initiatives. Kram describes how both mentor and protege see this change:

> For the senior manager, the young manager is proof of effectiveness in passing on important values, knowledge, and skills; there is pride in seeing the young manager move on to greater responsibility and career advancement. Both individuals acknowledge that what was is no longer; they also recognize a new bond that is more responsive to their current needs... . For the young manager, the ability to relate in a more peerlike fashion with the senior manager and the ability to function effectively in new settings without the immediate support of the relationship reflect greater competence, self-confidence, and autonomy. (1983, pp. 620-621).

A third development involves changes in the psychodynamic relationship between mentor and protege which enable the latter to feel like the former's equal. After aggressively and perhaps sexually challenging the mentor, the protege makes peace with him. Hunt and Michael describe this change simply: "The former protege takes on some of the best qualities of his or her mentor, and an amicable friendship continues" (1983, p. 483; emphasis added). The protege comes to see the mentor as neither fantastic nor threatening, but as admirably competent, and the protege "takes on" the mentor's good qualities - becomes like the mentor in realistically beneficial ways. Becoming like the mentor in these ways permits an "amicable" equality.

But, as Levinson et al. argue, the process of "taking on" is both conscious and unconscious:

> Following the separation, the younger man may take the admired qualities more fully into himself. He may become better able to learn from himself, to listen to the voices from within. His personality is enriched as he makes the mentor a more intrinsic part of himself. The internalization of significant figures is a major source of development in adulthood" (1978, p. 101; emphasis added).

Missirian (1982), too, emphasizes the "internalization" of the mentor. Kram interviewed a woman who describes the ambiguous position of her former mentor, both separate from her and yet part of her:

> Well to me he will always be the boss. Like I don't really see myself so much as his peer because he was the boss for so long. I will probably always look toward him for advice because I have a lot of respect for him... . We are peers now, but to me he will always have a part as the boss - even if I were to get promoted and he weren't (1983, p. 620; emphasis added).

The psychological "internalization" of the mentor represents a conclusion to the social mentoring relationship. It is most successful when it accompanies resolution of aggressive or sexual conflicts between mentor and protege. The mentor must recognize that the protege has the knowledge and skills necessary for autonomous practice. But, further, the protege must acknowledge the mentor's intellectual and organizational authority, and the mentor must agree that the protege has appropriate values to be trusted to practice alone. Then the protege can identify the mentor's "admired qualities" with himself. The former protege can then "look toward him for advice" by "listening to the voices from within." Consciously and unconsciously, the protege asks himself, "What would my mentor do in this situation?" and his internalized mentor offers an answer. Where this inner dialogue which replaces external discussion is generally "amicable," the mentor is strengthened in confronting the former mentor and others as equals at work. (12)

This process has two unconscious meanings. First, following extended confrontation with a mentor, the internalized mentor represents a more realistically supportive ego ideal than earlier fantastic idealizations. It enables the former protege to feel equal to the mentor in competence. But there is a second meaning to identifying with the mentor's "best qualities," namely, accepting his or her "values." In exchange for the mentor's authorization to practice autonomously, the protege internalizes the mentor's ethics as part of his or her superego, or conscience. In this way, the former protege can feel the mentor's moral equal, sanctioned to act as competently as possible.

These developments are analogous to the child's resolution of the Oedipus complex and venturing into latency by sublimating, or redirecting, aggressive and libidinal wishes into socially valued work skills (Erikson, 1963 and 1968). The protege gives up enough of the fantasies that the parentlike mentor is perfect and omnipotent to engage organizational reality and develop an appropriate "sense of industry." The former protege can now begin to develop his or her own "sense of identity" as a member of the organization (Baum, 1990). When successful, mentoring enables a protege to be "reborn."

Mentoring Failures

Mentoring may fail in two ways. Mentor and protege may become so involved with one another that they become isolated from the rest of the organization and the protege never emerges as an independent worker. This possibility is likely when the pair prefer the apparent perfection of the idealized relationship or the sexuality of the Oedipally framed relationship to the limits and disappointments of work. Alternatively, even with a mentor's encouragement to advance, a protege may be so anxious about the aggression, or the sexuality, of the latter stage in the relationship as to avoid dealing with differences and conflicts. As a result, he or she will be unable to master organizational reality.

Whether a mentoring relationship is successful or not depends on the maturity of the protege. For example, has he relatively successfully mastered narcissistic and Oedipal challenges in his childhood? Does he already have a sense of competence and identity elsewhere? In addition, the success of the relationship depends on the maturity of the mentor. For example, does he already have experience in rearing children or supervising people, or, at least, is he prepared to meet the challenges of what Erikson (1963 and 1968) calls "generativity" (see Baum, 1990)? A mentor who cannot both hold a protege and let go appropriately will force the protege to do some of the mentor's work as well, and probably not very well.

Organizational psychological structure also matters: every organization's social structure encourages typical patterns of conscious and unconscious feelings and assumptions among members, and some patterns are more conducive to mentoring than others (Baum, 1987). The "good enough" mentor, like the "good enough" mother (Levinson et al., 1978; and Winnicott, 1965), permits the protege to make a transition from idealizing dependence to realistic acceptance of a separate existence and independence. However, bureaucracy, where authority is hierarchical and where those who exercise the most authority are often invisible and inaccessible, arouses in many workers an Oedipal anxiety about the power and punitiveness of everyone in authority (Baum, 1987). Encountering others, particularly those with authority, feels like an aggressive act likely to be punished.

Insofar as bureaucratic work or politics evokes anxieties about Oedipal relationships, proteges will have special difficulty giving up idealizing the mentor or will become enraged on discovering his shortcomings and then cynically consider normal organizational politics a second-best state of existence. Bureaucracy does not inevitably defeat mentoring, and former proteges can become productive and politically effective, but bureaucracy can interfere with developing working relations with others based on empathic, realistic appreciation for them. In particular, proteges may feel moved and free to treat those separate, imperfect others as targets for the rage of their disillusionment. Moreover, they may find venting their rage sometimes more important than getting work done. Or else, finding anger and conflict so frightening, they may idealize the mentor still more intensely. Some formal mentoring programs encourage idealization by couching the relationship as an instrumental exchange of information.

CONCLUSIONS

There are both realistic and fantastic aspects to mentoring relationships. Realistically, a mentor can provide a protege with knowledge, skills, protection, and access that launch the latter's career. Proteges (and mentors) unconsciously bring fantastic meanings to these relationships for the same reasons that people think unconsciously anywhere in life. First, regressive fantasies, particularly the idealization of the mentor and the relationship, defend the protege against real dangers in entering and advancing in an organization.

In addition, these fantasies which lead away from reality can also assist in engaging reality; they can be regressions in the service of ego interests. Nonpsychoanalytic reporters on mentoring relationships produce an account which clearly resembles not just narcissistic regression, but progression to an Oedipus-like relationship, and then latency and the establishment of a realistic social identity. Unconsciously, proteges seem to believe that a pattern of development which worked in the past can serve them again when they enter an organization. The ego ideal, in offering perfection and love, is regressive, but it is also the beginning of a path toward realistic ambition.

Implications for organizational policy are clear. If managers value mentoring, they must accept the private, potentially subversive nature of the relationship. They must allow protege and mentor the time and space to initiate and work through a passionate relationship that may temporarily interfere with work. At the same time, managers must give up the illusion that formal mentoring programs can reap the gains of successful mentoring while avoiding these risks. Formal programs may facilitate mentoring, but they cannot lead to maturity and independence in new workers without allowing them emotional space for development. An organization that nurtured mentoring would be quite an innovation.

NOTES

(1) It is possible that income and career advancement are associated with being mentored because ambitious competent people are especially likely to seek mentors. Note also Strober's (1982) finding that being mentored was not significantly correlated with total annual salary and was significantly slightly negatively associated with job satisfaction among MBA graduates she studied. In short, the role of mentoring in a personal career is more complicated than most studies consider.

(2) Phillips-Jones suggests the extraordinary character of mentors in the introduction to her book of mentoring: "About three years ago, I rediscovered Jesus Christ, a mentor I once had and then ignored for some years. His effect on my life has been tremendous. My husband, Dr. G. Brian Jones, is the most comprehensive human mentor I've had..." (1982, p.11)

(3) Levinson et al. refer in passing to "homosexual meanings that are actually involved or that may be attributed" to a mentor by others. (1978, p. 237)

(4) See Schwartz (1990) on the "organizational ideal," a projection of the ego ideal onto a workplace and its managers. Schwartz argues that the narcissistic wish to regain perfection encourages workers to substitute identification with an idealized manager for realistic assessment of an organization and instrumental action.

(5) Levinson et al. (1978) call attention to "parallels" between a man's relationship with a mentor and that with a special woman.

(6) There has been little research on how frequently sexual relations have developed from mentoring relations. Fitt and Newton (1981) found sexual involvement among 10% of a sample of 30 women executives. Collins (1983) reports sexual involvement among 20% of a sample of 400 women executives and professionals. Probably women underreport their involvement in these relationships, in which one or both partners may be married and which, at any rate, are often disapproved of by co-workers or company norms.

(7) Calculated sexual exploitation, which is another possibility, particularly on the part of the mentor, is not puzzling theoretically or otherwise.

(8) Winnicott (1965) observes that a child's growth depends on a mother who is "good enough" to permit and help him to move securely from feeling completely dependent on her to being independent of her. Levinson et al. (1978) argue that a mentor must work analogously.

(9) A minority of these women mentors, but data are often presented in a way that makes it impossible to distinguish the course of the two types of relationships.

(10) For other examples of transference in organizations, see Baum (1987); Hirschhorn(1988); Hodgson, Levinson and Zaleznik (1965); Kets de Vries and Miller (1984).

(11) For discussion of male and female differences in Oedipal relationships, see Fenichel (1945); Freud (1920/1977; 1924/1989; 1933/1965); Heimann (1959); Klein (1928/1948; 1945/1948), and Tyson (1989).

(12) If the conclusion of the mentoring relationship is not amicable, a former protege, feeling both gratitude or affection and anger or resentment toward the mentor, may internalize a tormentor, an inner voice with ridicules, belittles, or discourages. In this case, the internal dialogue may lead the former protege to doubt his or her ability to act and cause the protege to become immobilized, certain he or she is not the mentor's equal. Schafer (1968) discusses the variations in internalization processes.

REFERENCES

BAUM, H.S. The invisible bureaucracy; The unconscious in organizational problem solving. New York: Oxford University Press, 1987

BAUM, H.S. Organizational politics against organizational culture: A psychoanalytic perspective. Human Resource Management, 28, 1989, 191-206.

BAUM, H. S. Organizational membership: Personal development in the workplace. Albany: State University of New York Press, 1990.

BAUM, H. S. Creating a family in the workplace. Human Relations, 44, 1991, 1137-1159.

BOWEN, D.B. Were men meant to mentor women? Training Development Journal, 1985, 39, 30-34.

BURKE, R. J. Mentors in organizations. Group and Organization Studies, 9, 1984, 353-372.

CHASSEGUET-SMIRGEL, J. The ego ideal: A psychoanalytic essay on the malady of the ideal. Translated by P. Burrows. New York: W. W. Norton and Company, 1985.

CHASSEGUET-SMIRGEL, J. Sexuality and mind. New York: New York University Press, 1986.

CLAWSON, J.G., & KRAM, K.E. Managing cross-gender mentoring. Business Horizons, 27, 1984, 22-32.

COLLINS, N.W. Professional women and their mentors: A practical guide to mentoring for the woman who wants to get ahead. Englewood Cliffs: Prentice-Hall, 1983.

DALTON, G.W., THOMPSON, P.H., & PRICE, R.L. The four stages of professional careers - A new look at performance by professionals. Organizational Dynamics, 6, 1977, 19-42.

ERIKSON, E.H. Childhood and society. Second edition. New York: W.W. Norton and Company, 1963.

ERIKSON, E.H. Identity: Youth and crisis. New York: W.W. Norton and Company, 1968.

Everyone who makes it has a mentor. Harvard Business Review, 56, 1978, 89-101.

FENICHEL, O. The psychoanalytic theory of neurosis. New York: W.W. Norton and Company, 1945.

FITT, L.W., & NEWTON, D.A. When the mentor is a man and the protégée a woman. Harvard Business Review, 59, 56, 58, 60, 1981.
FREUD, S. Introductory lectures on psychoanalysis. Translated by J. Strachey. New York: W. W. Norton and Company, 1977. (Originally published 1920.)
FREUD, S. The dissolution of the Oedipus complex. In The Freud reader, edited by P. Gay. New York: W.W. Norton and Company, 1989. (Originally published 1924.)
FREUD, S. Some psychical consequences of the anatomical distinction between the sexes. In The Freud reader, edited by P. Gay. New York: W.W. Norton and Company, 1989. (Originally published 1925.)
FREUD, S. New introductory lectures on psychoanalysis. Translated by J. Strachey. New York: W.W. Norton and Company, 1965. (Originally published 1933.)
HEIMANN, P. A contribution to the re-evaluation of the Oedipus complex - The early stages. In New directions in psychoanalysis, edited by M. Klein, P. Heimann, and R. E. Money-Kyrle. New York: Basic Books, 1959.
HENNIG, M., & JARDIM, A. The managerial woman. New York: Pocket Books, 1977.
HIRSCHHORN, L. The workplace within: Psychodynamics of organizational life. Cambridge: M. I. T. Press, 1988.
HODGSON, R.C., LEVINSON, D.J., & ZALEZNIK, A. The executive role constellation. Boston: Harvard University, The Graduate School of Business Administration, 1965.
HUNT, D M., & MICHAEL, C. Mentorship: A career development tool. Academy of Management Review, 9, 1983, 475-485.
JOFFE, W.G. A critical review of the status of the envy concept. International Journal of Psychoanalysis, 50, 1969, 533-545.
KETS DE VRIES, M.F.R. The motivating role of envy: A forgotten factor in management theory. Fontainebleau, France: INSEAD, 1988.
KETS DE VRIES, M.F.R., & MILLER, D. The neurotic organization. San Francisco: Jossey-Bass, 1984.
KLAUSS, R. Formalized mentor relations for managerial and executive development in the federal government. Public Administration Review, 41, 1981, 489-496.
KLEIN, M. Early stages of the Oedipus conflict. In Contributions to psychoanalysis, 1921-1945. London: The Hogarth Press and the Institute of Psychoanalysis, 1948. (Originally published 1928.)
KLEIN, M. A contribution to the psychogenesis of manic-depressive states. In Contributions to psychoanalysis, 1921-1945. London: The Hogarth Press and the Institute of Psychoanalysis, 1948. (Originally published 1935.)
KLEIN, M. Mourning and its relation to manic-depressive states. In Contributions to psychoanalysis, 1921-1945. London: The Hogarth Press and the Institute of Psychoanalysis, 1948. (Originally published 1940.)
KLEIN, M. The Oedipus complex in the light of early anxieties. In Contributions to psychoanalysis, 1921-1945. London: The Hogarth Press and the Institute of Psychoanalysis, 1948. (Originally published 1945.)
KLEIN, M. Envy and gratitude and other works, 1946-1963. New York: Dell, 1975.
KOHUT, H. Thoughts on narcissism and narcissistic rage. Psychoanalytic Study of the Child, 27, 1972, 360-400.
KRAM, K.E. Phases of the mentor relationship. Academy of Management Journal, 26, 1983, 608-625.

KRAM, K. E. Mentoring at work; Developmental relationships in organizational life. Glenview, Illinois: Scott, Foresman, & Company, 1985.

KRIS, E. Psychoanalytic explorations in art. New York: Schocken, 1952.

LEAN, E. Cross-gender mentoring: Downright upright and good for productivity. Training and Development Journal, 37; 1983, 61-65.

LEVINSON, D.J., DARROW, C.N., KLEIN, E.B., LEVINSON, M.H., & MCKEE, B. The seasons of a man's life. New York: Ballantine Books, 1978.

The mentors. Public Management, 61-62, 1979, 2-16.

MISSIRIAN, A. K. The corporate connection; Why executive women need mentors to reach the top. Englewood Cliffs: Prentice-Hall, 1982.

PHILLIPS-JONES, L. Mentors & proteges. New York: Arbor House Publishing Company, 1982.

RAGINS, B.R. Barriers to mentoring: The female manager's dilemma. Human Relations, 42, 1989, 1-22.

RANGELL, L. Aggression, Oedipus, and historical perspective. International Journal of Psychoanalysis, 53, 1972, 3-11.

REICH, M.H. Executive views from both sides of mentoring. Personnel, 1985, 62, 42-46.

REICH, M.H. The mentor connection. Personnel, 63, 1986, 50-56.

ROCHE, G. R. Much ado about mentors. Harvard Business Review, 57, 1979, 14-28.

SCHAFER, R. Aspects of internalization. New York: International Universities Press, 1968.

SCHWARTZ, H.S. Narcissistic process and corporate decay. New York: New York University Press, 1990.

SHAPIRO, E.C., HASELTINE, F.P., & ROWE, M.P. Moving up: Role models, mentors, and the "patron system." Sloan Management Review, 19, 1978, 51-58.

SPIELMAN, P.M. Envy and jealousy: An attempt at clarification. Psychoanalytic Quarterly, 40, 1971, 59-82.

STROBER, M. H. The MBA: Sure passport to success for women and men? In Women in the workplace, edited by P. A. Wallace. Boston: Auburn House Publishing Company, 1982.

TYSON, P. Infantile sexuality, gender identity, and obstacles to Oedipal progression. Journal of the American Psychoanalytic Association, 37, 1989, 1051-1069.

WINNICOTT, D. W. The maturational processes and the facilitating environment; Studies in the theory of emotional development. New York: International Universities Press, 1965.

ZEY, M. G. The mentor connection. Homewood, Illinois: Dow Jones-Irwin, 1984.

The Social Character of Bureaucracy: Anxiety and Ritualistic Defense

Michael A. Diamond

INTRODUCTION

In analyzing the social character of bureaucracy, one must examine the psychodynamics of obsessional neurosis in the individual and ritualistic practices in the bureaucracy. Much of organization theory either implicitly or explicitly characterizes bureaucratic behavior as ritualistic. [See, for example, Weber (1947); Hummel (1977, 1982); Merton (1940, 1963); Crozier (1964); Argyris and Schon (1974, 1978); and Zaleznik and Kets de Vries (1975).] A more complete appreciation of the role of ritualistic behavior in bureaucracy recognizes its origins in the human personality. "The culture of the system reflects:...the types of people the organization attracts" (Burke, 1982, p. 76).

My purpose is to examine psychoanalytically the notion of "fit" between social character and "ideal type" bureaucracy. The social character of bureaucracy symbolizes the outcome of interpenetration between psyche and organization. Ritualistic behavior in bureaucracy arises from unconsciously motivated obsessional thinking and compulsive behavior aimed at defending one's self from anxiety about losing control (Diamond, 1984; Zaleznik and Kets de Vries, 1975; Sperling, 1950). It serves to contain anxiety, which is the unpleasant experience of a momentary loss of self/object boundaries and identity (Freud, 1959a; Klein, 1975; Erikson, 1968; Kafka, 1983). This occurs in the organizational recruit at the moment of entry into the bureaucracy where he acts to deny reality by "undoing" the self-alienation that has occurred (signal anxiety) and "isolating" its affects (Freud, 1959a).

At the point of organizational entry the recruit displays ritualistic behavior that serves as a defense against the anxiety of self-fragmentation. This anxiety arises in the entrant due to the ambivalent feelings and feared loss of individuality, which are linked to the personal meaning of assuming membership in an organization or group (Freud, 1921/1959b). Furthermore, this intrapsychic process may influence the newcomer to submit to the organizational or professional culture.

Reprinted by permission of publisher, from Political Psychology, Vol. 6, No. 4, 1985. Office of Rights/Permissions, Plenum Publishing Corp., New York.

Preliminary Discussion

In her case study of a nursing service, Menzies (1960) reports that the nursing staff utilized defensive techniques including obsessional rituals (ritualistic behavior) in coping with anxiety. She observes: "A necessary psychological task for the entrant into any profession that works with people is the development of adequate professional detachment. He must learn, for example, to control his feelings, refrain from excessive involvement, avoid disturbing identifications, maintain his professional independence against manipulation and demands for unprofessional behaviour" (p. 102).

Menzies is not concerned with supporting or opposing this organizationally enforced detachment and denial of feelings in the nursing profession, but in pointing out the excessive degree of preoccupation with impersonal norms and behavior patterns among the nurses. She concludes that the level of denial of feelings and detachment imposed on the newcomers by the experienced professional nurses greatly contributes to the stress and high rates of turnover among nursing trainees. Menzies' study illustrates the extent to which organizational members construct social systems characterized by obsessional rituals (ritualistic behavior) that serve as a defense against anxiety.

Another example of ritualistic behavior evoked in the entrant is found in Ritti and Funkhouser's text on organizational behavior entitled "The Ropes to Skip and the Ropes to Know." The authors claim: "The first problem faced by the new member is that of gaining entry into the men's hut - of gaining access to the basic organizational secrets. A key episode here is the rite of passage. This is more or less an affirmation to the individual of the fact that he has been accepted into the men's hut" (1977, p. 3).

The authors describe how a new member of the organization must selectively focus his energy and attention on doing whatever is necessary to gain acceptance to the "men's hut." The "men's hut" refers to the ruling norms in a typically patriarchical and hierarchical organization, where socialization of the new member depends on his ability to assimilate the values of the organizational culture. He must prove to the organizational elites that he is deserving of membership and entrance to the "men's hut." Organizationally sanctioned performances and impressions by the new member take priority over his substantive work output. "The hut is a symbol of, and a medium for maintaining, the status quo and the good of the order" (1977, p. 3). The new member's compulsion to be accepted by and allowed entrance to the "men's hut" forces him to "learn the ropes" (1977). This means that a new member contains his anxiety at the point of organizational entry by exchanging his individual ego ideal for that of the organization and is motivated by the latent "hope" or "idea" that he may one day enter the "men's hut."

Other circumstances that might jeopardize the integrity of the organizational member's identity range from the anxiety of entry to changes of organizational leadership and political philosophy caused by the appearance of a new administration. Here, the member who identifies with the norms and values of his public agency, its previous mission statement and policy commitment, may perceive the change as an attack on his ego integrity and self-esteem.

He must now resolve the conflict between himself (his ego ideal) and the new organizational culture. If, on the one hand, professional opportunities are available and his degree of self-esteem and ego strength remain adequate, then he may choose to leave the agency. On the other hand, a combination of his need for security and his low self-esteem could motivate him to remain with the agency regardless of his apparent conflict with the new policy direction. In the latter case, he may repress and deny his conflicts by selectively attending to routinized bureaucratic practices and ritualistic performances that are often disconnected from practical purpose.

For example, Menzies (1960) observes nurses of a general hospital relying on "ritual task performance" as a defense against the anxiety of taking responsibility for decision-making in nurse-patient relationships. The "ritual task performance" may often be disconnected from the needs of patients, but serves the nurses' need to avoid the anxiety of personal responsibility. The "ritual task performance" characterized by its lists of prescribed actions and rigid routines is analyzed as a "reacetion formation" to the ultimate anxiety of losing control. In the stressful climate of a nursing service, assuming personal responsibility for one's actions and decisions may represent too great a risk to the individual nurse's identity and his or her membership in the profession.

The salience of ritualistic behavior for organization theory in the critical analysis of the social character of bureaucracy must be adequately explored in order to open up systems to analysis according to ritualistic content. Organizational analysts interested in understanding bureaucratic behavior should pay attention to the ritualistic (obsessional and compulsive) behavior of new members during the socialization process in order to delineate dysfunctional, meaningless, and conformist activities from functional meaningful, and adaptive activities. The former signify symptomatic and (neurotic) obsessive-compulsive bureaucratic practices, while the latter connote non-neurotic, purposeful, organizational practices. This enables us to distinguish ritualistic behavior as symptomatic administrative action from mere repeated actions that are practical and functional. A conceptual distinction between cultural ritual and ritualistic behavior must now be established.

CULTURAL RITUAL AND RITUALISTIC BEHAVIOR DEFINED

Cultural ritual is defined as the established form; a system of rites; a ceremonial act or action; and a customarily repeated act or series of acts (Merriam-Webster, 1974, p. 604). Cultural rituals (such as religious and magical ceremonies) function to confirm and accept human emotionality (Kafka, 1983). Ritualistic behavior is defined in organizational terms as "dysfunctional and obsessional, bureaucratic practices," such as the habitual observance of an established form or process for doing things and the repetition of acts. Cultural rituals control and make the unknowable appear knowable and are meaningful to the collective (Siggins, 1983). Ritualistic behavior is experienced as meaningless routine that serves to suppress and deny genuine feelings. A major distinction therefore exists between socially useful cultural rituals and what become obsessional and compulsive features of ritualistic behavior by bureaucrats.

The rationally organized and routinized character of bureaucratic behavior is tantamount to the defensive action taken by the ego in the symptom formation of obsessional neurosis. (1) For example, when we discuss ritual in the situational and social context of bureaucracy, we are more precisely describing what psychoanalyst John Kafka (1983) called "ritualistic behavior." In his article "Challenge and Confirmation in Ritual Action," Kafka clarifies the distinction between the terms "ritual" and "ritualistic."

> Rituals can produce a feeling of completeness - a whole act, a finished sequence, the achievement (at least for a while) of satisfaction, satiation, perhaps serenity. But sometimes as in "ritualistic behavior," they may instead generate a feeling of mechanical repetition or the absence of a meaning achieved, a sense of being enmeshed in an endless series of aborted sequences. (p. 31)

Kafka's clarification distinguishes purposeful and meaningful social action from dysfunctional bureaucratic action. Cultural rituals differ from ritualistic behavior by both confirming and challenging everyday reality. Ritualistic behavior functions to deny the presence of a "reality principle" in life and death, love and hate, conflict and growth. Cultural rituals, such as the celebration of puberty rites, represent the healthy adaptive recognition and affirmation of human development and change. Ritualistic behavior symbolizes the emergence of psychological defensive tendencies, as illustrated in bureaucratic performances of symptomatic repetition, which stress rationality differentiated from feeling, and routine, stability, and control (Menzies, 1960; Jaques, 1955). Ritualistic behavior symbolizes the attempt to overcome by repression the ambivalent feelings that threaten one's self, in contrast to some cultural rituals that encourage tolerance and awareness of ambivalence (Kafka, 1983). For Kafka, the difference between ritual and ritualistic concerns the psychological function of boundaries between the individual and the group. The individual is motivated to overcome ambivalence and to establish an "unambiguous set of signals" (p. 35). Kafka interprets these ritualistic actions as "regression in the service of the ego." This distinction is crucial for identifying the prevalence of symptomatic rituals (ritualistic behavior) in modern bureaucratic organizations. It is argued that complementary human needs are served by the perpetuation of ritualistic behavior and bureaucratic practices.

In his article "Rite, Ritual and Defense," Smith (1983) writes: "The defensiveness of belief, rather than the literality of belief is the proper object of study for distinguishing between individual pathology and culturally sanctioned ceremonials." For Smith, this distinction "could be framed within the concepts of regressive and progressive play/work" (p. 17) and defensive or nondefensive behavior (p. 18). In her article "Psychoanalysis and Ritual," Siggins defines "personal ritual" (what we distinguish here as "ritualistic behavior") as a symptom of an obsessional-compulsive disorder (1983, p. 3). "It is a personal and not a cultural construction though the form may well have cultural symbolic meaning" (p. 3). Dysfunctional (obsessive-compulsive) bureaucratic action is a "pseudo-social ritual" where instrumental human relations and impersonality promote the suppression of intersubjective meaning and mutual understanding among organizational participants. Identification of the nuances of ritualistic behavior in the self and in the bureaucracy illuminates the origins and concomitant actions of symptomatic organizational behavior.

THE PSYCHOLOGICAL ORIGINS OF RITUALISTIC BEHAVIOR

R. D. Laing (1969) describes "primary ontological security" as the existential position of a person with a "centrally firm sense of his own and other people's reality and identity." According to Laing, it is precisely the lack of this security that distinguished the psychotic from others. In the cycle of human development, ritualistic behavior in the child integrates the self by differentiating self and other. For instance, Erik Erikson (1966) notes that the earliest ritualization (ritualistic behavior) occurs in the mother-infant greeting and recognition behavior. According to Erikson, a "sense of basic trust" or "mistrust" emerges out of the interpersonal experiences of the first year of infant development (1968, p. 96). Hence, if the mother/ caretaker is emotionally healthy and the emotional bonding between mother and infant is good, then a primary sense of security and trust originates from the earliest ritualistic act. More specifically, if the necessary "trust" and sense of personal security is established during the first year to approximately 18 months of infancy, the baby comes to trust with minimal anxiety the mother's periodic absence. In the ritualistic performance one observes playful interactions between the mother and her child in coping with her mutual absence and presence. These playful interactions may take on a rather serious quality if we acknowledge their necessary ego function in challenging and confirming the child's sense of security and awareness of its separateness from the mother.

Ritualistic behavior in the form of greetings and recognition between mother and infant carries great implications for the crucial psychological foundations and genesis of self. Initially ritualistic behavior symbolizes a decisive moment in the early object relationship between mother and infant, wherein the psychodynamic process of separation and individuation, the necessary establishment of boundaries between self and other(s), makes its appearance .

Thus ritualistic behavior in its earliest manifestation is both purposeful and meaningful. It shares much in common with cultural rituals as meaningful celebrations and ceremonials with a common aim to control and make manageable that which appears life-threatening (loss of the "good" object-mother). Siggins (1983, p.3) states that ritual acts serve common personal needs "to control, to make manageable that which is unknown, frightening, overpowering." "The more helpless one feels," she writes, "the more one calls upon outside magical aid." Surely, cultural rituals in society and ritualistic behavior in infancy share this in common. On the other hand, individuals engaged in ritualistic acts (obsessional symptomatic rituals) may also wish to satisfy these personal needs for control and manageability, but institutionalized actions may lack meaningfulness, purposefulness, and human intimacy. As Siggins writes: "In the structured situation, ritual is an integral part of the organization. When a person or group revolts against the confines of the structure and wishes to be free and unfettered, he wants to be part of an individualized community based on personal intimacy, which tends to be antiritualistic" (p. 10). She continues: "This is one aspect of the paradoxical relationship between form and freedom that continually occurs in human life and institutions."

BUREAUCRATIC CONTEXT OF RITUALISTIC BEHAVIOR

Managers' attempts at promoting integration between individuals and organizations are much more complex and emotionally loaded than (the simplistic notion of) striking a balance between individual interests and organizational goals. This apparently innocuous problem of modern organizations includes, to the contrary, a complex phenomenon known in psychoanalysis as the "return of the repressed," in which individuals experience the return of primary impulses and uncanny emotions; the reemergence of ambivalent feelings and a renewed search for the "good" lost object .

The difference between cultural ritual (a series of meaningful ceremonial acts) and ritualistic behavior (psychologically regressive, repressive, defensive and, seemingly, purposeless acts of repetition) is most notable at the point of entry for the organizational recruit. Entry is described as a transformation from social actor to bureaucratic functionary, which is a momentary but profound psychological event in which the entrant dons the cloak of an organizational role and identity by electing to participate in the institutional activities. From this moment, the organization-joiner is vulnerable to bureaucratic inducements to promote loyalty and control of subordinates. By reinforcing ritualistic behavior, bureaucracy ensures mechanisms to acculturate and indoctrinate organizational participants.

I do not contend that bureaucratization (the human construction of bureaucracy and the socialization of bureaucrats) represents an outcome of ontological insecurities arising (aboriginally) from a failure of "good enough mothering" (Winnicott, 1965). That conjecture is absurdly reductionistic. But I do contend that bureaucratization is understood as emerging from defensive psychodynamic processes (Diamond, 1984) that occur as a consequence of the person's crucial need to maintain self boundaries (identity) and ego integrity just prior to, and following, entry into the formal organization. In ritualistic behavior, bureaucratic routine and repetition serve no organizational purpose. Yet that behavior plays a decisive role for the recruit in managing self boundaries and defending against anxiety felt during entry into the complex organization. At the moment of interface between the individual recruit and the organization, signal anxiety is felt in response to a fear of losing one's self boundaries and identity. At this decisive moment, any recruit must decide whether to affiliate with (by becoming a part of) the organization, or to remain separate from (and not part of) the institution.

This choice, regardless of how seemingly rational or irrational, invokes some dissonance and affects the integrity of the ego. The existential and psychological foundations of self are momentarily uprooted. Primitive human needs for attachment, merger, and dependency are reawakened. Such initial human motives encourage the nascent bureaucrat to locate his or her identity outside the self in the external quarter of bureaucracy. Along with the decision to join and accept membership in the formal organization, a renewed attachment is formulated by hierarchical arrangement. A "merger relationship" is established between superordinate and subordinate that contains libidinal energy and ambivalent feelings by bureaucratic practice and ritualistic behavior.

At the outset, ritualistic behavior ensures the management of self/object boundaries for the newcomer. Psychologically regressive dynamics of repetition and routine (reminiscent of primary process though essential to the child's need for object constancy and his development of focal attention) emerge in service to the vulnerable adult self. As Kafka notes: "Ritualistic" action represents striving for "object constancy" and "reality-anchoring" that appears to defend one against "massive confusion and total disorganization" (1983).

Accounts from organizational theorists of dysfunctional consequences in bureaucratic organizations often depict human behavior that is rigid and defensive. Viewed from a psychoanalytic perspective as an outcome of human needs (often, symptomatically expressed in human behavior), this phenomenon represents a wish to maintain the status quo, avoid anxiety-provoking conflict, and deny reality.

RITUALISTIC BEHAVIOR AND ORGANIZATION THEORY

Many organization theorists examine ritualistic behavior in modern bureaucratic organizations from different but mutually consistent perspectives. Such behavior is explicitly identified as a key factor in perpetuating dysfunctional consequences and ineffectiveness within bureaucratic institutions; at the same time, it achieves a necessary defensive equilibrium for organizational participants by managing self/object boundaries and alleviating anxiety over losing control. The following discussion outlines the arguments of prominent organization theorists and attempts to draw parallels and develop a consistent underlying pattern of thought.

Phenomenologist Ralph Hummel, for example, views the implications of Max Weber's characterization of modern bureaucracy as symbolizing a historical transition from socially organized action to rationally organized, efficient, stable, and controlled action (Weber, 1947; Hummel, 1977). He writes

> Society imposes general rules for proper social behavior, but personal discretion is allowed, providing plenty of room for actions based on mutual understanding. As society becomes more bureaucratic, however, rationally organized action finally collapses that room: in its never-ending search for control over its functionaries, bureaucracy must destroy discretion. (Hummel, 1977, pp. 33-34)

Hummel's warning is clear: as bureaucracy penetrates society it usurps individual freedom. Cultural rituals that regularly celebrate life (rites of passage) or death (funeral rites) often succumb to dysfunctional, irrational bureaucratic forms of action. In place of celebrating life and acknowledging death, ritualistic behavior facilitates individual attachment to hierarchy and conformity to impersonal rules, regulations, and procedures. Bureaucratic managers function to perpetuate hierarchy and ritualistic behavior by selectively attending to control and accountability of subordinates. Thus, managers treat subordinates as "part" human and one-dimensional for purposes of domination. Hummel illustrates this with the complaints of a functionary in the personnel department of the Cleveland, Ohio, Board of Education, who proclaims

> For a long time, I felt my role within the bureaucracy was to deal with human needs. In recent years, accountability has become so important, however, that I now must spend more and more time completing forms and compiling records. In many instances this work is duplicated by others and there is less time devoted to rendering service. My program director is caught up in this control situation and is constantly seeking new control methods and reactivating dormant rules. We had the sign-in and the sign-out procedure, the daily log, weekly, bi-weekly, monthly and yearly reports; now, we have a management information retrieval system. When similar information about all workers in the program is placed in the system, management can then analyze this (sic) data and attempt to control the daily work schedule and work distribution. Before all this paperwork there was more productivity. It

> seems that accountability and productivity are not compatible. (Hummel, 1977, pp. 26-27)

Management's obsession with bureaucratic control, accountability, and efficiency often results in duplication and lower productivity. Bureaucratic behavior among organizational participants replaces intersubjectively meaningful, collaborative, and effective social actions (cultural ritual) with meaningless, rigidly conformist, and routine (ritualistic) actions. In Hummel's analysis the functionary is a product of bureaucratic ritualism.

Sociologist Robert Merton (1940) criticizes the dysfunctional and purposeless aspects of bureaucracy. He warns that dysfunctions arise from the bureaucrat's preoccupation with control over his subordinates and his insistence on the "reliability of response" and predictability of bureaucratic behavior. According to Merton, sentiments of loyalty and conformity in bureaucracy can be "more intense than is technically necessary." In a later work, Merton explains:

> There is a margin of safety, so to speak, in the pressure exerted by these sentiments upon the bureaucrat to conform to his patterned obligation, in much the same sense that added allowance (precautionary overestimates) are made by the engineer in designing the supports for a bridge. But his very emphasis leads to a transference of the sentiments from the aims of the organization onto the particular details of behavior required by rules. Adherence to the rules, originally conceived as a means, becomes transformed into an end-in-itself; there occurs the familiar process of displacement of goals whereby "an instrumental value becomes a terminal value." (Merton, 1963, pp. 258-259)

For Merton, the bureaucrat's reliance on impersonal rules and prescribed actions fosters ritualistic attitudes. This results in diminishing effective responses to clients, personnel, and the task environment of the agency. (2) This phenomenon is comparable to the "ritual task performance" (mentioned above) in the Menzies case study of the nursing service. According to Merton, bureaucratic behavior (characterized by the functionary's extraordinary dependency on rules and prescriptions for action) often results in goal displacement. Originally intended to produce rationally organized and efficient action, bureaucracy deteriorates into dysfunctional, inefficient, and irrationally organized impersonal action. Bureaucrats emphasize means over ends; form (process) takes priority over substance. From a sociological perspective, Merton observes that ritualistic behavior is characteristic of bureaucracy:

> Discipline, readily interpreted as conformance with relations, whatever the situation, is seen not as a measure designed for specific purposes but becomes an immediate value in the life-organization of the bureaucrat. This emphasis, resulting from the displacement of the original goals, develops into rigidities and an inability to adjust readily. Formalism, even ritualism, ensues with an unchallenged insistence upon punctilious adherence to formalized procedures. This may be exaggerated to the point where primary concern with conformity to the rules interferes with the achievement of the purposes of the organization, in which case we have the familiar phenomenon ol the technicism or red tape of the official. (1963, pp. 258-259)

In a psychoanalytic framework, one might suggest that ego integrity, autonomy, and a sense of reality are unwittingly sacrificed to a collective wish for certainty and predictability in a changing environment. Managers in bureaucratic organizations tend to control and dominate their functionaries and their task environment. This is symptomatic of the ego's need in an obsessional neurosis to control "impulse activities" from the inside and distort reality from the outside. Bureaucratic managers stress conformity to impersonal rules and procedures (official behavior). This results, on the one hand, in goal displacement and, on the other hand, in destruction of individual discretion. Unlike cultural rituals that enhance a feeling of completeness and achievement, bureaucratic rituals (ritualistic acts) promote mechanical repetition and suppress feelings from thoughts and behavior. Compulsive routine and impersonal action among organizational members symbolize the bureaucrat's reliance on formalism, conservatism, cases, technicism, and red tape as a defense against anxiety about losing control. These defensive actions illustrate psychological repression and unconscious denial of reality among bureaucratic participants.

French sociologist Michel Crozier in "The Bureaucratic Phenomenon" further enhances our understanding of the significance of ritualistic behavior for bureaucracy. He writes:

> ..a bureaucratic organization is an organization that cannot correct its behavior by learning from its errors. Bureaucratic patterns of action, such as the impersonality of rules and the centralization of decision-making, have

> been so stabilized that they have become part of the organization's self-reinforcing equilibrium. Finally, when one rule prevents adequate dealing with one case, its failure will not generate pressure to make it more complete, more precise, and more binding. (1964, p. 187)

For Crozier, a typical feature of bureaucracy is its tendency to produce "vicious circles" where organizational participants repeat errors and do not learn from their mistakes because of an overwhelming propensity to defend themselves against the necessity for and the reality of change. The bureaucrat's common response to failure is reinforcement and/or expansion of his routine structural arrangements and normative assumptions - illustrated by a "more of the same" attitude.

Crozier identifies four basic components that comprise the "vicious circle" of bureaucracy: "impersonal rules, the centralization of decisions, strata isolation and concomitant group pressure on the individual, and the development of parallel power relationships around remaining areas of uncertainty" (1964, p. 187).

In his empirical analysis of dysfunctions in the French bureaucracy, Crozier views ritualistic behavior as predominantly the result of peer group pressure on individual members among the numerous strata of the hierarchical system. He expands Merton's notion of goal displacement and Hummel's assertion of limits to discretion by arguing that the displacement of goals is enforced by peer groups emerging in "the isolation of different strata" as a way of protecting group members against other groups and against the organization (1964, pp. 190-191). Furthermore, he suggests this isolation allows the unit to "control its own domain and to ignore the organization's wider goals" (1964, p. 191). Crozier explains:

> ...in order to get the best bargain for its own members, the peer group must pretend that their partial objective is an end in itself. The member's ritualism provides good means to achieve such an end. It enables the group to assert its own functions are the most crucial for the success of the whole organization. Then, finally, it helps develop and reinforce group solidarity among the group's own members. (1964, p. 191)

For Crozier, the function of ritualistic behavior in bureaucracy is both a response to and a perpetuation of bureaucratic centralization and impersonal norms. Ritualistic behavior is a dysfunctional consequence of peer group pressure intended to enhance group or unit cohesion and promote power relationships for bargaining purposes. Such behavior reinforces isolationist tendencies and defensivc attitudes among the strata of bureaucracy, which in turn promote competition and divisiveness between organizational units and peer groups. This leads to intraorganizational boundaries among units (or departments) becoming increasingly rigid and protective with communication and coordination becoming increasingly difficult. This outcome is illustrated by the narrow-minded and parochial (often territorial) ritualistic attitudes among organizational group members.

From a psychoanalytic perspective at the organizational level, these findings suggest that meaningful reality-testing is unlikely and the organization finds itself incapable of responding to environmental demands for change. Peer groups surface as havens in an alienating and depersonalizing organizational climate. As a symbol of the organizational ego, management inadequately functions to balance internal and external systemic pressures. At the individual level, a so-called "bureaucratic personality" emerges among functionaries: someone who respects power relationships throughout the organizational strata, but who is predominantly motivated by interpersonal security needs and defense against anxiety over losing control.

In their books "Theory in Practice" (1974) and "Organizational Learning" (1978), social psychologists Chris Argyris and Donald Schon discuss (what I interpret as) ritualistic behavior and bureaucratic dysfunctions by examining "constancy-seeking" behavior and "single-loop" learning of individual and organizational "model 1 theories-in-use" and "0-1 learning systems" (1978).

According to Argyris and Schon, model 1 assumptions and governing values produce behavioral outcomes in the organization that foster limited learning, decreasing effectiveness, and the promotion of rigidity. These governing variables that effect intraorganizational behavior include the following tendencies: to achieve purposes as the individual perceives them; to maximize winning and minimize losing; to minimize eliciting negative feelings; to be rational and minimize emotionality (1976, p. 31). Action strategies of model 1 include: efforts to design and manage the environment so that the individual is in control over the factors relevant to him; acts to own and control tasks; and, unilateral protection of self and unilateral protection of others from being hurt (1976, p. 31).

The consequences of model 1 theory-in-use further portray ritualistic behavior. For example, the individual is viewed as defensive; defensive interpersonal and group relationships are commonplace; defensive norms must prevail; and "low freedom of choice, internal commitment, and risk taking" persist (1976, p. 31). Finally, Argyris and Schon (1978) point out that model 1 theory-in-use and its counterpart 0-1 learning systems result in the inability to "double-loop" learn; therefore, individual members of these systems perpetuate "self-sealing processes, single-loop learning, and, little public testing of theories" (1976, p. 31).

Hence, ritualistic behavior in modern organizations represents tacit skills of defense against the anxiety of uncertainty and predictability associated with problem-solving and change in the status quo. At the same time that cultural ritual serves to control or make manageable that which is unknown or frightening, ritualistic behavior (as symbolized by model 1 and bureaucratic organizations) serves a defensive function for bureaucrats of psychologically repressing and denying the necessity (often the inevitability) of organizational and interpersonal change. From a psychoanalytic viewpoint, change means loss at the personal (often unconscious) level of experience. Ritualistic behavior among bureaucrats functions, thereby, to avoid anxiety connected with consciously painful recognition of loss. Defensive psychological activities of denial and selective inattention operate to repress feelings and narrowly focus one's thoughts on meaningless and repetitive tasks, while functioning to meet the unconscious desire for interpersonal security in maintaining stability and the status quo. Under these circumstances, organizational and individual reality-testing surrenders to a collective fantasy of control and (what some might call) immortalily (Denhardt,1981).

Psychoanalysts Abraham Zaleznik and Manfred Kets de Vries write in "Power and the Corporate Mind":

> Any collective experience, such as organizational planning, with its capacity for changing the atmosphere and the imagery ot power conflicts, can fall victim to rigidities. The rigidities consist mainly of the formation and elaboration of structures, procedures, and other ceremonials that create the illusion of solving problems but, in reality, only provide a basis for the discharge of valuable energies. (1975, p. 135)

For Zaleznik and Kets de Vries, ordinary organizational activities like planning and decision-making inevitably produce change and influence power relationships. Consequently, "ritualistic" approaches to solving real problems arise as a common feature of modern organizations, where, for example, people come together in committees "in the naive belief that the exchange of ideas is bound to produce a solution" (1975, p. 135).

It is not the mere formation of organizational committees for the purpose of solving problems which Zaleznik and Kets de Vries view suspiciously, but, rather, "that the faith that is invested in such proposals deflects attention from where it properly belongs" (1975, p. 135). Following a proposal to form the committee to examine a particular problem, organizational participants may ritualistically perceive the simple idea of the committee itself as the solution to the problem - a "magical formula" to alleviate the anxiety of uncertainty. The idea of the committee may, for the moment, serve as the object of a collective (organizational) wish to be rid of the anxiety-provoking event.

If undetected, ritualistic behavior in modern organizations literally can act as a blinder to reality - a defensive "screen" that conceals problems and denies conflicts. Human energy (cognitions and emotions), otherwise channeled into the correction of errors and actual problem solving, is often displaced by the influence of anxiety onto substitute objects promoting the illusion of safety and security without substantive reflection and change. Under the stress of uncertainty and neurotic anxiety, bureaucratic form (procedures, regulations, impersonal rules, red tape, etc.) takes precedence over organizational mission and substantive output (problem-solving, provision of services, personal responsibility).

Ritualistic action involves obsessional thinking and compulsive behavior, with which individuals defensively act to deny reality by "undoing" the self-alienation and "isolating" its affects (Freud, 1959a). As we have already seen, ritualistic action is commonplace in modern bureaucracy. Bureaucratic characteristics actually facilitate symptomatic rituals that unintentionally promote human tendencies to deny reality, and displace cognitions and emotions, in order to maintain security by momentarily avoiding anxiety. Ritualistic behavior serves a common purpose for both the individual and the organization. It functions as an instantaneous defense against personal fragmentation and organizational disequilibrium. Like rigid and "overdetermined" defensive operations in the obsessional neurotic, ritualistic behavior in the organization appears to reestablish equilibrium by securing the status quo (reinforcing individual and organizational boundaries). Actually, ritualistic behavior is indicative of symptomatic administrative behavior identified by organization theorists in the occurrence of "vicious circles," "self-sealing processes," "single-loop learning," and the generalized "displacement of goals." These organization theorists have identified such ritualistic phenomena in bureaucracy as decisive to dysfunctional consequences, ineffectiveness, and organizational pathology.

CONCLUSION

I have attempted to illustrate not only how ritualistic behavior that is commonplace in bureaucracy contributes to dysfunctional consequences such as goal displacement and the like, but also that it is symptomatic of obsessional-compulsive neuroses in the human personality (Freud, 1963) and symptomatic of the individual's need to control ambivalence and manage boundaries between self and other(s) (Kafka, 1983; Erikson, 1968).

Further, I have located the crucial moment of recurrence of these psychological needs in the adult at the point of entry into the bureaucratic system of organization. It is at this stressful moment that one's self is most vulnerable to the anxiety challenging the recruit's ego strength and self-esteem. Here, the management of self boundaries and the control of ambivalent feelings are a most prominent motivating force influencing the entrant's actions. Consequently, the extraordinary security needs of the new organizational member promotes conformity and overdependency or exaggerated and psychologically regressive demands for protection and defense against anxiety. A highly structured and often rigid institution designed for control and accountability like the "ideal type" bureaucracy may unwittingly facilitate and perpetuate such action.

The ultimate organizational paradox which the analysis of ritualistic behavior helps to illuminate is that the human construction of and adherence to a bureaucratic form of institution is the outcome of the obsessional neurotic's need to preserve and secure the self against anxiety about losing control. In the article, "The Absurdity of Ritual," Zuesse (1983, pp. 40-50) states: "In all ritual, it is evident people voluntarily submit to their bodily existence and assume very specific roles with highly patterned rules - roles and rules that end up making the self one with an infinite series of others who have embodied these 'typical' roles." The author suggests that the "free self voluntarily submits to particular boundaries and enters servitude to otherness and to an entire world of objective relationships and moral imperatives" (1983, p. 40). Zuesse concludes that ritual "may be self-alienating, but it is finally self-accepting in the deepest sense. The self that is accepted is the actual finite self of boundaries and limits, the self defined through others, and destined to die" (1983, p. 42).

In this paper, I have attempted to point out that while both cultural ritual and ritualistic behavior are self-limiting, only cultural ritual is truly self-accepting. In the cultural ritual, we construct a consensually validated system of meanings," whereas, in ritualistic behavior, group and organizational participants perpetuate a defensive social system against anxiety that fosters the suppression of collaborative human action by depersonalization and unilateral protectiveness.

NOTES

(1) Obsessional neurosis is a form of psychoneurosis in which the predominant symptoms are obsessive thoughts and compulsive behavior (obsessive rituals). Obsessional thoughts differ from normal thoughts in that they are experienced by the patient himself as unspontaneous, distracting, repetitive, ruminative, and as coming from elsewhere than himself; their subject-matter is typically absurd, bizarre, irrelevant, and obscene. Compulsive behavior is repetitive, stereotyped, ritualistic, and superstitious (see Rycroft, 1968).

(2) Such ritualistic attitudes and overprecautions will not only produce rigidity and a lack of spontaneity necessary to organizational adjustment, but, at the individual level and the organizational level such attitudes are symptomatic of obsessional processes at work that promote narrow-mindedness, parochialism, and selective inattention - cognitive processes attending to interpersonal security needs and avoidance of anxiety-provoking circumstances like that encountered by change and problem-solving activities.

REFERENCES

ARGYRIS, C. Leadership, learning, and changing the status quo. Organizational Dynamics, 4, 1976, No. 3.

ARGYRIS, C., & SCHON, D. Theory in Practice. San Francisco: Jossey-Bass, 1974.

ARGYRIS, C. & SCHON, D. Organizational Learning. Mass.: Addison-Wesley, Reading, 1978.

BAUM, H.S. Autonomy, shame, and doubt: Power in the bureaucratic lives of planners. Admin. Soc., 15(2), 1983, 147-184.

BOWLBY, J. Volume 1. Attachment. New York: Basic Books, 1969.

BOWLBY, J. Volume 2. Separation. New York: Basic Books, 1973.

BOWLBY, J. The Making and Breaking of Affectional Bonds. London: Tavistock Publications, 1979.

BURKE, W. W. Organization Development: Principles and Practices. Boston and Toronto: Little, Brown and Company, 1982.

CROZIER, M. The Bureaucratic Phenomenon. Chicago: University of Chicago Press, 1964.

DENHARDT, R.B. In the Shadow of Organization. Lawrence: University of Kansas Press, 1981.

DIAMOND, M.A. Bureaucracy as externalized self-system: A view from the psychological interior. Admin. Soc., 16(2), 1984, 195-214.

DIAMOND, M.A., & ALLCORN, S. Psychological barriers to personal responsibility. Organ. Dynamics, 12(4), 1984, 66-77.

ERIKSON, E. Childhood and Society. New York: Norton, 1963.

ERIKSON, E. Ontogeny of Ritualization. In R. Loewenstein, et al. (eds.), Psychoanalysis - A General Psychology: Essays in Honor of Heinz Hartmann. New York: International Universities Press, 1966.

ERIKSON, E. Identity, Youth and Crisis. New York: Norton, 1968.

FAIRBAIRN, W.R.D. Psychoanalytic Studies of Personality. London: Tavistock Publications, 1952.

FREUD, S. Group Psychology and the Analysis of the Ego. New York: Norton, 1921/1959b.

FREUD, S. The Ego and the Id. New York: Norton, 1923.

FREUD, S. Inhibitions, Symptoms and Anxiety. New York: Norton, 1959a.

FREUD, S. Character and Culture. New York: Collier Books, 1963.

FREUD, A. The Ego and the Mechanisms of Defense. New York: International Universities Press, 1966.

GREENSON, R. Explorations in Psychoanalysis. New York: International Universities Press, 1978.

HUMMEL, R. The Bureaucratic Experience. New York: St. Martins Press, 1977,1982.

JAQUES, E. Social systems as a defense against persecutory and depressive anxiety. In Klein, M., Heimann, P., and Money-Kyrle, R. E. (eds.), New Directions in Psychoanalysis. New York: Basic Books, 1955.

KAFKA, J. Challenge and confirmation in ritual action. Psychiatry, 46(1), 1983, 31-39.

KERNBERG, O. Regression in organizational leadership. Psychiatry, 42, 1979, 24-39.

KETS DE VRIES, M.F.R. Organizational Paradoxes. London: Tavistock Publications, 1980.

KLEIN, M. The Psychoanalysis of Children. Seymour Lawrence, Delacorte Press, 1975.

KOHUT, H. The Analysis of the Self. New York: International Universities Press, 1971.

LABIER, D. Bureaucracy and psychopathology. Polit. Psychol., 4(2), 1983, 223-244.

LAING, R.D. The Divided Self. Middlesex, England: Penguin Books, 1966.

LEVINSON, H. Executive. Cambridge, Mass.: Harvard University Press, 1981.

MAHLER, M.S., et al. The Psychological Birth of the Human Infant. New York: Basic Books, 1975.

MENZIES, I.E.P. A case in the functioning of social systems as a defense against anxiety: A report on a study of the nursing service of a general hospital. Human Relations, 13, 1960, 95-121.

Merriam- Webster Dictionary. New York: Pocket Books, 1974, p. 604.

MERTON, R. Bureaucratic structure and personality. Social Forces, 17, 1940.

MERTON, R. Bureaucratic structure and personality. In Smelser and Smelser (eds.), Personality and Social Systems. New York: Wiley, 1963.

REIK, T. Ritual: Psycho-Analytic Studies. New York: International Universities Press, 1946.

RITTI, R. R., & FUNKHOUSER, G. R. The Ropes to Skip and the Ropes to Know. Studies in Organizational Behavior. Columbus, Ohio: Grid, Inc., 1977.

RYCROFT, C. A Critical Dictionary of Psychoanalysis. Middlesex, England: Penguin Books, 1968.

SCHWARTZ H. Job involvement as obsession-compulsion. Acad. Management Rev., 7(3), 1982, 429-432.

SIGGINS, L. Psychoanalysis and ritual. Psychiatry, 46(1), 1983, 2-15.

SLATER, P. Microcosm. New York: Wiley, 1966.

SMITH J. H. Rite, ritual, and defense. Psychiatry, 46(1), 1983, 16-30.

SPERLING, O. Psychoanalytic aspects of bureaucracy. Psychoanalytic Quart., 19, 1960, 88-100.

SULLIVAN, H.S. The Interpersonal Theory of Psychiatry. New York: Norton, 1953.

WEBER, M. The Theory of Social and Economic Organization. New York: The Free Press, 1947.

WINNICOTT, D. W. The Maturational Processes and the Facilitating Environment, New York: International Universities Press, 1965.

ZALEZNIK, A., & Kets de Vries, M. Power and the Corporate Mind. Boston: Houghton Mifflin Co., 1975.

ZUESSE, E. M. The absurdity of ritual. Psychiatry, 46(1), 1983, 40-50.

Organizational Identity - A Psychoanalytic Exploration of Organizational Meaning

Michael A. Diamond

Organizational studies are undergoing change. Organization theory and research are moving toward greater sensitivity to subjective perceptions of the world, as illustrated by the current focus on "organizational culture." (1) This development shifts the analysis of organizations from the study of empirical "objective" data to "intersubjective" data. Scholars want to know what organizational members experience and how that experience influences their decisions and actions. Contemporary organizational research is, therefore, composed less of "factual" statements from detached observers about administrative behavior and more of statements from participants themselves.

This shift in the level of analysis is creating a new field of organizational analysis. Organizational analysts want to understand organizational settings that promote anxiety and encourage repression, denial, and the splitting of participant feelings and thoughts (Zaleznik and Kets de Vries, 1975; Kernberg, 1979; Kets de Vries, 1980 and 1984; Kets de Vries and Miller, 1984). These psychologically defensive responses protect organizational members from threatening or potentially threatening interpersonal and organizational situations. At the same time, these defenses damage self, self-other, and organizational relationships by fostering inauthenticity. Consequently, a false self may emerge (Winnicott, 1965) in which interpersonal and organizational defensive and repressive dynamics conceal feelings and thoughts of organizational members.

Modern organizational analysis focuses on the tension between the "true self," which modern organizational norms and values often negate or suppress, and the false self (Diamond, 1985b). Acknowledgment and communication of repressed (inaccessible) feelings and thoughts about the "true" (actual) experience of the interpersonal or organizational events alleviate anxiety and minimize psychologically defensive behavior. Such therapeutic consequences result from collaborative inquiry between organizational analyst and client, and among clients themselves. The collaborative search for

---

Reprinted, by permission of publishers, from Administration & Society, Vol. 20, No. 2, August 1988,

organizational identity produces shared meanings and consensual validation, which aid clients in problem solving and conflict resolution. A way of better understanding the importance of authentic and inauthentic states of self to organizations and organizational members is through the concept of organizational identity.

By advancing the concept of organizational identity, this essay contributes to the organizational literature a theory and practice for analyzing the intersubjective meaning of organizational behavior. It advances an explanation of individual feelings rooted in infancy about organizations, what Winnicott (1965) calls the "holding environment," and an explanation of interpersonal relationships grounded in adulthood but with origins in infancy and childhood - what Kohut (1977 and 1984) calls "selfobject transferences." It further proffers the notion of transference of emotions in hierarchical organizations as an instrument for observing and explaining key interpersonal relationships between organizational superordinates and their subordinates and between organizational analysts and their clients. Such relationships are grounded in the unconscious desires and expectations of both parties to the relationship. This is the essence of a transference of emotions. Understanding transference of emotions between superordinates and subordinates is a key ingredient in organizational identity, which distinguishes it, most prominently, from the popular use of organizational culture in the analysis of organization. Finally, for the purpose of organizational change and development an awareness of organizational identity is essential to the organizational member's willingness to assume responsibility for his or her actions and change the status quo. This willingness to take responsibility for one's actions is both the result of a mutual understanding of displaced (transferred) emotions between superordinates and subordinates, and often among peers, in the organization, and the outcome of one's recognition of his or her unconscious expectations and the desires of others. Knowing the identity of an organization evokes the personal meaning, experience, and perception of organizational life in the mind of individual members, which helps us understand unconscious motivations that govern behavior and that distinguishes one organization from another.

Organizational identity defines who we all are in a group and who (or what) we can be as members of groups (role identity). Organizational identity is the network of repetitive interpersonal strategies for coping with (defending against) interpersonal and organizational events that are stressful and perceived as threatening. Organizational identity represents the means by which work groups orient themselves toward the organization and from which individuals acquire their own sense of security and identity.

Organizational identity, it will be shown, may be found in the difficult-to-observe patterns of (interpersonal) interaction within organizations. Discovering organizational identity involves interpreting how people handle themselves and each other, especially under conditions of stress and change within organizations. Organizational analysis focuses upon individual behavior and interpersonal relationships that must be interpreted to find underlying meaning in the actions of others and make sense of complex organizational dynamics.

The concept of organizational identity is not entirely new (see Kets de Vries, 1984; Levinson and Weinbaum, 1984; Larçon and Reitter, 1984). Psychoanalytic organizational theorists and consultants, however, do not always share similar conceptions of organizational identity even when they set their sights on the same phenomenon. Levinson and Weinbaum, for example, emphasize the role of the ego ideal in organizational identification, while Larçon and Reitter (1984) stress major themes upon which the organizational identity is based. These themes include structural factors, political factors, action systems, and organizational imagery. Although my conceptualization incorporates many of these ideas, I wish to offer an alternative conceptualization.

My intent is to contribute to the organizational analyst's and administrative practitioner's way of thinking about and seizing hold of the intersubjective data collected in the process of observing self and others at work. Gaining an appreciation of these data enhances the psychoanalytic conceptualization of organizational identity. I turn to the latter subject first.

DEFINING ORGANIZATIONAL IDENTITY

Organizational identity is the totality of repetitive patterns of individual behavior and interpersonal relationships that taken together comprise the unacknowledged meaning of organizational life. These patterns of behavior include both consciously and unconsciously motivated actions that must be interpreted in order to have meaning for organizational members. This definition emphasizes organizational identity as the product of both conscious and unconscious thoughts and feelings that motivate behavior. The definition focuses upon interpreting individual actions in an interpersonal context. Organizational identity, it is asserted, evolves from narcissistic (self-other) needs for self-cohesion and integrity in work groups of two or more persons communicating and interacting with the intent of meeting an organizational (formal or informal) objective. Organizational identity, it will be seen, is a work group's coping response to critical incidents and everyday stressors. This is consistent with "the speculation that the evolution of affects serves the adaptive needs of the group" (Modell, 1984, p.184), which means that group performance in organizations must always be considered in a situational context.

Organizational identity is, therefore, the product of interpersonal strategies (defensive and adaptive) for coping with critical incidents. Such incidents may influence power and authority, responsibility and accountability, or may produce greater uncertainty and helplessness. Regardless, these incidents are changes from the status quo in organizations and consequently generate anxiety among organizational members.

Moreover, organizational identity is a solution to contradictory motives and conflicting aims of organizational participants. By this is meant that organizational identity represents a compromise formation. The assertion that organizational identity is a compromise formation means that it is the product of conflict that partially expresses both (or the collective) parties to the conflict (Rycroft, 1968, p.20). These collective defenses organize experience, shape perceptions of oneself and others, and, ultimately, influence administrative decisions and actions. It therefore develops from competing narcissistic needs and psychological defenses against threatening situations (situations perceived as particularly threatening to self-esteem and integrity; Diamond, 1984 and 1985a).

In sum, organizational identity implies that many repetitive (frequently ritualistic) patterns of interactions within work groups and among participants are, for organizational members, purposeful (but not necessarily conscious) psychological defenses against threatening events and interpersonal activities. These patterns of defenses constitute rational administrative processes of organizations that regulate threats to personal security (self-integrity) by structuring organizational life.

In the next section, the psychological origins of the concept of organizational identity are located in the so-called holding environment of infancy (Winnicott, 1965). The significance of this childhood holding environment both impacts behavior in organizations and, equally significant, the holding environment of organizations affects human behavior and adult development in much the same way.

CHILDHOOD AND ORGANIZATIONAL HOLDING ENVIRONMENTS

The holding environment may be regarded as the first organizational matrix of the nascent self. It becomes the unconscious symbol of the human artifact called "organization." An individual's first contact with organizations occurs in infancy. Organizational identity (adulthood) is grounded in the early psychological origins of conflict between the individual and the organization. The origins of organizational identity are rooted in the baby's first awareness of self as separate from others, an awareness that results in feelings of ambivalence and separation anxiety for the infant. The degree of success of separation and individuation depends upon the adequacy of the child's holding environment and the establishment of object constancy, the quality of "good-enough" parenting. The baby must feel secure and safe enough in the parent's presence to practice his or her newly discovered autonomy and independence. Both psychoanalytic concepts imply the need for reliability and authenticity of parenting ("good-enough mothering") during the child's separation and individuation (Winnicott, 1965). The importance of attachment, separation, and individuation, and the "good-enough" holding environment requires further elaboration.

An adequate holding environment consists of the parent's empathic (mirroring and idealizing) responses to the needs of the infant's nascent self. The parent satisfies the infant's narcissistic needs for (mirroring) self-confirmation and (idealization) merger with greatness, strength, and calmness by a willingness and ability to authentically and compassionately react to the baby's preverbal cues. The parent can facilitate the infant's cognitive and emotional self-development by establishing a secure and relatively anxiety-free attachment from which the baby can separate and individuate with confidence. Consequently, the parent's availability for safety and contact comfort facilitates the baby's sense of himself as separate from the loving parent, and, therefore, as separate from others and the environment.

In contrast to the "good-enough" holding environment, an inadequate ("not-good enough") holding environment does not provide for the baby's primary narcissistic demands. The infant' s emotional safety and security needs are not met. In fact, the parent may demand that the infant respond to the mother's or father's frustrated childhood narcissistic needs. The parent is not emotionally accessible to the infant and perhaps manipulates the child into meeting her or his needs. This anxious attachment to the parent (primarily to the mother) compromises the infant's efforts toward separation and individuation.

Intense feelings of ambivalence and separation anxiety are experienced. As the primary relationship to the parent is filled with uncertainty, successful differentiation between self and other, and self and environment becomes very difficult. The baby becomes depleted without the narcissistic supplies he needs for self-sustenance and individuation. As a result, a "false self" emerges that intends to protect the "true self" now filled with rage and loss due to separation anxiety. The preverbal holding environment is the psychological foundation for future self and other, and self and environmental relationships; a fact disregarded by scholars of mainstream organizational behavior and contemporary proponents of organizational culture. Because of the similarity of the organizational holding environment to that of the infant's relationship to the parent, organizational themes of attachment, separation, loss, and anxiety will reenact earlier developmental anxieties and perhaps create new ones.

In sum, organizational identity is a theory of self and other relations. It guides practitioners and organizational analysts in the practice of analyzing self and other relations in organizational settings. Its basic theoretical premise is that the model for understanding unconscious adult actions in organizations is found in the dynamics of self-other relations in infancy. Similar to the role of parenting in establishing a safe and "good-enough" holding environment for the emergence of the baby's sense of self, the organizational environment of the adult may either help or hurt self-integrity. Furthermore, psychological dilemmas of organizational membership may revive the infant's earlier anxieties arising from his or her relationship to the parent.

In order to appreciate the significance of early object (self-other) relations more fully, the usefulness of transference for organizational analysis should be stated. Transference, as defined in the next section, provides for the understanding of many unconscious aspects of interpersonal relations. In this regard, transference is used as an analytical technique for studying organizational identity. The primary unit of analysis of organizational identity is interpersonal (but not interpersonal in the traditional social psychological sense), transference enables the organizational analyst and practitioner to understand the unconscious meaning of human interactions in empathy and counter-transference. By placing himself in the other's experience through identification (empathy) and by acknowledging how he is responding to others (countertransference), the organizational analyst and administrative practitioner are more responsive to (interpret) how organizational members feel and think in present circumstances. These dimensions of transference encourage public testing of assumptions intended to confirm or disconfirm the meaning of the experiences of the other members, which include unconscious themes from early self-other relations. These transference themes are categorized into three patterns: mirroring, idealizing, and twinship (alter ego). In the final analysis, the study of transference is especially appropriate to exploring the psychodynamics of repetitive self, self-other, and environmental relations that comprise the organizational identity.

In the following section, transference is defined and discussed.

TRANSFERENCE OF EMOTIONS

Transference of emotions is an everyday occurrence of human interaction. It is an unconscious (often preconscious) phenomenon that typically occurs between two persons in which one transfers feelings from significant past relationships (to mother, father, siblings, etc.) to another person in the present. According to psychoanalyst Ralph Greenson (1978, p.201), "Transference is the experiencing of feelings, drives, attitudes, fantasies, and defenses toward a person in the present that are inappropriate to that person and are a repetition, a displacement of reactions originating in regard to significant persons of early childhood. I emphasize that for a reaction to be considered transference it must have two characteristics: It must be a repetition of the past and it must be inappropriate to the present." The notion of transference helps explain the infant-parent relationship. John Bowlby (1979) describes the prolonged dependency of infancy as "attachment" behavior in which the infant "clings to" and "follows" the mother. From the beginning of life, this universal human condition sets the stage for a dynamic and contradictory psychological structure of selfhood. It is the dilemma of self-identity derived from the (cognitive-affective) negotiation of one's self-image in the developmental process of separation and individuation, differentiation and integration. Adult interactions are, therefore, bound to renew feelings of attachment, separation, loss, and anxiety that promote the splitting-up or repression of such feelings. These phenomena are often psychoanalytically understood as a form of repetition-compulsion, or simply the compulsion to repeat earlier conditions. The outcome of these human interactions are unconsciously affected by the interpersonal quality of the relationship. For example, a subordinate may have unconscious expectations of his superordinate. These expectations may originate in his frustrated need for idealization during childhood, where his need to merge with greatness, strength, and calmness was unfulfilled. Such painful disappointment is often pushed out of conscious awareness (repressed) until a significant adult relationship revives feelings and thoughts unconsciously associated with earlier events between a child and his parents. In this instance, the subordinate may admire and idealize his supervisor as superhuman and infallible. Inevitably, his admired supervisor makes mistakes that result in the subordinate's feeling severe disappointment, rage, and depression. His needs to merge with greatness, strength, and calmness are once again frustrated. His feelings of rage and depression are linked to his experience as a child, when he experienced the holding environment between himself and his mother and father, himself and others, as dangerous and unstable. Such feelings are inappropriate to the present (transferred). In sum, transference is often an expression of frustrated narcissistic (developmental) needs or narcissistic injury that results in damaged self-integrity and lowered self-esteem.

Before describing the nuances of transference phenomena observable in the organizational setting, I will explain the underlying developmental rationale for recurrent transference of emotions in adults.

Narcissistic Needs of the Bipolar Self

In Figure 1, Kohut's conceptualization of narcissistic development known as the bipolar self is presented.

FIGURE 1: Bipolar Self

pole of ambitions	----------	intermediate area of skills and talents	----------	pole of idealized goals

CORRESPONDING SELF AND OTHER NEEDS

mirror transference	--------------	twinship and alterego	-------------------	idealizing transference

Kohut's categories of transference, while incomplete, provide a basis for analyzing organizational identity. (2) The bipolar self consists of ambitions at one pole and ideals at the other pole. These are connected by an "intermediate area" of talents and skills (Kohut, 1977 and 1984). Certain types of transference (mirroring, idealizing, and twinship) correspond to each pole and the intermediate area of the bipolar self. Explaining these transferences and their relationship to components of the bipolar self, Kohut writes, "The individual developmental lines of our three major self [other] object needs should therefore be examined . . . via a detailed investigation of the needs of man for the sustenance of his self in these three areas (i.e., his need to experience mirroring and acceptance; his need to experience merger with greatness, strength, and calmness; and his need to experience the presence of essential alikeness) from the moment of birth to the moment of death" (1984, p.194). Parental responsiveness in the early childhood environment to the child's narcissistic need for mirroring and confirmation encourages the establishment of ambitions. Responsiveness to the child's need for merger with greatness, strength, and calmness promotes the development of ideals. The experience of the presence of essential alikeness facilitates the development of personal talents and skills. All of this supports self-cohesion and integrity essential to personal security and self-esteem. Among adults, "the selfobject transferences arise . . . in consequence of the fact that certain developmental needs were not responded to adequately in childhood but, on the other hand, were not frustrated completely"(p. 201). For Kohut, the needs of the bipolar self are crucial developmental components of healthy narcissism.

Narcissistic needs of the bipolar self persist in organizational life (as illustrated in the above example) and are analyzable through the study of transference. Whether their expression is healthy or pathological depends on many factors, but, most important, the degree to which narcissistic demands are satisfied or frustrated depends upon superordinate-subordinate relations. For example, needs for mirroring and acceptance are satisfied or frustrated depending upon a manager's ability to communicate recognition and appreciation for the performance of subordinates. When satisfied, needs for mirroring and acceptance are important motivators of organizational members. Needs for merger with greatness, strength, and calmness found in normal idealization are satisfied or frustrated depending upon the degree of a manager's perceived charisma and integrity. Such perceived and actual leadership characteristics encourage identification with managers and with managerial ideals and values. Finally, needs for talents and skills are satisfied or frustrated depending upon the adequacy of training and development opportunities, employee orientation, and mentoring between supervisors and their subordinates. Satisfaction of these needs encourages the desire for twinship and the experience of alikeness, which may strengthen self-competence and integrity, and affiliation of organizational members. Satisfaction of narcissistic needs in organizational life is not necessarily healthy, ethical, or efficacious. Frustration of narcissistic needs in organizational life is not necessarily unhealthy, unethical, or ineffective. The merit and quality of each case must be independently examined. Therefore, the need for interpreting organizational identity is paramount. The case illustrations presented later will help.

In the following section, I define and analyze the psychoanalytic notion of transference within the organizational context.

TRANSFERENCE PHENOMENA IN ORGANIZATIONAL HIERARCHIES

The analysis of transference is critical to understanding organizational identity. Attention to the "invariance" (Atwood and Stolorow, 1984) of human interactions, such as that found in the transference of emotions between superordinates and subordinates, is central to organizational analysis. Transference occurs in super-subordinate and peer relations, and between organizational analyst and client. In particular, transference phenomena are best understood by the analysis of leader-follower (superordinate-subordinate) relations. These relationships are filled with many reenactments of the dependency, attachment, separation, and individuation dilemmas of the parent-child relationship.

Transference in Organizations

Hierarchy, which is characterized by super-subordinate relations, encourages overdependencies and psychologically regressive (parent-child) interactions among adults (Freud, 1922; Fromm, 1941; Argyris, 1957; Kernberg, 1979; Diamond, 1984). As a result, these structurally imposed "inferior-superior" (Fromm, 1941) role relationships trigger reenactments of early childhood authority and narcissistic relationships. For example, superiors and subordinates displace frustrated needs onto each other. Superordinates and subordinates serve each other's unconscious and preconscious needs. The "heart" of otherwise impersonal hierarchical dynamics is found in narcissistic and infantile needs brought to and created by these relationships. These (prereflectively) unconscious and reciprocal transferences comprise the interpretable transference phenomena of complex organizations. The organizational identity embedded in these patterns of interpersonal hierarchical relationships must be discovered and described in order to achieve intentional change in the status quo.

This requires superordinate and subordinate coming to share a common understanding, explanation, and interpretation of their transference of emotions. This is provided by insightful practitioners and organizational consultants who are able to analyze the transference in order to facilitate learning.

Analysis of Transference in Organizations

The analysis of transference in organizations involves the assembly of a coherent image of interpersonal patterns of human interactions. The practitioner and organizational analyst must, momentarily, shift the center of experience away from himself in order, in the role of participant-observer, to empathically comprehend the intersubjective experience of organizational participants. Acquiring empathy by the process of identification (organizational identity), the practitioner reaches an interpretive understanding of interpersonal and organizational dynamics by seeing from the point of view of the other's experience of self and others, self and environment. The usefulness and truth value of such qualitative (intersubjective) data depends upon a practitioner's or organizational analyst's willingness to test his assumptions about the other's experience publicly. This requires the analyst to confirm or disconfirm interpretations acquired by identification (organizational identity) and empathy. Practitioners and organizational analysts focus on transferences that are repetitive, psychologically regressive, and counterproductive. These transference phenomena are especially observable in organizational responses to stressful events or critical incidents. Kets de Vries and Miller (1984, p.18) comment, "The focus is on clusters or behavior that remain relatively stable over the years, as opposed to simple dimensions of behavior."

To summarize: In organizational life transference phenomena contribute to the construction of organizational identity. Authority and peer relations rekindle frustrated (infantile) narcissistic needs in adult behavior. Stressful organizational events such as changes in leadership, retrenchment, cutbacks, policy or budgetary revisions, and shift of political climate foster psychologically regressive and defensive responses.

To better understand how transference phenomena are interpreted, we can look at three patterns of interpersonal relations: mirroring, idealizing, and (alter ego) twinship (Kohut, 1977 and 1984).

Interpreting Mirroring and Idealizing Transference in Organizations

The first two patterns of transference, mirroring and idealizing, are two sides of the same pattern of human interaction and therefore are discussed together. Mirror transferences derive from infantile needs for acceptance. If these needs are frustrated in adulthood, a manager may strive to support a narcissistic deficit by surrounding himself with admiring and loyal subordinates. Depending upon the degree of narcissistic injury and deficiency of adequate mirroring, mirror-hungry managers may develop a leadership style that is autocratic, paternalistic, and authoritarian. Subordinates are expected to admire and appear forced into a position of overdependence upon their managers. In these circumstances, staff loyalty and admiration encourage idealized images of their managers, which distorts staff capacity to recognize limitations. Staff members may respond by becoming "as-if performers," false and inauthentic. Their superior's overdetermined need for admiration is internalized by subordinates in an attitude that dictates: "I will be as you desire me" (Sullivan, 1953). In such instances, organizational subordinates become preoccupied with meeting the confirmation needs of their manager, thus being similar to infants who must respond to the mothers' narcissistic needs in the inadequate holding environment, the origins of (what Winnicott calls) a false self. In adulthood, this sort of role conformity is indicative of human interactions in organizational hierarchies in which managers unwittingly perpetuate inauthentic false-self systems among their membership.

In the above situation, the transference is reciprocal. The manager has assumed his leadership post with extraordinary needs for acceptance and recognition because of earlier deprivation. Subordinates respond with admiration and praise or they are eliminated as undesirables. The manager unwittingly seeks out staff members whose hunger for mirroring and acceptance gives them needs for merging with greatness, strength, and calmness. In this case, organizational identity is predicated on a mirror-hungry leadership style. The manager in this instance requires a staff in search of idealizable authority. He or she encourages and accepts such idealization so that, eventually, staff members come to merge psychologically with the imagined strength, greatness, and calmness of the manager. In return the manager receives love, admiration, and loyalty from the staff. This example of narcissistic (self-other) transference in organizational hierarchy is a persistent and repetitive pattern of super-subordinate interaction. A similar trend is found with the twinship or alter-ego transference.

Interpreting Twinship (Alter-Ego) Transference in Organizations

Failure of an adequate mirroring response often produces a wish to merge with a twin (or alter ego) instead of with an idealizable other. Merger is sought with a person or group viewed as essentially alike. An absence or minimum of differentiation between self and other is characteristic of this transference experience, in which pairing and merger occur among two or more people. This response solves the problem of inadequate parenting by repairing the perceived self--deficit with collective reassurances of self-importance and superiority.

In adulthood, the twinship transference is a defensive response to threatening situations. For example, twinship needs in organizations are evoked by perceived failure, or loss of leadership, mission, political or financial support. Consequently, members feel disappointed and hostile, taking flight from their intense feelings and potential conflict. This group or organization flight from a critical incident produces twinship or pairing with select others. Such motives can lead to homogeneity, uniformity, and group or dyadic cohesion.

Group cohesion becomes an important issue for organizational members. A retreat into "the presence of essential alikeness," momentarily repairs the perceived deficit in organizational participant's talents and skills. Identification with peers who have been similarly trained and educated often repairs the perceived deficit with collective reassurances of the importance and superiority of the like-minded member's contribution to the organization.

Interpretation of organizational identity is possible because of these transference phenomena. (3) We must now proceed to examine organizational analysis in theory and practice.

ORGANIZATIONAL ANALYSIS: THEORY AND PRACTICE

Organizational analysis centers on the acquisition of reflective knowledge, which is derived from attempts at illuminating, by working with organizational participants, the structures of interpersonal meaning and purpose that comprise an organization's identity. Awareness of organizational identity, and the place of one's role identity in it, is necessary for the assumption of personal responsibility and claimed action on behalf of individual organizational members. This assumption is crucial in promoting genuine democratic administration of public and business services (Diamond, 1985b). The fundamental intent of the psychoanalytic enterprise is that of unlocking meanings (1986, p.48), while the concepts of function, purpose, and meaning of experience and behavior make up psychoanalytic theory (p. 51). But it deserves highlighting that "what endows words and other symbolic structures with significance is the communication of affects" (Modell, 1984, p.173). Therefore, psychoanalytic organizational analysts, in contrast to nonpsychoanalytic organizational analysts, know that "interpretation can be effective only when there is, in Strachey's terms, a "point of urgency," that is to say [when] affect is genuine and communicated" (p. 90). (4) This is consistent with the emphasis upon the analysis of critical incidents as a strategy for reaching affects otherwise screened-off by repression and denial. In sum, the primary unit of analysis is interpersonal, the primary language is that of activity and relationships (Klein, 1976), and the primary transmitter is that of affects (Modell, 1984). These efforts make sense of the perceptual and emotional world (interpersonal experience) of organizational members and the influence of that inner organizational world on organizational action.

The analyst functions as a "reteller of narration" who brings to the surface the participant's "disclaiming of actions" (Schafer, 1983). The disclaiming of and discomfort with actions alerts the analyst to inauthenticity: a retreat into the public world that consequently "relieves one [the manager or public administrator] of personal responsibility" (Chessick, 1986, p.87).

For example, one manager requested a consultation to resolve an ongoing conflict between two departmental assistants. The administrator described his (rational) role as that of managing organizational boundaries between his department and the (operating environment) public. He complained that his two assistants constantly quarreled and were unable to manage the activities of their departments effectively. Nevertheless, he was rarely in the office and spent most of his time in the field. His actions were perceived not only by the consultant but also by his two assistants as flight from a threatening situation that persisted unresolved (role identity = one who flees from conflict). Moreover, his two assistants avoided raising the issue with each other and with the director himself. The organizational consultant's intervention consisted of eliciting this flight theme (defensive theme of organizational identity) and helping the managers to acknowledge their responsibility for the situation and claim their flight-oriented actions. Once that was accomplished it was possible to investigate the reasons and motives for their past actions so they could learn. This meant exploring feelings and underlying assumptions and attributions about each other.

The organizational analyst and management practitioner assist organizational participants, who share a common organizational history, in elaborating and consensually validating interpersonal experience. He literally helps them "'come to terms" with the psychic or affective base of their relationships. The complex role of analyst and practitioner is, therefore, that of participant-observer (Sullivan, 1953; Havens, 1976; Diamond, 1985b; Hirsch, 1985) and coauthor (Schafer, 1983) in the context of organizational dynamics. This interpretive role requires the establishment of a working alliance (Greenson, 1978) with organizational participants to reach, by way of interpretation, some clarification and mutual understanding of interpersonal experience in present organizational life. In the above case, the analyst offered the interpretation that regardless of their individual differences and disagreements, the three executive administrators shared in avoiding conflict. They had constructed an organizational identity characterized by mutual flights. This was responsible for deteriorating administration of departmental activities.

Organizational analysts and practitioners participate in and observe distinctive interpersonal configurations that produce and perpetuate organizational identity. The analyst and practitioner assumes that (prereflectively) unconscious (Atwood and Stolorow, 1984) actions of organizational members are primarily responsible for producing organizational identity. If not for the intervention, organizational members would remain unaware of the meaning and consequences of their actions and decisions and, therefore, lack the necessary information for change.

In the next two sections, I offer two case illustrations that incorporate three categories of transference phenomena in complex organizations. Both case illustrations are drawn from the author's consultation experiences.

CASE EXAMPLE: MIRRORING AND IDEALIZING TRANSFERENCE

A state agency had a history of detached and passive leadership. For nearly 15 years each of the 5 agency directors who had served as chief administrator was assigned the post only a few years before retirement. Each had little or no executive mandate to plan for the future of the agency. Because of their ages (all over 60 years) and lack of political support, they resisted the role of representative (proactive and supportive) leader. Because of a lack ol vital leadership, the agency could be described as a "depressed" organization (Kets de Vries and Miller, 1984) in which stagnation and apathy became deeply embedded in the organizational climate. Interviews with staff members revealed that they were dedicated public servants who genuinely cared for their clients and whose personal ethics supported the espoused mission of the agency. Turnover was not unusually high for such a lifeless agency because the staff were professionals in a vocation that offered little opportunity for mobility. This socioeconomic fact left them with little choice: in order to change, they had either to move out of state or change vocations. Consequently, staff members either selected-in and appeared to accept the situation, or "burned out" from frustration and disappointment and left.

Many of the staff members had been with the agency for more than 5 years, and they were eager for change and repeatedly expressed a desire for "real" leadership. Then, as a consequence of the election of a liberal, progressive state administration, the public agency acquired (it was assumed) proactive leadership and a policy mandate in support of the agency's provision of services.

The new chief administrator, a 45-year-old male with previous experience as a respected political manager and state lobbyist, took charge of the agency with the intent of revitalizing policy commitment to client service and reorganizing the agency. The reorganization limited the discretion of caseworkers (and other key professionals) and increased the chief administrator's authority and control by holding all unit supervisors and regional supervisors directly accountable. Where staff professionals previously had significant discretion and responsibility but no representative leadership, they now had limited discretion and responsibility. Yet the agency's adjustment to renewed bureaucratic leadership was relatively smooth. It took about three or four months for staff members to shift from stagnation to a revitalized commitment to the espoused policy of the agency. Change occurred with surprisingly little overt conflict and resistance, somewhat unusual for a change of such magnitude. In fact, staff members glorified their new leader, bestowing upon him exceptional respect and admiration. It was evident that agency members had displaced frustrated feelings of idealization onto the new chief administrator, who, in turn, relished the aggrandizement.

In this example, ideal-hungry staff professionals unwittingly satisfied frustrated needs for idealization by merging with a mirror-hungry leader. The staff's desire for merger with a leader of perceived greatness, strength, and calmness was reciprocated by the new chief administrator's desire for mirroring and acceptance. The mutual transference of emotional needs was complete, and a concomitant pattern of interaction followed. Below the level of unchanged organizational structure and sameness of mission, a new organizational identity was created.

We need not view this transference pattern in a complelely negative fashion; as Kets de Vries and Miller (1984, p.83-84) point out,

> It is possible to distinguish two types of idealization, which we shall call "normal idealization" and "clinging behavior. " These are progressively more extreme in the amount of passivity and dependence shown by followers. In "normal" idealization, the follower respects the leader and tries to emulate many of her general characteristics. But it is still possible for him [follower] to maintain a reasonable amount of initiative (especially if the leader is independent and strong) as he strives to be like the boss. In a more extreme type of transference, respect gives way to deification, and emulation is replaced by slavish subservience and ritualistic imitation. Here much initiative is lost as the subordinate becomes suitable only for simple and routine functions, with obvious impairment in his capacity for sound decision making.

What was previously described as characteristic of an "as-if performer," a false and inauthentic self (in subordinate idealization of superiors) is typical of this more extreme type of transference, which Kets de Vries and Miller call "clinging behavior" in contrast to "normal" idealization. In the case example, it is premature to conclude anything more than a "normal" idealization, particularly, when the agency's organizational history is taken into account for rendering its members hungry for idealizable leadership. On the other hand, knowledge of current transference patterns of idealization and past history should alert the organizational analyst and management practitioner to potential symptoms of organizational pathology.

CASE EXAMPLE: TWINSHIP (ALTER-EGO) TRANSFERENCE

Members of a department of a medical school found themselves in trouble after their new chair was rejected for tenure and promotion. The dean of the school had offered an untenured faculty member the position knowing that the other faculty members in the department, particularly the tenured faculty, were unwilling to take charge. The department was the least supported and most vulnerable in the school at a time of budget cuts and retrenchment. The department members, a mix of M.D.'s and Ph.D.'s with clinical, teaching, and research responsibilities, expected their new chair to take charge. The chair felt ambivalent about the leadership responsibilities, power and authority of his new position. He experienced painful disappointment because of the unsuccessful tenure decision and consequently questioned the justifiability of his appointment. His actions contradicted his statements to the faculty. On the one hand, he espoused a proactive, representative leadership role and the wish to be a "good" administrator at a time of uncertainty. This pleased the faculty, but, on the other hand, he did not operate as a leader. He became increasingly passive and resigned, putting off decisions and actions, and unwittingly produced feelings of ambiguity and uncertainty in faculty members.

Pairing and subdivided group cohesion located in departmental subcultures (characteristic of the twinship transference of emotions in groups and organizations) left the department paralyzed and, therefore, incapable of confronting its problems. The disappointed departmental faculty felt enraged and increasingly hostile, provoking splitting and polarization of the department into opposing camps - the M.D.'s and the Ph.D.'s. Faculty were unwilling to confront the chairman about their disappointment and frustration. Feeling guilty, responsible, and protective toward their weak leader, faculty took flight from the problem and turned their frustrations inward, producing the departmental split. These countervailing subcultures were the result of splitting represented by the group's regressive and compensatory response to frustrated mirroring and idealizing. On the one hand, faculty members retreated into "the presence of essential alikeness" and the safety and security of the mirror image of each in the other. On the other hand, the department resorted to a vertical split between two factions: Each faction perceived itself as all good and the other faction as all bad. (5)

This case example of twinship (or alter-ego) transference illustrates a dysfunctional consequence, but as with mirroring and idealizing transference phenomena, all twinship or alter-ego transferences are not as counterproductive as in the case illustration. The persecutory nature of the department's psychological response to a lack of leadership and unsupportive environment helps to explain the destructive and dysfunctional organizational consequences.

Some twinship (or alter-ego) transferences in complex organizations are essential in order to learn from experience and to accumulate talents and skills necessary for administrative and professional competence. For example, mentoring is possibly the most productive use of twinship or alter-ego transference in organizations. Supervisors who successfully negotiate psychological contracts (Levinson, 1981) with subordinates are engaged in nurturing the intermediate talents and skills necessary to the self-organization of ambitions and ideals. This interpersonal organizational phenomenon ultimately fosters self-cohesion and self-esteem, and is similar to the young child's alter-ego relationship to the parent. The child experiences "essential alikeness" as he or she stands by and watches carefully and lovingly the skillful actions of the parent at work in the kitchen or in the workshop (Kohut, 1984). The child, as does the adult later in life, needs a supportive and facilitative environment where he or she can learn by trial and error without losing self-confidence or experiencing narcissistic injury.

SUMMARY REMARKS

One purpose of organizational analysis is the discovery of organizational identity. Organizational identity consists of the repetitive structures of intersubjectivity located in human interactions that are affected by both conscious and prereflectively unconscious thoughts, feelings, and perceptions that in turn influence decisions and actions. Organizational identity is a structural solution or compromise formation to contradictory aims, motives, wishes, and desires among organizational participants. It consists of the collectivity of self and other needs of organizational members located in the transference of emotions in hierarchical relationships. These self and other needs include ambitions, talents and skills, and ideals (which originate in the relationship between infant and parent) that are intimately linked to the self-integrity of organizational members. Awareness of organizational identity is necessary for the assumption of personal responsibility and claimed action by organizational members, which is crucial to initiating intentional change in the status quo. In hierarchical organizations, organizational identity is most accessible to interpretation through the analysis of transference phenomena between organizational subordinates and their superordinates.

Unconscious narcissistic expectations are transferred to interpersonal relationships within the organizational setting. Here, the internal organizational environment replaces the parental object. Frustrations of self-other needs stimulate transference dynamics between organizational members that influence the pattern of interactions comprising the organizational identity. Ambitions and ideals of organizational members surface in continuous, in-depth conversations between supervisors and subordinates about mutual expectations and career objectives. Talents and skills are evaluated by examining personnel policies and training procedures for employee orientation and searching for mentoring relationships between supervisors and subordinates. Understanding organizational identity offers a glance behind the organizational curtain of complexity where personal motives and reasons for action reside.

NOTES

(1) See, for example, Administrative Science Quarterly 28, September 1983, Journal of Management Studies 20, September 1983; Organizational Dynamics 13, Summer 1984, Journal of Management 11, Summer 1985; and the Journal of Management Studies 23, May 1986 and recent organizational literature such as Zaleznik and Kets de Vries (1975), Argyris and Schon (1978), Schon (1984), Maccoby (1976), Kets de Vries (1980), Levinson (198l), Mitroff (1983), Schein (1985), Kets de Vries and Miller (1984), Srivastva and Associates (1983), Kets de Vries (1984), and Diamond (1985a).

(2) Kohut's categories of transference phenomena are, in my view, insufficient to encompass all features of leader-follower interactions. The persecutory transference needs consideration. Idealizing and mirroring transference phenomena may explain the predominance of a dependency fantasy or basic assumption underlying the group (unit or organizational) psychodynamics; twinship (alterego) transference phenomena may explain the predominance of a pairing fantasy (or basic assumption); but persecutory transference is necessary to explain a predominance of fight/flight fantasy (or basic assumption) governing decisions and actions. On the other hand, my experience in working within troubled organizations suggests concurrence between persecutory and twinship transference phenomena, the former often preceding the latter in critical incidents.

(3) Interpreting organizational identity involves assessing self-other needs (including ambitions and ideals, talents and skills) through the analysis of transference in work groups. Interpretation comprises an analysis of self and other relations in a sociocultural context. As G. S. Klein states, "Identity must always be defined as having aspects of both separateness and membership in a more encompassing entity, and as developing functions that reflect one's role in and relationship to that larger entity" (1976, p.179) Because of the assumption that we experience ourselves in the world in the company of others, the approach shifts from that of the psychology of the individual to an interpersonally based group psychology with individual ends.

Interpretation of organizational identity, therefore, depends not so much on words as upon affects: "Affects are at the heart of the problem of psychoanalytic knowledge. Words by themselves do not constitute the primary data of psychoanalysis," and "what endows words and other symbolic structures with significance is the communication of affects" (Kohut, 1984, p.172). The data of organizational identity are based upon the healthy narcissistic needs of organizational members, on the one hand, and frustrated, overdetermined narcissistic needs, on the other hand. In order to learn about these data, organizational participants must collaborate to construct a coherent story (Schafer, 1983). Within the story are the reasons and motives underlying current patterns of transference that comprise organizational dynamics. Organizational identity relies upon its underlying theory of affects (transference) to decode assumptions, myths, stories, and dreams. This theory of affects acknowledges the contradictory nature of human action in groups and organizations.

(4) In previous work (Diamond and Allcorn, 1985a; 1985b), it was submitted that organizational behavior can be understood when a critical event (or set of events) provokes adaptive and defensive actions by organizational participants. These anxiety-provoking incidents cause organizational defenses momentarily to fail. This results in the surfacing of previously screened-off thoughts, feelings, and perceptions. With the aid of informed practitioners or organizational analysts, repression of thoughts and feelings may be lifted. This intervention permits the organizational analyst and practitioner to observe (Havens, 1976; Diamond, 1985b and 1986) and redescribe (Schafer, 1983) unconscious and unacknowledged linking patterns of organizing work and interpersonal relations. Consistency and meaning are discovered out of the chaos and disorganization of the moment. This framework for organizational analysis is consistent with the notion that organizational member's "affects are the transmitter of data" (Modell, 1984, p.160-161) and that critical incidents are loaded with affects and are, therefore, signifiers of organizational identity. The practitioner and organizational analyst, therefore, function as receivers of the transmission of affects of organizational participants influenced by critical incidents.

(5) In the case example of twinship transference, narcissistic injury is felt collectively by faculty members. Both the school of medicine and the university are experienced by the department as hostile and inadequate environments; consequently the department faculty feel persecuted and victimized. This experience, aggravated by the chairman's inability to lead, causes a "schizoid" withdrawal and "splitting" described by psychoanalytic object relations theory (Guntrip, 1969) and is often produced by a "persecutory transference" (Kets de Vries and Miller, 1984). Persecutory transference is not recognized by most psychoanalytic self psychologists, but it does offer another dimension of understanding and explanation for what we (Diamond and Allcorn, 1987, p.525-543) call the tendency for group "homogenization," which is a collective response to annihilation and persecutory anxiety. Homogenization is characterized to some extent by the desire for "essential alikeness" found in the twinship (alterego) transference. But it cannot account for the initial response of narcissistic rage and aggression stemming from the group's disappointment in their leader: the leader who is unable to lead the group in fight or flight. Therefore, a fourth transference phenomenon, the persecutory transference, may be called for in order to explain more fully the initial regressive and defensive group response to the shared experience of operating in a hostile, unacceptable environment, and of being leaderless.

REFERENCES

ARGYRIS, C. Personality and Organization. New York: Harper & Row, 1957.

ARGYRIS, C., & SCHON, D. Organizational Learning. Reading, MA: Addison-Wesley, 1978.

ATWOOD, G.E., & STOLOROW, R.D. Structures of Subjectivity: Explorations in Psychoanalytic Phenomenology. Hillsdale, NJ: Analytic, 1984.

BION, W. R. Experiences in Groups. New York: Basic Books, 1959.

BOWLBY, J. The Making and Breaking of Affectional Bonds. London: Tavistock, 1979.

CHESSICK, R.D. Heidegger for psychotherapists. Amer. J. of Psychotherapy 40 (January), 1986, 83-95.

DIAMOND, M.A. Bureaucracy as externalized self-system: a view from the psychological interior. Administration & Society 16 (August), 1984, 195-214.

DIAMOND, M.A. The social character of bureaucracy: anxiety and ritualistic defense. Pol. Psych. 6 (December), 1985a, 663-679.

DIAMOND, M.A. Psychological dimensions of personal responsibility for public management: an object relations approach. J. of Management Studies 22 (November), 1985b, 649-667.

DIAMOND, M.A., & ALLCORN, S. Psychological responses to stress in complex organizations. Administration & Society 17 (August), 1985a, 217-239.

DIAMOND, M.A. & ALLCORN, S. Psychological dimensions of role use in bureaucratic organizations. Organizational Dynamics 14 (Summer), 1985b, 35-59.

DIAMOND, M.A. Resistance to change: a psychoanalytic critique of Argyris and Schon's contributions to organization theory and intervention. J. of Management Studies 23 (September), 1986.

DIAMOND, M.A. & ALLCORN, S. The psychodynamics of regression in work groups. Human Relations 40 (8), 1987, 525-543.

FREUD, S. Group Psychology and the Analysis of the Ego. New York: Norton, 1922.

FROMM, E. Escape From Freedom. New York: Holt, Rinehart & Winston, 1941.

GREENSON, R. Explorations in Psychoanalysis. New York: International Universities Press, 1978.

GUNTRIP, H. Schizoid Phenomena, Object Relations and the Self. New York: International Universities Press, 1969.

HAVENS, L. Participation Observation. New York: Jason Aronson, 1976.

HEIDEGGER, M. Being and Time (1927). New York: Harper & Row, 1962.

HIRSCH, I. The rediscovery of the advantages of the participant-observation model. Psychoanalysis and Contemporary Thought 8 (3), 1985, 441-459.

KERNBERG, O. Regression in organizational leadership. Psychiatry 42(1), 1979, 24-39.

KETS DE VRIES, M.F.R. Organizational Paradoxes. London: Tavistock, 1980.

KETS DE VRIES, M.F.R. [ed.] The Irrational Executive. New York: International Universities Press, 1984.

KETS DE VRIES, M.F.R., & MILLER, D. The Neurotic Organization. San Francisco: Jossey-Bass, 1984.

KLEIN, G.S. Psychoanalytic Theory. New York: International Universities Press, 1976.

KOHUT, H. The Analysis of the Self. New York: International Universities Press, 1971.

KOHUT, H. The Restoration of the Self. New York: International Universities Press, 1977.

KOHUT, H. How Does Analysis Cure? Chicago: Univ. of Chicago Press, 1984.

LARÇON & REITTER Chapter 16 in M.F.R. Kets de Vries (ed.) The Irrational Executive. New York: International Universities Press, 1984.
LEVINSON, H. Executive. Cambridge: Harvard Univ. Press, 1981.
LEVINSON & WEINBAUM Chapter 12 in M.F.R. Kets de Vries (ed) The Irrational Executive. New York: International Universities Press, 1984.
MACCOBY, M. The Gamesman. New York: Simon & Schuster, 1976.
MITROFF, I. Stakeholders of Organizational Mind. San Francisco: Jossey-Bass, 1983.
MODELL, A.H. Psychoanalysis in a New Context. New York: International Universities Press, 1984.
SCHAFER, R. A New Language for Psychoanalysis. New Haven: Yale Univ. Press, 1976.
SCHAFER, R. The Analytic Attitude. New York: Basic Books, 1983.
SCHEIN, E. Organizational Culture and Leadership. San Francisco: Jossey-Bass, 1985.
SCHON, D. The Reflective Practitioner. New York: Basic Books, 1984.
SRIVASTA, S. and Associates. Executive Mind. San Francisco: Jossey-Bass, 1983.
SULLIVAN, H. S. The Interpersonal Theory of Psychiatry. New York: Norton, 1953.
WINNICOTT, D. W. The Maturational Processes and the Facilitating Environment. New York: International Universities Press, 1965.
ZALEZNIK, A. & KETS DE VRIES, M.F.R. Power and the Corporate Mind. Boston: Houghton Mifflin, 1975.

Field Independence/Dependence Reconsidered

Leopold Gruenfeld

INTRODUCTION

This essay evaluates Witkin's (1978) theory of the field independent-dependent cognitive style (also called the global-articulated dimension) in the domain of group social behavior. The essence of social behavior is manifest in the influence process. Leadership and teaching roles are used to illustrate how cognitive style and styles of influence are related. The present binary and polarized construction of the field independent and dependent style limits progress in this area of study. What is required is a more precise multi-dimensional taxonomy. To provide such a taxonomy, this study makes distinctions between stressed and composed field independent and dependent styles. Chronic or situational anxiety and stress are suggested as orthogonal moderator variables of cognitive styles. It is argued that stress affects the field independent and dependent style in such a way that expression of these styles reveals an altered typology.

This newly hypothesized sub-types of the Field Independence/ Dependence cognitive styles have previously been observed and measured by Bales (1970, 1979) through his SYMLOG method, (a reliable and valid system for the observation of behavior in groups). Behavior thus observed may subsequently be correlated with perceptual and cognitive performance measures. It is hoped that this reverse strategy (correlating from observed behavior to perceptual measures) can enrich the study of individual differences in cognitive styles. To complete this essay a number of methodological dilemmas that aggrieve reviewers of research on cognitive style are discussed.

WITKIN'S PARADIGM AND TAXONOMY FOR THE STUDY OF COGNITIVE STYLES AND SOCIAL BEHAVIOR

Witkin's (1978) theory of field independent and field dependent cognitive style distinguishes between two major intellectual traditions in Western thought. One tradition subscribes to an internally focused explanation for cognitive processes. Its major proponent was Freud (Gardner, 1983), who focused on the internal (biological) development of the individual's cognitions. For the internally inclined Freud, the key to knowledge was self-control and a willingness to confront pain and paradox with a "tragic" internal cognitive style. The classic Freudian psychoanalytic exercise was one of turning inward toward self examination. The metaphor of field independence as self-reliance, self-sufficiency, and introversion is indicative of the Freudian mode of knowing and coping.

Another contrasting vision subscribes to an externally focused explanation of cognitive processes. Its major proponent was William James (Gardner, 1983), who focused on the external (social) development of the individual's cognitions. James stressed the importance of relationships with other individuals in the evolution of modes of knowing: "a man has as many social selves as there are individuals who recognize him and carry an image around of him in their minds." For the externally oriented James the key to knowing oneself was through others. In his view, confronting one's relationships with others and making appropriate environmental changes were the means for promoting self-actualization. James's optimistic fulfillment model, which turns outward toward an examination of, and orientation toward culture, contrasts with Freud's pessimistic interpsychic conflict model (Maddi, 1976). The metaphor of field dependence as conformity, adjustment and extroversion, is indicative of James's mode of knowing self and others. (Gardner, 1983).

A third view, professed by Jung (Hall and Lindzey, 1978), distinguishes between introversion and extroversion and suggests their coexistence. According to Jung, all persons are capable of both internal and external perspectives, but for each person one attitude may be more or less prominent. In accord with oriental, especially Confucian, philosophy, Jung suggested that cognitive styles are influenced by the thesis and antithesis of inner and other orientation. In other words, whenever major emphasis is given to one attitude, the other "opposing" attitude is mobilized in a compensatory manner. One attitude is dominant and conscious while the other is submerged and unconscious (Hall and Lindzey, 1978). Moreover, both attitudes are necessary for the wholeness of living. They are complimentary but function in opposition (Munroe, 1955). It is the manner in which these opposing cognitive styles are integrated or complimented that defines the person's mode of knowing and attention deployment. The spatial metaphor Jung employs is that of wholeness and completion, of the integration of opposites. Jung's concept runs contrary to Freud's and James's binary metaphor of either field independent or dependent cognitive styles. In oriental philosphy, individuals are defined in terms of their complexity, that is their ability or inability to consolidate several styles. In fact, it is indeed sound to assume that persons cannot function without some attention to both internal and external relationships (Gardner, 1983).

WHAT IS COGNITIVE STYLE?

Cognitive styles denote the focus and domain of a person's attention. According to Witkin (1978), attention may either be focused interoceptively (inward) or aleocentrically (outward). Inwardly focused individuals ruminate and reflect or pay attention to their feelings or internal bodily cues as a guide to behavior and experience. Outwardly focused individuals ruminate and reflect or pay attention to external cues as a guide to their behavior and experience. Internal or external orientations are alternative modes of cognition. The process that informs these alternative modes of processing information is "disembedding" or differentiating among elements or between figure and ground. According to Witkin, this disembedding process can be observed in several areas of psychological functioning, including the affective, intellective, and social domain.

In the social domain, which is the major concern of this essay, persons can or will either disembed self from others or fail to do so. Persons who differentiate between self and others are presumed to have an articulated sense of self. According to the spatial metaphor of a polarized dimension for cognitive style, individuals with an inner orientation maintain boundaries between their inner sphere of experience and potentially distracting external social influences. They are presumed to be "inner directed" like the 19th century western character type Riesman (1961) described as attentive to efficiency, materialistic achievements and social independence. Freud described his corresponding anal character as one who is obsessed with control or the loss of it (Gardner, 1983). Jung described his corresponding introvert as oriented toward the inner subjective world (Gardner, 1983). Fromm (1947) placed this character type functionally and historically into the period of industrialization along with the rise of capitalism. He described his corresponding hoarding type as frugal, hard working, and capable of delaying gratification.

Field dependents, on the other hand, have been described as unable to maintain firm boundaries between their inner and outer sphere of experience and thus as having a tendency to succumb to external social influences. They are presumed to be "other directed" like the 20th century western character type Riesman (1961) described as attentive to external guidance, social support, and contact with people. Freud described his corresponding character type as the oral type who is obsessed with pleasing others and optimistically dependent on them for nourishment and affection. Freud's oral person is conflicted about being abandoned and/or rejected by others. Jung described his corresponding extroverted type as oriented toward the objective external world. Fromm placed his corresponding dependent character type functionally and historically into the feudal age which was governed by principles of inequality. He described his dependent type as either submissive or paradoxically, caring for others through paternalism.

Witkin derived his types from a program of research that was informed by Gestalt psychologists' concern about inner and outer determinants of perception (Asch and Witkin, 1948a, 1948b). Witkin was impressed by individual differences in attention deployment and perception on the Tilted Room - Tilted Chair apparatus. He inductively built up a body of knowledge that initially relied on clinical observations for the construction of his theory. He drew attention at first to differences in adaptive ego-defenses between field dependent and field independent perceivers. Dependents used the defenses of denial and regression. Independents used the defenses of intellectualization and isolation. Lewis (1971) studied the social control mechanisms of shame and guilt and demonstrated that shame, a relatively other-directed and communal tactic of social control, was typical of field dependents, whereas guilt, a relatively inner-directed and autonomous tactic of social control, was typical of field independents.

Much of what later became known as the interpersonal theory of cognitive style (Witkin, 1978) was first observed from the interaction of therapists and their patients. It was found, for example, that therapists and patients who shared similar styles were more compatible. Field dependent therapists provided social support and sympathy; field indendent therapists were more confrontational and autonomous (Witkin, 1962). Many of these initial observations have subsequently been confirmed in a variety of settings including child rearing (Witkin, 1978; Seder, 1957)

Cognitive styles are operationally defined by means of perceptual tests like the Rod and Frame Test (RFT) or intellective tests like the Embedded Figures Test. What these tests have in common with each other and with the construct of cognitive style is the presentation of conflicting clues that bring on a predicament in the disembedding of a figure from its distracting context. This predicament causes individuals to fall back on their "archaic" perceptual problem-solving style. On the RFT, for example, many subjects cannot ignore a tilted or otherwise distracting visual framework in their efforts to adjust a rod to the true upright. They seem differentially to take account of the conflicting visual and gravitational clues. Those individuals categorized as field independent employ a discriminating perspective. By actively disregarding the tilted frame, they disembed the rod from its terrain; they are able to isolate the rod from its "context"

(Gruenfeld and Lin 1984). Those who cannot isolate the rod from its background respond globally to the entire field. They (the field dependents), incorporate figure and ground and thus accommodate to the compellingness of the entire perceptual configuration.

What is observed in the visual perceptual domain is also hypothesized to occur in other modalities of aural, kinesthetic, intellectual, and especially, social functioning. Goodenough (1985), for example, showed that field dependents prefer to work with, and in the proximity of, others. The spatial metaphor he used pictures field dependents as blending with the social field. Maintenance of one's autonomy was more typical of field independents. His spatial metaphor described field independents as being aloof from the social field. Witkin and Goodenough (1977) have summarized these and related conclusions as follows:

> "Field-dependent people make greater use of external social referents, but only when the situation is ambiguous and these referents provide information that helps to remve the ambiguity; field-independent people function with greater autonomy under such conditions. Field-dependent people are more attentive to social cues than are field-independent people. Field-dependent people have an interpersonal orientation: they show strong interest in others, prefer to be physically close to people, are emotionally open and gravitate to social situations. Field-independent people have an impersonal orientation: they are not very interested in others, show both physical and psychological distancing from people and prefer non-social situations."

There is considerable evidence that supports these hypotheses in the interpersonal domain (Witkin, 1978). Moreover, there is also evidence that field dependent-independents adopt situations to which they elect to respond in order to activate their dispositional cognitive styles. A number of studies that correlated measures of cognitive style with vocational interest and choice (Arbuthnot and Gruenfeld, 1969; Zytowski, et al., 1969; Witkin, 1973; Levy, 1969) clearly support these hypotheses. Surgical, field-independent nurses and pediatric field-dependent nurses inhabit different environments (Quinlan and Blatt, 1973). Managers in different hierarchical levels of a manufacturing organization are sifted out and select themselves to live in environments that require differing cognitive styles (MacEachron, 1977). At the lower levels of management the fair enforcement of rules and regulations maybe the appropriate field dependent cognitive style. At higher levels of management initiation of rules and articulation of the environment may represent the appropriate field independent cognitive style (Katz and Kahn, 1978). Relatedly, and consistent with these conjectures is the well-established observation that social class membership also accounts for some variance in the field independence/field dependence cognitive style (Gruenfeld and MacEachron, 1975). In an international comparative study of managers and technicians from developing countries, Gruenfeld and MacEachron, (1975) show that mean levels of field independent and dependent styles as measured by the RFT and EFT correlate substantially with various indices of socio-economic status of individual managers and level of economic development of their home country.

In view of these findings, the conceptual distinction between cognitive style and personal style is no longer tenable. We share the view of the "New Look" psychologists (Bruner, 1951; Klein, 1951) who objected to the treatment of perception and personality as if they were in fact two separate domains. We advocate "the view that personality affects the way an individual functions in all areas of life" (Goodenough, 1985) including the perceptual and cognitive domain.

Gardner (1983) emphasizes a somewhat different metaphor of intrapersonal and interpersonal intelligence, in which the field independent person is hypothesized as having a "core capacity" to access his or her feelings and "to discriminate among these feelings to draw on them as a means of understanding and guiding her behavior. That is, to become more or less involved in an interpersonal situation" (Gardner, 1983, p.239). The field-dependent interpersonal intelligence turns outward. Its core capacity is to make discriminations among other individuals. This type of cognitive style entails the capacity to detect various moods, and especially others' approval and/or disapproval. The commonly observed correlations between measures of field independence/dependence and vocational interest or choice elucidates these judgments. Field independents prefer work in the other-directed helping professions like the ministry, nursing and social work. Field dependents prefer more solitary inner-directed work like forest ranging, mathematics or writing novels. Gardner makes it intelligible that these stylistic preferences are expressions of differing types of "personal intelligence." Witkin (1978) would have approved of this value-free distinction among forms of cognitive style.

The distinctions between intrapersonal and interpersonal cognitive style explicated here are frequently tainted by prejudicial judgments. Unlike other forms of "knowing", cultural norms place a heavy premium on interpersonal styles of knowing or attention deployment.

Culturally "inappropriate" modes of interpersonal cognitive styles invite sanctions (Gardner 1983). Relatedly, "culture-shock" usually refers to encounters with "incomprehensible" modes of cognitive style. An intra-interpersonal mode of knowing also "... denotes that capacity about which individuals have the strongest and most intimate views; thus it becomes a sensitive (as well as elusive) target to examine" (Gardner, 1983, p.243). It was one of Witkin's major accomplishments that he drew psychologists' attention to these intra-interpersonal modes of knowing - "forms that have, however, tended to be ignored or minimized by nearly all students of cognition" (Gardner, 1983, p.241).

Although Witkin (1978) deplored value judgments about the field independent-dependent construct, field dependents have not fared well in social-psychological research, which has described them, by and large, as if they were dumb, but nice. Field dependents have often been labeled and operationalized on the Rod and Frame or Embedded Figures Tests in terms of what they cannot do. Field dependents have often been construed as immature infants who are subordinated and undifferentiated. They have been shown to be submissive to authority and peers and global, or stereotypical, in their perceptions of others (Witkin, 1978). Field dependency was mainly inferred from the ability of its antithetical binary opposite to disembed figures from their ground and the field dependent's inability, or lack of motivation, to do so. This deplorable state of affairs was due primarily to a failure to comprehend these variables from a functionalist perspective and to ground them in biological and/or ecological moorings (Berry, 1976). The evidence shows clearly, however, that the present cognitive style construct of field independence/dependence is culturally anchored in social class (MacEachron and Gruenfeld, 1978) as well as in ecologically different subsistence-level societies. From this perspective, cognitive styles are simply different and functionally appropriate strategies of attention deployment and problem solving (Berry in this volume 1989).

Sampson (1977) and Hsu (1983) have both concluded that the research like that on field independence/dependence is biased by an overidealized ego-ideal that favors rugged individualism and is cynical about people's social concerns and solidarity. This bias is not merely "cultural"; it is also cognitive and analytical, due to a failure to articulate fully several types of field-dependent and field-independent cognitive styles. It is one of the pitfalls of robust bi-polar typologies that they divide individuals and cultures into good and evil or superior and inferior, rather than simply different or functional only under certain specified conditions.

The strategy entertained in this essay is to articulate a more refined typology of the field independent/dependent cognitive style than the simple bi-polar and value-tainted one presently in vogue. It is hoped that a refined, more differentiated typology will also draw attention to an alternative measurement paradigm, namely the operationalization of constructs, that unlike current binary and polar measurements, will permit the identification of what both dependents and independents can do, rather than inferring differences based merely on an ability or inability to do perceptual disembedding tasks (Wachtel, 1987).

LEADERSHIP AND TEACHING STYLE: STUDIES OF THE INFLUENCE PROCESS

Before we explore an expanded typology of field independence/dependence, we turn first to an evaluation of findings in the domain of leadership and teaching style research that demonstrates an already impressive body of knowledge in the social psychological applications of Witkin's (1978) paradigm. Leadership refers to the influential increment over and above formalized rules and procedure that some group or organization members employ to get work done. Because these improvisations are freely chosen rather than prescribed they are likely to reflect cognitive style predispositions. The influence process that embraces leadership/followership and teacher/student cognitive styles is central to interpersonal research in social psychology and personality.

Research on leadership and teaching styles commands a considerable amount of face, and especially ecological, validity because it deals by-and-large with noncontrived, enduring, organic, and social relationships (Gruenfeld and Lin, 1984) where cognitive style differences are likely to emerge and to determine results. These situations contrast with contrived, superficial, and temporary mechanistic relationships where stylistic differences are unlikely to emerge or to determine results. These latter conditions, although methodologically elegant because they appear to be rigorous, are inappropriate for the study of individual differences because they obliterate them (Ickes, 1982; Snyder and Ickes, 1975; Weiss and Adler, 1988).

A considerable body of knowledge supports the working hypothesis that the field-independent/dependent cognitive style affects the interpersonal influence process. Field independents have "a sense of separate identity." They show greater self-nonself segregation. There is, therefore, presumed to be a "distant" relationship between self and other. For field dependents the boundaries between self and nonself are permeable. Therefore, there is presumed to be a close relationship between self and others. Also, field independents tend to rely on internal standards whereas field dependents rely more on others for self-definition. Field dependents are "more social", more likely to seek to influence others, and more susceptible to influence from others than field independents. Field dependents are also more likely than field independents to seek the fellowship of others because they need information to guide their behavior. In comparison to field independents, they are therefore, more personal. Field independents are presumed to be more impersonal and detached from others because they can rely on their analytical skills and standards to generate their own information. It follows from these theoretical presumptions that leaders and teachers who differ in cognitive style will use differing methods to influence others.

COGNITIVE STYLE AND LEADERSHIP STYLE

Research on groups usually distinguishes between two types of goals: 1) the goal of accomplishing the assigned, manifest task; and 2) the emergent goal of maintaining group membership and the strengthening of the group itself (Cartwright and Zander, 1968; Bales, 1970, 1979). Most group members attend selectively to either of these tasks although a few may integrate the two goals and alternate between them. "Some individuals focus on the first category; they may emphasize the task, initiate action, set standards, or develop procedural plans. Other individuals focus on the second category, they may emphasize harmonious interpersonal relations, arbitrate disputes, or maintain a pleasant membership atmosphere." (Gruenfeld and Lin, 1984). The most consistent finding, so far, is that field independent leaders or teachers are subject matter oriented. In other words, they initiate structures, or interpolate structures (Katz and Kahn, 1978) in large part because they have high levels of skill in structuring and restructuring situations. Field dependent leaders or teachers are follower oriented. They are considerate, in large part because they have high levels of skill in relationships with others. They are socially sensitive (Witkin, 1978).

Some validating confirmation was found by Weissenberg and Gruenfeld (1966) for the hypothesis that field dependents attend to a high concern for group leadership activity that emphasizes member maintenance and support. Conversely they found that field independents did not attend to a high concern for group leadership activity that emphasized member protection and comfort. Differences between field independence/field dependence and concern for leadership activity that emphasizes attention to group task were not supported apparently because field independents and dependents construe the tasks of the group differently. They attend to dissimilar tasks. Gruenfeld and Arbuthnot (1968) demonstrated that field independent males with masculine sex-role orientations (instrumental), but not males with feminine sex-role orientations (expressive), discriminated sharply in their judgments among the work performances of their peers. Relative intolerance in rating others on task performances has also been described by Fiedler (1964) to show regard for and attention to group tasks. Field dependent subjects, presumably because they attend to the maintenance of harmonious interpersonal relationships, did not discriminate sharply among the ratings of task performances of their peers. They were tolerant. Gruenfeld and Arbuthnot (1968) concluded that field dependence and field independence are good indicators of task and socio-emotional orientation. Relatedly, Gruenfeld and Weisenberg (1966) asked a group of production supervisors to describe successful supervisors in their plant. High ranking of the traits "imaginative" and "independent" were significantly and positively associated with field independence, and high ranking of "cooperative" and "tactful" were positively and significantly correlated with field dependence. The major presumption of this study was that supervisors are likely to endorse those traits that they themselves attribute to their own successful performance. Field independent and field dependent supervisors did indeed see themselves as the theory of the global-articulated cognitive style predicts they would.

Correspondingly, Fiedler (1964), in his advancement of a contingency theory of leadership effectiveness, distinguished between leaders who held more or lesser esteem for their least- and most-preferred coworkers. Those who held their least-preferred coworkers in high esteem failed to discriminate among the performances of their group's members. They were also tolerant and considerate in their treatment of others. Conversely, supervisors who had low esteem for their least preferred coworkers discriminated distinctly among the performances of their group's members. They were uncharitable and demanding in their concerns for the tasks of the group.

Some contradictory evidence was provided by Erez (1980), however, who, in a study of managers with engineering backgrounds, concluded that "field independent personalities may actually be employee-centered leaders when the situation requires attention to interpersonal stimuli, with the cognitive factor of social intelligence playing a role." The employee-centered style (consideration) was significantly and positively correlated with field independence but was not significantly related to social intelligence. This conclusion differs from the expected results that an employee-centered style is more field dependent. By adding the dimension of social intelligence,

Erez showed that field independents were able to behave in a more "considerate" manner if the situation required it.

Another style dimension - that which describes one's locus of control - is similar to the cognitive style of field independence and field dependence. "Those who ascribe control of events to themselves are said to have an internal locus of control and those who attribute control to outside forces are said to have an external locus of control" (Spector 1982). Anderson and Schnier (1978) found that individuals with an internal locus of control were more likely to emerge as group leaders, performed better in class, and were more task-oriented than those with an external locus of control. In addition, groups led by "internals" performed better than groups led by "externals." Goodstadt and Hjelle (1973) found that internals attempted to use personal persuasion to a greater extent than externals, and externals used coercion more. These latter studies, have not been tested with the traditional RFT and EFT measures. But, Rotter (1966) has claimed that the locus of control dimension is similar to Witkin's cognitive style dimensions, however. Specifically he suggests that internal locus of control is similar to the field-independent cognitive style and external locus of control is similar to the field-dependent cognitive style.

The bulk of studies on psychological differentiation and leadership style reveal that there are definite relationships between field independence/dependence and leadership style. Much work needs to be done, however, to clarify these relationships. The findings reveal some of the leadership style differences between different cognitive types, but the question of which leadership style is most effective has not yet been answered. Are different styles more effective depending on the styles of subordinates or the work environment or the task?

As mentioned before, an important study by McEachron (1977) showed that managers in manufacturing organizations who inhabit different levels in the organizational hierarchy differ in cognitive style apparently because they are preselected. Thus, differences in behavior and experience at dissimilar hierarchical levels are, due, at least, in part to the incumbents' cognitive style differences.

Field dependent workers might be more productive in group settings because they are relatively less aroused in the presence of others. Field independents, who have a lower threshold for arousal, might withdraw or distance themselves from others in groups because they are overwhelmed or overstimulated or anxious in the presence of "too many others" (Eysenck and Eysenck, 1985; Eysenck and Wilson, 1978; Fine, B, 1972). Correspondingly, field dependent managers derive job satisfaction from such external rewards as pay and job security, whereas field independent managers do not; they are more likely to find the intrinsic nature of their work satisfying (Gruenfeld and Weissenberg, 1971)

On the other hand, there is also some suggestion that leaders who can adjust to their followers' cognitive styles or whose own style is compatible with those of their followers are better liked and perhaps also more influential (Goodenough, 1985). Some tangential evidence in support of the compatibility hypothesis has been garnered by Gruenfeld and Alpert (1989), who show that mating is selective: Mates of similar cognitive styles are more likely to be involved in enduring (six months or more) friendship relationships.

Peterson and Scott (1975) have concluded, however, that the study of leadership style differences is inhibited by a paucity of typologies of leadership patterns. The exclusive emphasis on task and socio-emotional orientation is not sufficient to account for the numerous styles that are observable. The status of leadership research thus parallels that of cognitive style: insufficient analytical categories.

TEACHING STYLES

The inquiry into teaching style provides an alternate avenue for investigating the relationships among cognitive styles and leadership behaviors. The teacher's attention deployment toward various tasks and his or her strategies for communicating and organizing knowledge are convenient foci for research on individual differences in cognitive style.

Several studies have shown that teachers with different cognitive styles differ in their preferred method of teaching. Field-dependent teachers favor teaching situations that encourage interaction with students, for example. Field-independent teachers, on the other hand, prefer situations that are impersonal and attentive to the intellectual aspects of teaching, not the social aspects (Witkin, Moore, Goodenough and Cox, 1977). Moore (1973) found that field-dependent teachers use questions as instructional tools, (to introduce a new topic or to respond to a student), whereas field-independent teachers use questions primarily to check on student learning following instruction. Another important difference between field-dependent and independent teachers emphasizes their use of reinforcement strategies. Emmerich (1984) found that field-independent teachers view corrective feedback as a useful learning tool that provides students with valuable information for improving their performance. Field-independent teachers also display negative evaluations (expressing displeasure when a student's performance is below capacity) as a technique of teaching. Field dependent teachers, on the other hand, do not emphasize corrective feedback or negative evaluations. They seek to avoid antagonizing others (Witkin, Moore, Goodenough and Cox, 1977) by displaying social supportiveness and encouragement.

The categories of task and socio-emotional orientation used in teacher studies overlap considerably with similar dimensions in leadership behavior. It is also in the teaching domain that the link between cognitive style and subject matter choice for instruction has been firmly established. By-and-large field independent teachers gravitate to the teaching of mathematics and science. Field-dependent teachers gravitate to the teaching of humanities and social sciences (Witkin, Moore, Goodenough and Cox, 1977). Hudson (1968) compared two cultures of students, those in the physical sciences and those in the liberal arts. Science students were described by Hudson as convergers and liberal arts students as divergers. Convergers, who are similar to field independents, are intolerant of ambiguity. They prefer mechanistic tasks for which there are known right answers. Divergers, who are similar to field dependents, seek out ambiguous situations. The inexactness of the arts attracts them.

With regard to the effectiveness of varying cognitive styles as teaching strategies, the research findings are mixed. Witkin et al. (1977) point out that teachers of contrasting styles do not differ in teaching competence. Saracho and Dayton (1980) did find a relationship, however, between teachers' cognitive style and the achievement gains of their students. Students of field independent teachers achieved consistently higher scores on standardized learning tests. Saracho and Spodek (1981) added the element of student cognitive style to their study. They found the following hierarchy in student achievement (from high to low):

1. Field-independent students of field independent teachers
2. Field-dependent students of field independent teachers
3. Field-independent student of field dependent teachers
4. Field-dependent students of field dependent teachers.

An extension of these studies dealt with the matching or consistency of students' and teachers' cognitive styles. Teachers and students of like cognitive styles viewed each other more favorably than those whose styles were mismatched (DiStefano, 1970). In addition there was greater interpersonal attraction in matched student-teacher pairs than there was in mismatched pairs. It is also noteworthy that teachers gave higher grades to those students whose cognitive styles matched their own (James, 1973).

Provost (1981), in a study of teaching effectiveness and cognitive style, revealed impressive gender differences for active and passive teaching-treatment effects, which were the independent variables in his study. Females, rather than field dependents, preferred a passive teaching treatment. Males, rather than field independents, preferred a more active teaching treatment. Provost also reported that a literature review revealed a moderate correlation between IQ and performance on the EFT, a measure of the field-independent/dependent cognitive style. (Goodenough and Karp, 1961; Karp, 1963). The failure to control for general intelligence in the Provost study leaves his results with ambiguous and even controversial interpretations.

Despite the fact that there is considerable evidence that shows that the field-independent/dependent cognitive styles are significantly and importantly related to teaching behavior, these studies also reveal some of the troublesome methodological problems that stigmatize this kind of research. The bipolar typology of field dependence (task) and field independence (socio-emotional) orientation can no longer be considered sufficient to account for the many nuances of influence (i.e. leadership) behavior observed in groups. Moreover, their mutual exclusivity simply does not correspond to what can be even superficially observed, i.e. that there are mixed types which are both dependent and independent. A considerable body of knowledge both theoretical and empirical has identified several additional leadership styles: Schutz (1958), Reddin (1970), Blake and Mouton (1964) and their related cognitive strategies. Attempts at integration of stylistic dimensions have also been reported by Blake and Mouton (1964) and Bakan (1966). They theorize that some persons can deal with both analytical-task and interpersonal-membership concerns. Sowell (1987) also describes mixed types of the contrasting constrained and unconstrained visions. Gruenfeld and Kassum (1973) have shown that hospital nurses who are both task and socioemotionally oriented are most likely to be high performers. Social behavior is stylistically more varied than the mutually exclusive by polar and unidimensional conception of the field independent/dependent cognitive style currently suggests. In addition, most of these studies did not account for, or control, intelligence and/or gender differences, or similar constructs that are differently measured.

Wachtel (1987) has reported, for example, that various tests of field independence, like the Kohs, EFT, and RFT, correlate less with each other than with measures of general intelligence. Thus, general intelligence may have to be considered as an alternative and simpler framework for the interpretation of the findings reported above. Gender also may have confounded these results. For example, Emmerich et al. (1984) found that students and teachers of the same sex valued each other more highly than students and teachers of the opposite sex. In the Emmerich study the sex match-mismatch effect was more potent and took precedence over the cognitive style match-mismatch effect. These results are especially pertinent because of evidence that females in the North American middle class culture are more field dependent than their male counterparts. Social class, which is related to the field-independent/dependent style, may also have confounded the results noted above (MacEachron and Gruenfeld, 1978). The social class variable is a surrogate for almost every conceivable psychological variable and, therefore, unless subjects are matched for social class in the studies reported, the studies are subject to alternate interpretations. Such alternatives will have to be empirically refuted in future studies. These equivocations are not unique in their applicability to research on the field-independent/dependent cognitive style. They apply to the main body of findings about the relationship between personality and social behavior, as well (Wachtel, 1987).

TOWARD A RECONSTRUCTED TAXONOMY OF FIELD-INDEPENDENT/DEPENDENT COGNITIVE STYLES IN GROUPS: THE STRESSED AND COMPOSED STYLES

We turn now to a restructuring of the field independent/dependent typology to map out a more discriminating taxonomy of cognitive styles. Extensive observation of behavior and experience in self-analytic study groups (Gruenfeld and Lin, 1986; Gruenfeld and Seibert, 1988) has revealed that many field independents did not behave in the autonomous, self-controlled, analytical style expected on the basis of Witkin's conception. Some of them were intellectually immobilized, interpersonally reactive, and irritable, rather than analytical and reflective in their cognitive orientation. They were brittle, thin-skinned, judgmental, and overly sensitive to group member and leader evaluation of their performances. Many field dependents were actively and even analytically engaged in their interpersonal task. Other field dependents were conforming, but their conformity emulated a style that was by-and-large appropriate for the task that faced the members of the group. These observations drew attention to an apparently over-simplified binary taxonomy of both the field-independent and field-dependent style. We concluded that a great deal more research and conceptual work was still needed to map out a detailed taxonomy of field independence and dependence.

Our assessment of the present status of theory and research about the global-articulated cognitive style is predicated on the notion that univariate schemata or binary typologies are not sufficient to explain social interactions. Schein (1985), in a treatise on group culture and leadership has sharply defined the issue as follows: "In fact, one of the reasons why organization theory may not have progressed further than it has is that most of the typologies which are published tend to be unidimensional" (p. 111). The following statement quoted by Pervin (1984) also highlights the apparent value-laden and premature impressions of the global style as "dumb," regressed, and infantile, and the articulated style as intelligent, progressed, and mature: "Field dependent subjects show either inhibitions of impulses or uncontrolled expression of hostility while field independent subjects show an ability to express their impulses in a relatively controlled manner" (Pervin, 1984, p.119). This view is inconsistent with findings in cross-cultural psychology that show members of field dependent subsistence level cultures to behave "appropriately" in accord with the demands of their ecological environments (Berry, 1976). Moreover, Gruenfeld et al. (1988) show field independent subjects in a self-analytic, unstructured group environment to be immobilized by anxiety and fear, which was frequently acted out by fight/flight behavior - much of it "nasty" and even violent. Some field dependents behaved by-and-large in a controlled, task-oriented, and cooperative manner in this environment. The major intervening variable was the interpersonal nature of the task and the attendant level of anxiety it elicited in group members. Fiedler (1987) in his recent revision of his leadership resource theory has also proposed that level of anxiety immobilizes analytically-oriented group members. Millon (1981) proposed that independence and dependence can take on different stylistic expressions under conditions of chronic or situational stress. There are at least two versions of the stressed field-independent style: egotism (narcissism) and the antisocial syndrome. According to Millon there are also two versions of the stressed field-dependent type: submission and sociability. In addition, there are evidently two other types: the originally postulated independent type described by Witkin, modelled after the ancient Greek character type, and the dependent type, modelled after the character type of the European middle ages (Rosenthal, 1971). For purposes of convenience we have labeled these unstressed cognitive styles as composed.

A substantial body of research about social behavior in groups summarized by Bales, (1970, 1979) suggests three exhaustive dimensions of behavior, attitudes and, by implication, cognitive styles: active-passive (U/D), positive-negative (P/N) and controlled-expressive (F/B). The controlled-expressive dimension is isomorphic to the global-articulated dimension portrayed by Witkin

(1978) but it is only one of three major dimensions and it may, therefore, take on varying expressions depending on its association with activity and/or negativity (in other words, aggression and/or anxiety). Gruenfeld and Lin (1984) have reported a correlation of .67 (N=20) between measures of field independence (Rod and Frame Test) and Bales's (1970, 1979) controlled-expressive dimension, based on direct observations of behavior in non-contrived groups. But, passive (submissive) anxious (unfriendly) and controlled (field independent) persons behave quite differently from active (dominant), composed (friendly) and controlled (field independent) persons. We draw substantially on Bales's research (1970, 1979) to muster the evidence for our revised taxonomy. The multivariate typology proposed here will, it is hoped, provide an expanded source of imaginative and testable hypotheses.

THE EGOTISTIC VERSION OF THE STRESSED FIELD INDEPENDENT SYNDROME

Under conditions of chronic (trait) anxiety or situational (state) anxiety, some "egotistic" field independents attend mainly to themselves as their source of information and perceptional orientation. Mitchell (1988) has recently integrated various theoretical orientations to narcissism from an interpersonal style perspective that could be assimilated to expand present metaphors and research on cognitive style. According to Mitchell, the egotistic narcissist entertains illusions of self aggrandizement. He views himself as the center of the universe, perfect and exuberant, including a "grand overestimation of his capacities." The result is an idealized self attribution of a grandiose, self-sustaining, field independent "who is prone to exploit and use others." But, these overvalued self-attributions interfere with encounters between the narcissist and other people. The field independent, stressed narcissist remains inflexible and perpetuates "stereotyped patterns of integrating interpersonal relationships" (Mitchell, 1988, p.194). The greatest fear of the narcissist and indeed, the source of his anxiety is to be dependent on another. However, these cognitions and attributions predispose the narcissist to distancing others rather than being genuinely independent of them. Interpersonally, the field-independent self-centered egotist is stressed by relationships that are determined or conditioned by another. He is fearful of the loss of self determination and turns inward to rely on himself rather than others for gratification and esteem. He expects others to cater to him and to the high self esteem to which the egotist holds himself (Millon, 1981, p.158). The stressed field independent egotist is also self absorbed. He shows a "self-centered pattern of attention deployment."

Several students of culture have described this narcissistic type as the "social character" of the post-industrial middle class who deploys attention toward the exploitation and manipulation of others rather than showing open anger and hostility. Maccoby (1976) has described this cognitive orientation as "Gamesmanship" in employment organizations and Christie and Geis (1970) refer to a similar syndrome known as "Machiavellianism." This type finds his cultural habitat in the affluent, post-industrial consumer societies rather than the subsistence level cultures (Bell, 1976)

THE STRESSED FIELD-INDEPENDENT EGOTIST IN GROUPS

According to the group research reported by Bales (1970, 1979), the UNB character type (active, negative, expressive) behaves in a "provocative, egocentric, show-off" manner, similar to the behavior of a stressed field-independent egotist. This UNB type is concerned with "rugged individualism" and "self gratification". He employs a good deal of exploitative hostility in his interpersonal relations. He has been observed by Bales and subsequently by Gruenfeld and Lin (1984); and Gruenfeld et al. (1988), to move against authority in groups because authority appears to stifle and constrain his impulse for self-indulgence and personal pleasure seeking. Others see him as "favoring self expression and gratification." Group members find him entertaining, but also deficient in egalitarianism. According to Bales (1970, 1979), he is usually a central participant in group activity. He speaks a lot to the group as a whole rather than addressing individuals personally. In responding to him, however, others are not likely to reciprocate his high rate of activity. Because of his potential status as an "outlaw" brought on by his rejection of conventional rules and morality, others are fascinated by his behavior but intimidated and cautious about getting too close to him. The quality of his interactions is denoted by his low rate of asking for information and suggestions according to Bales. Being unfriendly and showing disagreement are salient features of his behavior: "In response to his dramatizing and joking, others are likely to be markedly high on showing tension and laughing" (Bales, p.240). Unlike the composed independent "archetype," he does not pursue arguments by analytic reasoning but by "provocative and suggestive words" and by shocking metaphors that give expression to his lack of self-restraint. He is most likely to come into conflict with task-oriented group members who seek to contain, socialize or isolate him. According to Bales, the "outlaw" is a potential leader or even collaborator with those who wish to bring about change. Significantly, and in accord with our present emphasis on stress as the debilitating cause for the field-independent cognitive style, Bales's research confirms that the "outlaw" is "high on the trait of nervous tension." With regard to group goals, the UNB type undermines member satisfaction with interpersonal events and tends to distract the group from accomplishing its task. His over-talking and self-absorption induces others to tread lightly with him.

These observations by Bales suggest a more elaborate multi-dimensional reconstruction of the field-independent cognitive style typology, because the original typology advocated by Witkin (1978) is unable to account for anxious or aggressive subtypes whose interpersonal boundaries and styles are quite brittle and different from the "composed" version of field independents initially described by Witkin. Many of these components of the narcissist's presumed cognitions are measureable and directly observable by the SYMLOG method. But with the exception of Gruenfeld and Lin (1984), this work has not yet found its way into the mainstream of research on the global articulated cognitive style.

TOWARD THE ANTISOCIAL PATTERN OF THE STRESSED FIELD INDEPENDENT SYNDROME

In contrast to the relatively exploitative, egotistic field-independent cognitive type, the antisocial version of the stressed field independent exhibits a vigorous and aggressive cognitive style. The antisocial field independents feel protected if they can establish independence from those who may do them harm, but their resentments toward others fester and persist. They are indignant. Millon, (1981, p.181) suggests that only a minor subset of the antisocial independent type come into conflict with the law." Many find themselves commended and reinforced in a competitive society, where tough, hard-headed 'realism' is admired as an attribute necessary for survival" (Millon, p.181). These "rugged" individualists may find a place for themselves in the world of business or politics, but what they fear most is humiliation. Many of these antisocial independents act on their hostile impulses. "Therefore, they are prone to counterattack the distrust of others which they have learned to expect" (Millon, 1981). They have an impetuous temper that flares easily into argumentativeness and battle designed to degrade and derogate others. They "are contemptuous toward authority, tradition, sentimentality and humanistic concerns". Certainly this cognitive style was not contemplated by Witkin (1978). Gruenfeld and Lin (1984) have observed that people with this stressed field independent cognitive style are unaware of the impact they have and impressions they make on others.

THE ANTISOCIAL PATTERN OF THE STRESSED FIELD INDEPENDENT IN GROUPS

According to Bales (1970, 1979) one can expect the UNF character type (active, negative and controlled) to behave in an "authoritarian, controlling, disapproving" manner similar to that if the stressed field-independent anti-social type. Although task-oriented, he takes a judgmental, dominant and dogmatic interpersonal stance. He is probably the most frequently studied and quoted type, the typical authoritarian personality (Adorno, Fraenkel and Brunswick, 1950). It is noteworthy that measures of authoritarianism are more or less consistently correlated with the RFT and EFT tests, the marker variables of the field independent cognitive style (Vernon, 1969, 1972). We interpret this to mean that authoritarianism is one of the dimensions of the global-articulated syndrome. Bales (1970, 1979) reports that of all the types this one is the most disliked by group members.

The UNF character type views others as being "stupid and immature" and, thus not a good source of information. He desires to impose discipline on them. The essence of this type, as viewed, for example, by Fromm (1941, 1947), is that they are intolerant of ambiguity. They are impervious to shades, nuances and the tentativeness of others, those who are presumed to be "weak." They are dogmatic, conservative, and anti-intellectual, perhaps even anti-scientific. They do not trust others, especially outsiders "who seek to infiltrate, confuse and overthrow the task and its authorities" (Bales, 1970, 1979). They entertain grandiose leadership ambitions and take responsibility for unpleasant but necessary tasks of the group. Indeed they usually have a prominent place in the group's interaction network. Bales (1970, 1979) reports that they overtalk by addressing the entire group rather than individual members. Others do not reciprocate this high activity level. "Either he tends to prevent replies by overtalking, or others tend to withhold replies, or both" (Bales, p.220). The quality of his interactions are informed by being unfriendly and disagreeing. He provides many suggestions and opinions. Bales noted that others seldom ask him for information or give it to him. He is not interested in information. Rather than discussion, debate and talking things over, he prefers to get into the thick of it by professing values (morality) and seeking action. He encounters strong resistance from others who are "markedly likely to disagree with him and to seem 'unfriendly'." His antisocial nature is reciprocated and sustained by others: "no other member is so likely to receive disagreement and unfriendly acts" (Bales, p.225). The UNF type promotes conflict because he tends to polarize group members. The socially gregarious members who seek to promote emotional warmth and cameradery are especially offended by him. His apparently elitist and hierarchial views are opposed by those members who seek a more egalitarian group atmosphere and who are appalled by the stressed field independent's propensity toward violence. In accord with our own observations of the anti-social, field dependent type, Bales reports that this UNF type is anxious, rigid, and tense. As can be excpected, the UNF style does not promote interpersonal satisfaction among group members, although, if the group does not polarize, he will promote group member satisfaction with task accomplishment (Bales, 1970, 1979). His ability to assume leadership in the group depends largely on the level of attachment to him and the good will that others have toward him.

THE STRESSED SUBMISSIVE FIELD DEPENDENT TYPE

Millon (1981) suggested a distinction between the field-dependent submissive and field-dependent gregarious patterns of social behavior. The present authors share Millon's conviction that field dependence can take on different stylistic expressions under conditions of chronic (trait anxiety) or situational (state anxiety) stress. There are at least two versions of a "stressed" field dependent cognitive style: the submissive and the gregarious syndrome.

Millon (1981) describes the dependent (submissive) character type as attending to a salient claim for social approval and affection. This type seeks to please those on whom they depend. "Losing the affection and protection of those on whom they depend leads them to feel exposed to the void of self-determination" (p.107). Relatedly, they also show fear of abandonment. To elaborate further, stressed field dependents "often submit to abuse and intimidation in the hope of avoiding isolation" (p.107). These descriptions are reminiscient of masochistic character traits (Fromm 1941, 1947). Millon (1981) also asserts this hypothesis: "Many dependent individuals search for a single, all powerful 'magic helper', a partner in whom they can place their trust and depend on to protect them from having to assume responsibilities or facing the competitive struggles of life alone" (p.107).

Interpersonally, submissive field dependents are mild and loving, admiring as well as willing to "give their all." Loyalty to others is the essence of their conformity (Witkin, 1978). It may be this loyalty that is one of the major determinants of the communalism-individualism syndrome posited by Triandis (1989) that overlaps with Witkin's cognitive styles. As a function of their differing preferences for loyalty to others, communalists place high value on group goals while individualists place high value on personal goals.

THE SUBMISSIVE FIELD-DEPENDENT IN GROUPS

According to Bales (1970, 1979), one can expect the D (submissive) character type to behave in a self-deprecatory manner similar to that of the stressed field dependent submissive type, that is to accept whatever exists, to be obedient to authority, and to work submissively with others. Acceptance of others is neither dutiful nor enthusiastic, but simply inactive and inert (Bales, p.377). Group members actually see this type as accepting authority. He is not emotionally involved in the lives of the group; others are curious about him, but he lacks curiosity (Bales, p.378).

The D member addresses other individuals but rarely the group as a whole. He is neither a central figure or actor in the group nor a strong supporter of others. Bales's studies show him to be uninvolved and unconcerned about the power struggles that go on in the group. He is more like a passive observer than an active participant. His anxiety immobilizes him. He does not look anxious and agitated to observers, but rather depressed and withdrawn (Gruenfeld, et al., 1978).

The D member is very low in the rate of interaction received and emitted. He is high in asking for direction and consistent with our present position, he appears anxious, shows tensions, and laughs. He is left pretty well alone and others are not likely to disagree with him. In group conflict situations, he is likely to play the role of silent partner. "Both to and from him one must look for minimal cues, silent glances, unobtrusive acts such as the choice of seating position, bodily position vis-a-vis the other, gestures..." (Bales, p.380). He is the recipient of a great many fantasies and mystifications. He is immobilized by his defensive strategy against stress, and it is mainly for this reason that we have chosen to classify him as the stressed and submissive type.

In terms of group member satisfactions, he makes neither a positive nor negative contribution. He is more or less acceptable to others. His contribution to satisfaction with members' task accomplishment is phlegmatic.

TOWARD THE STRESSED, SOCIALLY GREGARIOUS FIELD DEPENDENT SYNDROME

Under conditions of chronic (trait) anxiety or situational (state) anxiety, some dependents attend to being socially engaging. For example, they are hyperactive and over-talk. They "know" a lot of people and their social networks are the source of much "inside dope" and gossip, which titilates others, but does not analyze events.

Socially gregarious, stressed field-dependent types are sensitive to the moods and feelings of others whose attention they actively solicit (Millon, 1981). Rather than overtly manipulating others and therefore incurring the risk of being rejected by them, the gregarious dependent seeks to attract others by pleasing them. His/her attention is deployed toward others' approval or disapproval. This strategy is employed as an ingratiating search for information. The stressed gregarious field dependent's greatest fear is the possibility of being rejected by others on whom he depends as a major resource for information and know-how. However, his attachment to others is fickle. He seeks a conveniently large network of informants to provide the "inside dope" for his way of knowing, or his cognitive style. He knows a lot about many things but has difficulty developing knowledge that is bounded, specialized and intensive. He can sustain many casual acquaintances whom he entertains with tidbits of witty comments and commentary but he lacks analytically restrained and logical thought patterns. He appears to be very charming, but lacks loyalty and devotion to others. His interests shift precipitously and depend on what is approved or currently faddish. "Though they adopt convictions strongly and readily, their judgment is not firmly rooted, and they often play hunches" that invite others' attention and approval (Millon p.132). The major source of their anxiety is fear of evaluations that disconfirm their cognitive style. Many gregarious dependents are quite at ease in "playing the game" but they may become confused and flustered in their thinking when others take them seriously. They more or less avoid introspective reflection and responsible concentrated thinking" (Millon, p.140).

SOCIALLY GREGARIOUS FIELD DEPENDENT IN GROUPS

According to the Bales (1970, 1979) (SYMLOG) schemata the UPB (active, friendly, expressive) character type has been observed to display a dominant optimistic, and demonstrative behavioral and attitudinal pattern of action in groups similarly to the gregarious field-dependent cognitive style. Based upon considerable direct observation and research of behavior in groups, Bales summarizes the UPB pattern as "entertaining, sociable, smiling and warm" (Bales and Cohen, 1979). His values expressed in a group context are designed to "make others feel happy" (p.504). Specifically: "He takes the initiative in protecting or nurturing others, gives unconditional praise or reward, boosts the status of the other, gives approval and encouragement, gives warm acceptance without regard to the excellence or failure of performance of the other, or gives support, reassurance, comfort, or consolation" (Bales and Cohen, p.365). "He gives off nonverbal signs; gives emotional support by touching, feeding, protecting, or helping physically; or shows emotional warmth in facial expressions in other words, he smiles or laughs warmly and supportively..." (p.365). Some group members like him, but others are "put off" by too much "ascendance" in the service of socio-emotional support and friendliness. We conjecture that the emotional support provided may be seen by others as the UPB member's defense against his own anxiety. The UPB member has a prominent place in the group. "He is high in addressing remarks to the group as a whole rather than to particular members and is high on receiving in return" (Bales, p.253). His interest and concern for others is exemplified by asking frequently for information and opinion. But, paradoxically, he is also low in providing information and giving opinions. "He apparently tends not to engage much in rational analysis or arguments" (Bales, p.254). Surely, and not surprisingly, he does not disagree much with others. In return for his apparently low contribution to the task of the group, others are low in agreeing with him" (Bales, p.254). Bales also reports that the UPB type (similar to the gregarious, but anxious field-dependent type) is most likely to come into conflict with the UNF type (similar to the stressed, field-independent antisocial type). Although negative and stressed the UNF (autocratic antisocial type) is usually task-oriented and therefore views the UPB as "a warm and fuzzy playmate" who distracts members from their tasks by introducing a frivolous and lighthearted, even playful, atmosphere in the group. In terms of accomplishing the group's tasks, the UPB member's contribution is seen by other group members as negative. The UPB member is seen as "too ascendant, too talkative, and tends too much to crowd others out to make a predictable contribution to group membership satisfaction (Bales, 1970). Although he performs an important function in the group (the management of interpersonal stress and the provision of lighhearted distractions from the harsher demands of the task), he is unlikely to emerge as leader. Blake and Mouton (1964) label this cognitive style as appropriate for "country club" management. Country clubs, after all, exist for the enjoyment, fun and comradery of members. The socially ingratiating and convivial style of the UPB manager "leads" by "following" the desires and expectations of the country club membership.

THE COMPOSED, FIELD-INDEPENDENT COGNITIVE STYLE

The composed field independent originally described by Witkin resembles the ancient Greek character type. According to Rosenthal (1971), the ancient Greek field independent had strong convictions that helped him resist public opinion. He was committed to vigorous debate, which in turn was informed by reason and logic. He was indeed analytical and independent. The Greek independent respected authority, but also believed in high standards of excellence and self-development, as well as the inevitability of the tragic way of life, in other words, failure. This type is quite different from the rugged independent narcissist who arrogantly overestimates his right to enjoyment and unlimited self-actualization. The narcissist and anti-social type, unlike the Greek field independent, are bereft of a sense of duty to the community of others. The ancient Greek independent was, however, also communally-oriented or other directed. Rosenthal (1971) has described this composed cognitve type as balanced, or able to integrate or moderate egotism and social concerns. A similar position is taken by Bakan (1966), who relies on the discernment between agentic (field independent) and communal (field dependent) cognitive style. Bakan's description of the agentic field-independent style (which he derives from religious mythology and clinical observations) is far less "flattering" and idealized than Witkin's (1978) field independent. Extreme field independence and dependence, according to Bakan, lead to despair. The field-independent strategy, which is based on a metaphor of self-mastery, is unrealistic and socially destructive. The field-dependent strategy, which is based on pleasing others, is unable to take care of itself and thus also induces despair. Bakan, who relies on Witkin's findings of gender differences in cognitive styles, argues that field independence is, or should be, mitigated by a communal orientation. The evolving type is clearly interdependent.

THE COMPOSED FIELD-INDEPENDENT STYLE IN GROUPS

The composed field "interdependent" derived from ancient Greek culture, represents a two-sided, but complementary type of cognitive style (Rosenthal, 1971). It combines group immersion and commitment with traits of independent thought and conviction. In this culture, to give in to group pressure without reasoned argument or merely for the sake of maintaining harmony was considered an inappropiate form of cognitive style. Vitality and balance of ideas were sought through vigorous debate and self-assertion; thus a clash or conflict of ideas was welcomed as a form of acquiring knowledge. Acceptance of individual differences, rather than their supression was conceived of as the essence of group solidarity. Social life in groups was visualized as requiring "the best of men" and invited the kind of self-assertion that favored group goals rather than egotistic self-interest. "As individualism was so highly prized, there was no necessity for submerging the ego into the morass of group commonality or for playing the cat and mouse game of permitting one's genuine ideas to show only when confident of not arousing group disapproval." (Rosenthal, 1971, p.73) Guilt, according to Lewis

(1971), is the constraining "moral" incentive of the composed field-independent cognitive style. Thus, the courage to defy group sentiment and persevere in one's own convictions became esteemed qualities" (Rosenthal, p.74). Therefore, interdependence as visualized in this essay was fostered by respect for others on the basis of a person's uniqueness and special abilities. This cultural setting promotes integrity, thus fostering the composed field-independent style.

According to Bales (1970, 1979), one can expect the F character type (controlled) to behave in an "analytical, task oriented, problem solving" manner similar to that of the composed field-independent type. He or she is concerned with the group's task as externally and conservatively defined. He or she is impersonal, but committed and tentative, and seriously and curiously testing hypotheses to promote the task of the group.

Paradoxically and contradictory to Witkin's (1978) expectations, the F character type is not especially introspective about himself. He lacks understanding of repressed tendencies. He is empirical and focuses attention on what is manifest, cognitive and observable, although others do arouse his inquisitiveness. He is conflicted about others because they embody his temptations and potential distractions. "He rates himself low on favoring expression and gratification" (Bales, p.274). Interestingly, according to Bales, he does not hold a central position in the interaction network. He is inclined to address specific individuals and his frequency of acts received and emitted is average. He identifies with the rules and constraints of the group "by reason of the existence of common values or social norms" (Bales, p.274). The quality of his interactions are informed by the F member's conception of the group as a task force. He conservatively accepts the goal as assigned to the group by the environment. He defines authority in terms of these group goals. He reasons deductively from given premises and helps to generate detailed programs of action to be followed. "For him the most characteristic type of interaction in the small work group is giving opinion..." These opinions are supported by value judgments, logical and rational classification, and impersonal inference. He is also inclined to ask for and give suggestions and information. He receives and offers considerable agreement. Paradoxically, he also receives quite a bit of disagreement from others. The most likely opposition and source of conflict for the composed field independent type (F on the Bales SYMLOG typology) comes from the stressed field-dependent type (the various expressive B types on the Bales SYMLOG typology).

THE COMPOSED FIELD DEPENDENT STYLE

The global field dependent type has an idealized and preeminent regard for the group. He corresponds keenly to Triandis's (1989) definition of the communal character type. According to Triandis the communal character favors group goals over personal goals, reciprocal allegiances, and status obligations. Conformity, for the communal type, is informed by duty and responsibility, the "secular counterparts" of sacred obligation to God (Rosenthal, 1971). The presumptive paradigm is that of family: a complex system including status, hierarchy, and fraternal, as well as paternal discipline or maternally reciprocated care and protection. "From such influences emerged a group milieu in which conflict, envy, resentment, social aspiration, etc. were substantially deemphasized" (Rosenthal, p.151). Such a social system commits and integrates the individual "making him coextensive with the group." The emergent character type resembles the Japanese employer-employee relationship as described by Pascal and Athos (1981) and Hofstede (1980).

Similarily, the concept of collectivism, which we consider here as a manifestation in the social realm of the global cognitive style, is deeply rooted in the ethos of Chinese culture, which assumes that maintaining the group's well-being is the best guarantee for the individual (Hsu, 1981, 1983). The loss of face (shame) in Chinese culture is the result of the individual's failure to meet requirements consonant with his or her social status in the group. Shame is clearly the constraining moral motive of the global cognitive style. Unlike the field-independent articulated style the global field-dependent cognitive style is not empirical, pragmatic, or scientifically detached. Rather the global person is speculative, idealistic, and interpersonally or socially engrossed. The interpersonal world of the middle ages, the cultural habitat of the global field dependent, was ideologically inspired and well-ordered. The person's self-conceptions were, contrary to the current view, well defined (Rosenthal, 1971). The traditional field dependents were not afflicted by an inability to maintain interpersonal boundaries. Conformity was based on well defined rules and enforced or consecrated by divinely established authority. Composed field dependents were highly principled rather than obtuse in their conformity, as currently believed.

Those with the traditional field-dependent cognitive style were informed by kindness and compassion - virtues that sustained them in a world of evil persecution and economic hardships. These conditions "...produced a psychological view in which the immaterial, the symbolic, and the spiritual preoccupied cognition and emotion, leaving the medieval (composed field dependent) mind largely oriented to metaphoric or intellectual perception and judgment while depreciating their empirical and materialistic counterparts" (Rosenthal, p.114). From a socialpsychological perspective, this system of cognition emphasizes psychological stability and security through reciprocal obligations and respect for social roles not unlike those that are observed in Japanese culture and enterprises today (Atsumi, 1980). To construe this system of mutual obligation and interdependence as mere "submission" and "conformity," as is often implied in research and theory about cognitive styles, is inaccurate. The global field-dependent style attends to a set of basic a priori assumptions that are "reasoned manifestations" of the global field-dependent cognitive style. Such a system of thought makes empirical criteria of proof irrelevant. Thus we would expect the global style to be conceptual and theoretical and not attentive to methods of proof. Composed field dependents resemble "intellectuals." The composed field-independent cognitive style would be the opposite: preoccupied and attentive to method of proof but aversive to theoretical construction or meaningfulness of results. Composed field independents resemble "empiricists."

The cognitive intellectual skills of the dependent type in medieval Europe (Rosenthal, 1971) were manifested in symbol creations, or allegorical, metaphorical references to events. The empirical was spurned and the imaginative and intuitive became the dominant mode of "analysis." Not unlike contemporary hermeneutics or the psychoanalytic method, the composed dependent type relied on scrutiny of words, symbolic insights, interpretations of disguised action, and language analysis for discovery. Measures of verbal, ideational and projective skills thus appear to be potentially valid operational indicators which may either replace or supplement perceptual measures of disembeddedness. Finally, it needs to be pointed out again that although the global-dependent cognitive style is not empirical and scientific, it does serve the important psychological function of ordering the universe especially when the universe is chaotic and psychologically overwhelming. It helps "to support tenets that would give meaning and hope to the human life... " (Rosenthal, 1971, p.126.).

THE COMPOSED FIELD DEPENDENT IN GROUPS

According to Bales (1970, 1979) the UF character type is ascendent and task-oriented but seeks to promote group loyalty and cooperation in a neutral rather than a friendly or unfriendly manner similar to that of the composed field-dependent. Consistent with Rosenthal's (1971) description of this type in the middle ages, the UF identifies himself with a larger plan in which he seeks to reconcile whatever conflict and disharmony exist among group members. He attempts to preserve group cohesion by promoting loyalty rather than positive and affectionate interpersonal bonds. He is an "ideologue" who professes values of unity by direct suggestion, rather than tailoring his appeal to the particular needs and motives of others (Bales, 1970). His method is rather simplistic, uniform, and impersonal - it is simply to insist that cooperation is necessary, that there is and must be a larger plan, and that individualism of all varieties must be curbed in the interests of the larger plan and unity (Bales, p.214).

The UF group member, according to Bales, usually plays a prominent role in the group. He is inclined to address the group as a whole rather than individuals alone. Others are fairly high in addressing him, although the UF member's initiation of verbal remarks to specific other individuals is low. He is high in giving suggestions and may ask the group to attend to its task as if he were an authority, a position he sometimes assumes in the group (Gruenfeld and Lin, 1984). He concentrates on informational aspects of the problem facing the group. He asks for information rather than giving it. Bales points out that giving much information is also the essence of social conversation "and it may play a large part in dramatizing and joking as well." Thus, the UF leader helps to prepare the groundwork of camaraderie and group fellowship, which facilitates the accomplishment of the group's task.

As previously mentioned, the UF composed field dependent is neither friendly nor unfriendly. He tries to present a balanced and controlled affective view of himself. "In responding to the UF leader, other group members are markedly low on asking him for information and on asking him for his opinion. Cautious attempts to bring him into the group are unnecessary. He is already "in as he can be, by self definition" (Bales, p. 216). The interchange between the UF member and others is "legalistic and cooperative." He gives and receives much agreement. Nonetheless, he is a serious player in the group. He is most likely to come into conflict with ascendent and expressive types who are more playful and distracted and less loyal to the task than the UF composed field-dependent type. The field-independent UNB egotist types and the UPB gregarious dependent types are also likely to annoy him or be annoyed by him. He is clearly committed to both the task and its role members. But he is also impartial and self-controlled and therefore not likely to engage in either personal friendships or animosities. He has a conservative view of the group and its task. He does not move the group toward satisfaction with its interpersonal relationships. He is too detached and not particularly affectionate or sensitive to the feelings of others. He does move group members toward task achievement and that, according to Bales, is his virtue. He seeks unity of purpose rather than being united with others.

It is our conjecture that the composed independent and dependent cognitive styles unlike their stressed derivatives, are not split and segregated, rather they are integrated and inform each other. They may differ in their particular emphasis, but we find it probable that task settings require some emphasis on both the internal and external personal environment, as suggested Gardner (1983). As Blake and Mouton (1967) have suggested, sociability for the mere sake of togetherness, or status totally devoid of work and task accomplishment, is intolerable in groups, families, and organizations. Task and production emphasis without concern for others is also intolerable because it is tyrannical and results in isolation and withdrawal. The composed and integrated field independent/dependent cognitive style blends social solidarity and task accomplishment. A good group is one that is viewed as accepting its authority, other group members, and the shared task of the group. Similarily, an integrated cognitive style would be one that is flexible and moves from dependence to independence. A person with this style would not be rigidly and dogmatically locked into a compulsive repetitive pattern. We suspect that such a pattern, if it exists, is rare and both culturally and personally unique. Most people, cultures, groups, and organizations appear to be more or less specialized.

We conclude this section by gratefully acknowledging the contribution of Professor Bales's (1970, 1979) writings and research to our work on cognitive style. We have been able here to provide only a cursory flavor of his contribution to our taxonomy. The SYMLOG schemata is a remarkably useful breakthrough in the study of individual differences of behavior in groups. His taxonomy also provided us with the metaphors, images and data that helped us reconceptualize our thinking about cognitive and personal styles in groups. Professor Richard Polley has been enormously helpful in teaching us how to use the SYMLOG method and has provided us with invaluable help by letting us share his computer software. Both Bales's and Polley's work has encouraged us to observe individual differences in social behavior directly and systematically, and to work our way backward from the observation of behavior to perceptual measures of cognitive style and personality. Dr. Hy Witkin's work, as well as my personal contacts with him have inspired my research, teaching and pleasure in my academic career. Witkin's own cognitive style nicely integrated profound analytical and integrative abilities as well as humane and socially interested concerns. His sudden and unexpected death in 1979 left an enormous void for all of us who knew him and worked with him. This essay was inspired by Witkin's work and confidence in his theory of Psychological Differentiation. It is hoped that he would have approved by and large of the concerns, criticisms and modifications of his original theory of cognitive styles presented here. We turn now to several methodological issues that are relevant to the study of the field-independent/dependent cognitive style.

METHODOLOGICAL CONCERNS AND CRITIQUES OF RESEARCH ON COGNITIVE STYLES - THE INAPPROPRIATENESS OF THE TIGHTLY CONTROLLED COERCIVE RESEARCH SETTING

The apparent sparsity of current research that relates cognitive style to behavior in groups is due, at least in part, to research designs that undermine the hypotheses that were to be tested. Wachtel (1987) calls into question the appropriateness of tightly controlled social settings for the study of cognitive styles. He draws attention to the range of possible choices and intentions that are normally encountered when one faces another human being. This range of choices is restricted in most social psychological experiments and precluded in the very measurement of cognitive style that is based on pass-fail criteria. Groups, however, are loosely coupled role systems that require choices among adaptive strategies. The more controlled the research setting, the more likely that subjects will feel coerced to respond in a manner that is atypical for them (Argyris, 1980). Research conditions that limit alternatives, either of choices or behavior, cannot account for individual differences in predispositional cognitive styles. Such experiments expurgate individual differences. Thus, the presumed "rigour" of the project "rigs" its findings when it concludes that individual differences in cognitive style make no difference.

Unlike the precise instructions given to task groups which aim to measure speed and accuracy of productivity, the task instructions given to group members in the analytical self study group we observed are left deliberately vague because the ambiguity of the task is designed to encourage the expression of stylistic dimensions of personality functioning (Lazarus, Baker, Broverman and Mayer). Pervin (1984) has defined the appropriate setting for research on individual differences as follows: "While the underlying personality organization may be expressed in all behaviors and in all situations, it will be particularly apparent in unstructured situations and in areas associated with conflict for the individual" (Pervin, p.18). Pervin also encourages the use of "loosely coupled" research settings in which subjects can choose and formulate their own conditions and activate their preferred problem solving styles and abilities. Pervin urges inclusion of conflict situations, not only because it enhances personal construal and choice but a!so because it promotes "ego involvement." Ickes (1982) has shown how the use of an open-ended, precipitating, interpersonal paradigm, unlike a highly structured study situation, permits observation of personality disposition. Gruenfeld and Lin (1984) have also shown how an open ended, conflictual, and precipitating research study setting produces substantial correlations between field independence/dependence and behavior in groups. Ickes (1982) distinguishes between psychologically strong and weak test situations and suggests that only the unstructured "weak" situation is appropriate for the study of individual differences of behavior in groups.

Burns and Stalker (1961) have identified two contrasting settings for the study and observation of behavior in work groups, the mechanistic task environment and the organic one. The mechanistic task environment is described as consisting of stable conditions with specialized and "tightly" prescribed tasks and roles. In the mechanistic task groups, subjects are mainly concerned with technical improvements of the means rather than specifications of ends. These are the task groups that are governed by concerns for efficiency. These tasks are usually closely supervised and otherwise restricted by rules, duties, and obligations. Interaction in the mechanistic setting is mainly hierarchical, between superior and subordinate. In contrast to the mechanistic task environment is the relatively more fluid, organic one. The organic task environment gives rise to unforeseen problems that leave the definition of means and ends to the participants who must reconstruct their environment so that they can pragmatically deal with it. "The organic setting requires the continual renegotiation of tasks by bargaining with others. Interaction is horizontal and control of behavior is derived from a presumed community of interests in the progress of the relationship. The atmophere is marked by consultation rather than command, advice rather than instruction" (Gruenfeld and Lin, 1984). The organic form of social setting is distinguished by anxiety and conflict among the members about what they should be doing. This environment is appropriate for the study of cognitive style in groups.

CLASSIFICATION OF ORGANIC TASKS: ENVIRONMENT FOR THE STUDY OF COGNITIVE STYLE DIFFERENCES

McGrath (1984) has provided a circumplex of tasks for the study of behavior in groups. McGrath proposes four general performance processes that are engaged by the group task: to Generate (alternatives); to Choose (alternatives); to Negotiate; and to Execute (p.61). This process-focused typology identifies the tasks that are liable to precipitate observable cognitive style predispositions. For example, the Choose process is distinguished by either intellective tasks for which there is a correct answer or the discussion tasks for which the right answer is the group's consensus. These tasks are subdivided further into cooperative- and conflict-inclined interaction. Under conditions of conflict, the group task is less to choose than to negotiate. Furthermore there are conflicts of viewpoint, both cognitive conflicts and conflicts of interest or motives. These types of tasks are remarkably well-suited for the study of cognitive styles and are contrasted with tasks in which there are demonstrably right answers and "the group's task is to compute the correct answer" (McGrath, p.63).

It is banal by now to assert that behavior and experience are functions of both person and situation. Witkin has provided a fertile theory of personal dispositions. Moreover, McGrath has generated an appropiate process oriented theory of tasks that will permit systematic assessment of interactive effects between cognitive style variables and task variables on social behavior. Progress in the study of the effects of field independent/dependent cognitive style will depend considerably on the use of precipitating, loosely-coupled research paradigm conditions. In any event, future research studies should investigate and report how free subjects felt to display their stylistic predispositions (Wachtel, 1987).

SUMMARY AND CONCLUSIONS

This essay calls for a reassessment of the polarized unidimensional construction of the field independent/dependent cognitive style. The emergent impresice and "idealized" conception of exclusively depersonalized or totally individualized notion of psychological functioning limits the progress of research because it oversimplifies and often caricaturizes a vital strategy of social behavior and experience. Moreover, the field independent and dependent stylistic qualities coexist because, it is proposed, persons cannot function without some attention to both internal and external concerns. Future research and theorizing should therefore seek to integrate the independent and dependent dimensions of psychological functioning and "differentiate" the bipolar typology by postulating several nuances of the field independent/dependent cognitive style. A precisely calibrated integrated and multidimensional typology is however not a theory. A great deal of conceptual and theoretical work which will describe both the antecedent and consequent characteristics of cognitive style will therefore be required if research in this area is to make significant progress. Based on both formal and informal study of subjects behavior in self analytic study groups

(Gruenfeld and Lin, 1984) this essay is an initial attempt to articulate a multidimensional typology of cognitive styles.

A selected review of research in the domain of leadership and teaching styles demonstrates the utility of the field independent/dependent dimension to predict stylistic preferences in social influence behavior. On the positive side these findings show that field independence/dependence is not merely a visual or purely intellective orientation, as some critics have claimed. The entire body of knowledge provides considerable evidence for the construct validity of the Rod and Frame test and the Embedded Figures Test that is consistent with Witkin's theory. On the negative side the many nuances of stylistic leadership and teaching style differences previously identified are profoundly underestimated. Considerable, as yet unexplained "error" variance in the relationship between cognitive style and influence (leadership) behavior bids for explanation.

The present authors call for the modification of the stereotypical orientation of researchers in this field who describe field independents as merely analytical, rigorous and managerial and field dependents as merely intuitive, facile and ministerial. Both, formal as well as informal observation of field independent and dependent group members shows that these interpretations are value biased grossly exaggerated and misunderstood (Gruenfeld and Lin, 1984).

The future research strategy suggested in this paper is to observe social behavior directly and to index these observations with measures of the field independent/dependent perceptual style. To this end we proposed that anxiety and stress be employed as moderators of the field independent/dependent style.

The system we have adopted for the observation of field dependents/independents behavior in groups is SYMLOG (System for the Multiple Level Observation of Behavior in Groups) developed by F. Bales. The behavioral and attitudinal (images) variables which both guide and abstract these observations are based upon considerable research and theoretical development (Bales, 1978).

Based on our observation that anxiety and stress may undermine the performance of independents and augment the performance of field dependents in self analytic groups, we propose in this essay a discernment between composed (integrated) and stressed (fractionated) personal styles. Stressed field independents are either egotistical (self centered-narcissistic) or anti-social (aggressive-authoritarian). Stressed field dependents are either withdrawn (submissive-phlegmatic) or gregarious (succoring-social).

Finally, there are two composed or integrated types. The composed field independent and the composed field dependent. The composed field independent is committed to group goals and the authority structure. He reasons analytically, independently and with conviction within the constraints of the tasks and the social norms of the group. He is a (conservative) empiricists. The composed field dependent is coextensive with the group. He is idealistic about the group, speculative rather than analytical and interpersonally engrossed rather than detached from other group members. He is kind and compassionate. He is a (liberal) intellectual. According to Sowell (1987) the expressive liberal-intellectual and constrained conservative-empiricist subscribe to different and conflicting visions about knowledge and reason, as well as the social process. Sowell, has provided a fertile assembly of hypothesis about the composed field independent and composed field dependent type which are testable and should provide an enriched view to supplement Witkin's original work.

Last but not least future research on field independence and dependence will be well advised to test hypothesis in relatively conflicted and unstructured social situations not only because these permit personal construal and choice (a basic assumption of the manifestation of stylistic behaviors and preferences) but also because they are "ego involving" and therefore more likely than "rigorous" experimentally controlled situations to engender stylistic individual differences. McGrath (1984) has provided a circumplex of group tasks that should be useful for the description of various research settings in which individual differences have been observed. Relatedly, it will also behoove investigators to describe and vary systematically the population parameters on which research was conducted in terms of gender, age and social class because these variables are implicated and correlated with cognitive styles.

REFERENCES

ADORNO, T.W., FRENKEL-BRUNSWIK, E., LEVINSON, D.J. & SANFORD, R. N. The Authoritarian Personality. NY: Harper, 1950.

ANDERSON, C.R., & SCHNEIER, C.E. Locus of Control, Leader-Behavior and Leader Performance Among Management Students. Academy of Management Journal, 21, 1978, 690-698.

ARBUTHNOT, J. & GRUENFELD, L.W. Field Independence and educational-vocational interests. Journal of Consulting and Clinical Psychology, 33, 1969, 631.

ARGYRIS, C. Inner Contradictions of Rigorous Research. NY: Academic Press, 1980.

ARMSTRONG, D.G. Team Teaching and Academic Achievement. Review of Educational Research, 47, 1977, 65-86.

ATSUMI, R. Patterns of personal relationships: A key to understanding Japanese thought and behavior. Social Analysis, 6, 1980, 63-78.

BAKAN, D. The Duality of Human Existence. Chicago: Rand McNally & Co., 1966.

BALES, R.F. & COHEN, S.P. SYMLOG - A System for the Multiple Level Observation of Groups. NY: Free Press, 1979.

BALES, R.F. Personality and Interpersonal Behavior. NY: Holt, Rinehart and Winston, 1970.

BELL, D. The Cultural Contradictions of Capitalism. NY: Basic Books Inc., 1976.

BERNARDIN, H.J. & BOWNAS D.A. Personality Assessment in Organizations. NY: Praeger Publishers, 1985.

BERRY, J.W. Human Ecology and Cognitive Style. NY: John Wiley & Sons, 1976.

BLAKE, R.R. & MOUTON, J.S. The Managerial Grid. Houston, TX: Gulf Publishing Co., 1964.

BRUNER, J.S. Personality Dynamics and the Process of Perceiving in Perception - An Approach to Personality, Robert Blake and Glen Ramsey (eds). NY: The Ronald Press Co., 1951, 121.

BURNES, T. & STALKER, G.M. The Management of Innovation. London: Tavistock, 1961.

CAMPBELL, D.T. & FISKE, D.W. Convergent and Discriminant Validation by the Multitrait-Multimethod Matrix. Psychological Bulletin, 56, 1959, 81-105.

CHRISTIE, R. & GEIS F.L. Studies in Machiavellianism. NY: Academic Press, 1970.

DiSTEFANO, J. Interpersonal perceptions of field independent and field dependent teachers and students (Doctoral dissertation, Cornell University, 1969). Dissertation Abstracts International, 1970, 31, pps. 463A-464A. (University Microfilms No. 70-11, 225).

EMMERICH, W. & SHEPARD, K. Cognitive factors in the development of sex-typed preferences. Sex Roles, 11, 1984, 11-12.

EMMERICH, W. & SHEPARD, K. Development of sex- differentiated preferences during late childhood and adolescence. Developmental Psychology, 18, 1982, 406-417.

EREZ, M. Correlates of leadership style: Field-dependence and social intelligence versus social orientation. Perceptual and Motor Skills, 50, 1980, 231-238.

EYSENCK, H.J. & EYSENCK, M.W. Personality and Individual Differences. NY: Plenum Press, 1985.

EYSENCK, H.J. & WILSON, G.D. The Psychological Basis of Ideology. Lancaster: Medical and Technical Publishers (Baltimore: University Park Press, 1978), 1978.

FIEDLER, F.E. & GARCIA, J.E. New approaches to effective leadership: cognitive resources and organizational performance. Wiley, 1987.

FINE, B. Field-dependent introverts and neuroticism: Eysenck and Witkin united. Psychological Reports, 31, 1972, 939-956.

FINE, B.J. & DANFORTH, A.V. Field-dependence, extraversion and perception of the vertical: Empirical and theoretical perspectives of the rod and frame test. Perceptual and Motor Skills, 40, 1975, 683-693.

FINE, B.J. & KOBRICK, J.L. Note on the relationship between introversion - extraversion, field-dependence-independence and accuracy of visual target detection. Perceptual and Motor Skills, 42, 1976, 763-766.

FINE, B.J. & KOLBRICK, J.L. Field-dependence, practice and low illumination as related to the Farnsworth-Mussell 100-Hue test. Perceptual and Motor Skill, 51, 1980, 1167-1177.

FINE, B.J. Field-dependence, extraversion, Eysenck and autarky. Personality and Individual Differences, 4, 1983, 359-360.

FISHBEIN, M. & AJZEN, I. Attitudes Towards Objects as Predicators of Single and Multiple Behavioral Criteria. Psychological Review, 81, 1974, 59-74.

FISHBEIN, M. & AJZEN, I. Beliefs, Attitude, Intention and Behavior: An Introduction to Theory and Research. Addison-Wesley: MA, 1975.

FORSYTH, D.R. Group Dynamics. CA: Brooks/Cole Publishing Co., 1983.

FROMM, E. Escape from Freedom. NY: Farrar and Rinehart, Inc., 1941.

FROMM, E. Man For Himself. NY: Rinehart and Company, Inc., 1947.

GARDNER, H. Frames of Mind: The Theory of Multiple Intelligences. NY: Basic Books, Inc., 1983.

GOODENOUGH, D.R. & KARO, S.A. Field dependence and intellectual functioning. Journal Abnormal Soc. Psychol., 63, 1961.

GOODENOUGH, D.R. & KARP, S.A. Field dependence and intellectual functioning. J. Abnorm. Soc. Psychol., 63, 1961, 241-246.

GOODENOUGH, D.R. Styles of Cognitive-Personality Functioning. In: Personality Assessment in Organizations, edited by H. John Bernardin and David A. Bownas. NY: Praeger Publishers, 1985.

GOODSTADT, B.E. and HJELLE, L.A. Power to the powerless: Locus of control and the use of power. Journal of Personality and Social Psychology, 27, 1973, 190-196.

GRUENFELD, L. & KASSUM, S. Supervisory style and organizational effectiveness in a pediatric hospital. Personnel Psychology, 26, (4), 1973, 531-544.

GRUENFELD, L. & LIN, Thung-Rung. Social Behavior of Field Independents and Dependents in an Organic Group. In: Human Relations, Vol.37, No. 9., 1984, 721-741.

GRUENFELD, L. & SEIBERT, S. Analysis of Unconscious References to Leadership and Authority in Groups: A Case of Evaluation Anxiety (unpublished paper), 1988.

GRUENFELD, L. & WEISSENBERG. Relationship Among Leadership Dimensions and Cognitive Style. Journal of Applied Psychology, 50, 1966.

GRUENFELD, L. Cognitive Style - Field Dependence/Independence as a Framework for the Study of Task and Social Orientations in Organizational Leadership. In: Managing for Accomplishment, edited by Bernard M. Bass et al., Heath Lexington Books, Publishers, 1970.

GRUENFELD, L.W. & ALPERT, R. Cognitive Style and Accuracy of Interpersonal Perception. (1989 unpublished manuscript).

GRUENFELD, L.W. & ARBUTHNOT, J. Field Independence as a Conceptual Framework for Prediction of Variability in Ratings of Others. Perceptual and Motor Skills, Vol. 28, 1969.

GRUENFELD, L.W. & MacEACHRON, A.E. Relationship between age, socioeconomic status, and field dependence. Perceptual and Motor Skills, Vol. 28, 1975.

GRUENFELD, L.W. & NEDD, A. A Study of Differences Among Six Different Ethnic Groups in Trinidad. Journal of International Psychology, 1976.

GRUENFELD, L.W. & WEISSENBERG. Field Independence and Articulation of Sources of Job Satisfaction. Journal of Applied Psychology, 1971.

HALL, C. S. & GARDNER, L. Theories of Personality. NY: John Wiley & Sons, 1978.

HOFSTEDE, G. Culture's Consequences. Beverly Hills, CA: Sage, 1980.

HOLLANDER, E. P. Leadership Dynamics. NY: The Free Press, 1978.

HSU, F.L.K. American and Chinese: Passage to differences. Honolulu: University of Hawaii Press, 1981.

HUDSON, L. Contrary Imaginations. London: Metheun, 1966a.

HUDSON, L. Frames of Mind. Methuen and Co. Ltd, 1968.

ICKES, W. A Basic Paradigm for the Study of Personality, Roles and Social Behavior. In: W. Ickes and E.S. Knowles, eds. Personality, Roles, and Social Behavior. NY: Springer-Verlag, 1982.

KARP, S.A. Field dependence and overcoming embeddedness. J. Consult. Psychol., 27, 1963, 294-302.

KATZ, D. & KAHN, R.L. The Social Psvchology of Organizations. NY: John Wiley & Sons, 1978.

KLEIN, G.S. The Personal World Through Perception. In: Perception - An Approach to Personality, Robert Blake and Glen Ramsey (eds.), p. 328. NY: The Ronald Press Co, 1951.

LEVY, S. Field independence-field dependence and occupational interests. Unpublished masters thesis, Cornell University, 1969.

LEWIS, H.B. Shame and Guilt in Neuorsis. NY: International Universities Press, Inc., 1971.

LONDON, H. & EXNER, Jr., J.E. Dimensions of Personality. NY: John Wiley and Sons, 1978.

MACCOBY, M. The Gamesman. NY: Bantam Books, 1976.

MacEACHRON, A.E. & GRUENFELD, L.W. The effects of family authority structure and socioeconomic status on field independence. Journal of Social Psychology, 104, 1978, 49-56.

MacEACHRON, A.E. Two Interactive Perspectives on the Relationship between Job Level and Job Satisfaction. Organizational Behavior and Human Performance, 19, 1977, 226-246.

MacEACHRON, A.E. Two Interactive Perspectives on the Relationship between Job Level and Job Satisfaction. Organizational Behavior and Human Performance, 19, 1977, 226-246.

MADDI, S.R. Personality Theories: A Comparative Analysis, 3rd Edition. Homewood, IL: The Dorsey Press, 1976.

McGRATH, J.E. Groups: Interaction and Performance. NY: Prentice Hall, 1984.

MIKLLON, T. Disorders of Personality, DSM-111; Axis 11. NY: John Wiley & Sons, 1981.
MILLON, T. Disorders of Personality. Wiley-Interscience, 1981.
MITCHELL, S.A. Relational Concepts in Psychoanalysis: An Integration. Harvard University Press, 1988.
MOORE, C.A. Styles of teacher behavior under simulated teaching conditions (Doctoral dissertation, Stanford University, 1973). Dissertation Abstracts International, 34, 1973, pps. 3149A-3150A. (University Microfilms No. 73-30, 449).
MUNROE, R.L. Schools of Psychoanalytic Thought. NY: Holt, Rinehart and Winston, 1955.
NISBET, R. Twilight of Authority. NY: Oxford University Press, 1975.
PASCALE, R.T. & ATHOS, A.G. The Art of Japanese Management: Applications for American Executives. NY: Simon & Schuster, 1981.
PERVIN, L.A. Personality: Theory and Research, 4th Edition. NY: John Wiley & Sons, Inc., 1984.
PETERSON, C. & SCOTT, W.A. Generally and Topic Specificity of Cognitive Styles. Journal of Research in Personality, 9, 1975, 366-374.
PROVOST, G.L. Teaching strategies, modes of evaluation, and field-dependence factor. Perceptual and Motor Skills, 52, 1981, 163-173.
PROVOST, G.L. The effects of two teaching strategies and of two modes of evaluation on the performance of learners of different cognitive styles. Dissertation Abstracts International, 40, 1980, 5834-5835.
QUINLAN, D.M. & BLATT, S.J. Field articulation and performance under stress: Differential predictions in surgical and psychiatric nursing training. Journal of Consulting and Clinical Psychology, 39, 1972, 517. .
RIESMAN, D. The Lonely Crowd. London: Yale University Press, 1961.
ROSENTHAL, B.G. The Images of Man. NY: Basic Books, 1971.
SARACHO, O.N. & DAYTON, C.M. Relationship of teachers' cognitive styles to pupils' academic achievement gains. Journal of Educational Psychology, 72, 1981, 544-549.
SARACHO, O.N. & SPODEK, B. The teachers' cognitive styles and their educational implications. Educational Forum, 45, 1981, 153-159.
SCHEIN, E.H. Organizational Culture and Leadership. NY: Jossey-Bass Publishers, 1985.
SEIBERT, S.E. Master's Thesis entitled, The Utility of an Unstructured Setting for the Assessment of Personality and Interpersonal Behavior, 1988.
SHEPEL, L.F. & JAMES, W.H. Persistence as a function of a locus of control, task structure and reinforcement schedule. Proceedings of the 81st Annual Convention of the APA, Montreal, 8, 1973, 301-302.
SNYDER, M. & ICKES, W. Personality and Social Behavior. In: G. Lindsey & E. Aronson (Eds.), Handbook of Social Psychology, 32, 1975, 637-644.
SPECTOR, P.E. Behavior in organizations as a function of employee's locus of control. Psychological Bulletin, 91, 1982, 482-497.
TRIANDIS, H.C. The Self and Social Behavior in Differing Cultural Contexts. Psychological Review, 96, 1989, 506-520.
VERNON, P.E. Intelligence and Cultural Environment. London: Methuen, 1969.

VERNON, P.E. The Distinctiveness of Field Independence. Journal of Personality, 40, 1972, 366-391.

WACHTEL, P. Action and Insight. NY: Guilford Press, 1987, 296-314.

WEISS, H.M. & ADLER, S. Personality and Organizational Behavior. Research in Organizational Behavior, Vol. 6, 1984, 1-50.

WITKIN, H.A. Cognitive Styles in Personal and Cultural Adaptation. Clark University Press, 1978.

WITKIN, H.A. et al. Psychological Differentiation. NY: John Wiley & Sons, Inc., 1962.

WITKIN, H.A. The role of cognitive style in academic performance and in teacher-student relations. Educational Testing Services Research Bulletin. Princeton, NJ: Education Testing Service, 1973.

WITKIN, H.A. The role of cognitive style in academic performance and in teacher-student relations. Educational Testing Services Research Bulletin. Princeton, NJ: Education Testing Service, 1973.

ZYTOWSKY, D.G., MILLS, D.H. & PAEPE, C. Psychological differentiation and the stress vocational-interest blank. Journal of Counseling Psychology, 16, 41-44.

Leaders and Followers in a Postindustrial Age: A Psychodynamic View

Larry Hirschhorn

INTRODUCTION

Of the many demands posed by the postindustrial milieu (Hirschhorn, 1988), perhaps the most poignant is the need for leaders and their subordinates to recognize their dependence on one another. The rationale for this need is simple and pragmatic: The pressures dictated by postindustrial technological advancements; the pace, depth, and accumulation of change; and the complexity and consequences of decisions all require the maximum use of resources, particularly human resources. In brief, the leader no longer charts the organization' s work, with subordinates lined up to do the bidding. Instead, the leader and the subordinates must collaborate.

As Krantz (1990) suggests, collaboration requires that the parties recognize the need to collaborate - that is, the need to actively depend on each other. In addition to an explicit dependency built into the subordinate's role, the subordinate often brings to that role an implicit assumption of "leader as authority." If, however, the leader attempts to make a more collaborative connection by acknowledging dependence on the subordinate, that leader in effect exposes a kind of vulnerability. The subordinate may cease to perceive the leader as omnipotent, and may ignore - or even thwart - the leader's attempts.

Likewise, if followers attempt to develop a more collaborative process and thereby alter their relatively passive and dependent role, they also expose their own vulnerability. Furthermore, they risk alienating their leader, who may feel that her or his authority is being undermined, and may experience a sense of impotence. Thus, leaders may also ignore or thwart their followers' attempts.

This article explores - primarily from the leader's perspective - the delicate dynamics of leaders' and followers' situations as they grope toward more collaborative relationships. The rewards of collaboration are numerous, both for business and for furthering a fuller sense of community in the workplace. A price is paid for this, however: Such collaboration requires sophisticated psychological work. All participants must be willing to acknowledge the individual

---

Reprinted with permission from NTL Institute, "Leaders and Followers in a Postindustrial Age: A Psychodynamic View" by Larry Hirschhorn, pp. 529-542, Journal of Applied Behavioral Science, Vol. 26, No. 4, copyright 1990.

vulnerability that accompanies their recognizing their true dependency, and must confront the shame, anger, and disappointment that stem from exposing that vulnerability.

The first section of this article presents a series of vignettes showing the difficulties leaders experience in coming to terms with vulnerability, both as individuals and as leaders. In the second section, I discuss how followers can hamper leaders as they seek to expose their vulnerability. In two vignettes, leaders try to share their uncertainties (i.e., acknowledge a "we're-in-this-together" atmosphere), only to have their efforts foiled. The third section describes an extended case in which a leader and his subordinates try to reach out to each other. When they ultimately connect, their subsequent interactions are refreshed, the clarity of their work increases, and their respect for one another is manifested.

The concluding section discusses evolving forms of workplace relationships, the mechanisms fostering them, and their implications. For the collaborative approach, I speculate on how personal feelings and role need to be integrated differently, particularly on the leader's part.

LEADERS

The Leader as a Person: The Need for Vulnerability

The purpose of the first encounter I had with Frank, a vice president of a large division in a pharmaceutical company, was to assess whether we could work together productively. He began by sketching the company's various divisions on a flip chart, and then indicated how much revenue each division generated. I was struck by his control of the facts and how easily he described the company's organization. He seemed comfortable discussing the billions of dollars generated by the different divisions and describing management' s resource allocation decisions. This man seemed to be "in charge."

As Frank continued, however, I became increasingly confused about his role. When he finally identified his position - senior executive of a division within a subsidiary - I realized that his ease of presentation had led me to believe that his rank was much closer to the company's most senior executives than it actually was. Moreover, I realized that he had never mentioned his own subordinates, the people he worked with every day. I began to suspect I was discovering a fantasy he had about himself: that he worked only with numbers and dollars and was a grand strategist collaborating with the company's top management.

Hoping to gain more insight, I stopped Frank in the middle of his story and asked him to tell me about the people he worked with. To my surprise, he sat down as if deflated, and then began to describe the confusion he felt in leading his own team. The senior management had dramatically restructured the company in the last five years, and required the divisions to produce more profit, greater revenues, and better-quality products, but with fewer people and greater attention to productivity and safety. The company had sponsored many programs to improve effectiveness in areas such as quality, safety, and work simplification, and these programs had greatly complicated the task of managing his division's activities.

In addition, following the example of other division vice presidents and responding to pressure from his own team, Frank had started a "visioning process," working with those reporting directly to him and some of their subordinates to produce a vision for his division. Yet he felt uncertain about the value of this activity. He asked me what I thought of vision statements. Could they be written without being linked to a business plan? Had he been right to "yield" to his subordinates' pressure to write such a statement? If the statement affirmed employees' rights to a better quality of work life, would he be "shooting himself in the foot"? After all, following several years of cutbacks, his employees could only feel overworked and exploited, and what could he do about that?

Listening to him, I understood that his subordinates were painful reminders of the confusion he faced in linking all these corporate programs and objectives to the day-to-day work of his division. Feeling confused themselves, his subordinates wanted a vision, but Frank was unsure of whether he could give them one. Perhaps he could not lead them, he felt. It now became clear why I had overestimated his position when he first spoke. He was feeling uncertain of his own role. By appearing to be more important than he was, he was not simply trying to impress me. Rather, he was projecting a defensive fantasy that made him feel more in control of his situation than he actually was. In doing so, however, Frank not only distanced himself from me, he distanced himself psychologically from the very people he had to depend on to do his work successfully. As our conversation came to an end, he said he wanted me to help him "stay ahead" of his subordinates. How could he lead them otherwise? I told him that as I had been listening to him I had thought, "Frank is asking for answers, but I keep wondering, 'What are the questions?'"

This vignette exemplifies many of the dilemmas and challenges leaders face today. Pressed to advance on many different fronts -

quality, revenues, profits, productivity, and safety - Frank did not know how to integrate these efforts. Aware that his employees felt overworked and exploited, he was afraid to raise their expectations, yet he wanted to relate to them effectively through some shared vision of the division. His confusion made him feel ineffective, and to compensate for this feeling he identified with the senior management of the company. He imagined that by internalizing their strategic vision and projecting it as his own, he could delimit his own sense of vulnerability. But he could not develop an effective connection to his subordinates, his own management team. Their confusion stimulated his, and when they pressed him to lead (i.e., asked him to give them a vision), he was wary. To break out of this vicious circle, Frank needed to affirm his confusion - his vulnerability - and see it as a starting point for his development rather than as a signal of defeat.

Frank, I suggest, was facing the dilemmas of leading in a postindustrial age. The individual leader needs talent and imagination, but today cannot grasp the complexities of the social field alone. The leader needs subordinates. This requirement challenges leaders' sophistication and maturity. All leaders must have sufficient self-regard to cope with the disappointments ambition inevitably produces. Their "narcissism" helps them sacrifice current pleasures for the sake of an ideal image of their lives while protecting them from the psychological damage competitors want to inflict. Today leaders must also acknowledge their dependency on - and thus their vulnerability to - the strengths and weaknesses of others so they can get the help they need. They therefore face the complicated task of simultaneously identifying with their ambitions and their limitations. They must step beyond their formal roles and present themselves to their subordinates as human beings having not just strengths, but also limits and uncertainties.

The Leader as Role: The Need for Organizational Authority

Leaders must be vulnerable to their subordinates, which requires leaders to reveal more of their "personhoods." They cannot hide behind the role of leader, but instead must bring more of their passions, fears, and values to it. Yet the role cannot be ignored. Leaders can neither pretend to be "just one person talking to another," nor act as if differences in power and authority between them and their subordinates can be ignored.

Consider Harry, the senior partner of a public relations firm, an enormously charming man who was well liked by his associates. Several of the women in particular felt comfortable remonstrating with him; for example, at times they told him not to talk for other women at the firm's meetings and to let associates finish their sentences. I felt drawn to the firm's family atmosphere and to the camaraderie that encouraged humor and spontaneity.

Yet, as I learned at a two-day retreat, this informality was matched by a feeling that secrets and cabals shaped much of the firm's development. For example, one year earlier the firm's three partners had nominated two associates to the partnership but neither was able to generate business, and both left the firm before the retreat. The remaining associates were enraged. Why had these two people been made partners? What criteria were used? Why were these decisions seemingly made behind closed doors? Why did the firm have no public criteria for advancement? Why did the partners' decision making often seem arbitrary? The subject of the firm's promotion policy was paramount during the retreat. In effect, because the partners - particularly the senior partner - related to the firm as if it were their family, they also treated it as their private domain. Harry's personableness and warmth deprived the firm of the qualities of an organization, of the roles, rules, and procedures that help people feel secure. Indeed, because it lacked organization, the firm was not growing as rapidly as it could. Although they were experts in public relations, the partners were unable and unwilling to actually shape a marketing plan and process that could discipline the work of all the firm's members. Ultimately, the firm suffered from Harry's excessive personalism and his inability to take on a more formal role.

Consider also the following situation. I was working with an architectural services firm that was growing quickly and faced organizational and planning challenges. Perry, the senior partner and a majority owner of the firm, was an immensely charming man with the gift of gab and a capacity to sell the firm's services to a wide range of customers. As we worked together, I imagined that I was getting close to him. He confided many of the firm's "secrets" to me. After a complicated planning retreat, I wrote him a "hot" letter full of feeling and rich in thought (or so I believed) about the firm's dynamics. I regretted doing so, for Perry called me two days later, said he was appalled that I could write such a letter, and proposed that he send it right back.

What was going on? Just as he sold services to his clients, Perry had "sold" me on the character of our "special" working relationship. I believe my experiences highlighted the character of his leadership. He led his group by means of seduction, using "secrets" and special conversations to maintain personal control over the direction of the firm. Far from taking a formal role and acting through a formal structure, he developed special relationships with several partners so that each imagined he or she was especially close to him. The resulting feelings and fantasies people developed about him did not empower them, nor did they encourage critical thinking, much less collaboration. Instead, as I discovered, people wanted to please him so that they could maintain their individual special relationships with him. When they got too close, however, Perry could control the relationships and indeed regulate their moods by simply cutting off communication. In other words, by acting too much out of his person rather than his role, and by mobilizing his charm rather than his authority, he created a nearly toxic environment that lacked order and structure.

In a postindustrial milieu, leaders cannot use their role defensively to hide their uncertainty and vulnerability. But, as these vignettes suggest, if they deny the salience of their formal role and the differences between them and their subordinates, they can create a climate of uncertainty and insecurity. Frank hid behind his role as leader to such an extent that he conjured up another leadership position, even while his subordinates clamored for collaboration (i.e., the "visioning process"). Harry and Perry each set up a false intimacy that mimicked collaboration, but in fact barred their followers' participation. The followers were trapped in the dynamics of pleasing these men and were denied the organizational structure leaders must provide.

This section describes types of leaders ranging from those who lean too much toward the role to those who lean too much toward the person. Followers also have responsibilities when they attempt to collaborate, yet if their leader asks for help (unlike Frank, Harry, or Perry), does that mean that they can respond? What are the anxieties of followers?

FOLLOWERS

Consider the following vignette. A co-consultant and I were working with Greg, a superintendent, and his principals on the challenge of decentralizing school district governance. During a critical meeting, we first met with the principals and asked them to develop questions for Greg about "site-based (i.e., school building-based) management." The questions were sensible and conveyed the principals' core anxieties. Most important, they wanted to know how Greg would evaluate their performance in this new system of governance, and what level of confusion in school buildings he would tolerate.

Greg then joined the meeting. As he examined the list of questions and talked with the principals, it soon became obvious that he had no clear answers. He was not sure how his role and theirs would be shaped by the politics of the board of education. He noted that at a time when taxpayers demanded objective measures of teacher performance, the entire evaluation system could be revised. He seemed comfortable, however, with his own uncertainty and periodically said, "I don't know. I am thinking out loud here." He did, however, emphasize that even as they promoted teacher participation in their own buildings, the principals should have control over basics such as bus schedules, supplies, and the budget. He argued that without these basics in place, teacher participation would never work.

Curiously, when Greg was present the principals seemed tongue-tied and their conversation was stiff. After Greg left and the principals examined their encounter with him, they were genuinely puzzled over their own passivity. They felt certain, however, that Greg had warned them, in an almost punishing way, to get control of the basic management tasks in their buildings. I asked the principals, "Did you feel that Greg was punishing you just now?" Several said that indeed he was. I suggested that Greg's thinking, although not completely coherent, was certainly complex, and could not be reduced to a few simple injunctions or remonstrations. I also said that Greg was exploring difficult issues in the same way they were.

What was going on? The principals were clearly anxious about their ability to function in a decentralized setting. Perhaps they were passive because they had hoped that Greg would tell them how to function in this new setting and assure them, despite their confusion, that they were indeed good managers. When he did not meet their needs for dependency, when he did not give them answers, they were unable to talk directly with him. Adults who assume professional roles expect to feel competent. When they feel incompetent - as when the principals were tongue-tied - they feel ashamed. This suggests that the principals interpreted their incompetence as a sign that they were bad managers.

That is also why when Greg suggested that a participative climate could develop only in a setting where the basics were secured, the principals considered this a reproach, a statement that they were bad building managers. In short, when their leader revealed his confusion as well as his willingness to collaborate with his subordinates, this frightened them. Consequently, they grew passive and "incompetent" and, instead of regarding Greg as open, they felt he was punishing their perceived incompetence.

Clearly, the prospect of decentralized decision making in the schools (i.e., of site-based management) made the principals feel insecure and anxious. Indeed, while Greg was being shown the flip chart with their questions, one principal named Fred whispered frequently to a colleague on his right, like a schoolboy, but never contributed to the group discussion. He then stood up, walked to the flip chart, and added the word "my" to the question "How will this program affect our evaluations?" I was struck by Fred's willingness to expose his anxiety. Because of his whispering during the meeting, I believe that when he added "my" to the phrase on the flip chart he acted not as an adult taking a risk, but as a dependent child who simply wanted protection. He was first and foremost concerned about his performance, and thus was not ready to collaborate with Greg. Rather than remaining silent in Greg' s presence, he asserted his competence in a counterdependent manner by periodically whispering.

Undermining the Leader's Vulnerability

Subordinates may also resist the leader who exposes her or his vulnerability - and thus brings one' s person to the role of leader - in other ways and for other reasons. For example, consider Marie, a senior professional in a work methods division of a large engineering services company, who asked me to help facilitate the division's executive retreat. The group members accounted for 25% of the company's profits, but felt neglected by upper management and exploited by their clients. Asked frequently to go to on long, remote assignments, the group members felt isolated from one another and burdened by clients who wanted work done "now!" They felt as if they were part of a "body shop" in which they, as interchangeable parts, were simply "rented" out to clients as technical assistants on narrowly defined job-analysis tasks. Particular pieces of their work might be satisfying, but overall the group members felt alone and uneasy.

At the retreat the group members spent a lot of time discussing their malaise. Although they had a good sense of their problems, they seemed unable to act as a group to improve their situation. Marie described an example in which the group members, facing a downturn had developed some good advertising copy for their services and obtained several inquiries from potential clients, but then simply failed to follow through with them.

They also talked of developing new task-analysis software and committing division funds for this project, but Tom, the most successful senior manager in the group, was wary. Using the group's lingo of "green" as billed time and "nongreen" as unbilled time, he noted that if any members were allocated to work on this software, "The more nongreen someone else is, the more green I have to be." I concurred, adding that they were struggling with the dilemmas involved in acting collectively. Reflecting on these problems earlier, Lynn, a senior work methods specialist, had told the group, "Did you ever try to coach soccer with seven-year-olds? Well, we're like that: No matter what someone tells us, we do what we want."

As the retreat unfolded, I saw that the group members felt trapped partly because they were disappointed in their group leader, Hal. He was a highly respected professional and had written a classic textbook in the field of industrial methods. But he appeared to be too easygoing and soft on the people around him, and did not fight for his group's rights when dealing with the corporate office.

I observed the dilemmas resulting from his leadership and from the group's incapacity to support him on the first morning of the retreat. As the group members continued to discuss their dilemmas, their malaise deepened. John, a long-term member of the division, who had been standing at the door for much of the time, said, "This is the same old shit. I need to go back to the office. I have to leave." Hal protested and asked him to stay, but John walked out anyway. Hal then told everyone else to take a break. I responded by saying that just because John left the others did not have to, and encouraged them to think about this before choosing what to do. They continued to talk, but the group began to fragment: Some people went to the washroom, others went to get refreshments, and finally Hal called for a break.

After the break, Hal made his most passionate statement of the day. "We have only one life to live," he said. "I want you all to grow and develop. We can only work and live with others." I was moved by his passion, by the way in which he powerfully brought his feelings, commitments, and values into the room. He had been challenged to take up his leadership role and he was doing it.

Then Kathy, a staff member, replied, "Well, if we can solve the travel problem, then that would be good for me, for sure." I was shocked by her remarkably self-centered response; it seemed incompatible with Hal's statement and indeed obliterated its impact. Hal, seemingly unperturbed, responded, "You are right." Then the discussion quickly reverted to the more pragmatic and often-repeated dilemmas of marketing.

I suggest that the group was frightened by Hal's passion. He and the group had established a stable, albeit unsatisfactory balance between each professional's individual domain and the group's collective life. As the leader, Hal had been too nice and had failed to confront the senior managers of the company. People adjusted by securing their own niches, establishing their own practices - doing "what they want," in Lynn's words - while warily monitoring, as Tom did, one another's activities. In the absence of a more intense group life centered on and stimulated by their leader, they had arrived at a modus vivendi. They had obtained control over their individual domains while sacrificing the integrity and potency of the larger collective. Hal's passion frightened them because it threatened to upset the balance. If the group members had acknowledged the strength of his statement, they might have had to exchange the little control that they had achieved for the uncertainty of a more complex, although potentially richer group life. Meanwhile, of course, the business suffered.

Note the content of Hal and Kathy's statements. Hal raised the stakes. He affirmed both the importance of his subordinates' experiences (i.e., they were not just discussing "jobs") and then argued, as a leader should, that group members would find satisfaction only by building a group life: "We can only work and live with others."

Kathy responded not simply by reducing life to travel dilemmas but by turning Hal's appeal to collective life into a discussion of her needs. Content and process came together. Kathy undermined Hal's passion with a comment that was not only pragmatic, but reinforced each member's penchant for looking out for oneself alone. Ironically, it seemed as if Kathy had acknowledged Hal ("What you said means I might have to travel less"), but in fact she denied his passion and presence. Hal, as the leader, risked exposing himself. For a moment he brought his feelings, his passion, and his person to his role. He was foiled by followers who would not risk following him.

Summary

In a postindustrial milieu, leaders need followers - that is, they must acknowledge their dependence on followers. They must do so, however, without simultaneously eliminating the role differences that differentiate them from followers. The organization needs both the leader's person (feelings) and role.

Similarly, when facing leaders who make themselves vulnerable by asking for help and commitment, followers must struggle with their own ambivalence. They may be disappointed in leaders who do not know everything; they may be frightened by leaders who bring feeling and passion to the role; they may be angry at leaders who, despite their accessibility and personableness, insist on delineating the role differences that separate leaders from followers.

EXAMPLE OF COLLABORATION

The following is the case of a group of people who had to work with the founding partner of a small strategy-consulting firm in a sophisticated way. The case examines how the followers and the leader both felt vulnerable and dependent as each wrestled with the leader's probable resignation. The case also shows how group members, unable to work with these feelings in the first phase of the retreat, appeared stiff, unspontaneous, and close to despair. In contrast, when the senior partner and his subordinates finally confronted their feelings and acknowledged their vulnerability, the group became spontaneous and productive.

The Retreat

The seven partners of a strategy-consulting firm employing about twenty-five people were organizing a retreat to discuss their plans for growth and business development. Their last meeting had been extremely difficult. Six of the partners had hoped to hire Bob, an expert in finance, as the eighth partner, but one partner, Jim, had vociferously objected. The other partners did not understand Jim's seemingly capricious and arbitrary arguments, but were reluctant to offer a partnership to an outsider if one of their own was so opposed. The meeting left everyone feeling uneasy. Anticipating that they would have to address the issue again and clarify its implications for the firm's policy, the partners asked me to facilitate their retreat. I interviewed each of the partners and wrote a brief diagnostic note, which I sent to them several days before the retreat. The note placed their failed attempts to hire Bob in the context of broader challenges they faced in developing the firm. In particular, the note emphasized the partners' great dependence on the firm's founder and leader, Brandon, who was 62 years old and had indicated that he had been working too hard. I suggested that the difficulty they faced in promoting associates or hiring partners was linked to the anxiety they felt when they thought about Brandon's prospective - although not necessarily imminent - retirement.

The retreat was held in a hotel room, with Paul, a member of the executive committee of the firm, in charge. Expecting the partners to discuss my note, I remained silent so that I could observe how they worked. To my surprise, however, both the note and my presence were ignored. Instead, Paul led those present through a brisk review of markets and sales opportunities. Cooperating with Paul, the group seemed compliant and passive, while Paul himself appeared tense. By conducting the meeting in the spirit of "business as usual," the partners ensured that their recent failed experience, my note, and my presence would not stimulate their anxiety or disrupt their ability to talk rationally. During the first hour, feeling excluded and even extruded, I intervened only once, suggesting that Paul slow down and allow some discussion rather than simply march through the agenda. He grunted to show he understood me and tried to comply, but his attempt was partial and inadequate.

Brief moments of thinking and feeling broke through the facade of this business discussion. For example, during a discussion on growth, Brandon offhandedly said he wanted to reduce his activity level over the next three years. Nancy, the partner in charge of administration, said that Brandon's statement came as a revelation to her. I asked if anyone else found it to be a revelation. Henry, another partner, said that he, too, was feeling tired and wished he could cut back. I said that they seemed to be talking about dissolution rather than growth. The partners were silent and seemed depressed, but this mood was quickly altered when Will, a partner specializing in health care, stepped in and revealed a model he had developed showing the links between the number of partners, associates, revenues, and profits. The group gave Will their complete attention and appeared somewhat animated, and the depression that had almost engulfed them was put aside. The issue of their dependence on Brandon's plans was suppressed.

At lunch the partners discussed the economics of frequent-flying plans and traded tips on how to maximize their mileage, during which they became quite lively. But after lunch they returned to their dilemmas. At Henry's prompting, they discussed various "voting rules" they could use to help break stalemates whenever they could not reach a consensus. Brandon, who had been very angry at Jim for blocking Bob's nomination for partnership at the earlier meeting, suddenly suggested that someone be made a partner only when that person had garnered the unanimous vote of the partnership. Expecting to be lambasted in the discussion, Jim was, as he later said, completely surprised. It suddenly seemed as if the basic reason for this retreat and for the partners' lengthy discussions and disputes after the last one could now be forgotten. The group seemed to be, to use Bion's (1961) terms, in complete "flight" from its dilemmas.

Nancy still was dissatisfied. "There may be a problem with all this," she said. "Are you going to throw a monkey wrench into this?" Paul asked. "A big one, I'm afraid," she answered. She then asked, "Can we really tolerate this unanimity rule? I'm not sure we really can." Jim, anxious to protect the agreement, was quick to answer, "I've thought about this, and I think we can trust the partners to take each other's feelings into account. It really can work." Seemingly resigned to the partners' retreat from their dilemmas and differences, Nancy said nothing.

I then noted that, in my interviews, several partners had wondered whether they should rely on structures - such as voting rules - or should find a better process to solve their problems in working together. I said that Nancy was discussing process and Jim was discussing structure, and asked them, "What choice do you want to make?" Brandon responded by asking me what I thought about their process.

Sensing that the group was finally inviting me to work, I told them how hard I had found it to enter the group and contribute to its discussion all day. I said that they had ignored me and the note, and I wondered if this said something about how they worked with one other. Jim indicated that he had found the note reassuring; he had read it twice and it had calmed him down. Then Nancy asked me to review the three key points I had made in the note. Uncertain if and how I should reply, I was silent for a moment. Paul asked what I meant by the word "process." I replied, "the group's process," and Brandon launched into a vigorous discussion of the group's process that morning. He was frustrated with the morning's discussion. He said that the discussion had not worked, and then blamed Paul for cutting it off. I suggested that Paul had led the group in a manner everyone supported. He had not done anything the group did not want him to do. Perhaps they were not prepared for more.

The discussion intensified. Jim then turned to Brandon and said, with considerable tension in his voice, that Brandon too frequently waited until everyone else had spoken and then, by having the last word, controlled the discussion' s outcome. Having already broached the issue of process, Brandon addressed Jim ' s comment and, instead of simply defending himself, he said that in his previous partnership he had often been "paranoic," and had tried to control the group. He was determined not to let this happen again. He spoke last, he said, so that everyone else could say what was on their minds without worrying about what he thought. I noted the irony of Jim's and Brandon's different interpretations of the same process. Brandon turned to Jim and thanked him, saying, "I need to learn from all of you about this."

Brandon's openness led Nancy to talk directly to him. She told him that she was unhappy that he had not talked to her sooner about his retirement plans. Jim added that if Brandon had been more direct about his retirement planning, the group could have had a more intelligent and informed planning discussion that morning.

After I heard these two comments, I wondered if openness would turn to hostility and rancor, but Brandon was steady. He listened to the two and told them, "You all have to continue to give me feedback." He then talked at greater length about retiring. He noted quite poignantly that he had grown up with his clients and that as company executives retired he would lose his network of referrals. He felt it was time for others to step in. Speaking hopefully about teaching at a local business school, Brandon's tone was personal and honest. For the first time, the group seemed calm and focused.

Brandon then turned to me and asked, "Well, how should we use you? Do we need you any longer? We can do some of the technical work we face on finances without you." I thought Brandon's question reflected a sense that the group was satisfied with its last discussion yet uncertain and anxious about how they could deepen and sustain the conversation. Continuing might spoil that feeling of satisfaction. I suggested that they try an experiment. They should talk about an important issue they faced, and I would take up the role of a process facilitator, helping them deepen their understanding of how they worked together. They responded with eagerness and decided to discuss the problems an inactive partner posed for their practice.

The discussion's tone differed considerably from that morning's work. The partners were active and zestful. Most strikingly, Brandon no longer held back, but talked freely and without inhibition. I noted that the discussion seemed more lively because Brandon was more active and others spoke and dealt with him directly. The group was pleased by my comment. Feeling more as if the group had authorized me to work with them, I intervened several minutes later. Jim had said to Brandon, "With all due respect, I differ," to which Brandon responded, "Well, there really isn't a big difference." Then I said, "Brandon is not letting Jim meet him in the open."

In contrast to the structured conversation of that morning, the afternoon's discussion flowed spontaneously from issue to issue. The group talked at some length about the supervision of an associate and then discussed Nancy' s role as the administrative partner. I suggested that one reason Nancy was reticent at many partner meetings was that people used her as a go-between. She was "filled up" with people's concerns, I suggested, and felt inhibited when meeting with the group as a whole. "Like a battered wife," Nancy muttered under her breath, to which Paul - who had been the least sensitive to the psychological issues shaping the group' s experience that day - noted with real spontaneity, "That's interesting!"

Finally, after the group members had completed their discussion and were contemplating the end of their work with me, Henry noted with some satisfaction, "Having a cold, I expected to be tired, but I have the energy to tackle more issues." I suggested that when they had been able to talk freely and were no longer fighting their impulses, they actually did have more energy. Affirming this interpretation, Jim noted that in the last hour "there were no mine fields."

Case Interpretation

Both Brandon and the partners faced significant uncertainties. The partners were naturally anxious about their ability to develop the business once Brandon retired. In my pre-retreat interviews, many employees emphasized Brandon' s creativity and his capacity to stimulate both colleagues and clients. Brandon had significant anxiety: He was feeling less effective as his own contacts in the marketplace were retiring and he, too, worried about the firm's development as he progressively cut back on his work. Not only did he want his partners to succeed for their own sake, but his retirement income depended significantly on the continued success of the firm. The interviews suggested that the partners' differences over whether to make Bob a partner were linked to these core anxieties. Jim was particularly eager to prove that the firm could do without Brandon and was taking an increasingly active role in the partners' affairs to help shape a leadership system that could replace Brandon. He thus represented the hope and fantasy that the partners could flourish without Brandon and might as well begin to prove it immediately.

Brandon and the other partners depended deeply on one another to make this leadership transition a successful one; neither could do it alone. Yet, as the description above suggests, they had difficulty acknowledging their dependence on one other. They did not know how to be vulnerable and acknowledge that none of them alone could control or contain the process. Brandon had tried to control the process by not clearly discussing his retirement plans. Working on the assumption that he should not alarm people prematurely - particularly when he was uncertain about the timing of his retirement - he shared little with his partners. Paradoxically, this only made them feel more anxious and angry, and had results such as stimulating Jim's fantasy that the partners could easily do without Brandon. In effect, their mutual dependence produced enough anxiety to allow each side to fantasize that, in fact, they did not need the other. Feeling angry, the partners did not know how to engage Brandon in a conversation. While discussing the future of the firm, they were unable and unwilling to turn directly to him and ask him what he was thinking and feeling.

Certainly, aspects of their mutual dependence "leaked out" in the morning's conversation. Brandon mentioned offhandedly that he was thinking of cutting back on his work over the next three years. Nancy replied that this was news to her (although actually it was not), then Henry said he was thinking of cutting back as well. Indeed, the mood was so depressed I told the group they were talking about firm dissolution rather than firm growth.

This leakage was telling. Unable to collaborate, they simply made one other angry and depressed. Indeed, the highly structured way in which Paul led the group can be interpreted as a defense mechanism whereby the group sought to function as rigidly as possible, even to the point of excluding me from its process, to protect itself from these feelings.

Dimensions of Development

Yet the group did progress, the group process developed, and how it developed helps us understand the dynamics of leader-follower relationships. Working to contain its feelings, the group reached a cul-de-sac. Expecting that the problem of the group's relationship to Brandon would finally be exorcised by a discussion of the "voting rule," Jim, the other partners, and I were surprised the group reached an agreement so quickly. Brandon, sensing that he would be dragged into another fight, simply withdrew, and the group had no issue to deploy as a symbol of its dilemmas. The group could not even stimulate or support a conflict, as it had in the previous meeting when Brandon and Jim confronted each other. Nancy, sensing the stalemate, tried to restimulate the fight, but got nowhere. I suggested that the partners could choose either a structural or a process solution, and Brandon invited me to join the group psychologically by asking what I thought of its process.

Feeling authorized to work, I announced that I had felt excluded, and the group's work took off. In quick succession, and with Brandon as their "process leader," the partners confronted their disappointment in their own process. Jim felt free to confront Brandon about his apparently controlling manner, and, after some hesitation, the partners further authorized me to work with them on their process.

This sequence is telling. My statement that I had felt excluded helped the partners reflect on how they might have excluded one another by psychologically stepping away from one other. Brandon could then reflect on how he felt excluded (he was frustrated with that morning's discussion). Jim, sensing that Brandon had finally expressed his feelings, confronted Brandon, and their interchange was the turning point for the group's work. Once they directly highlighted Brandon's tendency to conceal his thoughts and feelings, Jim and the others learned that Brandon had withheld his comments so he would not dominate the group. That is, this was Brandon's conscious understanding of his behavior; by suggesting that he was "paranoic" about dominating, he pointed to unconscious motives as well. As many leaders do who struggle with their narcissism, he may have exaggerated the consequences of his aggression on others. But Brandon stayed with the group, accepted Nancy and Jim's challenges, led the group in defining my role, and finally allowed me to become free to work intensively with the group. The group then began to work on a new basis. Brandon was engaged, I had a role, Jim encountered no more land mines, Nancy's suffering could be addressed, Paul gained insight, and Henry felt energized.

Consider, finally, one of the last important interchanges between Brandon and Jim. As he discussed a marketing dilemma, Jim said to Brandon, "With all due respect, I beg to differ." I suggest that his choice of words highlighted his intuitive feeling for the way in which a leader brings his person and his role to the table. He was aggressive, but also acknowledged Brandon's authority. He did this, I suggest, because - having experienced Brandon' s effective leadership, particularly the way in which Brandon took leadership by being vulnerable - he respected Brandon at that moment. Ironically, although many leaders imagine that if they bring their feelings to their role they will lose control and respect, once Brandon revealed his concerns, Jim treated him with more respect than before. Moreover, Jim subsequently found it easier to challenge Brandon because Brandon himself felt more secure. They had established the foundation for a more charged and lively leader-follower relationship.

This vignette suggests that in postindustrial settings successful leader-follower relationships are charged ones. When leaders and followers truly work with one other, they cannot check their unconscious fantasies and sometimes primitive feelings at the door. The leader and the follower must each bring these feelings and fantasies to their encounters and then work through them to produce a shared, rational understanding of their interdependence.

A TYPOLOGY

The challenge of building collaborative relationships can be seen as part of the broader challenge of building the postindustrial organi-zation - the organization in which the person and the role, the informal and the formal, and feelings and rational thought are more intricately combined. This new organization creates new sources of authority and new relationships.

Table 1 presents three "ideal types" of authority: the traditional, modern, and postmodern. Although these terms suggest that they are related to one other historically and emerged one after another, one should think of them in developmental terms - that is, as stages in which each transcends what went before, yet also contains elements of the previous stage.

TABLE 1
Ideal Types of Authority

	Forms:		
	Traditional	*Modern*	*Postindustrial*
Source of Authority	The Office	The Role	The Person/ Role
Organizational Mechanism	Coercion	Obligation	Collaboration
Individual Responses	Obedience	Self-discipline	Negotiation
Sanction and Benefits	Punishment and Reward	Guilt and Relief	Alienation and Com-munity

Let us examine each column in Table 1 in detail. In traditional settings - such as the Army, many schools, and early industrial operations - authority is attached to the office, represented by figures such as the general, the teacher, and the foreman. People in such settings experience authority as coercive. They comply with the organization by obeying authority, and are either rewarded or punished for their behavior. The problems of authority are simplified in the traditional milieu because those in authority focus on external behavior in the present and reward and punish people according to how well they obey stated criteria (e.g., you must do your homework, work at your station, sit still at your desk).

The modern setting poses new psychological demands. Here people coerce themselves by disciplining their impulses. As Schwartz (1983) suggests in his deontic theory of motivation, people come to work psychologically prepared to feel obliged to authority, and they feel guilty when they do not successfully fulfill their duty. In contrast to the traditional form, employees now monitor themselves, and feel rewarded in part simply by experiencing relief when work is completed. In psychodynamic terms. people have more developed superegos. They identify authority figures with disciplining and loving figures from their past (e.g., parents, teachers) and thus satisfy the former just as they sought to satisfy the latter. As David Reisman noted in his classic, "The Lonely Crowd" (1950), such employees have an "internal gyroscope" that enables them to work without constant external supervision and direction. Compared to the traditional form, the modern form of organization can therefore achieve higher levels of productivity and faster rates of change. Self-disciplined employees seeking to fulfill their duty will take more initiative than will employees who feel coerced.

The postindustrial setting poses even greater psychological demands. Here, as authority itself appears pyschologically vulnerable and open to influence, people are asked to collaborate with authority in shaping the organization' s direction and understanding its past. To help the organization adapt and develop, people can no longer simply fulfill their duty; instead, their duty - the psychological meaning of their roles - must be negotiated with authority. People cannot simply rely on internalized images of authority, which are derived from a time when, as children or students, they were small and weak and those in authority were big and strong. Instead, as they are offered a chance to collaborate with authority, they may have to overcome unconscious wishes derived from early experiences to rebel against authority, to comply with it passively, or to seduce it to win special favors. In the examples presented above, the principals had to overcome their feelings of inadequacy in the presence of the superintendent, employees of the public relations firm had to fight their feelings of not being "special" in the eyes of an authority figure, and a member of the industrial methods group (Kathy) wanted to attack authority when faced with a leader who passionately represented the collective life of the group. The postindustrial form thus offers participation, but only in exchange for more sophisticated psychological work. To work with authority that is more open to influence, people cannot simply rely on who they are. Rather, they must develop themselves further by becoming in touch with their feelings. This work, when successfully completed, can help create a psychological sense of community. When people cannot or will not complete this work, they are likely to feel estranged and alienated from one another and from themselves.

SUMMARY

Leaders and followers face new challenges in collaborating with one another. Leaders must be vulnerable, and followers must acknowledge their own complex responses to authority. To create the new postindustrial form, leaders and followers must produce participative processes, but only by first engaging in sophisticated psychological work. We are now at a cultural turning point. Dissatisfied with the modern form of organization in which coercion is internalized and leaders embody organizational discipline, we want a more flexible system of relationships. But going forward is difficult. We are in a transitional zone, and organizations of all types face deep dilemmas of aligning leaders and followers.

REFERENCES

BION, W. Experiences in groups. New York: Ballatine, 1961.

HIRSCHHORN, L. The workplace within. Cambridge: MIT Press, 1988.

KRANTZ, J. Lessons from the field. An essay on the crisis of leadership in contemporary organizations. Journal of Applied Behavioral Science, 26(1), 1990, 49-64.

REISMAN, D. The lonely crowd. A study of the changing American character. New Haven, CT: Yale University Press, 1950.

SCHWARTZ, H. A theory of deontic work motivation. Journal of Applied Behavioral Science, 19, 1983, 203-214.

The Impostor Syndrome: Developmental and Societal Issues

Manfred F. R. Kets de Vries

INTRODUCTION

Throughout history, impostors have fascinated the public at large. People leading fraudulent lives or engaging in fraudulent action always seem to have had a fatal attraction. One reason for this popularity may be that there is an element of recognition present in the encounter of impostors and their audiences. It often seems as if the impostors show us something about ourselves which we may prefer not to see under normal circumstances. And to some extent (given the differences between the public and private self), we are all impostors, we all play roles (Goffman, 1971). Presenting a facade and misleading the audience is part and parcel of everyday life. However, this does not explain the ease with which impostors can make fools of the audience in situations of true imposture. It often seems as if the audience is all too willing to be victimized.

The term impostor actually has two connotations which are often present concurrently. In the Oxford English dictionary we find a description of the impostor as someone who imposes on others, a person who is a deceiver, swindler, or cheat. The other meaning is that of a person who assumes a false character or passes him- or herself off as someone other than he or she really is. However, we can find situations where the two roles are combined, in that a person takes on a false identity in order to swindle others. But we also encounter individuals who pass themselves off as someone else without obtaining any visible benefits. The situation in which a person assumes a false character in order to engage in some form of swindling is more common. Nevertheless, financial gain should probably be looked at as a means to an end, not as the principal reason for the impostor's actions. Psychological gratifications often seem to be much more important.

Examples of imposture can be found in many different sources. Already in the Old Testament we find a famous example of a kind of imposture, i.e., Jacob's impersonation of Isaac. But probably one of the best known examples of an impostor in early literature is the story of Till Eulenspiegel. This most beloved of German folk heroes,

---

Reprinted, by permission of publisher, from Human Relations, Vol. 43, No. 7, 1990. Office of Rights/Permissions, Plenum Publishing Corp., New York.

whose name means "owl mirror," was a professional confidence man, jester, and self-styled philosopher who is said to have actually lived in the forteenth century (Oppenheimer, 1972). Eulenspiegel's name is symbolic in that he "wisely reflects" aspects of the audience's character, warts and all, at the same time as he is duping them.

Novelists have been fascinated by imposters. Cervantes's Don Quixote de la Mancha is a famous literary example of a form of imposture. His is the story of an elderly knight confused by having read too many romances, who replaces reality with fantasy, acting out a life filled with delusion, fighting windmills along the way. Then we have "The Confidence Man" by Herman Melville (1954), which takes place in a fictive world populated by impostors where everyone seems to play a role. The naive reader is deceived by the novel as much as the victims of the confidence man. A more specific example of the impostor in literature is the well-known "Confessions of Felix Krull, Confidence Man". This is Thomas Mann's (1969) uncanny description of the archtypical impostor, a person remarkable for his ability to win the favor and love of others by playing whatever role they desire, and taking advantage of everyone he encounters seemingly without experiencing a trace of guilt.

Apart from literature, we can find more contemporary examples of imposture in daily life. A famous case, later made into a movie starring Tony Curtis, was the career of Ferdinand Waldo Demara, alias the great impostor (Crichton, 1959). Reading his life history we can marvel at the ease with which this individual took on an amazing variety of aliases. Demara managed to play the roles of a Trappist monk, a doctor of psychology and dean of the school of philosophy at a small college in Pennsylvania, a law student, a zoology graduate, a cancer researcher and teacher at a junior college in Maine, a surgeon-lieutenant in the Royal Canadian Navy (actually successfully performing major surgery at sea), an assistant warden of a Texas prison, and a schoolteacher.

A memorable example of imposture in a business setting was the case of Anthony De Angelis whose manipulation of millions of gallons of nonexisting salad oil sent two Wall Street brokerage houses to bankruptcy, caused the failure of a subsidiary of the American Express Company, and led to plummeting futures prices on commodity markets in New York and Chicago (Miller, 1965). Although financial gain certainly played a role in this instance, De Angelis also created a remarkable world of make-believe to satisfy his need for recognition. He outsmarted dozens of the shrewdest bankers, brokers, and businessmen. While his con game was going on, however, nobody wondered how he could make money by selling salad oil at such impossibly low prices. Financiers rushed to loan him more money for the next deal. The wish to believe, fueled by greed, made even the most astute businessman suspend reality. Eventually, the financiers were holding papers for astounding quantities of salad oil, more than could be accounted for according to government reports about existing stocks. But still nobody was alarmed. Only after 8 years of operation did the bubble burst, after De Angelis could no longer maintain his position in the future vegetable oil market and the authorities discovered that his salad oil tanks were empty.

There is even a rather unusual psychiatric classification of imposture, the Münchausen syndrome, a condition named after a mythical German baron and soldier-adventurer who lived in the eighteenth century and became known as the hero of many tall tales (Lehmann, 1975; Swanson, 1981). Here, the medical field is chosen as the stage where these individuals play out their conflicts centered around aggression and dependency. The condition is characterized by repeated fabrication of clinically convincing symptoms and a false medical and social history. The wish of these people is to be given surgical or other forms of treatment for a nonpsychiatric medical illness.

When we review the lives of impostors with hindsight it often seems incomprehensible how others can fall for their machinations. Nonetheless, while the confidence game is taking place, the impostor seems to weave a magical spell like the Pied Piper and people are willing to follow. Impostors appear to be able to awaken otherwise dormant qualities by means of which we may be swept away, blinded to existing reality. Moreover, imposture may be more universal than would have been expected. Clinical investigation suggests that it may be a characteristic with a range going from feeling like a fraud without there being a reason to actually be actively involved in imposturous activities.

How does one become an impostor? What do impostors want? Why do impostors behave the way they do? What makes for their fascination? Why can they be so self-destructive? Is there an element of the impostor in all of us? It is the objective of this paper to find some answers to these questions. First, the literature on the impostor will be reviewed to be able to draw a personality sketch of this type of individual. Subsequently, in order to illustrate imposture in a business setting, a case study will be given.

PSYCHODYNAMIC INFERENCES

The earliest known clinical paper on the impostor was written by Karl Abraham (1925) who described the adventures of a conscript in the army. As an army doctor, Abraham was requested by a military court to make an investigation of the conscript. He wrote in his case history how impressed he was by the person's ability to gain the trust of others (including his jailers) and to betray such confidence immediately through deception. Abraham was particularly struck by his " ... genius at phantastic story telling" and his " ... uncontrollable desire for aggrandisement" (p. 294). As an explanation he suggested that since this particular individual " ... felt himself unloved in his childhood, he had an inner urge to show himself 'lovable' to everybody ... to prove to himself and to show them soon afterward how unworthy he was of such feeling" (p. 300). Abraham also pointed to the individual's longing for rich parents, symptomatic of what is called in clinical literature the "family romance," meaning the perpetuation of a relatively common childhood fantasy that one's parents are not the real ones and one is really of noble or royal descent. The parents are consequently viewed as frauds. The fantasy that somewhere out there, there must be some other, better, more understanding parents lingers on. What triggers this feeling is that the parents are experienced as not being really responsive to the child's needs for recognition and independence. Family romance fantasies can be looked at as forms of compensatory narcissistic self-enhancement, attempts to regulate self-esteem (Kaplan, 1974). These fantasies contribute to the development of a "personal myth" (Kris, 1975), a fusion of early memories and fantasies, which serves as an organizer of later experience. Abraham also commented on the strong self-defeating streak in the conscript's behavior in that ". . . he never showed much aptitude for eluding the arm of the law" (p. 292).

In her discussion of impostors, Helene Deutsch (1955) inferred that they assume the identities of others " ... not because they themselves lack the ability for achievement, but because they have to hide under a strange name to materialize a more or less reality adapted fantasy" (p. 332). She suggested that " ... the ego of the impostor, as expressed in his own true name, is devaluated, guilt-laden" (p. 332). No wonder such a person feels compelled to function under other, more glorious covers more in line with his or her magnificent ego ideal, i.e., his/her conception of how he/she really wishes to be. Deutsch inferred from her case example that the unusual behavior of the impostor is caused by the emotional "overfeeding" of the child by the mother, the former being smothered by all her affections. The father's behavior may have aggravated the situation, since he may have overburdened the child by making him or her the recipient of his unfulfilled desires. In her discussion, Deutsch also referred to individuals who, after having achieved success, are troubled by the feeling that they are impostors. In the case of her patient she commented that " ... the more effectively [he] functioned in reality, the more anxiety he developed ... he felt like an impostor in his new role, that of doing honest work" (p. 333).

Phyllis Greenacre (1958a, 1971) postulated the following basic constellations of disturbing symptoms in the case of imposture: "first, the dominant and dynamically active family romance; second, the intense and circumscribed disturbance of the sense of identity, a kind of infarction in the sense of reality, third, a malformation of the superego involving both conscience and ideals" (p. 96). She commented on impostors' apparent need for self-betrayal, struck as she was by the discrepancy in their abilities, where " ... skill and persuasiveness are combined with utter foolishness and stupidity" (p. 97). Greenacre recognized the necessity of the confirming reaction of the audience to help the impostor establish a realistic sense of self. She traced the genesis of this behavior to a family background where the parents are at odds with each other and where the child is treated with extreme possessiveness by the mother and used as an item of exhibitionistic display and not really as a separate person in his or her own right. At the same time, the mother may downgrade the father as being ineffective and disappointing. Greenacre postulated a serious imbalance in the Oedipal situation, with the child (in case of a male impostor) seemingly superseding the father's role in the family. She argued that the child is forced into an adult role prematurely. In order to maintain this position and gain and continue to capture the admiration of the grown-ups, astounding talents in mimicry will be developed, i.e., the ability to imitate adult behavior. Unfortunately, the price of such a developmental track is often the lack of a well-formed separate self and a poor sense of identity and reality.

In his discussion of imposture, Finkelstein (1974) presented one of his patients, self-described as "The Great Teddy," who was busily acting out typical family romance fantasies and demonstrating his narcissistic needs by, for example, elevating his parents' status. Finkelstein emphasized Teddy's great talents in the art of illusion and his ability to discover what his audience really wants. The psychological defense mechanisms of denial, rationalization, and splitting enabled him to act out his unconscious fantasies (Klein, 1988; Freud, 1966). Moreover, because of these defenses, he was able to deceive his audience without experiencing any conflict with existing reality. In explaining Teddy's behavior, Finkelstein highlighted the role of the parents. He describes how poorly the mother was attuned to Teddy's needs and used him almost like an extension of herself, turning him into a demonstration piece. Her relationship to him was characterized by superficiality, as she had no concern for real, substantial issues. Outside appearances were all that mattered. In addition, in this family constellation, mention must be made of the seductive nature of the mother-child interface, which left Teddy with the impression that his mother very much preferred him to his father.

Given the prevalence of such behavior, Teddy's parents instilled in him a highly unrealistic image of himself which became the basis for his later deceitful practices. In addition, Iying and pretending were a common pattern among all family members. All of them seemed to live out the fantasy of being a wonderful family, whereas the reality was quite different. Consequently, quite early in life Teddy became familiar with role-playing and imposture. To use Finkelstein's (1974) words, "[his] parents not only encouraged him to become an impostor; they also provided characteristics for him to identify with, particularly his mother's Iying and her interest in superficial appearance and his father's abilities as a glib talker" (p. 110). To be an impostor, to be a liar and pretender, was in a way behaving and acting exactly the way his parents wanted.

THE IMPOSTOR: A CHARACTER SKETCH

If we look at common themes among the various descriptions and take into consideration other observations about this type of person, we recognize that potential impostors come from families where there is often an ambiance of shared deception, lying, cheating, and make-believe. Appearance over substance is what really counts. Relationships tend to be superficial; showmanship becomes all-important. Impostors seem to have developed some kind of "screen identity" to ward off an underlying, more troubled one (Greenson, 1958). Such individuals may possess what can be called an overstimulated or overburdened self (Kohut & Wolf, 1978). They have never learned to moderate their grandiose self-images or idealized parental images. They want the world to treat them according to their ideals, not according to their real achievements. The real and the imaginary are not well integrated.

Some of these children appear to have become proxies of their parents, seemingly entrusted with the mission of fulfilling many of the parents' unrealistic hopes and wishes. Moreover, parents may have unconsciously encouraged amoral or antisocial behavior in their children (Johnson & Szurek, 1952); forbidden desires may consequently be acted out vicariously. In the family setting, mothers of future impostors may use their children to gratify their own narcissistic needs; showing them off becomes what counts. At the same time, these mothers can also be overseductive (Dupont, 1970). The fathers are frequently devaluated by the mothers and portrayed as ineffective. This particular family situation where there is a collusive relationship with the mother may create Oedipal problems making for a lack of phase-appropriate identification (Gottdiener, 1982). Adult behavior is expected of the children at a stage of development when they are not yet ready for it physiologically. Such children may later be confused about their true abilities and become victims of self-deceptive narcissism (Kets de Vries & Miller, 1985).

Impostors learn early to use mimicry and other techniques to imitate adult behavior, all ways to get and sustain attention. This talent continues to be present in adult life. Given this early training, the impostor becomes quite skilled in colluding with the audience to create an ambiance of make-believe and appearing more grandiose than he or she really is. Family romances take on an adult flavor since fantasies of aggrandisement continue to play a key role. Impostors' behavior also has overtones of what sometimes is called pseudologica phantastica (Fenichel, 1954; Deutsch, 1965) in which the content of the fantasies, usually elaborate fabrications to impress the audience, are really screen memories both revealing and concealing events which have actually happened. Here we should take note that pseudologica phantastica and pathological lying are different from normal daydreaming in that reality testing is suspended long enough to allow the individual to act on the fantasies. Fabrication of a new "truth" also becomes a way of covering up painful psychological material containing grains of historical truths (Weinshel, 1979; Spence, 1982; Blum, 1983). Lies serve a self-protective function in compartmentalizing threatening inner conflict. Somehow, the personal myth as organizer of life experiences has to be played out.

We notice how, by in acting the way they do, impostors seem to have lost the capacity to sharply differentiate between fantasy and reality. In fact, clinical evidence suggests that they often feel much better when they assume the identity of someone else. Their own identity, in spite of the existence of real gifts and talents, appears to be rejected or devaluated. They have never successfully negotiated the process of separation-individuation, becoming an individual in their own right, a crucial prerequisite to the development of a stable sense of identity (Mahler, Pine, & Bergman, 1975). Thus, impostors seem to suffer from a severe form of identity crisis (Wijsenbeek & Nitzan, 1968). Moreover, for some individuals, becoming an impostor is the victory of a dreaded but at the same time extremely tempting negative identity, meaning an identity one is warned not to become (Erikson, 1959; Gediman, 1985).

A corollary to this disturbance of the impostor's sense of identity is a deficiency in the acquisition of well-developed internalized standards and values. Facade and pretense will be substituted for real achievement. Impostors always seem to be on stage, engaged in a performance they may believe in themselves, relying on fiction for a temporary identity (Bursten, 1973; Martin, 1988). In acting the way they do, they have retained the make-believe quality of many childhood games, and the audience is needed to confirm their sense of identity and reality.

Impostors discover early in life the power of the word. Like the troubadours of bygone days or prose fiction writers they know how to fabricate illusions. Langer (1953) refers to the "mnemonic mode," the ability "to make that illusion convincing, i.e., make it, however far it may be from actuality, seem real" (p. 291). Structure, diction, imagery, the use of names and allusions are ways of making this happen. Descriptive expansion gives the stories of impostors their vitality and creates a suspension of disbelief. Langer mentions how the troubadours' audiences would ravel in their descriptions and ask for greater elaborations making, as it were, a three-dimensional painting. The impostor acts in a similar way. Given his empathic responsiveness, his ability to react to the cues of his audience, he will weave those cues into his tales, making for an increasingly believable tapestry of illusions. Porter (1987), in his study of the language of quackery, gives some insight into the reasons how this particular type of imposter, these pretended physicians, were able to fool their audiences. Quacks come across as truly verbal pyrotechnicians combining flattery with assurance. They use pseudo-scientific terms to obfuscate. They resort to religious allusions and superstitions, draw on the mystique of exoticism, of faraway places, and utilize as another source of prestige, social cachet, alluding to acquaintanceship with the high and mighty.

Due to their power of the word and their ability to listen, impostors have an uncanny talent for putting others under their spell. Somehow, in their own narcissistic pursuits, they have a great ability to satisfy the narcissistic needs of their audience. The optimistic way in which they are able to describe the supposed success of their exploits and how this success will enhance the lives of others can be intoxicating.

Symbolically, one can argue that impostors take on the role of the archaic, all caring mother, satisfying oceanic longings, gratifying the almost-forgotten, but never really relinquished wishes for total attention of early childhood. To the impostor, the greediness of the audience becomes another lever. It enhances the willingness of the other to share the fantasies of the impostor. In many instances, W. C.

Fields's statement that "you can't cheat an honest man" rings a bell of truth. Between impostor and audience there is an element of mutuality, a kind of unconscious conspiracy. The audience is made happy, presumably by thinking it will get what it wants, while the impostor needs the audience to counteract a sense of inner emptiness and reaffirm some kind of identity. Of course, the audience is most susceptible in times of upheaval, when imposture can really occur on a grand scale, given the dormant need for a savior.

However, the interface between impostor and audience also contains a strong aggressive component. Imposture is not only a way to repress and deny painful, unconscious material. Making a fool of the audience and the use of lies and deceit can also be seen as aggressive acts, a form of retaliation, of getting symbolically even with the ineffective, exploiting, overburdening parents of childhood.

But to be constantly on stage, engaged as it were in a continuous performance, can be very draining. The tension which accompanies deceit must come along with occasional feelings of just wanting to give up. This may explain the instability and self-defeating component we often find in the behavior of impostors. Many of them are no strangers to masochistic behavior. Frequently, there is a remarkable contrast between their great skill in creating situations of make-believe and "stupid" acts which cause exposure (Grand, 1973). The role of unconscious guilt and the existence of disturbances in their sense of identity probably play a role in their failure to protect themselves adequately against detection.

A Comparison with the "as if" Personality

There are strong resemblances between the impostor and what has been described as the "as if" personality (Deutsch, 1942; Reich, 1953; Sullivan, 1953). We are referring to a schizoid type of person who gives the impression of being well adjusted and emotionally involved, but is unfortunately only acting "as if." A closer look at such people indicates, however, that something is missing. These individuals express a lack of authenticity in their relationships with others. Their affective relationship with others has a stunted quality. These people appear to be emotionally involved but actually lack that capacity. They have a completely passive, almost plastic attitude toward the environment. No single integrated personality seems present. Instead, there appears to be a series of superficial imitations. Such individuals will shift with the tide, ready to adopt whatever attitudes and reactions are expected. Pseudoidentification seems to be the norm. And although they may appear well adjusted to the naive observer, displaying emotions in a very convincing way, they only behave as though they have normal emotional responses to others. Relationships are inconsistant, transitory identification is the rule. Behavior is continually changing, depending on what person, social group, or cause captures their attention.

Annie Reich (1953), referring to women, mentioned how some of them " ... have short-lived, dependent infatuations during which they completely take over the man's personality, only to drop him again after a short time and to 'deify' another subject" (p. 25). Here, impressions not substance are what counts. Reich blamed these transitory identifications on the inability of the child "to develop any feeling or depth in relation to the mother" (p. 36). The mothers have used their children for their own exhibitionistic displays requiring superficial imitations, and do not foster an in-depth internalization of values and behavior patterns. Thus, the basis of this disorder is a lack of stability in the earliest relationship with the primary caretakers. The difference between the self and the other becomes poorly delineated resulting in a defective development of the person's identity.

When we look at the differences between the impostor and the "as if" personality, we notice that the impostor tends to be warm and seductive, while the "as if" character possesses more cold, schizoid features. The lack of affect in the "as if" person becomes a main distinguishing feature. In addition, the "as if" personality seems to have a more transitional nature, very much dependent on whom he or she is in contact with. This differs quite a lot from that of the impostor who has a sense of identity based on a number of specific roles (Panel, 1966; Ross, 1967; Fast, 1970). To use Ross's (1967) words, "unlike 'as if' individuals, impostors do not show a proclivity for multiple identifications and they identify with objects corresponding to their ego ideal" (p. 70). The "as if" person is more dependent on the reality of the other while the impostor is doing his own thing, pursuing his or her personal myth, using very specific intrapsychic imagery to act out different roles. Of course, one may argue that the "as if" personality can be viewed as a very diffuse form of imposture.

FEELING IMPOSTUROUS

At times, a distinction has been made between the "true" and the "neurotic" impostor (Greenacre, 1958a, 1958b; Aarons, 1959; Gediman, 1985). While the first category refers to those people whose identity is based on impersonations, not on actual accomplishments and purposeful activity, the second group is different in that the individuals feel fraudulent and imposturous while actually being very successful in their pursuits. They feel that they have fooled everybody and that they are not as competent or intelligent as others think they are. Success is attributed to luck, compensatory hard work, or "superficial" external factors such as physical attractiveness or likeability. Some of them are incredibly hard workers; they are always overprepared. However, they cannot accept that they have intellectual gifts and ability. They experience a constant fear that their imposturous existence will be found out, that they will not be able to live up to others' expectations and catastrophe will follow. We are somehow reminded of Winnicott's (1975) description of people who develop a "false self," which can be seen as an attempt to hide and protect the inner core of the person's personality, an outcome of adaptive failure resulting in a deceptive false identity.

In describing the internal experiences of incompetence and phoniness of impostors, Gediman (1985) has suggested a continuum ranging from "the psychopathic impostor who may assume a false identity for conscious and deliberate purposes of deception, through a heterogeneous variety of individuals who are vulnerable to a shaky identity sense" (p. 912). For the "neurotic" group, it seems to be exceedingly hard to accept their own talents and achievements.

One of the tasks of childhood is to accomplish that "the infant's primary narcissism, the belief in his own and in his parent's omnipotence, ... gradually recede(s), that is to say, it must be replaced by autonomous functioning" (Mahler et al., 1975, p. 226). Individuals who feel like impostors have also experienced problems concerning the separation-individuation process, granted not to such a dramatic degree as we find among real impostors. However, true separation has never been accomplished. These people never had a chance to feel truly independent. They lack a cohesive sense of self. Their achievements and capabilities are experienced as phony and hollow and cause guilt, fear, and stress. Their view of themselves is that of being a fraud (Clance & Imes, 1978; Clance, 1985).

Such people are unusually sensitive to experiences of rejection; they are excessively afraid of social failure and suffer from lingering dependency needs. What should also be noted are their perfectionistic attitudes toward themselves. It is as if they have incorporated the excessive expectations of their parents which never have been properly "metabolized." In many instances, they may suffer from generalized forms of anxiety, lack of self-confidence, and depression.

In the case of women who feel imposturous, Clance and Imes (1978) hypothesize about the existence of two types depending on their family history. According to their study, the first group is victimized by a family myth whereby one sibling has been designated the intelligent one. In contrast, the person who later will feel imposturous is called the "sensitive" or socially adept one. In spite of her string of achievements, the family continues to attribute greater intelligence and ability to the "bright" sibling whose academic performance is often much poorer. It leaves the other with a sense of doubt about her true abilities and the lingering question of whether her family may after all be right.

In the second situation, the assertion is made that the person in question is superior in every way: intellect, personality, appearance, or other qualities. Many anecdotes are told about the person's precocity as an infant. Yet, at the same time, she experiences situations where she has difficulty in achieving. Given the indiscriminate manner in which she is praised, she begins to distrust her parents' perceptions and consequently her own.

Although we can argue that, concerning social expectations, the attribution of ability is subjected to sex stereotyping, women are defined by society as less competent than men and some women are worried that too much success will interfere in their relationships with men, one can seriously question if the two proposed dynamic constellations about feeling imposturous are limited only to women. Men may suffer from similar feelings often related to the unconscious sense of guilt about doing better than the father of childhood. This may lead to anxiety because of fear of his envy (Schafer, 1984). In such instances, it appears that the Oedipal drama has never been successfully resolved. Such infantile fears, which may contain a kernel of truth, often based on covert messages, may linger on into adulthood (Kets de Vries, 1989). What can add to these feelings is that these people's success may qualify them as very different from their family background, raising realistic fears of separation, estrangement, and rejection.

However, with respect to the gender question in imposture, one caveat is worth mentioning and it has to do with sexuality. While it is almost impossible for a man to fake orgasm, this form of imposture is quite easy for women. Women who experience difficulties in reaching orgasm and for various reasons take recourse to shamming it, may feel imposturous in other parts of their lives.

Like the true impostor, the person who feels imposturous adopts a survival strategy based on inauthenticity in order to win the approval of others. Sycophantic behavior, intellectual flattery, and charm become means of avoiding expected social rejection. Telling the other person what he or she wants to hear becomes the chosen strategy for gaining approval and postponing the dreaded moment of being found out to be an impostor. Here again, Annie Reich's (1953) earlier-mentioned formulations about narcissistic object choice in women come to mind.

Aspects of this way of thinking and acting also remind us of one of Freud's (1916) character types, "those wrecked by success," a group of people who fall ill when a long-cherished wish comes to fruition. There are some differences, however. These particular people may go further than merely feeling inauthentic and fraudulent and engage in self-defeating acts, achieving, as it were, "victory through defeat" (Reik, 1941). Instead of pleasure, their "success neurosis" causes them unhappiness when they are faced with their own accomplishments, at least at one level of consciousness. It can be inferred that the extravagant desires of their ego ideal can never be met. Of course, another way of looking at it is seeing their behavior as a form of rebellion, not wanting to submit to the expectations of the parents.

Both those "wrecked by success" and those feeling inauthentic, the latter fearing to be found out as not really so bright or competent and having a sense of fooling everybody despite outstanding achievements, possess a strong masochistic streak in that behaving in this way they inflict pain on themselves (Grossman, 1986; Simons, 1987). In the past, such behavior may have been a relational way of attracting attention or else a form of negative identification with an abusing or abused parental figure. Particularly in the case of women, some authors have mentioned in this context a Cinderella Complex (Dowling, 1981), a self-defeating tendency to wish to be taken care of or rescued from the responsibility of having to take care of oneself. However, expecting an external force to change one's life, waiting for the magic slipper and not having to take charge of oneself, may be a costly life strategy.

THE IMPOSTOR DIMENSION AMONG ENTREPRENEURS

It was suggested earlier that to some extent we are all impostors, we are all on stage. This stage role becomes more prominent when we move to a public setting such as an organization (Goffman, 1971). Entrepreneurs are more inclined than other businessmen to take on elements of the impostor role, given the inherent drama in the act of creation (after all, they are trying to turn their fantasies into some form of reality). In their intense need to pursue a vision and convince others of their ideas, they may resort to distortion of facts. However, the enthusiasm they generate in selling their dreams, unrealistic or ill-defined as they may be, is important because it makes them catalysts of change and, if successful, a main source of economic development.

Sometimes, however, these dreams may turn sour. Then the only thing remembered are the more fictional, imposturous parts of the project. One of the most dramatic examples in the past few years of how elements of imposture can affect business enterprise has been the case of Refaat El-Sayed, the former (now dismissed) chairman of Fermenta, the Swedish biotechnology firm. This Egyptian immigrant was able to dazzle the Swedish financial and industrial establishment, the media, and the public at large. El-Sayed became a folk hero to the man on the street because of his unpretentious lifestyle and his indifference to the trappings of wealth despite having become the richest man in Sweden. He would be photographed in his small apartment in a suburb of Stockholm drinking Coca Cola and eating pizza or be seen playing soccer with an amateur league. Because of his activities he had become the inspiration and pride of Sweden's large immigrant population. In 1985 he was even voted "Swede of the year" by Swedish television. Unfortunately, what initially looked like a tempest in a tea cup, the revelation that he never, as he had alleged, held a doctorate, turned into a fullfledged scandal when an increasing number of irregularities were revealed. Fermenta stock, once the darling of the investment community (having reached an incredible price earnings ratio of 56), plummeted more than 90% in one year, damaging many individuals and Swedish institutions (Wittebort, 1987; Sundqvist, 1987).

Very little is known of El-Sayed's early days. He was born in 1946, the youngest in the family, son of a teacher. His mother, who came from Czechoslovakia, died a year after his birth. According to him, there were two sisters and another two brothers in the family. The latter two are said to have died in the war with Israel. The father remarried and had nine more children. El-Sayed went to Czechoslovakia twice to participate in a youth camp. In 1966, he left Egypt for Sweden to study at a university. Before that, he had been enrolled at a School of Agriculture in Cairo. While in Sweden, he visited Russia a number of times in order to go to summer camp. In 1972, he married a Swedish social worker.

Whatever is fact or fancy in El-Sayed's description of his personal background, one thing is clear, it must have been a very confusing and turbulent one. There is the death of his mother at a very early age, an event that must surely have had a serious impact on the later course of his life. The fact that she came from a very different cultural background must have been a source of curiosity to him. To add to this sense of confusion there was, of course, the presence of a stepmother and more children. About the role of the different female figures in his life, we can only make conjectures. Also, not much is said about his father. But certainly, one male figure, according to him, his paternal grandfather, was quite important as a key transmitter of beliefs and values.

According to El-Sayed, at an early age, he had to be self-sufficient and behave like a small adult. One may infer from such a statement that age-appropriate development didn't really occur. He must have learned very quickly how to be a survivor, not relying on anybody. He has described how from early on he learned how to take initiative, how he possessed the ability to capture the attention of others and assume a leadership role given his wish to differentiate himself.

Although we will never really know the exact nature of the family dynamics, we may infer that his visits to Czechoslovakia and Russia and his eventual immigration to Sweden were ways of coming to grip with whom he really was, all attempts to stabilize a confused sense of personal and cultural identity. His later behavior shows, however, that this sense of confusion may have lingered on and also demonstrates the difficulty he had in distinguishing fact from fiction. The "wish to believe" and thereby fitting the facts to match his desires may have become so strong that it marred his sense of reality.

From early on in his business career, El-Sayed showed strong entrepreneurial inclinations. He worked as a consultant in microbiology and held several patents. In 1973, he started a company called Micro-Chem which probably gave him some of the contacts he found advantageous later on. In 1981, El-Sayed became interested in a penicillin factory owned by Astra, a Swedish pharmaceutical company. The factory, Fermenta, was losing money and Astra was willing to sell. Through ingenious representation of his financial solvency, since he didn't have any money, and a number of imaginative tax maneuvers, El-Sayed gained control over Fermenta, paying one Swedish crown for the shares. At that time, Fermenta was making the raw material for production of penicillin, a depressed market with worldwide overcapacity. El-Sayed's original business idea was to turn the factory into a producer of cattle vaccine, a product which offered high margins. However, he never really pursued this idea, concentrating instead on buying various antibiotics firms.

Surprisingly enough, the factory started to make profits, probably to a large extent a result of advantageous currency fluctuations. In 1984, El-Sayed decided to go public with Fermenta. In the prospectus, it was stated, probably to increase his credibility, that he had a PhD in chemistry. The offering was made at a time when the Swedish stock market was experiencing an unprecedented rise. Furthermore, in Sweden, there was a lack of companies in biotechnology. The issue was 16 times oversubscribed.

The year 1985 was a period of rapid expansion for Fermenta. El-Sayed frantically bought new companies or entered into joint ventures or marketing arrangements with companies in related fields. His idea was to become a major player in the antibiotics field so that he could influence world prices. In the meantime, he had succeeded in attracting to his board some of the most reputable businessmen in Sweden.

From all descriptions, El-Sayed seemed to come across as a bundle of energy, a man in a hurry, totally future-oriented. Some even portrayed him as a continuously moving target, a characteristic which may have made it hard to understand him. His speech was rapid, fragmented, accented, and often not very coherent. His mannerisms, and unorthodox behavior were a puzzle to many. But, like Andersen's story about the Emperor's new clothes, many labeled him a genius given their inability to understand him. In the context of Sweden, where people have a very different modus operandi, this unconventional outsider must have left his audience completely spellbound.

El-Sayed was also described as being extremely talented in reading people. There was a warmth and generosity about him that made him attractive. He had a great knack for appearing to give his audience what they wanted. He would dazzle others with his command of figures and tables. These qualities made him a very skillful negotiator. But with hindsight, it appears that his presentation was not always correct, and he often ended up taking advantage of the situation.

Paradoxically, El-Sayed's role of playing the anti-hero, not being part of the financial establishment and for all appearance's sake not being interested in the traditional trappings of power, got him more attention than would otherwise have been the case. It turned out to be a very effective way of satisfying his need to be in the limelight and be liked. And in the end, as a spokeman for Volvo said, ascribing more deliberate planning to his actions than was probably the case, El-Sayed "...more or less fooled all of Swedish society-politicians, businessmen, financial analysts, financial journalists" (Wittebort, 1987, p. 96). In the aftermath, everyone realized that what he sold was dreams and promises, that the stock price of Fermenta rose to a large extent on air and not on substance, and that his company was not really much of a high-tech firm but basically a very simple manufacturing enterprise. El-Sayed's persuasiveness, combined with the added inducement of the greed of others, enabled him to get the attention of everyone.

Meanwhile, Fermenta's stock price took off phenomenally. At the end of 1985, it was trading at 213 compared to an introduction price only a year and a half earlier of 21.25. With 44% of the stock (79% of the voting rights), El-Sayed had become the richest man in Sweden, at least on paper. El-Sayed reached the zenith of his career in January 1986 with the announcement of a spectacular deal. With Volvo's backing, Fermenta would take the lead in consolidating Sweden's pharmaceutical/biotechnology industry thereby gaining control over some of the major players in the field. It was soon after this announcement that an innocuous-looking article in an obscure paper appeared questioning whether El-Sayed really had obtained a doctorate.

For many, the small deception was hard to take. After an initial reaction of disbelief, those involved started to take a closer look at El-Sayed's various activities. The Volvo deal fell through and the "socialist dream," as he had been called because of his ability to play a capitalist game with a socialist touch, tumbled rapidly from his pedestal. An increasing number of irregularities came to the fore, such as long-term contracts with payments booked up in front, capital transactions recorded as profits, buy-back arrangements of Fermenta shares at guaranteed profits, and loans given to himself for other questionable transactions. It became clear that at Fermenta, imprecise reporting and selective forecasting had been the order of the day. Industrivärden, an investment company affiliated with Svenska Handelsbanken, discovered that Fermenta's assets were vastly overvalued.

It was also discovered that a part of Fermenta's profits were generated by deals that never existed. It became clear, too, that El-Sayed had played more than an active role in managing Fermenta's stock price. He had been a true master of the media, playing the rags-to-riches story for all it was worth. Thus, every journalist willing to listen had been receiving stories about future deals, mergers, and acquisitions, announcements which could not but influence the stock price.

In doing all this, however, it does appear that El-Sayed didn't see any wrongdoing in his actions. Like many entrepreneurs, seeing the boundaries, distinguishing what was his and what was the company's, was not his forte. He probably rationalized that what he was doing was in the best interest of the company. And that may have been correct at one level of analysis. (In spite of all his wheeling and dealing he doesn't appear to have benefitted much personally). In fact, El-Sayed's identification with Fermenta was so strong that he was unwilling to separate from it and enrich himself by selling out at a time when a deal was still possible. The way he mixed fact with fancy seems to indicate that his capacity for reality testing was to some extent marred. The lie about his credentials was certainly self-destructive given the likelihood, in the light of his self-perpetrated visibility, that he would be found out.

When we look at his behavior more closely, we can see how El-Sayed fits some of the characteristics of the impostor. For example, as described in the previous character sketch, we can see it in his showmanship, his talent in playing on the greed of others, and his ability to suspend the disbelief of his audience and create excitement about the supposed success of his ventures. The protean quality of his sense of identity is demonstrated in the way he was oscillated between playing the role of the average guy and being a wheeler dealer business tycoon.

It can be said, however, that in many aspects El-Sayed's behavior is not very different from that of the typical entrepreneur. Similar behavior patterns can be seen, particularly when the darker sides of entrepreneurship come to the fore (Kets de Vries, 1985). All entrepreneurs need dreams, but in dreaming they are not always effective in distinguishing fact from fancy. And there are, of course, limits to how far they can distort reality. In trying to resolve his own confusion and act accordingly to his "inner theater," El-Sayed seems to have transgressed. His personal myth increasingly led him into trouble. His own problems and those of his business became too intertwined. Self-deception eventually led to his downfall.

The paradox is that now El-Sayed is getting all the blame for the shattered illusions of his investors. As is often the case, a villain is being made out of one of our heroes. After all, being a hero is not a very stable position. One may argue, however, that the investors are as much to blame, having become victims of their own greed. And in the end, when he could no longer deliver, El-Sayed was turned into the scapegoat. Although we may hypothesize that he probably did not really act intentionally, but was swept away by unconscious forces, he has now been found guilty on 14 counts of financial misconduct and jailed for 5 years (International Herald Tribune, 1989, p. 12). As a postscript, one may add that in spite of the financial losses, it is people like El-Sayed who are the lifeblood of society, seeing "new combinations" where others don't and in doing so helping reevaluate existing patterns. Moreover, his legacy is that the scandal has inspired lasting changes in the Swedish financial system.

CONCLUDING REMARKS

The writer G. K. Chesterton once remarked very astutely that "... a really accomplished impostor is the most wretched of geniuses: he is a Napoleon on a desert island." We have seen, however, that most impostors are not of that ilk, they will not remain Napoleons for too long. Eventually, all too human foibles take over and impostors unmask themselves.

The potential marks, instead of waiting for that to happen and be victimized in the meantime would do better, to be prepared and be alert to indications of imposture. And, as we have seen from our previous discussion, there are many telltale signs.

The challenge for all of us becomes to maintain our capacity for rational thinking and not be swept away by emotional forces when the sirens promising instant love, wealth, and happiness are beckoning and we may be tempted to give in. When something doesn't really make sense and in spite of that, we are very tempted to suspend our sense of disbelief, it is high time to take a hard look and reevaluate the situation. However, it is not too easy to resist an individual who has as his or her message, "trust me, I will take care of all your needs." In particular, it is difficult to fight the force of greed. But when these powerful feelings arise, the time has come to distance ourselves, take another hard look, have discussions with outsiders and wonder what really is going on.

The mesmerizing power of the impostor is only one issue. There is also, as we have seen, the question of feeling like an impostor. At time we may all fall victim to such negative thoughts. When they become a grinding preoccupation, however, they can make for a miserable life. If that is the case, a lot of time and effort will be needed to break the spell and recapture a sense of authenticity. It is a difficult task to stop the vicious circle made up of feelings of inadequacy, the related hard work or procrastination, doubt, and guilt. But it is possible if we are willing to acquire greater insight into our own motivations and actions. It is the development of one's own reflective capacity, and the awareness of one's blind spots, sometimes with the help of insightful others, that will have a prophylactic effect on the mesmerizing power of the impostor and the paralyzing forces of feeling imposturous.

REFERENCES

AARONS, Z.A. A study of a perversion and an attendant character disorder. The Psychoanalytic Quarterly, XXVIII(4), 1959, 481-492.

ABRAHAM, K. The history of an impostor in the light of psychoanalytical knowledge. In Clinical papers on psychoanalysis. New York: Brunner/Mazel, 1955.

BLUM, H.P. The psychoanalytic process and analytic influence: A clinical study of a lie and loss. International Journal of Psychoanalysis, 64, 1983, 17-33.

BURSTEN, B. The manipulator: A psychoanalytic view. New Haven and London: Yale University Press, 1973.

CLANCE, P.R. The impostor phenomenon. New York: Peachtree Publishing, 1985.

CLANCE, P.R., & IMES, S.A. The impostor phenomenon in high achieving women: Dynamics and therapeutic intervention. Psychotherapy: Theory, research and practice, 15(3), 1978, 241-247.

CRICHTON, R. The great impostor. New York: Random House, 1959.

DEUTSCH, H. Some forms of emotional disturbance and their relationship to schizophrenia. In: Neuroses and character types. New York: International Universities Press, 1985.

DEUTSCH, H. The impostor: Contribution to ego psychology of a type of psychopath. In: Neuroses and character types. New York: International Universities Press, 1986.

DEUTSCH, H. Neuroses and character types. New York: International Universities Press, 1965.

DOWLING, C. The Cinderella complex. New York: Summit Books, 1981.

DUPONT, R.L. The impostor and his mother. The Journal of Nervous and Mental Disease, 150(6), 1970, 444-448.

ERIKSON, E.H. Identity and the life cycle. In: Psychological issues (Vol. 1, No. 1). New York: International Universities Press, 1959.

FAST, I. A function of action in the early development of identity. International Journal of Psychoanalysis, 51, 1970, 471-478.

FENICHEL, O. The collected papers of Otto Fenichel (2nd series). New York: International Universities Press, 1954.

FINKELSTEIN, L. The impostor: Aspects of his development. The Psychoanalytic Quarterly, XLIII (1), 1974, 85-114.

FREUD, A. The ego and the mechanisms of defense (revised ed.). New York: International Universities Press, 1966.

FREUD, S. Some character types met within psychoanalytic work. In J. Strachey (Ed.), The standard edition of the complete psychological works of Sigmund Freud (Vol. XIV). London: Hogarth Press and Institute of Psychoanalysis, 1957.

GEDIMAN, H.K. Imposture, inauthenticity and feeling fraudulent. Journal of the American Psychoanalytic Association, 33(4), 1985, 911-935.

GOFFMAN, E. Relations in public. New York: Harper Colophon Books, 1971.

GOTTDIENER, A. The impostor. Contemporary Psychoanalysis, 18(3), 1982, 438-454.

GRAND, H.G. The masochistic defense of the "double mask": Its relationship to imposture. International Journal of Psychoanalysis, 54, 1973, 445-454.

GREENACRE, P. The impostor. In: Emotional growth (Vol. 1). New York: International Universities Press, 1971.

GREENACRE, P. The relation of the impostor to the artist. In: Emotional growth (Vol. 1). New York: International Universities Press, 1971.
GREENSON, R.R. On screen defenses, screen hunger, and screen identity. Journal of the American Psychoanalytic Association, 6, 1958, 242-262.
GROSSMAN, W.I. Notes on masochism: A discussion of the history and development of a psychoanalytic concept. The Psychoanalytic Quarterly, LV(3), 1986, 379-413.
INTERNATIONAL HERALD TRIBUNE. From rags to riches to penitentiary. July 20, 1989.
JOHNSON, A.M., & SZUREK, S.A. The genesis of antisocial acting out in children and adults. The Psychoanalytic Quarterly, XXI, 1952, 323-343.
KAPLAN, L.J. The concept of the family romance. Psychoanalytic Review, 61(2), 1974, 169-202.
KETS DE VRIES, M.F.R. The dark side of entrepreneurship. Harvard Business Review, November-December 1985, 160-167.
KETS DE VRIES, M. F. R. Prisoners of leadership. New York: Wiley, 1989.
KETS DE VRIES, M.F.R., & MILLERD, D. Narcissism and leadership: An object relations perspective. Human Relations, 38(6), 1985, 583-601.
KLEIN, M. Love, guilt and reparation and other works: 1921-1945. London: Virago, 1988.
KOHUT, H., & WOLF, E.S. The disorders of the self and their treatment: An outline. International Journal of Psychoanalysis, 59,1978, 413-426.
KRIS, E.. The personal myth: A problem in psychoanalytic technique. In: Selected Papers of Ernst Kris. New Haven: Yale University Press, 1975, pp. 272-300.
LANGER, S.K. Feeling and form. London: Routledge & Kegan Paul, 1953.
LEHMANN, H.E. Unusual psychiatric disorders and atypical psychoses. In: A. M. Freedman, H. I. Kaplan, and B. J. Sadock (Eds.), Comprehensive textbook of psychiatry (Vol. 2, 2nd eds.). Baltimore: Williams and Wilkins, 1975.
MAHLER, M.S., PINE, F., & BERGMAN, A. The psychological birth of the human infant. New York: Basic Books, 1975.
MANN, T. Confessions of Felix Krull, confidence man. New York: Vintage Books, 1969.
MARTIN, J. Who am I this time: Uncovering the fictive personality. New York: Norton, 1988.
MELVILLE, H. The confidence man. New York: New American Library, 1954.
MILLER, N.G. The great salad oil swindle. Baltimore: Penguin Books, 1965.
OPPENHEIMER, P. A pleasant vintage of Till Eulenspiegel. Middletown, Connecticut: Wesleyan University Press, 1972.
PANEL, Clinical and theoretical aspects of "as if" characters. Journal of the American Psychoanalytic Association, 14, 1966, 569-590.
PORTER, R. The language of quackery in England. In P. Burke and R. Porter (Eds.), The social history of language. Cambridge: Cambridge University Press, 1987.
REICH, A. Narcissistic object choice in women. Journal of the American Psychoanalytic Association, 1, 1953, 22-44.
REIK, T. Masochism in modern man. New York: Farrer & Rinehart, 1941.
ROSS, N. The "as if" concept. Journal of the American Psychoanalytic Association, 15(1), 1967, 59-82.
SCHAFER, R. The pursuit of failure and the idealization of unhappiness. American Psychologist, 39(4), 1984, 398-405.

SIMONS, R.C. Psychoanalytic contribution to psychiatric nosology: Forms of masochistic behavior. Journal of the American Psychoanalytic Association, 35(3), 1987, 583-608.

SPENCE, D. Narrative truth and historical truth. New York: Norton, 1982.

SULLIVAN, H.S. The interpersonal theory of psychiatry. New York: Norton, 1953.

SUNDQVIST, S.I. Refaat & Fermenta: Dramat och Aktörerna. Stockholm: Författarförlaget, 1987.

SWANSON, D.A. The Münchausen Syndrome. American Journal of Psychotherapy, 35(3), 1981, 436-444.

WEINSHEL, E.M. Some observations on not telling the truth. Journal of the American Psychoanalytic Association, 27(3), 1979, 503-532.

WIJSENBEEK, H., & NITZAN, I. The case of Peter, an impostor. Psychiatria, Neurologia, Neurochirurgia, 71, 1968, 193-202.

WINNICOTT, D.W. Through pediatrics to psychoanalysis. New York: Basic Books, 1975.

WITTEBORT, S. Behind the great Swedish scandal. Institutional Investor, August 1987, 93-104.

Alexithymia in Organizational Life: The Organization Man Revisited

Manfred F. R. Kets de Vries

INTRODUCTION

More than 30 years have passed since Whyte (1956) wrote his classic work "The Organization Man". His depiction of what he perceived to be the typical executive very much resembled Sinclair Lewis's satiric but convincing portrait of Babbitt, the bland, totally conformist real estate man from Zenith Corporation, an individual glib and opportunistic both in business and private life. Lewis turned "Babbitt" into a moral tale of how compromising about conformity can become the price required for our business culture. The novel is a prime example of the creation of a personal wasteland, how an individual can lead an empty, thoroughly meaningless existence. Babbitt is a man who

> ... beheld, and half admitted that he beheld, his way of life as incredibly mechanical. Mechanical business - a brisk selling of badly built houses. Mechanical religion - a dry, hard church, shut off from the real life of the streets, inhumanly respectable as a top-hat. Mechanical golf and dinner parties and bridge and conversation ... mechanical friendships - back-slapping and jocular, never daring to essay the test of quietness (Lewis, 1922, p. 323).

Whyte's quintessential organization man seems to be quite similar: colorless, dull, and unimaginative. We are faced with a person afraid to make bold decisions, an individual far removed from his opposite, the conquistador of business or the entrepreneur. His description of the organization man also reminds us of Erich Fromm's speculations about the proliferation of a marketing orientation, a form of acting and behaving which he believed to be typical of modern life. Fromm's marketing-oriented person is someone with a shaky feeling of identity, an individual exceedingly superficial and very changeable in his attitudes. For this person, identity seems to be made up of the sum total of the roles he can be expected to play. Thus, "the premise of the marketing orientation is emptiness, the lack of any specific quality which would not be subject to change, since any persistent trait of

---

Reprinted, by permission of publisher, from Human Relations, Vol. 42, No. 12, 1989. Office of Rights/Permissions, Plenum Publishing Corp, New York.

character might conflict someday with the requirements of the market" (Fromm, 1947, p. 85).

This sense of depersonalization, automation, and emptiness of life comes across very well in Harrington's (1958) ironic presentation of "Life in a Crystal Palace". In the "crystal palace," a metaphor for a large organization, everything seems to be bland and mechanical. Life is deadening; conversation seems to be merely a "filler," a way of avoiding silence. Everybody automatically and completely accepts, and lives according to the organization's policies and procedures. From the author's descriptions, the crystal palace turns into a corporate theater where conformity rules, all the actors are interchangeable, and no one dares to call attention to himself.

In his book "The Gamesman", Michael Maccoby (1976) presents a more nuanced view of corporate man. He regards the company man as one among a number of types. In his analysis, this individual is less of a caricature; he portrays a person essential to the functioning of the large corporation. This person gives it its strength because of his strong identification with the organization's goals and values. At the same time, however, Maccoby warned against the company man's excessive reactions of dependency, since he tends to feel lost when separated from his organization. To use Maccoby's (1976) words:

> Although the company man's work tends to reinforce a responsible attitude to the organization and the project, it may also strenghten a negative syndrome of dependency: submissive surrender to the organization and to authority, sentimental idealization of those in power, a tendency to betray the self in order to gain security, comfort, luxury (p. 94).

The work of the cultural historian Christopher Lasch, echoes this theme of conformity and dependency, which he believes is accentuated by the fact that "the corporation takes on the appearance of a total institution, in which every trace of individual identity disappears" (Lasch, 1984, p. 70).

All these descriptions beg the question as to whether or not Whyte had identified a specific personality type or if he was merely trying to satirize organizational life. The appeal of his book and the continuing popularity of its theme do indicate, however, that Whyte must have hit a sensitive chord among businessmen and other people familiar with organizations. It seems that his view of organizational life led to immediate recognition of a pattern that was present in contemporary business culture.

Although he and others dealing with the same theme may sometimes have resorted to stereotypes or oversimplifications, there was something true in what they were saying. Given the kind of impact these authors had, the key question becomes why do people in organizational life behave in such a way? Is there something in organizations that accentuates this behavior pattern? What do organizations do to people? Are certain otherwise dormant personality characteristics more likely to come out into the open in organizations? Or should the question be put differently: is there a group of people with specific personality characteristics who are attracted to certain types of organizations? Can one compare given organizations to "holding stations" which offer a comfortable but unobtrusive shelter to people with specific predilictions?

In answering these questions, Whyte did not have the advantage of using some of the more contemporary conceptualizations of personality. Taking his sociological bent into consideration, he left in-depth psychological speculation to others. But perhaps the time has come to take up where he left off. Given the importance of the behavior patterns described, particularly since such behavior does not usually foster organizational creativity and innovation, the objective of this paper is to take another look at the organization man and make inferences about his or her existence. In order to arrive at a deeper level of analysis, the organization man's behavior will be explored in the context of a relatively recent clinical construct called alexithymia. The study of such a construct offers the opportunity to better understand the development of a specific style of interaction particularly as it relates to the emotions. As the subsequent discussion will show, there are many interesting parallels between the organization man and the alexithymic disposition. This exploration will also give us the opportunity to make tentative observations as to whether there are certain types of organizations which enhance this mode of behavior and whether there are specific jobs where the behavior is prominent. Such a study is, of course, by its nature speculative. Pursuing this line of investigation may, however, shed light on the reasons for the obstinate survival of the organization man and may also further understanding of the nature of the interface and fit between personality and organization.

THE NATURE OF ALEXITHYMIA

In 1963, two French psychoanalysts, Marty and de M'Uzan, identified a style of thought and expression which they named "pensée opératoire". In studying psychosomatic patients, they found a cognitive and affective style where there was a conspicuous absence of fantasy, little dream recollections, and an unusual, utilitarian way of thinking. They also noticed that in responding to questions, these people would behave in a rather robot-like manner and repeat in great detail past action without enlarging upon their activities. As de M'Uzan (1974) put it: "the patient's language is poor, flat and banal, glued to the present, and only producing facts stated chronologically" (p. 462).

Sifneos (1972, 1973) noticed similar patterns in his psychosomatic patients. He too stressed these individuals' inability to find words to describe emotions, as well as their use of action to express emotion and avoid conflict, their preoccupation with external events rather than fantasy or emotions, and their tendency to describe endlessly the circumstances surrounding an event rather than their feelings. To him goes the credit for having first coined the term alexithymia, a word constructed from the Greek meaning no words for emotions. He and a colleague pursued this line of research and viewed alexithymia as some kind of communication disorder (Nemiah & Sifneos, 1970; Nemiah, 1977, 1978).

Independently, Krystal (1968, 1974, 1982) was coming to similar conclusions while studying severe post-traumatic states. He noted that alexithymic individuals seem to have defects in affective and cognitive functioning and in interpersonal relationships, due to an impoverished intrapsychic life. Elaborating on these differentiating characteristics, Krystal (1979) stated that the people in question "are unable to distinguish between one emotion and another" (p. 17), but, "like the color-blind person, they have become aware of their deficiency and have learned to pick up clues by which they infer what they cannot discern" (p. 18). With respect to their cognitive problems, he mentioned that it almost seems as if these people are super-adjusted to reality. He continued by saying, however, that if one gets "past the superficial impression of superb functioning, one discovers a sterility and monotony of ideas and severe impoverishment of their imagination" (Krystal, 1979, p. 19). With respect to their relationships with others, Krystal noticed an impaired capacity for empathy: these people treat others with cool detachment and indifference. The pattern was supported by others, who observed that when dealing with such individuals one is left with a feeling of dullness, boredom, and frustration (Taylor, 1977). Encouraged by these findings, many other researchers and clinicians in the fields of psychiatry, medical psychology, and psychotherapy recalled and recognized similar behavior patterns (Brautigan & Von Rad, 1977).

In this context, it is important to mention the work of one clinician, McDougall, who, cognizant of the high degree of social conformity among alexithymics, used the words "pseudonormality" (1974), "robots" (1980a), and "normopaths" (1984) to describe these people.

She argued that:

> Instead of some form of psychic management of disturbing affects or unwelcome knowledge or fantasies, the ego may achieve complete destruction of the representations or feelings concerned, so that these are not registered. The result then may be a super adaptation to external reality, a robot-like adjustment to inner and outer pressure which short - circuits the world of the imaginary. This "pseudo-normality" is a widespread character trait and may well be a danger sign pointing to the eventuality of psychosomatic symptoms (McDougall, 1974, p. 444).

The origin of this behavior, she speculates, is due to a special kind of parenting whereby the mother tends to use the child as a "drug" (1974, 1980b, 1982a,b). In arguing her case, she presents clinical material demonstrating that from the beginning the mother seems to be out of touch with the child's emotional needs. Many other studies (Krystal, 1979, 1982; Gardos, Schniebolk, Mirin, Wolk, & Rosenthal, 1984) have supported her conjecture that the pathogenesis of alexithymia is created in the first and second years of life. What a number of clinicians suggest is that these mothers (and fathers) solve their own, often narcissistic conflicts through the child, who gets stuck in what may be described as an aborted symbiotic relationship. The child finds him- or herself in a sort of archaic double-bind situation, hence, a state of extreme dependency is artificially prolonged. Separation and autonomous feelings of identity are stifled and real individuation is prevented. The child is treated like an extension of the mother and is under her constant surveillance; his or her body is handled like someone else's property. Furthermore, the father may even covertly encourage this type of situation in order to be spared a similar "fate," afraid as he may be of the perceived "engulfing" qualities of his wife.

Given such childrearing practice, the mother is not what has sometimes been described as a "mére satisfaisante" (a satisfying mother), but instead becomes a "mére calmante" (a tranquilizing mother). Due to her own problems, the mother does not allow normal identification processes to occur. Consequently, the child never really learns how to feel at ease without being in continual contact with her. He or she does not internalize the "mére satisfaisante", a necessary process if he or she is going to be able to manage without needing continuous external stimuli (Fain & Kreisher, 1970). The overbearing treatment of the child can probably be looked at as the mother's way of arriving at some form of restitution for assumed defects of her own. Since separation is discouraged, any desire for exploration or any form of initiative are nipped in the bud. Predictably, such treatment has grave consequences for later personality development. Since the mother does not allow for satisfactory transitional space (Winnicott, 1975), she disrupts the process of play, exploration, and symbolization. Moreover, the child does not really experience whatever symbolizations are formed as his or her own mental productions but as something alien coming from the outside. Such a situation can lead to an arrest in affect development (Krystal, 1979, 1982). Differentiation, verbalization, and desomatization of emotions never properly occur, impeding construction of a highly complex matrix of signals essential for daily functioning (as opposed to experiencing emotions as dangerous, potentially uncontrollable forces). These people consequently ignore their bodies' signs and their minds' signals of distress. Symbol formation will be impaired and a stilted fantasy life may become a reality. Vague somatic sensations will frequently replace dream and fantasy material. Moreover, given their earlier situation of dependency, they may become addictively captive to external stimuli, a life line which can structure their world, unable as they are to resort to their own symbolic representations, fantasies, or dreams to work through mental conflict. To use McDougall's (1982b) words, what they "feel will appear in the people [they are] involved with. They are [their] mirror" (p. 88). They attempt "to make substitute objects in the external world do duty for symbolic ones which are absent or damaged in the inner psychic world" (p. 449). But it is her opinion that such attempts are "doomed to failure" and will lead "to endless repetition and addictive attachment to the outer world and external objects" (p. 449).

Hence, these people are preoccupied with the concrete and the objective; the use of metaphors, allusions, and hidden meanings is strange to them. They tend to negate and deny the existence of emotions (Von Rad, 1983). They somehow seem to be psychological illiterates lacking the capacity for empathy, strangers as they are to reflective self-awareness and needing to resort to action as a way dealing with conflicts (Neill & Sandifer, 1982; Lesser & Lesser, 1983; Taylor, 1984). Given their capacity to negate and deny emotions, they are probably not even aware of, or experience intrapsychic conflict.

Their behavior has a robot-like quality with stiffness of posture and often a lack of facial expressiveness. External details seem to be utilized as a way of filling their inner deadness. Due to the nature of their upbringing, their "true self" (Winnicott, 1975) has never been allowed to emerge.

Some clinicians have differentiated between primary and secondary forms of alexithymia. In the first instance, alexithymia is viewed as a specific character trait caused by possible genetic neurophysiological deficits, i.e., a disconnection between the left and right hemispheres due to a commissurotomy, or by early psychic trauma; while in the second instance, sociocultural factors may play a role. There, reference is made to alexithymic reactions which may develop after a specific stressful event or series of events. In this regard, some researchers have looked at rather extreme situations. Examples are the kind of emotional numbing that occurs in the case of concentration camp victims or Vietnam War veterans (Freiberger, 1977; Shipko, Alvarez, & Norrello, 1983; Krystal, Giller & Cicchetti, 1986).

What we can infer from these studies is that alexithymia as communication disorder tends to be relatively widespread. Like with most clinical syndromes, estimates of its prevalence among the general population vary, however. For example, one study using undergraduate students as subjects showed that 8.2% of the men and 1.8% of the women fell within the alexithymic range (Blanchard, Arena, & Pallmeyer, 1981). But this study raises questions about the validity and reliability of the instruments.

Whatever the exact percentage of alexithymics in the general population may be, this construct is used to described individuals with an extreme reality-based cognitive style, an impoverished fantasy life, a paucity of inner emotional experiences, a tendency to engage in stereotypical interpersonal behavior, and a speech pattern characterized by endless, trivial, repetitive details. This last characteristic seems to be the outcome of the need to find some kind of foothold in the external world due to the difficulty these people experience internally in describing what they feel. Whatever feelings they may have tend to be of a vague, diffuse nature. Here, however, is where agreement seems to end. Although psychodynamic inferences have gone a long way toward an explanation, there is still a considerable amount of confusion about the construct's etiology. Is it really a trait? Or is it a situation-specific form of coping behavior? Can it be both trait and state? (Von Rad, 1984; Ahrens & Deffner, 1986). The answers to these questions are not yet clear.

In spite of this confusion, however, what is clear is that the existence of alexithymia is based on a large body of consistent clinical and phenomenological observations. In addition, alexithymia is not an all-or-nothing phenomenon. On the contrary, it appears to be potentially accessible to everyone, admittedly to a varying degree. It seems to be a graded dimension whereby individuals will occupy different positions on a spectrum of cognitive/affective experience and expression (Martin, Phil, & Dobkin, 1984). Moreover, insidiously, these alexithymic inclinations may influence our perceptions and actions. Given what we now know about alexithymic individuals, what is particularly noteworthy for the purposes of this article is that, in their behavior, they resemble in an uncanny way the organization man.

THE ORGANIZATION MAN'S ALEXITHYMIC PREDISPOSITION

Many years ago, an astute observer of organizational life wrote the following lines about some of its characteristics:

> The dominance of the spirit of formalistic impersonality, "sine via et studio," without hatred or passion, and hence without affection or enthusiasm. The dominant norms are concepts of straightforward duty without regard to personal considerations. Everyone is subject to formal equality of treatment, that is, everyone in the same empirical situation. This is the spirit in which the ideal official conducts his office (Weber, 1947, p. 340).

Reading Max Weber's description of the bureaucrat, we recall the alexithymic's factual, unemotional, and unimaginative way of behaving and acting. We remember the wooden quality implicit in such behavior. Since alexithymics don't know how to manage their emotions, it is easy to perceive how little room they have for feelings. We can actually observe how the people in question will often substitute action, inappropriate as it may be, for feelings. Moreover, we have noted how, when asked how they feel, these people will usually resort to a description of external events. For them "facts" seem to be what counts. Some people pervert what originally may have been a realistic concern. They have difficulty going beyond this obsession with facts, unable as they are to use their imaginations. They seem to suffer from a deficiency in utilizing feelings and fantasies in their mental functioning. Their behavior appears to be almost overadaptive. But we may discover, that is to say, if we go beyond the first impression of excellent functioning, the sterility of their imaginations and the monotony of their ideas. We can also recall the impression of blandness, dullness, and colorlessness with which we are left when dealing with such people.

Organizational Types

Organizations give alexithymics great opportunities to blend into the organizational culture. These organizational environments legitimize what otherwise may be looked at as strange behavior. As such, they give relief in providing some kind of structure, thus making alexithymic behavior less conspicuous; organizations take on a "containing" function (Bion, 1961). Moreover, given the possibility of the existence of such a phenomenon as secondary alexithymia, it may very well be that certain types of organizations go even further in that they possess the kind of numbing quality which awakens dormant alexithymic tendencies in their employees.

In looking at organizational factors which can contribute to this kind of behavior, we are reminded in particular of two organizational "ideal" types described in earlier research (Kets de Vries & Miller, 1985, 1986, 1988): the "compulsive" and "depressive" organizations. In the former, we find an organization which is bureaucratic and tends to be inwardly focused. A strict hierarchy exists in which an individual manager's status derives directly from a specific position. The leadership tends to dominate the organization from top to bottom, insisting that others conform to tightly prescribed rules and procedures. Slavish adherence to programmed, standardized, routine practices are the norm. There is strategic reliance on a narrow, established theme to the exclusion of other factors. Rigid formal codes, ritualized evaluation processes, and an attitude of risk aversion makes any form of change an extremely difficult proposition.

The "depressive" organization is similar in many ways but is in worse shape. This type of organization drifts with no sense of direction and is often confined to antiquated "mature" markets. Various protectionistic practices are the only reason it still survives. Extreme conservatism, a very vague set of goals and strategies, and an absence of plans are the rule. Structurally, these organizations are bureaucratic, ritualistic, and inflexible. There is a leadership vacuum, a lack of motivation and initiative, and an attitude of passivity and negativity. Communications are poor and so is scanning, as there is ignorance of market trends. The organizational climate is impersonal, "decidophobia" being the rule, leading to a great resistance to change.

From the description of these two types of organizations, we can see how well they fit with the alexithymic disposition. They provide an ideal holding environment which makes alexithymics less conspicuous. At the same time, we should not forget the effect of the organization on the individual, with its potential to bring out otherwise dormant alexithymic characteristics. Although other types of organizations may have similar effects, none has that kind of numbing quality that we find in the "compulsive" and "depressive" organizations.

Individual Styles

The Detached CEO. Going from an organizational to an individual orientation, we can occasionally find top executives who experience great difficulty in dealing with emotions. To protect themselves from emotional involvement these people may use a detached style. McDougall (1982b) has already equated alexithymic symptoms "to a form of schizoid withdrawal from others and to the maintenance of a devitalized inner state of which the individual is unaware" (p. 88). This form of emotional isolation can, however, have serious organizational repercussions since such behavior may frustrate the dependency needs of the other executives, leading to feelings of bewilderment and aggressiveness (Kets de Vries & Miller, 1985, 1986, 1988). A highly politicized organizational culture may develop a playground for second-tier "gamesmen" (Maccoby, 1976). Warring and uncooperative fiefdoms may be the consequences. If so, self-imposed barriers to the free flow of information will prevail. With such an organizational culture, it is no wonder that there is insufficient scanning of the external environment; the focus of the organization is more internal. A vacillating, inconsistent, muddling-through type of strategy can usually be observed, its orientation depending on which clique managed to get the ear of the senior executive.

In this case, we can see how alexithymic behavior at the top, given the dynamics of power, can have serious organizational consequences. We don't have to go all the way to the top, however, to find this type of behavior. There are certain kinds of jobs which suit the alexithymic disposition very well. Here, two groups of people come to mind, both of which show a type of behavior also observed in the context of the schizoid condition (Kets de Vries, 1980).

The Systems Person. These people will disguise their interpersonal difficulties by resorting to jobs which are thing-oriented. Abstractions, tasks, ideas, and inanimate objects become of overriding importance. Feelings are superfluous here; what really counts is "the system." Their contacts with others are depersonalized and mechanical. Attachment to procedures and rules and regulations becomes their way of coping with the sterility of their inner world. The present information revolution is a great facilitator in making such behavior less conspicuous. The increasing importance of the human/computer interface becomes a marvelous disguise for some of the people in question. The systems person operates in an automaton-like way, hanging on to fixed routines or zealously advocating abstractions and thereby abolishing relationships with real people. His or her pace is directed, and stimulus provided by the terminal of his or her computer. Such people seem to be perfectly programmed. Unfortunately, with their often mindless and rigid pursuit of routines, curiosity and initiative are missing. Hence, they may not possess a sufficient adaptive capacity to cope with environmental changes, a deficiency which can have devastating consequences for the organization.

The Sociol Sensor. The behavior of these people has a chameleon-like quality. They are the role players par excellence, taking on new roles when it suits them. They are very astute in picking up signals from the outside world and adjust their behavior accordingly. The only structure they know seems to come from the external environment. They are the "as if" personalities described as having "a highly plastic readiness to pick up signals from the outer world and to mold oneself and one's behavior accordingly" (Deutsch, 1965, p. 265). They resemble the marketing-oriented people referred to by Erich Fromm (1947). They are also like the color-blind persons described by Krystal (1979, 1982), those who have learned how to cover up their deficiencies in affectual reactions. And they fit very well in service-oriented industries where "prescribed" emotions frequently become the norm. But in spite of all their efforts and notwithstanding their superficial adjustment, a sense of conviction is lacking in their actions. Although the first impression is one of complete normality and they seem to be superadaptive, under the veneer one quickly discovers a sense of desperate shallowness and lack of warmth. Changeability in their attitudes and their talent for mimicry seem to be their only permanent qualities. Their glibness in behavior makes for a notion of pseudo-sincerity and pseudo-authenticity. Their super-adaptability and pseudo-compliance seem to take place with only one goal in mind, that is, to avoid having to deal with feelings. What seems like adaptiveness is really insensitivity to the feelings and reactions of the people around them. The mask of extroversion becomes a disguise for the emptiness of their inner theater." Given the deadness of their inner world, creativity and insight will be found wanting.

SEARCHING FOR SOLUTIONS

Although the alexithymic predisposition, be it primary or secondary, is something that a number of executives possess or at least are susceptible to, albeit to varying degrees, this does not mean we cannot do something about it. Granted, we have seen how some individuals perpetuate the situation by finding jobs that shelter them from circumstance which may demand affective responses, and we have observed how some people manage to pursue rather stunted lifestyles. We have seen how such behavior, when it involves top managers, can sometimes influence the overall organization dramatically. We have also noted how organizations may take advantage of alexithymic predispositions and, through particular structural and strategic arrangements, even accentuate such a situation in their organizational cultures through the suppression or exact prescription of emotion (Hochschild, 1983). We have seen how the information and service revolution with all its accompaniments has very much facilitated this behavior.

In our assessment of alexithymic behavior we have observed that, in general, organizations do not appreciate it when people do own up to their emotions. In large bureaucratic organizations, affect is avoided, "greyness" in dress, behavior, and actions appears to be the norm, and conformity the prevailing pattern. Even sexuality seems to be eradicated (Burrell, 1984). All in all, the executive and "the man in the grey flannel suit" are apparently almost synonymous. Expression of emotion is feared to disrupt organizational processes, or emotion is carefully managed with all the associated strains due to the suppression of one's "true self" (Winnicott, 1975). The climb to the executive suite is not enhanced by eccentricity in behavior. Executives have to "fit," and that does not necessarily make for the best and the brightest. However, we should also take note that in this context, innovation and creativity in organizations do not come from alexithymic-oriented behavior, i.e., how convenient this "don't-rock-the-boat" attitude may be from a short-term perspective. For creativity in organizations we need bold moves, leaps of imagination, passion, and vision.

To break the vicious circle of emotionlessness is not going to be easy. Unfortunately, there are no quick fixes to the problem. This does not mean, however, that nothing can be done about it, that alexithymic behavior patterns in organizations are inevitable. But if change is desired, if there is a wish to enliven organizational life, it will need a sustained effort.

When we look at "ideal types," meaning in this instance the "heroes" of the business world, we notice that the ones who tend to be admired most are those who engage in bold action. It is leaders such as Iacocca, Jobs, and Ross Perot, people with "fire in their belly," who are chosen as examples of how to run corporations. And in light of their behavior and actions these people are no strangers to emotion.

What this tells us is that executives do not have to be alexithymic to succeed. They do not necessarily have to give in to potential alexithymic tendencies in their make-up. The negative sides of the organization man and the stifling effects of organizational life can be avoided. But in order to be able to do so, both the manager and the organization have a responsibility. The manager has to take the initiative and establish preventive steps. Here, Whyte went even further and argued for a combative attitude on the part of the organization man.

> The organization man is not in the grip of vast social forces about which it is impossible for him to do anything; the options are there, and with wisdom and foresight he can turn the future away from the dehumanized collective that so haunts our thoughts ... He must fight The Organization. Not stupidly or selfishly, for the defects of individual self-regard are no more to be venerated than the defects of cooperation. But fight he must, for the demands for his surrender are constant and powerful; and the more he has come to like the life of organization the more difficult does he find it to resist these demands, or even to recognize them. It is wretched dispiriting advice to hold before him the dream that ideally there need be no conflict between him and society. There always is; there always must be (Whyte 1956, p. 404).

We don't have to go that far and preach revolution. However, to create more effective organizations, an effort must be made to help executives own up to their emotions and practice their capacity for reflective self-observation. The tendency of many executives to merely give in to "flight into action" (Klein, 1935) without the balance of reflection has to be carefully monitored.

Executives have to discover or redsicover the ability to "play," learn how to use humor and how to engage in flights of fancy. It is from such characteristics that vision and adaptability derive. Executives should be able to confront their feelings and not remain prisoners of a fictitious balance for which they are partially responsible. They should not hide their true selves, but show authenticity in action. They should try to overcome infantile fixations and aims. To do so, imaginative experience and fantasy production must be encouraged, even if, paradoxically, this has to be done in a directed way. Not only therapists but also organizational leaders can play an important role fostering such practices. More importantly, organizational leadership can set the example that the expression of emotion is an acceptable practice by showing it themselves. They also should encourage a diversity in emotional expression and not just stick to prescribed routines. Of course, to make this work within the organization, a climate of trust becomes a necessity. Executives should come to realize that the expression of emotion in a business context does not have negative career implications, that there is room for critical give and take and space for imagination.

Other signals can be given by the organization through structural arrangements which encourage risk-taking, experimentation, and participation. In order to foster such behavior, there will also be a need for imagination in human resource practices with respect to hiring, training, and development, which will in turn avoid creating organizations populated by"clones." Encouraging a positive attitude toward change should become a central concern. For the purposes of establishing a culture of change, slack in the system will be needed to allow for continuous adaptation and development. Naturally, not only should structures be hospitable to change and adaptation, but so should individuals. To be able to do so, however, further exploratory work will be needed to better understand the nature and prevalence of alexithymia in organizations. A greater knowledge of this behavior pattern may be helpful to arrive at a more complete equilibration between individual style and organizational infra- and supra-structure. And in balancing these forces, we could keep in mind the words of Yeats who once said: "by logic and reason we die hourly; by imagination we live!"

REFERENCES

AHRENS, S., & DEFFNER, G. Empirical study of alexithymia: Methodology and results. American Journal of Psychiatry, XL(3), 1986, 430-447.

BION, S. Experiences in groups. London: Tavistock, 1961.

BLANCHARD, E.B., ARENA, J.G., & PALLMEYER, T. P. Psychosomatic properties of a scale to measure alexithymia. Psychotherapy and Psychosomatics, 35, 1981, 64-71.

BRAUTIGAN, B., & VON RAD, M. Toward a theory of psychosomatic disorders. Basel: Karger, 1977.

BURRELL, G. Sex and organizational analysis. Organization Studies, 5(2), 1984, 97-118.

DEUTSCH, H. Neuroses and character types. New York: International Universities Press, 1965.

FAIN, M., & KREISHER, L. Discussion sur la genèse des fonctions représentatives. Revue Francaise de Psychanalyse, 34, 1970, 285-306.

FREIBERGER, H. Supportive psychotherapeutic techniques in primary and secondary alexithymia. Psychotherapy and Psychosomatics., 20, 1977, 337-342.

FROMM, E. Man for himself: An inquiry into the psychiatry of ethics. New York: Fawcett, 1947.

GARDOS, G., SCHNIEBOLK, S., MIRIN, S.M., WOLK, P. & ROSENTHAL, K.L. Alexithymia: Toward validation and measurement. Comprehensive Psychiatry, 25(3), 1984, 278-282.
HARRINGTON, A. Life in a crystal palace. New York: Alfred A. Knopf, 1958.
HOCHSCHILD, A.R. The managed heart. Berkeley: University of Los Angeles Press, 1983.
KETS DE VRIES, M.F.R. Organizational paradoxes: Clinical approaches to management. London: Tavistock, 1980.
KETS DE VRIES, M.F.R., & MILLER, D. The neurotic organization. San Francisco: Jossey Bass, 1985.
KETS DE VRIES, M.F.R., & MILLER, D. Personality, culture and organization. Academy of Management Review, 11(2), 1986, 266-279.
KETS DE VRIES, M. F. R., & MILLER, D. Unstable at the top: Inside the neurotic organization. New York: New American Library, 1988.
KLEIN, M. A contribution to the psychogenesis of manic-depressive states. In: Contributions to psychoanalysis, 1921-1945. New York: McGraw-Hill, 1964.
KRYSTAL, H. Massive psychic trauma. New York: International Universities Press, 1986.
KRYSTAL, H. The genetic development of affects and affect regression. The Annual of Psychoanalysis (Part 2), 1974, 98- 126.
KRYSTAL, H. Alexithymia and psychotherapy. American Journal of Psychotherapy, 33, 1979, 17-31.
KRYSTAL, H. Alexithymia and the effectiveness of psychoanalytic treatment. International Journal of Psychoanalytic Psychotherapy, 9, 1982, 353-378.
KRYSTAL, J. H., GILLER, E. L., & CICCHETTI, V. Assessment of alexithymia in post-traumatic stress disorder and somatic illness: Introduction of a reliable measure. Psychosomatic Medicine, 48(1/2), 1986, 84-94.
LESSER, I. M., & LESSER, B. Z. Alexithymia: Examining the development of a psychological concept. American Journal of Psychiatry, 40(10), 1983, 1305-1308.
LEWIS, S. Babbitt. New York: Harcourt, Brace, Jovanovitch, 1922.
MACCOBY, M. The gamesman. New York: Simon and Schuster, 1976.
MARTIN, J. B., PHIL, R. O., & DOBKIN, P. Schalling-Sifneos Personality Scale: Findings and recommendations. Psychotherapy and Psychosomatics, 41, 1984, 145-152.
MARTY, P., & DE M'UZAN, M. La pensée opératoire. Revue Francaise de Psychanalyse, 27, 1963, 1345-1354.
McDOUGALL, J. The psychosoma and the psychoanalytic process. International Review of Psychoanalysis, 1, 1974, 437-459.
McDOUGALL, J. The anti-analysant in analysis. In: S. Lebovici and D. Widlöcher (Eds.), Psychoanalysis in France. New York: International Universities Press, 1980. (a)
McDOUGALL, J. Alexithymia, psychosomatics, and psychosis. International Journal of Psychoanalytic Psychotherapy, 9, 1982, 379-388. (a)
McDOUGALL, J. Alexithymia: A psychoanalytic viewpoint. Psychotherapy and Psychosomatics, 38, 1982, 81-90. (b)
McDOUGALL, J. The dis-affected patient Reflections on affect pathology. Psychoanalytic Quarterly, L*III*, 1984, 386-409.
DE M'UZAN, J. Analytical process and the notion of the past. International Review of Psychoanalysis, 1, 1974, 461-466.

NEILL, J.R., & SANDIFER, M.G. The clinical approach to alexithymia: A review. Psychosomatics, 23, 1982, 1223-1231.

NEMIAH, J.C. Alexithymia: Theoretical considerations. Psychotherapy and Psychosomatics, 28, 1977, 199-206.

NEMIAH, J.C. Alexithymia and psychosomatic illness. Journal of continuing Education in Psychiatry, 39, 1978, 25-27.

NEMIAH, J .C., & SIFNEOS, E. Affect and fantasy in patients with psychosomatic disorders. In: O. Hill (Ed.), Modern trends in psychosomatic medicine (Vol. 2). London: Butterworths, 1970.

SHIPKO, S.W., ALVAREZ, W.A., & NORRELLO, N. Towards a teleological model of alexithymia: Alexithymia and post-traumatic stress disorder. Psychotherapy and Psychosomatics, 39, 1983, 122-126.

SIFNEOS, P.E. Short-term psychotherapy and emotional crisis. Cambridge: Harvard University Press, 1972.

SIFNEOS, P.E. The prevalence of alexithymic characteristics in psychosomatic patients. Psychotherapy and Psychosomatics, 22, 1973, 255-262.

TAYLOR, G.J. Alexithymia and the counter-transference. Psychotherapy and psychosomatics, 28, 1977, 141-147.

TAYLOR, G.J. Alexithymia: Concept, measurement and implications for treatment. American Journal of Psychiatry, 141(6), 1984, 725-732.

VON RAD, M. Alexithymie: Empirische Untersuchungen zur Diagnostik und Therapie psychosomatisch Kranker. Berlin: Springer Verlag, 1983.

VON RAD, M. Alexithymia and symptom formation. Psychotherapy and Psychosomatics, 42, 1984, 80-89.

WEBER, M. The theory of social and economic organization (translated by A.M. Henderson and T. Parsons). New York: Oxford University Press, 1947.

WHYTE, W.H. The Organization Man, New York: Simon and Schuster, 1956.

The Managerial Couple: Superior-Subordinate Relationships as a Unit of Analysis

James Krantz

INTRODUCTION

The superior-subordinate relationship (called the "managerial couple" in this article) is pervasive in hierarchical organizations and essential to their effectiveness. Through this primary interpersonal link, the delegation of work, the division of labor, and accountability are all realized. Together, both members of the managerial couple must accomplish a job, but neither can control that job individually. Therefore, each must trust the other while coping with feelings of dependence on the other. The extent to which each relies on the other and can be let down by the other often touches upon deep-seated anxieties.

Managerial couples in work organizations take on a life of their own, replete with shared fantasies, hopes and disappointments, collaborative dialogue, and collusive, defensive patterns. On one end of a continuum is the productive, creative, evolving, and mutually stimulating couple. On the other is the rigid, stalemated, sometimes mutually punishing relationship characterized by excessive conflict, numbing detachment, or debilitating dependency.

The managerial couple is a unit of analysis which, I believe, organization theorists have generally underrepresented. This two-person field has its own systemic properties, and like other elements of a system, such as divisions or individuals, is in reciprocal relationship with its system and its parts. The couple is influenced by and influences its context. (1)

Consider the following managerial couple. Sarah, the president of a for-profit urban medical center, has been widely recognized for the innovative programs she initiated in the hospital. Al, a new vice president for community based programs, oversaw two major units. One unit had been actively involved in the restructuring and refocusing programs that received so much recognition; the other unit had been largely outside of this new strategic orientation. Al's predecessor had felt unable to intervene deeply in this second unit. Part of Al's new assignment, then, was to bring this unit into the

---

Reprinted, by permission of publisher, from Human Resource Management, Summer 1989, Vol. 28, No. 2 ,

hospitalwide change agenda. Sarah was eager to have this work begun and realized, along with Al, that he needed to develop a vision that would both embody the hospital's strategic orientation and could serve as a blueprint for the unit's development.

The following incident typifies the difficulties this managerial couple experienced. The hospital management was accustomed to developing strategic plans collectively, believing that it had produced good results. Sarah thus encouraged Al to benefit from the other top managers and to build on their experiences in planning and implementing programs appropriate to the hospital's mission. She also realized the others could contribute an understanding to Al's unit over time.

While Al agreed that he needed a "vision" for the unit, he responded to her suggestions and prodding in a way that made Sarah feel dismissed and unwanted. She encouraged him to set up a meeting with the senior management group and offered to help him design the meeting so that it would be effective and lively. She felt Al's reluctance, so she suggested several times that he call a consultant the hospital used to help in designing working meetings. Again, though he didn't say so to her, Al conveyed through his actions that he did not want to call the consultant.

Sarah and Al were heading towards a stalemate. Al claimed he felt increasingly pressured while Sarah reported she felt increasingly angry, dismissed, and aggressive toward him. Finally, Al scheduled a meeting in a deeply ambivalent way. He tried to line up others' schedules on very short notice for a busy executive group, selecting a day when the vice president of the large nursing unit, someone with an invaluable contribution to make, was typically out of the hospital. Moreover, the executive team's consultant was also unavailable.

The importance of the event, however, was generally recognized and the meeting was arranged. Sarah sensed that because Al had "not taken in" her supervision and direction, he did not really "own" the meeting. Instead, sullen and resentful, he appeared to be doing it out of obligation to Sarah, rather than in a spirit of collaboration and shared development. His inability to own his task was clearly illustrated by his scheduling the meeting in Sarah's office, as if it were her meeting, rather than his.

As the date approached there was no briefing or preparation for the group's work, and Sarah sensed that Al wasn't ready. She was anxious about the meeting failing, not only for the project itself, but for what it signalled about their relationship and Al's entry into the executive team. At this point, direct communication seemed impossible so she indirectly suggested to Al, through another member on the team, that if he wasn't ready, perhaps he should postpone the meeting. Al decided to go ahead knowing, by his own recounting, that he wasn't ready and that he would "get his behind kicked." Exactly this happened. As the meeting unfolded, Al was painfully unprepared and the meeting lacked a design or focus, leaving the other team members with no effective way to participate. This, in turn, enraged Sarah, who became quite punitive and critical.

What is happening here? The working relationship between Sarah and Al is unsatisfying for both and the work they are producing is of low quality. The two have developed a relationship characterized by certain patterns, anxieties, and defenses which gives it a recurrent, systemic quality. Each had some enduring tendencies, traits, and ways of taking up their roles that were observable across settings. Yet together they seemed to bring out the worst in each other and together create a pairing that continually elicited Al's passive, sullen ineptitude and Sarah's overbearing, punitive dissatisfaction. They were each depending on the other - Sarah on Al to accomplish an important job she had delegated to him and Al on Sarah for leadership and authorization. The experience of this interdependency was frightening because it entailed a mutual vulnerability to the other, including a susceptibility to other's irrationality and fears.

This paper attempts to unravel some of the strands that go into shaping this important relationship. First, I explore the central characteristics of the managerial couple, as distinct from other pairwise relationships either in or outside of organizations. Then I consider three psychodynamic frames of analysis useful for understanding the forces that shape the managerial couple: the interpersonal relationship, the pair embedded in the work group, and the pair as a function of intergroup relations. The impact of structure on the managerial couple is then considered .

CHARACTERISTICS OF THE MANAGERIAL COUPLE

Every managerial couple shares two features that distinguish it from other kinds of couples. First, every managerial couple contains a hierarchical boundary. Work in hierarchical organizations is divided into discrete segments to allow for the management of subtasks. Each successive structural differentiation creates a level of authority, with a manager retaining responsibility for the original sphere, and the subordinate being delegated a more delimited area to handle. The manager and subordinate meet, therefore, at a juncture in the organization where an internal boundary has been created, and each couple must manage the transactions across this boundary.

A superior's accountability for a subordinate's performance - the second feature of the managerial couple - is simultaneously the curse and blessing of the arrangement. On one hand, it enables organizations to adhere to a primary mission and to multiply effort efficiently through successive levels of delegation and accountability. On the other, it ties the subordinate and manager together in an emotionally charged, interdependent bond: they need each other to succeed. While the levels of influence obviously differ, each can damage or empower the other. What gives each couple its distinctive character is the way accountability, authority, and dependence coalesce within this human relationship and define its internal process as an element of the larger organization.

The subordinate has been delegated tasks, and the superordinate manager has responsibilities. These responsibilities include those delegated to the subordinate, but not vice versa. This is the sine qua non of the managerial couple - the superior is accountable to his or her own superior, in turn, for what the subordinate does. Superiors can only be held accountable if they have authorized their subordinates to be responsible for some subpart of their own responsibilities and have sufficient authority to hold the subordinate accountable. Thus, the boundary between the two is an authority boundary as well as a task boundary, and the two must handle the issues of authority between them. Equally, this is why the superior is vulnerable to and dependent upon the subordinate; inadequate work by the subordinate threatens the superior's position with respect to his or her own boss.

The impact of this task/authority boundary on the human relationships involved is enormous and differentiates it from other pair relationships in the organization, such as lateral or collegial ones. This boundary, and the need for the individuals in the couple to transact across it to accomplish work, elicits powerful emotions within the pair. Dependency, in both directions, is established and each individual's emotional response to authority is activated. The managerial couple, as a result, becomes a vehicle for expressing deep archetypal processes.

THE INTERPERSONAL WORLD OF THE MANAGERIAL COUPLE

Each individual in the managerial couple must tolerate the irrational substrata of complex authority relations if the pair is to be creative and productive. Those involved must confront inner conflicts associated with issues of independence and dependence, rivalry, giving and getting, controlling and being controlled, competing and cooperating, success, failure, evaluation, trust and accountability, sharing, mutual recognition of differences, etc. (Gould, 1985; Levinson, 1959; Zaleznik, 1966). And such dilemmas face not only the individuals in the couple but the pair itself, which establishes enduring patterns and propensities that define the two-person field as a unit of analysis with its own properties.

While the impact of interpersonal influence is pervasive, the means by which couples establish and maintain recurring patterns is enigmatic and elusive, precisely because the most profound influence is unconscious and not known by either party (Stern, 1989). An important clue, however, can be found in the research in group and organizational life, which shows that the anxieties and defenses elicited in such settings are of a powerful, early, and primitive sort (e.g., Bion, 1959; Jaques, 1955; Menzies, 1961; Kernberg, 1980).

Group life resonates with some of the earliest, most troubling conflicts of group members, including those which are reawakened when authority figures are symbolically equated with parents. Subordinates often relive and attempt to rework emotional experiences with their superiors that they had with their parents as young children. As these and other important very early feelings are revived, the resulting anxieties often lead members of the couple to engage in psychological maneuvers designed to reduce the painful feelings, maneuvers which often subject the pair to difficulty in working together.

The way these defensive maneuvers bind working couples to one another in a sort of joint enactment process has been conceptualized as "projective identification" by psychoanalytic writers (Horwitz, 1983; Ogden, 1979). Painful doubts and anxieties lead one or both of the pair to disavow some important but troubling aspect of their own selves and project it into the other. The recipient, also more susceptible under stressful conditions, actually enacts this projected part as if it were him or herself, absorbing the feelings and behaviors associated with the rejected parts. As a consequence, each party relates to some bothersome part of him or herself, which has been split off and projected into the other, as if it were actually a trait of the other, who then begins to enact that behavior. Thus one may despise or fear or even love some part of oneself that has been lodged in another, as if it actually were an attribute of the other.

Sarah and Al exhibited the kind of mutually reinforcing pattern of projective identification that results in a stable yet rigid pairing. Sarah was embarrassed by the failure of one hospital unit to align with the widely recognized changes, feeling this reflected unfavorably on her performance and reputation. Further, as is typical in such situations, she was anxious about her appointment of Al - would he be as competent and productive as she hoped? Al shared complementary feelings of worry about his becoming a fully respected member of this executive team and performing well at this new and higher level.

Sarah, as was her bent, tended to deny her own sense of uncertainty and doubts, a trait which heightened her confidence and enhanced her considerable leadership capacities in many situations. In this instance, however, she projected her doubts onto Al, whose already existing worries were amplified; he now felt especially doubtful and incompetent in relation to Sarah not only because of his own makeup but because of Sarah's disowned feelings, which he was taking on as well. She distanced herself from Al, and her contact with him took on a tense and slightly suspicious texture, partly because she was relating not only to Al but to certain unwanted parts of herself that were now lodged in him.

As Al became less able and more frightened, he grew more passive, splitting off his own aggressiveness and sense of mastery. The idea of acting authoritatively and risking possible failure under these conditions made him feel extremely vulnerable and exposed. As a consequence, he disowned these parts of himself and projected them into Sarah, who now had to manage not only her own aggressiveness, competence, and dominating aspects, but her subordinate's as well. Feeling as if she had to be aggressive for both of them, Sarah then felt and behaved in an overly responsible manner. In relating to Sarah, Al now not only had to face her frightening assertiveness but the frightening parts of himself which he had projected into her. Sarah became increasingly aggressive and critical while Al became more passive, self-protective, and incompetent. A stable but dysfunctional relationship is thus established.

In mild form, projective identification in the managerial couple, as in any pair, can promote sensitivity, empathy, and understanding as each is able to put themselves "into the other's shoes" (Gilmore and Krantz, 1985). But when it shapes the relationship with greater intensity and rigidity, the effects can be crippling to the collaboration. Not only is the interaction disabled by anxious withdrawal or excessive conflict and contempt, but the individuals are left depleted. The manager who disowns and projects away his or her aggressiveness, for example, will be unable to act decisively in managerial situations calling for action. Alternatively, if the superior's dependency and vulnerability has been split off and projected into the subordinate, as with Sarah, the boss will likely have trouble receiving bad news from the subordinate, and the subordinate is likely to be helpless and submissive. The resulting collaboration will be flawed as a result of the shared, two-person pattern created.

Thus, managerial couples create unconscious agreements in order to maintain mutual misperceptions as a defense against recognizing the underlying problems, conflicts, or differences (Alderfer, 1986) inherent in achieving and maintaining collaboration across lines of authority. While the degree to which these misperceptions are used and maintained depends partly upon each member's individual development (Gould, 1988), there are also a variety of organizational or systemic influences on managerial couples.

THE COUPLE IN THE GROUP

Managerial couples work and interact within a group context, and are therefore profoundly influenced by the group's dynamics. A variety of systemic and group-level dynamics can cause managers and subordinates to regress (Kernberg, 1980), rendering the individuals of the managerial couple even more vulnerable to disabling forces. Particular individuals, as members of groups, are induced into roles (Redl, 1963; Rioch, 1970) on behalf of the entire group. Thus every couple contends not only its own internal dynamics and interrelations, but must carry some degree of emotional freight for the group.

An important contribution to understanding the couple in the group is Bion's (1959) description of how groups tend to elicit pairings among their members and use them as projective targets for unconscious group emotion. What he calls the Basic Assumption Pairing Group will invest its hope and creative excitement in a group. In a sophisticated work organization, this emotional background can support many creative pairings, as leadership shifts around the group (Gould, 1985).

Managerial couples must often bear the weight of group fantasy. In a higher functioning group, this may support the couple and foster welcomed, stimulated collaboration between pairs within the group. Under the impact of intensified anxiety, however, its more primitive manifestation appears, in which the "pairing group" invests wildly grandiose hopes in one of its couples, who then become the repository for all possibility in the group. The managerial couple can easily then become burdened by these projections and overwhelmed with such high expectations, while the others passively await the pair's magical creation. The group's idealization of its messianic couple will, for example, create strong pressures for the pair to deny its aggressive and conflictual dimensions, rendering the couple less capable of achieving sophisticated collaboration. And of course it will be doomed to disappoint the expectant others. Finally, a creative pair may elicit jealousy and destructive envy from other group members, in part because of the measure of exclusivity inherent in any true interpersonal joining.

A good example of both dynamics can be seen in "Powerplay" by Mary Cunningham (1984), her story about the events at Bendix surrounding her meteoric rise and pairing with the chairman, William Agee. Agee was regarded as a "Wunderkind" who would save the endangered company. Both loved and despised, he went about changing the culture of managerial work in the company. He hired Cunningham, a bright young Harvard MBA, as his executive assistant whose analytical ability consistently outshone that of the older executives.

She and Agee grew increasingly closer, while the deep changes Agee pursued in a turbulent environment created enormous anxiety. From her description (p. 98), it seemed as if, over time, the two of them could trust only each other. The pair, according to this book and other sources, became an object of enormous interest and concern within (and outside) the company, representing both hope and danger at different times. From a group-as-a-whole perspective, certain factions invested the couple with great hope; it would produce the Bendix of the future, a firm making high-tech electronics rather than used auto parts. Yet the envy, hatred, and resentment grew fiercely, until finally the board forced Agee to fire Cunningham.

While the strong connection between the two may have been partly independent of the powerful emotional forces within Bendix at the time, the couple was unconsciously used by the group to contain, or enact, the hope for a magical renewal of the company. This, and the attendant envy and resentfulness toward them, clearly had a disastrous impact on their ability to collaborate effectively. Both the hope and the envy drove them together; they progressively became isolated from other resentful senior executives and simultaneously responded to the board's expectation that they would accomplish wildly grandiose results. As they came to enact these irrational dynamics they progressively lost touch with the company and became increasingly disabled.

Thus to the extent the managerial couple is "containing," or enacting, some aspect of the whole group's emotional life, it is subject to forces that can amplify powerful emotions. When the work group is in the grips of a too powerful unconscious process, the managerial couple will have to contend with the underlying fantasies being used defensively to evade task-based anxieties, and the corresponding emotional states will suffuse the collaboration.

THE COUPLE AND THE INTERGROUP RELATIONSHIP

Not only are managerial couples embedded within groups, they may also constitute the interface between two organizational groups - for example, structurally-based hierarchical and task groups such as headquarters and field units or marketing and sales, as well as "identity" groups such as women and men or blacks and whites. The superior and subordinate, while being members of the same group from one perspective, from another are members of two different groups, which in turn subjects them to another set of powerful dynamics.

The superior and subordinate each have their own peer-level groups, which are brought together by the managerial couple. By representing their work roles, each becomes imbued with the outlook and unconscious orientations of its group memberships and, equally, each symbolizes its group to the other. Inevitably, the historic intergroup relationship between the two units the couple represents will be enacted within its own relationship.

A vertical chain of three managers in a human service organization providing a range of services to an adolescent population is a good illustration. The commissioner, who oversaw the entire operation, had a tense relationship with the director, who headed up the long-stay center treating the most disturbed children in the agency. The director, in turn, had an equally tense working relationship with the heads of the dormitories.

These managerial couples were having difficulty in working effectively. According to the director, the commissioner-director couple was characterized by mistrust; communication and dialogue were poor, and as a result, the commissioner doubted his director's ability. Ultimately, the two discovered that their relationship was, in part, enacting a historic mistrust and suspicion between the field institutions and headquarters.

Hierarchical group as well as identity group relations were shaping relations between the pair. Historically, the central office was run by white managers identified with governmental affairs, while the field institutions were run by black managers, who identified more with the children and their plight. The task of forcibly institutionalizing poor black children, even if they were trying to help those in their control, was anxiety-provoking for socially concerned managers, black and white alike. Elements of social oppression and racism were inevitably manifested in the work of the organization; the feelings they engendered had to be managed by all segments of the enterprise.

The anxiety and pain were often culturally simplified through a process in which the field units attributed all the racism and oppression to headquarters staff, who were mostly white, came largely from a higher social class, and of course were more closely linked to the larger issues of political governance. Through such attribution, the field units were able to exonerate themselves psychologically from confronting the complexities of belonging to the enterprise. Senior headquarters staff managed their mixed feelings differently. They disavowed the part of themselves that was ill at ease with the agency's work and projected it onto the field managers, believing the latter weren't invested in the agency's overall well being but instead were parochially concerned with their own narrow interests. Field-headquarters relations were tense and adversarial, as one might expect. The commissioner and the director recreated this intergroup dynamic inside their own relationship, with each feeling both misunderstood and mistrusted. Only when they saw the link between their experience as a pair and the dynamics of headquarters-field relationships did they understand the chronic and seemingly obscure roots of their own strained working relationship.

THE COUPLE AND THE FORMAL ORGANIZATION

All human relationships involve irrational, unconscious dynamic processes, deeper connections in which the meaning of the relationship, for each, is rooted. The irrational, unconscious background to the managerial couple can be the wellspring of creativity, zest, and excitement or the source of destructiveness and detachment.

Traditional organization theory has excluded recognizing the irrational, affective dimensions of role relations. The legacy ot Weber's (1947) theory of bureaucracy is a normative orientation toward an impersonal, rational conception of organizational life, based on a foundation of rationally-derived structures. In this scheme, furthered by Taylorist approaches and the "scientific management" tradition, rationally derived structures allow for the elimination of irrationality and unwanted emotion from role performance (Levinson, 1959).

Yet we also know that people inevitably bring more to their work roles than only those capacities required by their tasks (Rice, 1965). People use their work roles to manage their anxieties and meet other socio-emotional needs as well as to satisfy their needs to accomplish work alone. Thus the irrational dimensions of life are brought into the workplace and find expression in social relations. Indeed, by emphasizing impersonality, an organization may drive emotional needs underground, thereby increasing people's irrational responses to work. In such an environment, a subordinate, for example, feeling punished by a superior's evaluation may sullenly withdraw from work or punish his or her own subordinate in turn. The "repressed returns."

While rationally-derived structures cannot eliminate the uncontrollable realm of human feeling and irrationality from organizational life, they can shape and channel it. The presence of the irrational bond between the managerial couple is shaped by the formal structure in which the couple is embedded and by the bit of the structure that is embedded within the couple - the boundary of authority and delegation between them. Structure can help link the irrational bonds to the managerial couple's work and thereby facilitate it, or it can enhance the potential disturbance within the working pair.

When role definitions are confused, vague, or inappropriate to an organization's tasks the result is regression on the group level to dysfunctional, anti-task cultures (Kernberg, 1980; Menzies, 1979; Hirschhorn, 1988). Unclear role definitions create significant conflicts between members of the managerial couple as well: people can easily arrogate authority to themselves, on the one hand, or deny accountability on the other, resulting in distorted internal boundaries.

The case of David, who managed a section of an R&D lab for a pharmaceutical company, illustrates how an inadequately structured situation can stir deep and disruptive interpersonal dynamics. As section manager, he was responsible for the unit's performance, though he had no authority to remove subordinates from their positions. He was in a particularly difficult situation with Mary, who worked below standards but not with such glaring incompetence that David's own superior would fire her. Yet the unit operated under very tight performance standards, and Mary could undermine David's performance without his being able to respond effectively, leaving David vulnerable and exposed for his own performance in relations to his boss.

Consequently, David felt persecuted by Mary and expressed his helplessness and rage by becoming suspicious and punitive. The situation touched on some of his very deep anxieties about control and dependence. The couple's interaction developed into a rigid pattern of suspicion and concealment; both were locked into dealing with each other's personal defense because the formal structure failed to enable

David to manage his dependence on her productively. With the requisite authority he might have removed her or, alternatively, been able to shape her performance through the process of genuine accountability.

Finally, the managerial couple is not only affected by the organization's structure, but affects it as well. When the couple is regressive, pressures will arise to blur or obfuscate the formal role relations even more. This leads to an increased avoidance of anxiety and confronting issues of dependability, accountability, and trust, which are inevitably painful in a failing collaboration.

The case of Sarah and Al illustrates this nicely. Sarah wanted Al to take more initiative with the strategic planning process. Over time, a considerable amount of anxiety had built up over this event. As both sides tended to engage in mutual projective processes and got locked into the stalemate described earlier, lines ot accountability tended to blur. Sarah did not feel she could trust Al to carry out her wishes, so she pushed him to do a task without really delegating it to him. Al then felt demeaned; he wasn't being given an authentic delegation but rather performing in a rote fashion, leading him to blur the lines of accountability from his side. This led to an odd set of actions conveying the confusion over whose meeting it was. For example, the invitation to the meeting from Al was: "Sarah wants me to have a meeting. . ." Thus, in this instance, the formal structure that lodged accountability and responsibility clearly within the supervisory structure gave way to a vague, fused sense of responsibility as the couple defended against confronting the painful realities of the collaboration at that moment.

Not only does investment in formal structure create the conditions in which people can work productively; it also provides an ongoing way to understand a working relationship. A considered formal structure provides a model against which the managerial couple's actual collaboration can be assessed. Though she had developed a difficult pattern with Al, Sarah was an exceptionally capable manager and supervisor. She was able to understand how off-track her relationship with Al had become, in part because she saw how cloudy the lines of accountability had gotten. The model of organizing and the clearly delineated boundaries to which their management group aspired and often reached stood in sharp contrast to the confused, blurred pattern of accountability she had with Al. This difference provided the essential diagnostic information. Her investment in formal structure provided a set of principles to help guide her in the relationship and thereby understand the defensive processes, which in turn enabled them to establish fuller, productive collaboration.

MANAGERIAL IMPLICATIONS

All members of any organization are involved in managerial couples and are inevitably affected by the forces discussed in this paper. The two person relationship can become very loaded, both because of what is inside it and because of what is projected into it by others. Managers trying to improve organizational functioning are likely to benefit from considering the managerial couple as a unit of analysis - both as a source of invaluable information as well as a locus for development.

This requires appreciating the many forces which are finding expression through, and shaping the pair's working relationship. Unbundling these various influences can be confusing and difficult. As the case of Sarah and Al illustrates, managerial of structure and boundaries provide a point of departure for sorting out different influences. One of the key functions of managerial leadership is to provide conditions which support accountability.

Accountability, and its capacity to harness social dynamics to task, occurs only in conjunction with certain patterns of authority and can be achieved only when the formal boundary across which the members of a managerial couple transact has certain characteristics (Jaques, 1976). Clearly defined roles and well negotiated distribution of shared responsibility enable members of the working couple to understand their interpersonal relationship in the context of the larger, shared task and its human meaning. An enabling formal organization and rationally derived structure allows members to bring their irrational, feeling-full aspects into productive relation to the task. Defensively derived structures and boundaries pit the inevitable irrational connection between the couple against the demands of task, and are thus disabling.

While inadequate structures are often the source of difficulties in the managerial couple, enabling structures can be undermined as the result of other regressive pressures that are rooted in interpersonal, group, and inter-group dynamics. These are more difficult to ferret out and understand, although managers often enhance their own competence by developing the reflective capacity to see how these wider systemic forces are enacted by working pairs. Outside consultation is often helpful in exploring these elements because of the unconscious nature of these powerful emotional undercurrents, or worse, because the pair has gotten locked into patterns dominated by projective identification.

CONCLUSION

As with all social realities, understanding the managerial couple requires taking multiple levels of analysis into account. The individual, interpersonal, group, and intergroup perspectives all help to untangle the many determinants of the managerial couple's life. Similarly, to appreciate the managerial couple in context as a systemic process, an understanding of the impact of the social and technical subsystems is necessary to explore the couple's experience.

The changing social, economic, and political situation is naturally represented microcosmically in the evolution of working couples, putting them under greater stress. Vastly greater diversity in the workforce means that many more couples will have to manage the tendency toward projection and splitting that racial, ethnic, and gender differences promote. Increasingly complex and unpredictable settings render ritualized, unexamined pair arrangements maladaptive (Hirschhorn, 1988). Turbulent environments make demands on both organizations as a whole and their constituent managerial couples to achieve an ongoing, active, adaptation and learning.

Every boundary in the midst of managerial couples contains the seeds of conflict; these are inherent in an organization's needs to make decisions based on function and efficiency rather than in their personal interests of people. Nonetheless, in deep and genuine collaboration there is also the possibility of creativity and mutual growth (Hirschhorn, 1988; Gould, 1988). Achieving this is the challenge for the pair and for the group in which it is situated.

NOTES

(1) This paper looks at the managerial couple relationship in its organizational context, and examines its major components from a socio-technical perspective. By socio-technical perspective I am referring to a frame of reference first developed by Trist and his colleagues at the Tavistock Institute (e. g., Trist and Bramforth, 1951; Trist et al., 1963), which emphasizes the interrelatedness of the functioning of the social and technological subsystems of an enterprise.

The social system refers to the people in the work situation and the relationships among them, including their particular physical and psychological characteristics and requirements. The social system includes the cultural mechanisms which govern social relations. The technological, technical system refers to aspects of formal organization such as procedures, policies, techniques, tools, and structures which are used by the social system to accomplish work. Sociotechnical studies show that the two subsystems are related to one another, serve as constraints on each other, and must be effectively fit to one another to achieve optimal functioning.

Typically used to describe manufacturing systems (Cummings, 1978), the design of jobs (Davis, 1978), methods of organizing overall enterprises, and a philosophy of work organization (Emery, 1982), socio-technical systems theory is a frame of reference which can be used to study the relationship between and within any level of a system. Although efforts have been made to explore the interpersonal dimensions of work relations (e. g., Bennis et al., 1979; Argyris, 1962; Baird and Kram, 1983; Gabarro, 1987), and the interpersonal aspects of authority relations (e.g., Rioch, 1970; Kernberg, 1980; Levinson, 1969; Kets de Vries, 1979), this is the first time I am aware of socio-technical systems theory being specifically used to shed light on the managerial couple.

REFERENCES

ALDERFER, C. An intergroup perspective on group dynamics. In: J. Lorsch (ed.), Handbook of Organizational Behavior. Englewood Cliffs, NJ: Prentice Hall, 1986.

ARGYRIS, C. Interpersonal competence and organizational effectiveness. London: Tavistock Publications, 1962.

BENNIS, W., VAN MAANEN, J., SCHEIN, E., & STEELE, F. Essays in interpersonal dynamics. Homewood, IL: The Dorsey Press, 1979.

BION, W.R. Experiences in groups. London: Tavistock, 1959.

CUMMINGS, T. Sociotechnical systems: The design of work and quality of working life. In: W. Pasmore and J. Sherwood (Eds.), Sociotechnical Systems: A Sourcebook. La Jolla, CA: Univerity Associates Press, 1978.

CUNNINGHAM, M. Powerplay. New York: Simon and Schuster, 1984.

DAVIS, L. Sociotechnical experimentation: A review of sixteen studies. In W. Pasmore and J. Sherwood (Eds.), Sociotechnical Systems : A Sourcebook. La Jolla, CA: University Associates Press, 1978.

EMERY, F. New perspectives on the world of work: Sociotechnical foundations for a new social order? Human Relations, 35(12), 1982, 1095-1122.

GABARRO, J.J. Socialization at the top: How CEO's and their subordinates evolve interpersonal contracts. Organizational Dynamics (Winter), p. 2.

GILMORE, T., & KRANTZ, J. Projective identification in the consulting relationship: Exploring the unconscious dimensions of a client system. Human Relations, 38(12), 1985, 1159-1177.

GOULD, L.J. Derivations of Bion's Basic Assumption Theory in Klein's developmental positions. Presented at the 7th Scientific Meetings, The A.K. Rice Institute, Arlington, VA, April, 1985.

GOULD, L. The capacity to work: Developmental origins of mature collaboration, prepared for the First International Symposium on Group Relations Contributions to Social and Political Issues. Oxford, England, May, 1988.

HIRSCHHORN, L. The workplace within. Cambridge, MA: MIT Press, 1988.

HORWITZ, L. Projective identification in dyads and groups. International Journal of Group Psychotherapy, 33, 1983, 259-279.

JAQUES, E. Social systems as a defense against persecutory and depressive anxiety. In: M. Klein, P. Heimann, & R.E. Money-Kryle (Eds.), New Directions in Psychoanalysis. London: Tavistock Publications, 1955.

JAQUES, E. A General Theory of Bureaucracy. London: Heinemann, 1976.

KERNBERG, O. Internal world and external reality: Object relations theory applied. New York: Jason Aronson, 1980.

KETS DE VRIES, M.F.R. Managers can drive their subordinates mad. Harvard Business Review, July-August, 1979.

LEVINSON, D. Role, personality, and social structure in the organizational setting. Journal of Abnormal and Social Psychology, 58, 1959, 170-180.

MENZIES, I. The functioning of social systems as a defense against anxiety. Human Relations, 13, 1961, 95-121.

MENZIES, I. Staff support systems: Task and anti-task in adolescent institutions. In R. Hinshelwood & N. Manning (Eds.), Therapeutic Communities. London: Routledge & Kegan Paul, 1979.

NEWTON, P. & LEVINSON, D. The work group within the organization: A sociopsychological approach. Psychiatry, 36, 1973, 115-132.

OGDEN, T. On projective identification. International Journal of Psychoanalysis, 60, 1979, 357-373.

REDL, F. Psychoanalysis and group therapy: A developmental point of view. American Journal of Orthopsychiatry, 33, 1963, 135-142.

RICE, A.K. Individual, group and intergroup processes. Human Relations, 22(6), 1965, 565-584.

RIOCH, M. All we like sheep.....[Isaiah 53:6]: Followers and leaders. Psychiatry, 33, 1970, 56-66.

STERN, D.B. The analyst's unformulated experience of the patient. Contemporary Psychoanalysis, 25(1), 1989, 1-33.

TRIST, E. & BRAMFORTH, K. Some social and psychological consequences of the Longwall Method of coal-getting. Human Relations, 4, 1951, 3-38.

TRIST, E., HIGGIN, G., MURRAY, H. & POLLOCK, A. Organizational choice: Capabilities of groups at the coal face under changing technologies. London: Tavistock Publications, 1963.

WEBER, M. The Protestant ethic and the spirit of capitalism. London: Oxford University Press, 1947.

ZALEZNIK, A. Human dilemmas of leadership. New York: Harper & Row, 1966.

Corporate Imagery and Corporate Identity

Jean-Paul Larçon and Roland Reitter

In any organization, the relationship between strategic, structural, and psychological factors centering around a common core of abilities leads us to postulate the existence of a "corporate identity" which, in the same way as an individual's personality, deeply influences its development. Corporate identity seems to be a series of interdependent characteristics of the organization from which it draws its specificity, stability, and unity.

No one would deny that in the history of Renault or of General Motors there is a specificity, a stability, and a unity which provide each of these firms with its own identity and permanence despite fluctuations in the general industrial situation. Whether seen from the viewpoint of its managers (i. e., Louis Renault or Pierre Dreyfus), or of academics or trade unionists, the firm appears as an entity having specific sociological, psychological, and political characteristics which themselves determine choices of product policy, trade-union relations, and industrial strategies.

What, then, are the foundations of this organizational identity and how does it change with time? How can such an identity be created or altered? These are all fundamental questions for the managers, consultant, or researcher.

The practitioner generally uses his intuition to understand the identity of the organization with which he is concerned, but we must take our study further than this intuitive approach in order to comprehend this fundamental aspect of the life of the organization.

Let us start with the individual executive. Once he has reached a certain level in the hierarchy, his life within the organization assumes crucial importance for his own self-image to the extent that he assumes responsibilities, has complex power relationships and exerts some influence on the activities of the company. His problems, successes, and failures have a profound effect upon his ambition and psychological equilibrium. The organization is part of his emotional life.

Now, the individual's life in the organization has three aspects: first, he is generally part of a restricted work group in which he spends most of his time and experiences most of his emotions (group identity); second, he encounters specific problems in his job which bring him specific satisfactions (role identity); finally, he is a member of the organization as a whole, and as such he shares his problems with others and obeys the rules of the game (corporate identity). These three elements determine the images the individual forms about his life within the organization. Of course, all these representations are both conscious and unconscious; they are important contributing factors to overall organizational identity.

As a member of a work group, the individual is emotionally involved; tasks are distributed and in turn received; places are assigned and coalitions are formed. The work group receives a certain amount of power related to the task to be done, and within the group a new division takes place. A certain mental effort is made. The group gradually works out a common mental definition, a common image of the structure of the group in which every member can find a place to his satisfaction. Thus everyone will have a specific and stable image of his group, and of himself as a member of this group.

The individual also carries on a professional role in which he exhibits the personal skills he has developed. This professional role is necessary for the execution of the task which the organization has set itself. The individual soon acquires the qualities necessary to carry on this role; he shares the rules of his professional role with others; he knows the pitfalls to avoid: he acquires an impression of what "we" are - "we" being his professional group, such as IBM systems analysts, or researchers at Polaroid.

Finally, the individual has an image of the organization as a whole, of what it is and what he himself is as a member of the organization. This image of the organization is the fruit of the individual's experiences and of his working life within the firm. It is formed from numerous messages which he decodes. These messages can be grouped according to their origin, for they come from two important and connected spheres in the life of the organization: the political power and the organizational context.

The political power is often differentiated. Behind the senior management there is a controlling power representing the owners, whether public or private. The strength, clarity, and cohesion of this "power constellation" is of interest to every individual in the organization. The very personality of the chief executive, his values, beliefs, attitudes, and personal conflicts cannot be a matter of indifference to those who depend on him, in the sense that it is he who eventually makes the major decisions for the organization and defines its aims and future.

We cannot lay too much stress on the fact that the strategy of an organization partly constitutes the basis of its future identity. It is therefore vital for each individual to know clearly the firm's aims and how it hopes to achieve them, to the extent that the individual's own identity depends partly on the identity of the organization.

This identity of the organization must be seen in what we can call the organizational structure, that is, the structuring of the life of the organization. Every practitioner knows that it is extremely important for the structure of an organization to be in harmony with its strategy and to be based on systems of management - administrative direction, selection, evaluation, remuneration of personnel, system of planning, etc. - which form a coherent whole and which can provide the individuals in the organization with a coherent and acceptable view of the rules of the game within their organization. If we add to this the working context and the manner in which time and space are treated, we arrive at a composite whole which is nevertheless felt by the individual to be one entity: the organizational structure, within which he acts.

Let us take some examples of the major themes on which the impressions of the organization's identity will be based:

- The institution may appear to be fragmented or, on the other hand,. to form a coherent unit: if fragmented, it contains parts which are alien, different, difficult to understand, mysterious, even hostile; if a coherent unit, it forms a familiar world, smooth in operation and presenting few dangers.
- The organization may appear powerful or weak. If powerful, some of its power will reflect back on to its members, unless it scares them. If weak, its members will experience its lack of power, unless they find in this an additional motive to fight the organization's cause.
- It can also be just or unjust, "good" or "bad." It can confer many or few benefits on its members.
- It may select and exclude, or attract and include people, it may give the impression that the hierarchy is important and rigid or, on the contrary, it may smooth over differences and conceal them, treating all its members as equals.
- The organization may be dynamic or inert. It may give its members the impression that they are in control of their environment, or, on the other hand, that they are very dependent on it.
- The organization may be strict or relaxed in the supervision of its employees. Does it follow a manager's movements closely, or does it allow a certain freedom of action ? Does it allow for self-expression? Conversely, if the manager loses control over his

emotions, how is he allowed to behave? Does it allow for a certain amount of distress? How does it deal with unconventional behavior? Are weaknesses allowed? Is there provision for regression in moments of stress?
- Does the organization permit confrontation and open conflict or does it rather impose a maze of bureaucratic procedures which stifle the shouldering of responsibility and the expression of conflict?
- Is the organization really special and different? Does it permit its members to be so in contacts with outsiders? Or is the manager merely one of many?

These are a few major themes. We shall take one example to illustrate their formation. Let us take the first of the themes we have just mentioned: a fragmented or unified impression of the organization - and relate it to the different categories of messages studied: what is it that makes an organization appear fragmented?

- Disagreement between the owners over what the identity of the firm should be and internal political conflict: this is frequently the case in France where joint ventures are favored (the company Genvrain constitutes a good example).
- Lack of unity at managerial level. First of all, of course, if there is a dyad or triad at the top and if the divisions between senior management are visible, the direction of the firm may be unclear and become a source of distress to those whose position in the firm is in jeopardy.
- However, even without multiple leadership at the top, there may be extreme ambivalence as expressed by the president. He may have doubts about himself and his own ability to act; he may be unconsciously trying to punish himself for his failures and even for his successes.
- The way strategy is determined. Some plans are ambiguous or obscure, or too many directions are issued at the same time. When the members of an organization ask themselves what their firm is doing - or what it is - and they receive conflicting messages without priorities for action, the firm may be seen as lacking identity or unity.
- The administrative systems and procedures. We have approached this subject via the topic of conflicting plans. Even if there is no conflict in the plans themselves, procedures may appear to contradict themselves or the plans. For example, a firm cannot at the same time preach the individual responsibility of employees, and then control their every action.
- Naturally those policies which relate to the process of differentiating or integrating units or to the solving of internal conflicts, also directly influence the perception of the firm's unity or lack of unity.

- Contradiction between the information which the firm issues about itself and the everyday reality of the situation. For example, the firm which tries to persuade itself that it has no conflicts will evolve rituals and taboos to conceal them; it preaches and publicizes certain values, but those who speak openly of conflict are rejected.

This lack of cohesion within the organization, which is also a lack of cohesion within oneself, is experienced traumatically by its members, and may lead to serious disturbances in behavior, such as psychological withdrawal, whereby the individual avoids suffering by refusing to make an emotional commitment, and seeks satisfaction outside the organization.

This last point leads us to a discussion of the relations between the organization's imagery, and the very functioning of the organization, in particular its capacity for strategic adaption. When the researcher looks at an organization, he does not at first see the imagery of the organization's members. What he sees are the concrete collective results of their actions and he can trace the daily habits revealed by what Crozier and Friedberg (1980) call organizational games. He can inquire as to the visible external symbols of the organization's culture. We feel that these fundamental aspects of the organization's functioning are closely dependent on its internal images.

A firm's ability to implement its strategy depends on the ability of its members, both individuals and groups, not only to carry out the specific job assigned to them, but also to coordinate and integrate their efforts - and adapt to external developments. In other words, the practices of each member must be in harmony with the organization's strategy. The games practiced by the individuals and groups must be stable and regulated, while at the same time they must be capable of evolving, if necessary. In short, an organization must have the ability to learn, and it is only able to learn if the structure of its policy games is not too inflexible, for reasons either rational (e. g., conflicting interests) or emotional.

These practices are not the only interesting aspect of organizational functioning. Like all human groups, the organization has a collective life style - a culture - which it manifests in symbolic form: myths, rituals and taboos. These symbols are very important since they provide clues to the collective imagery, their usual function being to allow for the tensions which may arise in the group from the organization's basic choices, and to assert the unity of the group over and above these differences and tensions.

The business firm, like any other human group, engenders myths, that is, stories about its history. The origins of the firm naturally constitute an ideal subject for myths, for it is there that the firm's values generally have their origin. But other key periods may also be evoked: economic crises, wars, interventions by governments (or approaches to governments). In very broad terms the purpose of the myth is to create - or to support - an ideal image of the firm. This image will cover problematic or obscure aspects and show them in a favorable light. The myth itself creates values.

Rites are practices which reflect the myth and which have no significance in themselves other than providing an occasion for a consensus on the important problem which the rite masks. A very good example is dissected by Trepo (1973). Taking four case studies of firms, he shows how a management style which is participative with regard to objectives may turn into a ritual when superiors and subordinates share anxiety regarding their respective situations of power and dependence; a system of Management by Objectives may enable them to hide this anxiety and this situation behind a screen of participation and "modern management." It is also very revealing to note how much such practices become emphasized when they have become rituals, for when an M.B.O. system is really successful, little is said about it. The same goes for the whole phraseology of "modern management": a real manager does not constantly boast of what he is doing.

Taboos can pinpoint the organization's sensitive spots; only those things which strike at the heart of the organization - its basic values, its secret conflict, its contradictions, its traumas - are taboo. Since the taboo is what should be denied, hidden, exorcised, wiped out, it is a fundamental part of the equilibrium of a company.

More generally, organizations have their own distinctive life style. They draw up their own code of values, their code of speech, their code of dress, which is not necessarily that which senior management would like to see applied. For the student of organizations, these symbols constitute an important aspect of identity; they are messages from the organization' s core. Thus the organization's identity appears as an aggregate of its interdependent characteristics, which give its specificity, stability, and unity. Of these characteristics, the policy and structural factors form the bases of the identity, whereas the imagery and the functioning of the organization are two facets of the reality of the identity (see Figure 1).

FIGURE 1
Organizational Identity

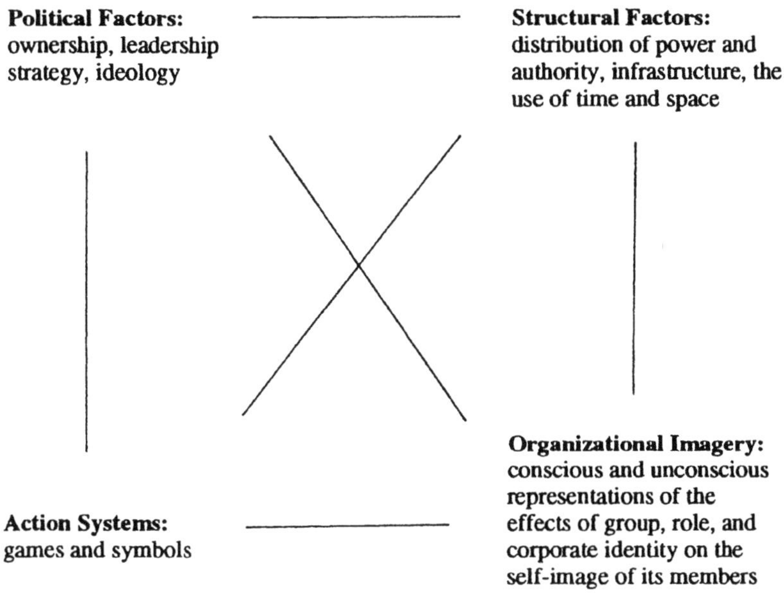

This chart is not easy to use. Policy and structural data must be collected with the patience of an entomologist in order to understand their unity and complexity. At the level of imagery, the researcher deals with human feelings and the unconscious, which is never easy to comprehend. A certain relationship inevitably develops between the researcher and the persons interviewed, in which the researcher takes on the role of a psychoanalyst, but in a very ambiguous context. These phenomena (transferences, countertransferences) are in themselves highly interesting to analyze. Finally, when the researcher examines the organization's functioning, he is both entomologist and analyst: he observes and describes practices, but he also interprets them in the realm of the actors' private mental world. He is doomed to move uneasily back and forth between these two positions.

We should like to illustrate this grid by briefly considering the case of Knoll France. Knoll, a firm well known in France for the sophistication of its contemporary furniture, belongs to an American company, Knoll International, which itself belonged from 1967 to 1975 to a conglomerate, the Walter E. Heller group. In 1973, Knoll France was a firm which had its own traditions and a very personal style within this group, a style created by one of its senior managers of the Sixties, Yves Vidal. At that time most individuals within Knoll France saw themselves as artists and Knoll as a design firm selling "craft works," mainly to the upper class. Organizational life seemed like a continuous party. Pedestrian concerns such as costs were unknown. Knoll meant beauty coming from Bauhaus; Knoll was not just a merchant. The 1972 exhibition of Knoll furniture held at the Louvre symbolized this tradition.

Knoll International, however, the parent company, was more concerned with mass marketing, and has mainly been involved in the office furniture market in the United States. This difference did not matter so long as the whole organization was profitable and shared the same long-term goals, but things became complicated when Walter Heller - who wanted to sell Knoll International - put on pressure to improve the group's short-term profits. Knoll International then informed Knoll France that they must "mass produce or die".

This mass production approach, more commercial than artistic, was achieved, not without difficulty, between 1973 and 1977 by a new management team which day after day came up against the old tradition and the image of "their" firm which is still held by its employees today, especially those on the marketing side. The launching of the "Pillorama" in 1976 can be seen as the symbol of these difficulties. Pillorama was a set of cushions which could be arranged in different ways to form a flexible and mobile system of interior furnishing. There is no doubt that this product corresponded to a developing section of the market and provided an original solution to the furnishing problem for people seeking a new lifestyle. This product, sold at a "moderate" price, was designed in the U.S. to appeal to a very large public. The new chairman of Knoll France, applying the new strategy of mechanization, was one of the first to mobilize his forces to sell this product. It was then that the effects on the individual internal image of Knoll France were suddenly experienced: the French salesmen felt that this product did not correspond to the image of quality or style which they had formed of "their products," and the production department saw the product as unfinished, slapdash, contrary to their tradition. Knoll agents thought the product "clashed" with other products in their shops. In short, it was generally felt that Pillorama was not "Knoll." This conflict in internal imagery might have been one of the contributing factors for the poor performance of Pillorama in France. However, by an irony of fate, an impressive order was won from the head of an important Arab state (where the cushion is a traditional product) for a personalized and luxurious version of the product. The desired "mass-produced" product once more became a "deluxe craft item." The organization had achieved a product in keeping with its identity and that still contributed to the company's success.

Thus it would seem that the firm's capacity to evolve and adapt to external conditions is profoundly affected by its identity, and in particular by those images which the employees form of the organization. A series of studies we made in medium-sized business concerns (Larçon and Reitter, 1979), of about 2.000 employees, has shown in particular that these images have a considerable bearing on the quality of commitment to the firm's general objectives, and on how choices are made between individual objectives and the interests of subgroups - subsidiaries, departments or sections - in relation to the aims of the organization as a whole. The imagery of the organization's members influences attitudes regarding the possible risks involved in investment decisions, diversification projects, the evaluation of new opportunities, the launching of new products. The imagery is decisive in matters of horizontal communication, interdepartmental relations, and cooperation between departments. This concept also appears to be very important when general management wishes to develop cooperation between different departments or to establish close internal cooperation on a specific project.

According to whether the organization appears to be united by a leader, purpose, or strategic plan, or fragmented into disparate activities or into competing feudal units, the attitude of its employees becomes more personal and political, or more cooperative and more oriented towards action and results.

While the small firm is relatively sheltered from these considerations to the extent that allegiance is directed towards the personality of the employer and the range of its products and markets is small, the firm which is both large and diversified may, on the other hand, create for its employees an image which is confused and in itself uninspiring.

One is astonished to discover to what extent objectives which appear clear at the level of general management are misunderstood or distorted at lower levels. The information and communications policy no doubt is partly to blame, but this rift between the firm's real or desired identity and the feeling of identity actually experienced by its members is far more than a simple matter of internal information. The image which employees form of the firm often reflects real inadequacies or contradictions in strategy, in styles of authority, and in the structure of the organization, or above all in the links between these three elements. Thus an analysis of this identity as experienced by others reveals to the chief executive the quality of the employees' participation in the firm's or subsidiary's overall policy and at the same time, the difficulties involved in achieving change. The identity of the firm constitutes a key factor in its survival, a force of inertia or a dynamic factor in its development.

REFERENCES

CROZIER, M., & FRIEDBERG, E. L'Acteur et le Système. Paris: Seuil, 1980.

LARÇON, J.-P., & REITTER, R. Structures de Pouvoir et Identite de l'Entreprise. Paris: Nathan, 1979.

TREPO, G. Management Style à la Française. European Business, Autumn, 1973.

Leadership Anyone?

Harry Levinson

Managers sometimes say,"I'm not the leader - the guy at the top is." Such managers make a serious mistake. They fail to see that organizations need people at all levels with leadership abilities - so much so that managers whose skills lie in following directives and sticking with established techniques will increasingly find their career futures bleak. The cliches are true: business today simply isn't what it used to be, and changes escalate quickly; economic conditions and markets shift with astonishing speed. And more important still, the organizational map has been transformed. Managers are no longer responsible only to their bosses and, ultimately, the stockholders. Today a range of groups is part of every business's natural constituency, each making demands on managers that must be met. Employee groups demand that managers improve the quality of worklife; consumers and community groups demand safer products and a cleaner environment; government agencies require managers to fill hiring quotas. Managers must meet all these demands, and more. And, of course, they still must protect profits.

The heat's on, and it will get hotter in coming years. Managers will be told to clamp down and cut back - and to keep everybody happy as the slices of the pie get smaller. What can managers do? The old ways don't satisfy the new constituencies; piecemeal answers don't much satisfy anyone. Organizations increasingly will need managers who can help them anticipate changes and chart new courses. They'll pressure managers to adapt, innovate, and take charge; they'll seek people with fresh ideas, a sense of purpose, and the desire to act. The business periodicals keep telling us that the old days of the organizational man have ended. Managers can no longer manage. They must exert forward force and pull their organizations into the fray. They must lead.

Leading the Way

Managers become leaders when they invest themselves in their work and convince others that their efforts can make a significant difference. They become leaders when they learn to take a stand and take risks, to anticipate, initiate, and innovate. Any manager who sees a need and says, "I want to do something about that," has the potential

---

The CEO appreciated the opportunity to talk about his executive problems, but shied away from those having to do with his family and his disappointment in them. He would not accept a referral to outside professionals to deal with his family problems, which is my usual practice.

He had little confidence in the people who reported to him and the contributions they had hoped to make in their joint efforts with him. His fantasy was that, in addition to working with them individually, as I did regularly, and from time to time as a group, as I also did, they would behave better toward their own subordinates because of my skill in exhorting them to do so.

As I worked with the people who reported to the CEO, it became clear to me that only one member of that top management group was sophisticated in management terms and could think in the longer range. The rest were pretty much confined to making their annual bottom line under the severe and continuous pressure of small margins. His was a far-flung organization. As a result, it intersected with many different governmental and regulatory bodies. Negative reaction from any one could have serious impact on the relationships with the others.

It's Different

Consultation with top management is a wide-ranging and varied task with frustrations beyond those that occur in most ordinary psychological counseling, but also with gratifications that arise from those very same issues. The psychological consultant is often in the position of having to evaluate and help make decisions about the age and stage of adult development in which his client and the client organization finds itself. Frequently, the consultant must deal with people whose characterological posture makes it difficult for them to become aware of the sensitivity of others. For much the same reason, the client may well not be able to accept psychological help for his own character problems and these, therefore, need to be dealt with obliquely so that the adaptive effort of the client and the client organization may be supported, while at the same time working around the more difficult character issues. The complexities of the transferences to the consultant must be managed in ways that are unlike those in individual and group therapy because they occur in the work context and frequently cannot be dealt with in the work group as a group. In times of change, the consultant has to be the rock of stability, though he or she can't manage the change, and often must deal with changes that are proposed by non-psychological consultants in strategy, marketing, finance, and so on. Finally, the consultant must be a teacher because often executives cannot act wisely without that input of knowledge that gives them an intellectual rationale for appropriate action. The top management consultant must do all this without losing his or her perspective as a psychologist and his or her very specific psychological role.

Power

There are many issues common in consulting with executives in top management. First, the nature of the people who rise to such levels. Obviously they must have a wish for power. That wish may arise out of identification with successful mentors and models, or it may arise for compensatory reasons, out of an intolerable unconscious sense of helplessness. When it arises out of identification with parental and other models, usually its pursuit is a more flexible effort, more amenable to adapting to changes in the environment and in the nature of the business. When it becomes a compensatory effort, then it is more likely to be both more rigid and more directed to becoming big and powerful unconsciously to becoming omnipotent. Indeed, a compensatory pursuit is so intertwined with the psychology of the chief executive that it is difficult to separate the organization from the individual. That was the case with my client.

Whichever the reason one seeks power, and I have oversimplified somewhat, working with senior executives psychologically means that one inevitably has multiple roles. As this example illustrates, on the one hand, one has to deal with the personal idiosyncrasies and pathologies of the key executives. On the other, one has also to be concerned with what is also fundamental to them, too, namely the perpetuation of the organization. That has a number of implications.

Power and Isolation

People who seek and gain power have a certain mystique about them for all the rest of us who serve them, envy them, or criticize them. They get a good deal of both envy and criticism because of their lifestyle. In addition, however, reaching such heights increases their distance from people on the street. Therefore, they risk losing touch with the feelings, wishes, and attitudes of ordinary human beings. Inevitably, they are caught up in the bureaucracies that necessarily arise as their organizations grow and find it increasingly difficult to have a direct effect on what goes on in those organizations. Corporate bureaucracies can become so big and so complicated that the senior executives have great difficulty managing them (Ginzberg & Vojta, 1985). Large organizations tend to lose their flexibility, their ability to adapt competitively, as criticisms of Roger Smith, the former chief executive of General Motors, illustrate.

In the process of building those bureaucracies, top management also frequently loses the confidence of its middle management. This problem has become exacerbated in recent years with repetitive downsizing and firing. Ginzberg and Vojta believe that many big companies have been in decline since the early 1960s and that the fault lies with the CEO who they see as an isolated, buffeted executive, so disconnected from his people that he rarely knows what has gone wrong until after it has occurred. Furthermore, given the competition for power, organizations are necessarily political scenes and, as in the example with which I began, that leads to various kinds of political sensitivity and in-fighting.

So, today's top management is highly visible and the subject of all kinds of criticism, as well as identification. Describing one CEO, the observer (Kleinfield, 1985) says he fills a wide range of roles: "Coach, politician, diplomat, Sun King, Roman god. Thousands of people, dozens of divisions, hundreds of products orbit around him and respond to his pronouncements, his whims, his vision."

My client was like that. On the one hand, he saw himself as a simple man. On the other, he had power and influence beyond his dreams. He knew that, but somehow it never seemed real to him. The greater his success, the greater his sense of inadequacy - and the less his lieutenants measured up. Part of my task was to help counteract his low self-image, another to help him see his subordinates more realistically, and still another to support their self-images in the face of his criticisms.

Control and Sensitivity

Business organizations are fundamentally instruments of control. By definition, one cannot have a business without accountability. Therefore senior executives are people who are devoted to control of themselves personally and of the financial and functional aspects of the organization. That control is threatened not only by the ups and downs of the marketplace, but also by the vicissitudes of international economics, unpredictable events ranging from revolutions to meteorological catastrophes, to corporate raiders, to regulatory decisions, to technological advances, to demographic shifts. The dedication to control means that characterologically many are highly controlled and therefore are less sensitive to their own subtle feelings, especially those related to unconscious longings and conflicts, than those who are not so tightly controlled.

Andrew Mellon, the famous Pittsburgh industrialist and banker of many years ago, once said, "In all my business enterprises, I have never once put an engineer in charge. The trouble with engineers is that they deal with specific facts and with problems that always have specific solutions...In business, however, the human element is very important and incalculable. You never know what men are going to do. For this reason engineers are not much use in handling human problems." (Hersh, 1978). One doesn't have to agree entirely with Mellon to understand why he reached his conclusion.

A fundamental of psychological consultation at all levels of management is the development among executives of greater awareness of their own feelings, of the feelings of others, and the influence of those respective feelings on each other. My client wanted me to manipulate and exhort. He could not understand, let alone enact, what he was supposed to so. Nevertheless, I had to help him try to understand some of his own feelings and those of others, then to work around his denials without exacerbating his depression or trying to get him to behave in ways that were inimical to him.

People Values

Although some executives are inconsiderate and some take pride in "I don't get ulcers, I give them" kind of behavior, by and large those with whom I work most closely have a very powerful value position. These men and women have personal convictions and personal boundaries for their behavior and their organization's behavior that are not going to allow them either to be bullies or to undertake activities which do not fall within those value boundaries. They manage their aggression well from a position of personal integrity. I find them quite sensitive to other people's concerns. In fact, sometimes too sensitive in the sense that they often find it most difficult to face up to the limits and deficiencies of other people and to move fast enough, both on behalf of their own organizations and on behalf of those people who aren't doing well, to allow the organization to function at its maximum. My client had that problem. He had great difficulty sensing his own and others' more subtle feelings, but he had great concern for people. In fact, when his subordinates fired people, many made a beeline for his office, knowing he would hear them and find another place for them - whether or not they deserved a second chance. His admirable sense of community responsibility also made him vulnerable to too many who would exploit him.

Such behavior puts a heavy burden on the consultant. He or she must help the client act realistically, yet cope with his inordinate guilt.

Issues of Fit

A major issue facing the consultant is the fit of the chief executive and also other executives to their particular roles in given stages of organization development. It is widely recognized that many founder-entrepreneurs do well starting their businesses, but do less well when they then have to manage growing concerns. It is less widely recognized that the urgent creativity of the innovative entrepreneur usually becomes somewhat less urgent and more mature in middle age with the decline of the restlessness and impulsivity that characterizes the earlier adult era (Jaques, 1970).

And, it is even more difficult in the later stages of an individual's maturation to tolerate that kind of departure from one's own evolutionary history that is necessary to adapt flexibly to changes in technology and business climate. More obscure to executives themselves is where they are in the trajectory of adult development. Frequently, it is even less clear to them in what stage of its development the organization may be (Greiner, 1972). Furthermore, senior executives, particularly chief executives, almost never get away from their businesses; even their social relations are a function of their positions in their organizations.

These factors taken together make it difficult for them to recognize the limitations of their skills and competences, of their personalities and characters, and therefore to step aside voluntarily when they no longer fit given roles in particular organizations. The psychological consultant is in the difficult position of sometimes having to conclude that an executive no longer fits the requirements of his role and then helping him or her to understand that fact. Then there is the obligation to help that person mourn his or her loss and to prepare himself for a role more appropriate to his or her personality and level of conceptual competence (Jaques, 1989), usually elsewhere.

True, executives of publicly held corporations are evaluated in the business press and in security analysts' estimates of their profitability. They are held accountable for return on stockholders' equity, on sales, on the management of assets, on how well they have organized the business and developed successors, on the development of new products, and on morale, as well as corporate image and growth potential. However, short of abject failure, few chief executives are fired, even though those who report to them might well be for not meeting previously established goals. Therefore, although they get quantitative performance data and critical feedback about those data, the more pressing and useful qualitative psychological data come about as a product of the work of the psychologist consultant. Unlike the therapist, the organizational consultant can't depend alone on those data the individual himself brings. In the case illustration, it was necessary to confront the CEO with the fact that the time had come for him to step aside despite his unwillingness to do so.

The Consultant's Need to Know

Unlike most other psychological consultants, the consultant to top management necessarily needs a range of knowledge and skills for this professional role. For example, he or she hears, sees, and must share in the discussion about a vast array of phenomena as they arise for his clients. He or she must become knowledgeable about a wide range of industries and the problems in each, as well as be familiar with political and socioeconomic issues of the global world. In my client's multi-billion dollar conglomerate, the subsidiaries were in varied businesses that included Japan and parts of Europe.

The need to know about different industries is much like the need of an anthropologist to know the customs, practices, and dialects of different tribes. One can't understand the behavior without also knowing the taboos, myths, established practices, and historic figures of an industry. That kind of knowledge also makes it easier to establish rapport with new clients in those industries. Much of my own gratification comes from being a psycho-economic-political explorer. The role, therefore, is a wide-ranging and highly stimulating one before one even gets to the underlying psychological issues.

But it requires reading widely and keeping up to date with the business press, general magazines and news sources, as well as the psychological literature. I am amused by the naivete of some psychologists that leads them to think they can just as easily consult with top managements as with any other client, and with those family therapists who similarly think they can merely extrapolate from family therapy.

And Suffer the Little Children...

The consultant to top management must also be a child psychologist. Inevitably, in their dependency relationships with higher authority, people act in ways which are consistent with their earliest forms of dealing with power. When most of the efforts of a work group are directed toward finding gratification for dependency needs by leaning on the leader or on each other, then not much gets done (Bion, 1959). When members of the group are preoccupied with fighting each other or running away from each other, the task suffers. When splitting occurs, those to whom black hats are attributed are scapegoated.

When people form competing coalitions and partnerships, they make enemies of the others and the work of the group deteriorates accordingly.

Every consultant encounters such phenomena, but at the highest levels in organizations one must deal with them forthrightly because lower level people have exaggerated fantasies about the power of top management and because of the tendency for the negative behavior to cascade downward. In an effort to counteract these phenomena by pointing them out and by not being drawn into letting people become overly dependent on the senior executive, the consultant incurs significant wrath. Furthermore, when he or she makes it clear that he has no magical talents and can't solve all problems, many won't believe that. They will expect him to do so and be angry with him because he doesn't. Others will insist on fighting him. Some will react negatively in various ways to test his strength. Then his consulting role is put to the painful test as people enact their ambivalences.

Of course, all psychological consultants incur such behavior. What is so painfully different for the consultant to top management is that these phenomena occur in a context of great personal, economic, social, and sometimes political responsibilities among often highly educated people who "should know better." The consequences of such high-level conflicts can be fraught with serious danger to both executives and the corporation. The consultant may be even more keenly aware of the threat and therefore more painfully burdened in his or her role.

Loneliness

The psychological consultant must live with his or her own loneliness in role and with the fact that, although he may be friendly, he cannot be friends with those with whom he has a professional relationship. Clients will constantly test and gauge the consultant's authority and his concern for them. They may become frightened of their own attack on him and his possible revenge, fearing his capacity to retaliate.

That problem becomes more pressing for the consultant to top management. Being on the client's premises and, therefore, more directly and intensely involved in the client's (and the clients') business, it is much more difficult to maintain professional distance. Frequently being in the client's setting includes taking meals together and being present for celebratory occasions. First names are often more likely. All these factors give rise to a level of familiarity not customary in other psychological consulting roles.

While all others go about their business, often collectively, the consultant to top management must accept a myriad of psychological data and work them out alone. Sometimes he or she does so quickly, intuitively; sometimes with much thought. Unless he is part of a team, his work is his alone. Even those who say they follow where the client leads them nevertheless choose among interventions, requiring psychological work on their part that only they can do.

When problems arise in the consultation that the consultant doesn't understand or are refractory to his or her interventions, the wise consultant consults his or her own consultant. I use one of my senior colleagues for that purpose and serve the same role for other psychologists.

Teaching the Boss

Executives and other employees want to be governed and directed by strong, competent authority. Nevertheless, they are careful of the power of anyone who has and demonstrates such ability because of the feeling that he or she can use that power for evil as well as for good.

In the face of the more powerful leader, subordinates tend to feel less adequate, for if, in their eyes, they were more adequate, they would be in his role and he in theirs. When the boss accepts the ultimate decision-making responsibility, then the subordinates can comfortably explore their differences. If not, they must fight with each other about who is right or who is best. He must be the stable figure or his subordinates are in confusion. Many simple actions become compounded out of attitudes toward the boss. The boss must always be alert to exaggerations or constrictions of the behavior of subordinates that are not appropriate to the work at hand. These must to be examined for the implications they carry of fear of the boss or the need for people to protect themselves. It is up to the boss to clarify issues and maintain a realistic picture of himself for the organization. Often he can see in perspective these aspects of behavior only with the help of the consultant.

The boss has always to balance the self-interest of those who report to him. Frequently, like children, they are much concerned about who gets what advantage from the symbolic parental figure. It is easy for members of a group to scapegoat other members or to blame others for difficulties when the problems lie within the group itself. The task of the boss is complicated by the need for each person to protect his own territory and autonomy against the continuous testing by others. The boss must set limits, define and reinforce boundaries, and make it possible for resistances to direction and control to be examined rather than to be turned into anger and displacement against lower level people or customers. When there are economic downturns and things are not going well, it will be up to the CEO to reassure people that their efforts will ultimately pay off, and to point out that the product of hard work is always slow to come to fruition.

Here is where the trust of the boss, developed over time, becomes a critical issue in the functioning of the group. This is particularly true when it comes to managing loss and change where the boss has to be the chief mourner (Shore, 1988) and enable people to speak their anger and depression. Here is also where the trust of the consultant becomes most critical for the turmoil of change heightens paranoid feelings in the organization.

There seems to be a need, when it comes to managing change, to teach chief executives, no matter what the organization, what change and loss mean to people and how they are likely to react. The implication, of course, is that there not only needs to be increased personal communication, but also a continuous and repetitive flow of information that will both reassure people and counteract rumors. Many executives are reluctant to undertake those activities, particularly when they require their own personal interaction up and down the organization. One of the consultant's roles in such circumstances is to coach the chief executive and others in managing the change process.

Another major role is helping the chief executive understand that there are many managerial fads. While certainly there are usually more positive results to be obtained when people are involved in decision making, when decisions are pushed down to the lowest possible level, and when responsibility is similarly moved downward, when such actions are taken without careful thought, they become destructive. The task of the consultant is to help the chief executive think about which people should be involved in which decisions, to whom what tasks should be delegated, and what responsibilities should be devolved on which units or persons. Often decisions are pushed down to people who are neither prepared nor conceptually able to make them and tasks delegated to those who don't have the power to accomplish them. Not a few subsidiaries have been given the responsibility for their own action, charged only to return with a good bottom line. Too late does top management discover that it has delegated too much and therefore must retract some authority, thereby demoralizing the unit to whom accountability had been delegated. The task of the consultant is to help top management think differentially and psychologically about those kinds of actions, meaning the consultant himself or herself must know a great deal about management.

The contemporary fad has to do with the presumed abolition of hierarchy. While indeed levels may be reduced, in most cases they are reduced arbitrarily without a solid psychological conceptual basis (Jaques, 1989) that increases the psychological distance between levels, often making it difficult for boss and subordinate to communicate. In addition, since business organizations are fundamentally structures of accountability, there is no way that hierarchy can be abolished (Jaques, 1990).

Chief executives, like all others in various disciplines, are heavily influenced by their peer groups. They need to please their peers and to be accepted by them. In trade associations, they are often reluctant to take stands against the trade association's stand even when it is in their own corporation's best self-interest to do so and sometimes when it is in the best interest of society to do so. Part of the task of the top management consultant is to help the CEO examine problems of this kind and to make his or her own independent choices out of self-interest and organization interest.

Helping Him Let Go

When the chief executive or other member of the top management group who has been long identified with his role and the organization must leave either or both, then the consultant must help with the task of detachment. As in almost all such cases, the client must be aided in reviewing and appreciating his accomplishments, which he or she often minimizes. As in the case with many others, the executive will regret the goals he or she didn't achieve, and the blunders that dimmed what might have been glowing successes. The consultant must help him or her recognize the close approximation of his achievement to his or her ego ideal to counteract the tendency to depreciate their achievement with resulting vulnerability to depression.

There must also be opportunity to mourn one's loss of status, position, power, and privilege. Ideally, that process should include the executive's spouse, especially if that spouse is a wife for she loses social power and perquisites as well.

Planning for the future at this time ideally involves both spouses. This task, however, is best done with another consultant. My own experience is that such couples profit from consultation away from home in two-hour sessions over a five-day week. In the time between sessions, they have a rare opportunity to talk together about many issues that have not previously been given sufficient attention. The result frequently is elation for what they have accomplished psychologically together.

Not the least problem in separation is that of the consultant. He or she must say good-bye, sometimes to groups as well as individuals, and do his or her own mourning. If the consultant has been wise, he or she has formulated a prognosis for his task which helps bound the professional effort against the sense of failure due to unrealistic expectations.

Post-Retirement

Inevitably, as in the case example I've been using, the chief executive must retire. That is never an easy task. It is even more complicated now when many chief executives, still in good health, must look for new roles where they can make social contributions by building on their skills and competences.

In such instances, the top management consultant becomes a career counselor whose task it is to help the executive evaluate those aspects of his life that now need to be fulfilled and the roles in which such fulfillment might occur. Often this means going into government, but just as often, to do so means that one has to assess the political forces, especially at a national level, and prepare himself to become both visible and acceptable for the prospective roles that he or she would like to pursue. Sometimes that requires making one's authoritative knowledge visible in the form of publishing articles that reflect his knowledge and understanding. In other instances, it may well mean taking a greater part in trade associations or other organizations where one's knowledge, understanding, and proficiency can be recognized. Here it is necessary for the consultant to help the client review his own ego ideal changes in the light of his present age and stage in life (Levinson, et al., 1978) and in the light of the gratification he seeks.

Although consultation with top management tends to be a long-term arrangement, when the chief executive leave the organization, the consulting relationship usually does not continue, except for two conditions. The first is when certain special problems arise in the new role in which the chief executive finds himself. The second is when the former chief executive continues to be in need of a friend. That was the case, for example, in the illustration I gave earlier. In his fantasy, I may have continued to be the "son" that the client wanted when his own son did not respond. Under the new circumstances of his post-retirement role it was not inappropriate that I should visit him from time to time to bolster his optimism as his health declined.

In Conclusion

Psychological consultation with top management is a many-faceted activity. It requires the consultant to become broadly familiar with many aspects of life, work, and behavior in organizations. In that role he or she must be anthropologist, sociologist, social psychologist, teacher, group therapist, and clinician. He or she is always involved in issues of individual personality and group relations in a context of power and power struggles. He or she has the particular problem of working with people who often have difficulty recognizing, let alone accepting, their own feelings and those of others. They also often have difficulty recognizing and appreciating their own achievments, and coming to terms with their feelings of guilt. The consultant must help them recognize their expression of residues of infantile feelings, and learn to deal with them. Often he must teach them to understand loss and change, and to help them manage complex change situations. Usually top management consultation involves long-term relationships. The consultant must help with the detachment and mourning process, as well as planning for the future. In short, top management psychological consultation is an exciting professional adventure.

REFERENCES

BION, W.R. Experiences in Groups. New York: Basic Books, 1959.
GINZBERG, E., & VOJTA, G. Beyond Human Scale: The Large Corporation at Risk. New York: Basic Books, 1985.
GREINER, L.E. Evolution and Revolution as Organizations Grow. Harvard Business Review, July-August 1972, 37-46.
HERSH, B. The Mellon Family. New York: William Morrow & Company, 1978.
JAQUES, E. Work, Creativity and Social Justice. New York: International Universities Press, Ch. 3, 1970.
JAQUES, E. Requisite Organization. Arlington, Va.: Cason Hall, 1989.
JAQUES, E. In Praise of Hierarchy. Harvard Business Review, January-February 1990, 127-133.
KLEINFIELD, N.R. What It Takes: The Life of a CEO. New York Times Magazine, December 1, 1985, 32-55.
LEVINSON, D. et al. The Seasons of a Man's Life. New York: Alfred A. Knopf, 1978.
SHORE, M. Personal communication, 1988.

Leadership Anyone?

Harry Levinson

Managers sometimes say,"I'm not the leader - the guy at the top is." Such managers make a serious mistake. They fail to see that organizations need people at all levels with leadership abilities - so much so that managers whose skills lie in following directives and sticking with established techniques will increasingly find their career futures bleak. The cliches are true: business today simply isn't what it used to be, and changes escalate quickly; economic conditions and markets shift with astonishing speed. And more important still, the organizational map has been transformed. Managers are no longer responsible only to their bosses and, ultimately, the stockholders. Today a range of groups is part of every business's natural constituency, each making demands on managers that must be met. Employee groups demand that managers improve the quality of worklife; consumers and community groups demand safer products and a cleaner environment; government agencies require managers to fill hiring quotas. Managers must meet all these demands, and more. And, of course, they still must protect profits.

The heat's on, and it will get hotter in coming years. Managers will be told to clamp down and cut back - and to keep everybody happy as the slices of the pie get smaller. What can managers do? The old ways don't satisfy the new constituencies; piecemeal answers don't much satisfy anyone. Organizations increasingly will need managers who can help them anticipate changes and chart new courses. They'll pressure managers to adapt, innovate, and take charge; they'll seek people with fresh ideas, a sense of purpose, and the desire to act. The business periodicals keep telling us that the old days of the organizational man have ended. Managers can no longer manage. They must exert forward force and pull their organizations into the fray. They must lead.

Leading the Way

Managers become leaders when they invest themselves in their work and convince others that their efforts can make a significant difference. They become leaders when they learn to take a stand and take risks, to anticipate, initiate, and innovate. Any manager who sees a need and says, "I want to do something about that," has the potential

---

to become a leader. And any manager who goes on to say, "I can do something about that," has started to become a leader.

Some managers are self-starters. They want to lead their organizations because they're driven from within to take charge, accomplish, and leave their mark. These people have powerful superegos and demanding ego ideals; that is, they expect much of themselves and feel much is expected of them. They drive themselves because psychologically they have no choice. In some cases, they are striving to live up to their parents' ideals or accomplishments; in others, to compensate for their parents' real or perceived inadequacies or their own. These leaders meet the powerful demands of their ego ideals by asserting their views and acting on events. They want to be leaders and they see themselves as leaders.

Other step forward from the crowd to become leaders in times of need or crisis. Some, like Harry Truman, never saw themselves - and were not seen by others - as leaders. But often such people rise to the occasion when thrust into a role that impels them to act. They find better ways of doing things when their backs are against the wall. A contemporary example is Frances Hesselbein who started as a volunteer and then became the leader who revolutionized the Girl Scouts of America (Byrne, 1990).

Some leaders gain the confidence to take charge when they see that others are no more insightful or powerful than they. Jimmy Carter is reported to have made just that decision after meeting other would-be candidates for the Democratic presidential nomination. Such leaders may or may not have long-held burning ambitions, but something awakens the feeling - shared by most of us, consciously or not - that they can do just as well as anyone else.

Many managers, however, don't see themselves as potential leaders. Nothing in their experience or imagination encourages that vision of themselves. Others are afraid to lead, some fearful of falling on their faces; others of making just one small mistake. They play it safe, but they sell themselves and their organizations short, never seeing what might be possible for both. Moreover, to accomodate their shortened vision, they misintepret what their organizations need and want.

As Gardner (1990) indicates, our open society needs many leaders of all shapes and sizes in a myriad of contexts. We must therefore draw out the leadership talent of those who don't yet see it in themselves or who are afraid. Organizations need leaders who - regardless of their positions or titles - can state needs, formulate goals, and institute realistic programs for reaching them. Subordinates, moreover, need leaders who can inspire and support them and help them develop the competence they will need to serve their organizations effectively. Despite all the talk about leaderless groups, there really is no such thing. Therefore, there certainly will always be a need for leaders.

What does an organization do to develop leadership among that vast body of managers who don't become leaders by themselves? I want to answer that question by telling you a story about a man named Ron. Unlike most case citations, that is his name. Some years ago Ron was a participant in one of The Levinson Institute seminars "...On Leadership." He reported himself to be stimulated by his participation. Not long after he returned to Minneapolis, he was recruited for a new role near New York. His wife, Judy, was dismayed at the prospect of moving. Taking a leaf out of his seminar experience, he talked with her at considerable length; he also had her read the handout on stress and change that complements the lecture on that topic in the seminar, and a reprint of my article,"Easing the Pain of Personal Loss" (Levinson, 1972). She found all of this quite helpful, made the move, and adapted successfully.

Ron was recruited from his second role to become executive vice president of a supermarket chain. That chain had to expand or its competitors would invade its territory and threaten its position.

It was obvious to him that he could not handle the projected expansion by himself. It was also obvious to him that the chain had little depth of leadership on whom he could depend to carry it out. Furthermore, the supermarket business is not one that is highly attractice to young MBAs. In fact, most of its managers and executives have risen from bag-boy positions. One can hardly know the supermarket business well enough to be a good executive without having come through those ranks. He had taken seriously my admonition, repeated often in the seminar and contrary to a widely held managerial myth, that good managers don't make fast decisions, they make good decisions. They think about what they must do. Once again, he did what now was his regular practice: he turned to the lecture handouts, the books, and reprints when problems confronted him.

He had two promising lieutenants. One managed produce and the other groceries. He told them that they were the standard bearers of the future. But if they were going to carry those flags, they had to do two things. First, they had to check the ranks of their own subordinates to be sure that when they were no longer in their respective positions, those subordinates could carry on without them. Second, they had to broaden their knowledge of the business. The produce man recognized that he knew nothing about groceries, and the grocery man that he was equally ignorant about produce.

Somewhat chagrined, they reported that among their subordinates there were indeed too many people who were not carrying their full loads. They themselves made up for their subordinates' inadequacies by working longer hours. They would have to define accountabilities more sharply, train people to meet them, and hold them to those obligations. Also, each would have to learn the other's business. They would have to interchange jobs. Furthermore, Ron would have to teach them what they needed to know about higher level management. They agreed and their leadership training is underway.

This is a simple story. No doubt it occurs in one form or another frequently in many contexts every day. What is its relevance here?

Management vs. Leadership

There has long been a debate about whether leadership can be taught. Some insist that management and leadership are so different, management being essentially a matter of maintaining efficient conformity, while leadership, requiring innovative initiative, requires that one be a maverick (Zaleznik, 1988). Kotter (1990) demonstrates with excellent case studies that they are indeed different. But John W. Gardner (1990) disagrees: "Many writers on leadership take considerable pains to distinguish between leaders and managers. In the process leaders generally end up looking like a cross between Napoleon and the Pied Piper and managers like unimaginative clods. This troubles me. I once heard it said of a man, `He's an utterly first-class manager but there isn't a trace of the leader in him.´ I am still looking for that man and I' m beginning to believe that he does not exist. Every time I encounter utterly first-class managers they turn out to have quite a lot of the leader in them."

Others contend that leaders are born, not made. Some sociologists would argue that leadership is not an idiosyncratic talent, but behavior that arises out of a group need. The group determines who shall become its leader. Under different conditions, different people in the same group can become leaders.

There is indeed evidence that leadership can be taught, but the psychological evidence is drawn from a scattered range of leadership studies (Clark, 1990). The fact that such leaders as Lee Iacocca and others who have turned major business organizations around can suceed where their predecessors have failed, tells us that we are dealing with a much more psychological than sociological phenomenon.

Having taught leadership for 34 years in four university business schools and in my own private organization, I would have to take the position that leadership can indeed be taught, and that many people can profit sufficiently from that teaching to advance to successful business leadership roles. I detailed 22 years ago (Levinson, 1968) how that might be done. Sashkin (1988) summarizes and describes more recent modes of training managers for leadership roles.

To understand how that might happen, let us return to Ron. How might we conceptualize what happened to him and what constituted leadership on his part?

What Does It Take?

In his case, we have to assume he had a certain motivation to lead, a wish to pursue his own ego ideal through the medium of executive achievement. In many people, as in the case of his two subordinates, that wish has to be aroused, for neither man necessarily saw himself as giving leadership to an expanding organization.

First, Ron immersed himself in a frame of reference, namely the concept of theory and practice that was advanced in the seminar he attended. He was deeply involved in the content material, as reflected in how he used that material in both his family and business settings. Furthermore, to adapt that material to his own needs, he had to identify with me as the agent who propounded the concepts and the role that he found useful.

Second, just as a good golfer continues to practice his swing and a good tenor his scales, so Ron continued to fall back on what he had learned, to refresh himself repeatedly in the context of the problems he had to deal with. The greater his success in applying the material, the greater the reinforcement of both the material and the identification.

Third, when he chose subordinate leaders, he lifted their sights to a horizon that they had not previously perceived. He confronted them with the whole business and its realities, and held out a challenge to which they had to rise or continue to be forever a produce man and a grocery man.

In so doing, he implicitly also took into account Elliott Jaques' (1989) theory of levels of conceptual capacity, making a judgement that they could rise to and perhaps even above a Stratum V level. Up to that time, they could not know that they had potential for executive roles. They had no idea of the behavior required at that level, nor how they might mature to executive competence. Given the widespread propensity for self-deprecation, it was highly likely that their aspirations were too modest for their capacities. He gave them permission to pursue the horizon he had illuminated, and, by so doing so, expressed his confidence in their ability to seek it. He brought to bear the wide range of his experience that would manifest itself in mentoring and coaching. That support, in turn, would strengthen them and encourage them to turn to him when the inevitable disappointments and defeats made turning to the boss psychologically wise.

Evidently, he also took into careful consideration the culture in which that organization operated, as well as the culture of the business itself, for these two, despite their conceptual capacity, might well fail in situations in which they could not capitalize on their talents, skills, experience, and abilities. In keeping with what he had learned about performance appraisal (Levinson, 1976), Ron is giving them frequent significant incident (Flanagan, 1954) feedback on specific behavior. I have no doubt that he will assess carefully the specific skills and competencies they will have to develop to master their new roles, and that he will send them to appropriate training programs to enhance their competence. All of that support will engender their identification with him and with the leadership role, as well as with their own organization.

Some contemporary writers decry the value of mentoring. Perhaps many formal mentoring programs do not produce the resulted expected of them. But, clearly, those that are personal efforts of leaders to rear other leaders, as in the case of Ron, can be eminently successful.

In "The Exceptional Executive"(Levinson, 1968), I sought to integrate all of the contemporary theories of motivation in management under a psychoanalytic umbrella. There I argued that the exceptional executive is a teacher whose fundamental task is to teach others to operate as leaders to enhance the forward momentum of the business. I argued further that that task called for psychological understanding of self and others. Although many organizations have formal management development and executive development programs, few yet take full advantage of that conception. The simple reason is because contemporary performance appraisal systems are inadequate to deal with performance, let alone recognize and compensate performance that involves the development of successor leaders (Levinson, 1976).

Performance Appraisal

To translate these practices into real time efforts requires that performance appraisal be based on specific behavioral incidents (Flanagan, 1954) that in turn are related to a comprehensive behavioral job description (Levinson, 1983). The incidents should then be organized into categories that are given weights. Those weights can then be factored into compensation. Once executives recognize that they are being evaluated and compensated for their effectiveness in developing others, then those activities no longer will be an unpleasant burden incidental to their performance, but actually a critical component of the role that they are supposed to carry out. Then, executive development will become an integral part of the managerial role and organizational practice.

But let's elaborate further what we have learned from Ron and from other experiences. How would one go about developing leaders out of managers?

How Now?

Over more than three decades, I have had the opportunity to talk with a wide variety of technical people who have moved up several steps in the hierarchical ladder, only to find themselves disappointed because movement within a discipline does not give them the same status, power, influence, and opportunity as moving into a management hierarchy. All too often, such people are then locked into their skill hierarchy. They can't move readily into management because they are too far along to start at entry management levels and without that managerial experience can't move into such roles at peer levels. Therefore, frequently they are extremely frustrated and too early disillusioned with their career and career opportunities.

In my view, all entry-level people, whether managerial or technical, should be put on a managerial track. That will give them an opportunity to test what they can learn and do managerially, as well as to prepare themselves for assuming managerial roles within their disciplines if they do not prove to be effective managers outside of them. Such an opportunity provides a way for them to calibrate themselves, as well as to be calibrated by the organization, and to get a better understanding of what management and managerial processes are all about. If they and others at the entry level then begin to demonstrate some leadership potential, then the organization can develop them with whatever resources it has. Not the least of these is the leader-mentor superior (Levinson, 1962).

They should be taught early to understand the politics of their organizations and their own use of political skills to develop networks that, in turn, can support them and through which they can support others. Too many people in low-level managerial ranks disdain what they speak of as organizational politics and, as a result, do not develop those kinds of contacts that are necessary in everybody's organizations to evolve cooperative relationships. All organizations are necessarily political. Mentors and superiors especially must help lower level people understand the complexities of power relationships in their organizations in the context of the historical character and culture of the organization. Often it is those who have the highest standards and who therefore disdain anything political, certainly if they see it as self-aggrandizing, who need the permission and support of superiors to learn to use themselves more effectively in an organization and therefore to become eligible for leadership roles.

Fundamental to superior-subordinate relationships and those with peers and others with whom one must work is the issue of trust. Trust means more than simply being honest. It means also the ability to give specific direction and guidance upon which people can depend; consistency of behavior that is predictable and reliable; and the sense that one can be counted on as a peer, a subordinate, a superior to put the interest of the organization first; and to support others in their role functioning.

Not long ago, one of my colleagues conducted a questionnaire survey of some former seminar participants to ask what content they would like to have in a subsequent seminar. One responded that he wanted "tools." This stance is not unusual among many managers. They view themselves as doers. They are held responsible for getting results, and they want to learn how to get those results most expediently. Therefore, the emphasis on tools. However, one can't use tools without knowing what one is going to use them for and how. A carpenter needs to know the kind of wood he is going to be working on, and a mechanic the kind of automobile. Only then can either choose tools. Unfortunately, managers don't read very widely and, by and large, don't conceptualize very readily. Therefore, it is imperative for someone in a mentor or leadership role to encourage the subordinate not only to read, but also to then discuss what he has read with his mentor-superior. Beyond that, the manager who would become a leader needs to have time to think. But he needs something else, as reflected in the remark of the chief executive officer of a bank who complained that he didn't have anyone to bounce ideas against.

Everybody who would be in a leadership role necessarily has to have a confidant, someone with whom he can exchange ideas, someone who can say "no," or cause him to review his thoughts, his plans, his ideas. Few of us can generate out of our own solitude a perspective on what's going through our heads. Unlike novelists, dramatists, and other creative artists who cast their ideas in the words of their characters, a leader must develop concepts and plans and test them either in his head or in the environment. The writer simply lets his unconscious flow and later edits to sharpen what he has written. But the leader can't do that. The leader must formulate and conceptualize where his unit is going, how to define its niche, which option to pursue, and so on. To do that, he or she needs reverberation, feedback, echoing, and critical examination. The person who would develop as a leader should be doing that early.

In the course of that kind of discussion and thinking time, the mentor-leader is in a position to judge how well the subordinate tolerates ambiguity, how far into the future he or she thinks and plans, and to what novel insights his thinking may lead him. The higher in the organization one goes, the greater the need for tolerating ambiguity, the farther ahead one must plan, and the more innovative one must become.

The crucial psychological factors they must learn about have to do with creating conditions for identification with themselves by providing direction, support, and the opportunity to grieve when change brings about inevitable losses. If there is to be a leader, there must be followers. People follow voluntarily or reluctantly or not at all. If they are to follow voluntarily, then they must be able to identify with their leader. It follows that they can do so only if the leader helps them move toward their ego ideals. Particularly for those people who are innovative and creative, and therefore the most likely to be highly self-critical, the leader must communicate his or her faith in the follower's ability and encourage the enactment of his or her potential.

The model I have in mind is the great British composer, Edward Elgar (Ledbetter, 1990). He was highly successful significantly because his wife, Carolyn, encouraged him to compose the greatworks that she knew he had in him, to aspire to the highest ideals. She helped him with practical matters, as well as providing encouragement. He became England's first composer of international stature in two centuries. Unfortunately, after she died, he was never able to complete another large work. Our prospective leaders should have greater survival potential.

One can find many examples in the lives of other people who have risen to leadership prominence. That kind of communication is not simply a matter of encouragement, but it also is fundamental to combatting the depression that results from change and loss. All change is loss and all loss needs to be mourned. A leader needs to be the chief mourner of a group or organization (Shore, 1988). Unless people can mourn their losses, then the depressions burden them and keep them from adapting effectively to change or recovering successfully from the losses. Leaders who fail to recognize this then have to fight feelings of depression among their followers, not knowing even that they exist, but seeing only the lessened spirit of malaise.

Finally, there is the issue of vision. We have heard a lot in recent years about leaders having to have vision (Bennis and Nanus, 1985). Indeed, there is some truth to that assertion. One can't lead unless one has a sense of where one is going. However, as Stuart Rosenthal and I (1984) discovered, none of the six chief executives we interviewed came into his chief executive role with a vision. Only when he came upon a problem to be solved did he develop a vision for how to go about doing so. Visions arise out ot contact with problems and the need to evolve modes of solving them. They do not arise fully grown from the head of a leader simply because he is in that position.

Conclusion

In sum, leadership can indeed be taught and developed, at different conceptual levels, for different roles, and different tasks. It requires immersion in a frame of reference that structures the role. That frame of reference ideally arises out of personal contact with a trusted identification figure who lifts the sights of a would-be leader, gives him or her permission to pursue that horizon, supports, encourages, teaches, stimulates and demands interchange of ideas. The identification figure also must help the follower-to-become-leader to understand and manage the politics of the organization and to mourn disappointments lest they become defeats. All else, however useful, is incidental. Leadership development, like all growth, requires effective cultivators.

REFERENCES

BENNIS, W., & NANUS, B. Leaders: The Strategies for Taking Charge. New York: Harper & Row, 1985.

BYRNE, J.A. Profiting from the Nonprofits. Business Week, March 26, 1990, 66-74.

CLARK, K.E., & CLARK, M.B., eds. Measures of Leadership. W. Orange, N.J.: Leadership Library of America, 1990.

FLANAGAN, J.C. The Critical Incident Technique. Psychological Bulletin, 51, 1954, 327-358.
GARDNER, J.W. On Leadership. New York: The Free Press, 1990.
JAQUES, E. Requisite Organization. Arlington, Va.: Cason Hall and Company, 1989.
KOTTER, J. A Force of Change. New York: The Free Press, 1990.
LEDBETTER, S. Boston Symphony Orchestra Program, Week 22, 1990.
LEVINSON, H. A Psychologist Looks at Executive Development. Harvard Business Review, September-October, 1962, 69-75.
LEVINSON, H. The Exceptional Executive, revised as Executive (1981). Cambridge, Ma.: Harvard University Press, 1968.
LEVINSON, H. Easing the Pain of Personal Loss, Harvard Business Review, September-October, 1972, 80-88.
LEVINSON, H. Appraisal of What Performance? Harvard Business Review, July-August, 1976, 30-36.
LEVINSON, H. Behavioral Job Descriptions. In: The Levinson Letter Addendum, 1983.
LEVINSON, H., & ROSENTHAL, S. CEO: Corporate Leadership in Action. New York: Basic Books, 1984.
SASHKIN, M. The Visionary Leader. In: J.A. Conger and R.N. Kanungo (eds.) Charismatic Leadership. San Francisco: Jossey-Bass, 1988.
SHORE, M. Personal communication, 1988.
ZALEZNIK, A. The Managerial Mystique. New York: Harper & Row, 1988.

Narcissism Project and Corporate Decay: The Case of General Motors

Howard S. Schwartz

INTRODUCTION

When I left graduate school and began teaching organizational behavior courses, I was struck by the irrelevance of what I had learned to the actual organizational experience of my students. My students experienced and understood organizational life as a kind of "vanity fair," in which individuals who were interested in "getting ahead" could do so by playing to the vanity of their superiors. One needed to do this in two respects. One needed to flatter the superior as an individual and as an occupant of the superior role. This latter process tended to trail off into an adulation of the organization in general.

Work either fit into this process of adulation, in which case it made sense; or it did not, in which case it did not make sense. Work which did not make sense in this way, my students felt, was best left to the suckers who hadn't figured out yet how to get ahead and who deserved whatever torment this system led them to inherit. If, through this process, important, valid information was lost to the system by being withheld or simply unappreciated, that was not their concern. Through luck or guile, the consequences would, or could be made to, occur on somebody else's watch.

At first glance, my students' attitude looked to me like cynicism. But closer analysis suggested that, although they had a great deal of cynicism in them, they were not simply being cynical, for they believed in the righteousness of what they were doing.

For them, getting ahead was a moral imperative, which justified any means necessary for its accomplishment. But more than this, the system itself which called upon subordinates to idealize it was held morally sacrosanct. A person who refused to go along with the system was seen as not only stupid and naive, but as morally inferior. And this was so even if the individual in question was offering a point of view that was essential for the organization to do its work effectively and efficiently.

It thus seemed to me that, for my students, the organization's

---

Reprinted by permission of New York University Press from Howard Schwartz, Narcissistic Process and Corporate Decay: The Theory of the Organization Ideal (New York: New York University Press, 1990).

often even aggressive.

The function that I will use to explain the concept of organizational commitment will be called the "ontological function", by which I shall mean the function of providing a sense of Being, or identity, to the participants. The idea that organizations can provide their participants with a sense of identity is certainly not a new one in organizational thought. What I wish to offer in this paper is a sense of why that function is required, what its psychology is, and what it means; for in understanding these features of the process we will be able to understand how this apparently beneficial phenomenon, and the organizational commitment which results from it, can turn sour and malignant and can lead to the most terrible consequences.

Why the Ontological Function is Required

The crucial step in the analysis of the ontological function is to ask the question why is it required? The answer has to be that, in many cases, as Lichtenstein (1977) has pointed out, people's sense of identity is tenuous in the extreme.

This seems absurd. How can a person's sense of identity be tenuous? Are not people what they are? Is that not their identity? The answer is that, for the most part, people are not what they are, or, what is the same thing, cannot permit themselves to be what they are.

Thus, it makes sense to us to say: "He has made something of himself", or "She has become somebody". What we have to notice about these expressions is the implication that, if the persons in question had allowed themselves to be what they were before they became something or somebody, they would not have been anything or anybody. They would not, that is to say, have had an identity. This is to say that having an identity, at least in our culture, is something of an achievement. Again, we have the notion of the "has been". The "has been" is somebody who once was somebody, but is no longer anybody.

Taking these things together, what we find is that having an identity is not something that we can take for granted, that is something which we must achieve if we are to have it at all , and that we must continue to achieve if we are to maintain it. In other words, having an identity is a status that is always in question.

Moreover, there is clearly a judgemental element in these assertions. Making something of oneself is good, not making something of oneself is bad. Being somebody is good, being a "has been" is bad.

Thus, the question of identity reflects acceptance or rejection, affirmation or denial. Finally, it seems at least plausible that if these sorts of judgements are common when we judge others, something similar probably goes on when we assess and consider ourselves. We not only have the possibility of denying identity to others, but of denying it to ourselves. Indeed, the question of our own identity would, like the question of the identity of others, be continually in question at all times. Never, apparently, can we simply permit ourselves to be simply what we are.

Now, not allowing ourselves to be what we are just because that is what we are, means that we cannot take ourselves as the measure of what we are supposed to be. We look outside ourselves to find out who we are supposed to be, if we are going to be anything at all - if we are going to have an identity. I shall submit that we fashion social institutions largely to provide an answer to this question. In this way, I shall argue, social institutions, and specifically work organizations, develop an ontological function. In the meantime, though, the question becomes, why is it that people are not what they are, or cannot permit themselves to be what they are?

The Existential Psychoanalytic Psychology of the Ontological Function

To understand that people cannot permit themselves to be what they are is to recognize that at our psychological base lies self-rejection. In order to understand this self-rejection we must come to an understanding of where and when it originates as a stable part of the psychological structure.

In psychoanalytic theory, self-rejection is not a component of our original psychological configuration. On the contrary, to begin with the infant experiences itself without any self-critical sense whatever. Its experience is that of being the centre of a loving world.

Freud (1957/1914) referred to the attendant sense of cosmic significance and self-love as narcissism. The response of others who are oriented toward the child gives the child its sense of importance. Moreover, the child's love of these "mirroring" others, its opening itself to them, allows it to bask in their love for it, and to experience that love as love for itself (Lichtenstein, 1977).

But while love for others permits self-love, it is also the lever by which self-rejection enters into the child's mental configuration. For as time goes on, and as the child comes to enter into more complex relations with its parents and with the world, certain spontaneous actions on the part of the child become unacceptable to the parents and to others generally, and the child's love for them, its openness to them, and its need for their love, leads to its experiencing their rejection as self-caused rejection, and therefore as self-rejection, or guilt.

In the course of coming to live with others, bringing them into our minds as the "internal objects" (Klein, 1948) with whom the meaning of our lives is transacted, their rejection of us becomes internalized as our rejection of ourselves to form a stable part of our psychological configuration. It is thus that a permanent wound to our narcissism is created, thus that we cannot permit ourselves to be what we are, thus that the locus of our identity shifts from who we are to who others will permit us to be, and thus that the need for the ontological function is developed.

The ontological function refers to the projection of the possibility of a return to narcissism, to being the centre of a loving world, to regaining a stable, self-contained identity and a sense of Being without self-rejection as its core. It refers to a specification of that person who will be able to be exactly who he or she is and will not be required, under penalty of rejection, to be someone else.

Freud (1957/1914, 1955/1921; Chasseguet-Smirgel, 1985) refers to the specification of the person one must become in order to return to narcissism as the ego ideal. Recognizing that the ego ideal is defined in terms of social interaction, it becomes possible to regard the pattern of ideal social interaction in which the ego ideal is embedded, and by which it is defined, as itself a discernible ideal entity. We can see this ideal entity taking various forms, as defined by ideology (Chasseguet-Smirgel 1985): the community of saved souls, the community of post-revolutionary society, etc. For our purposes, we may limit discussion to the case in which the ego ideal takes the form of an organization. Giving this ideal pattern of organization a name, we shall refer to it as the organization ideal (Schwartz 1987b).

Thus, the organization ideal is an idea (in Freud's terms a "leading idea") of organizational life characterized by an integration of spontaneity, on the one hand, and conformance with the requirements of loved others on the other hand. It represents a synthetic unity of subject and object, self and other, freedom and necessity, activity and passivity. We may now observe that the ontological function of the organization consits in specifying an organization ideal to serve as an ego ideal for organizational participants. Up to this point, we may also observe, there is no problem. All that we have described is benign.

There is no way yet to understand why a person would commit criminal and anti-social acts because of concern for the corporation.

In order to understand how that can happen we need to go more fully into the psychology of the ego ideal and organization ideal. The problem is that the ego ideal, whether considered individually or as the organization ideal, is never attained. In order to see why this is so, it is necessary to return to the discussion of the roots of the self-rejection which makes the ontological function necessary.

We saw before that self-rejection arises from the internalization of the rejection of loved others. But if this were all that it amounted to, then we could imagine that the return to narcissism could be a real possibility. If one pleases the loved others, they will love one in return and one will again be the centre of a loving world.

There are two problems here. The first is that orienting oneself toward pleasing others in order to gain their love means, already, that one is not the centre of their world. Rather, those whose love one organizes one's life around are the centre of one's own. For the fact is that by orienting my life around their love I am conceding my dependence on them, and conceding the fact that they do not, and I cannot make them, love me for myself alone. Rather, if they are to love me, they will love me out of motives arising from within themselves. Accepting that one cannot have ontological hegemony over the world, that in order to have the love of others one must limit one's claims and one's sense of self-importance, amounts to self-rejection. Thus, if the organization ideal is to succeed in offering a return to narcissism , it must be based upon a redefinition of the self and of others in a way which denies the differences among us - which defines us as being essentially the same and having the same motives and the same centre. The problem is that, as individuals, we all remain different from the abstract self so defined, and therefore stand in perpetual contrast to it.

The second problem is that, even if I give up centrality in an attempt to gain love, the outcome must ultimately be disillusioning. For ultimately, it is the facts of biology that determine that the world is not a loving place, and the love of loved others, early in life, served only to conceal this fact. The point is that the threat of loss of love on the part of the apparently omnipotent parents is experienced so powerfully because it reveals to the infant how vulnerable, finite and, ultimately, mortal it is; and vulnerability, finitude and mortality remain facts. In other words, what the loss of love establishes for the infant is that its narcissism was an illusion. This revelation may be repressed, but it can never be eliminated as a basic element of the psychological configuration. I think we can see from this where another part of our internalized self-rejection comes from. It consits in the rejection of the vulnerability, finitude and mortality that go along with one's organic identity. Thus, the ego ideal and the organization ideal ultimately symbolize immortality. Again we can see why the ego ideal, and the organization ideal along with it, can never be achieved. Immortality is, of course, out of the question.

Thus, the ontological function, which consists in the specification of an organization ideal as a project of the return to narcissism, essentially requires the creation of illusion. We may now add the obvious fact that this illusion, if it is going to serve its purpose, must be taken as a fact. Accordingly, the ontological function of the organization must also involve the shielding of the illusion from reality, the maintenance of the illusion as an apparent fact in the face of its illusory character. It is this dual process - the creation of illusion and the preservation of the apparent facticity of the illusion - that leads to the malignant consequences we wish to explain.

Organizational Aspects of the Ontological Function

We may now define the term "organizational commitment", in a way that is consistent with its usage in traditional organizational psychology, (e.g., Schein, 1983/1968; Mowday et al., 1982) as the situation in which a person's identity is specified by the organization's ontological function. It describes a person, in other words, whose ego ideal is the organization ideal. Our question then becomes, how is it possible to explain morally reprehensible actions on the part of organizationally committed individuals, in the course of their organizational activity?

Three features of the ontological function interact to permit this explanation. They are (1) the content of the organization ideal, (2) the relationship of the individual to the organization ideal, and (3) defense of the identity through defense of the organization ideal.

Content of the Organization Ideal

In the case of the work organization, we may observe that the content of the organization ideal must (a) be social - that is to say it must be an image of social interaction among individual ego ideals, relating to each other in frictionless, mutually supportive, job-specific interaction. This amounts to the reqirement, mentioned earlier, that the members of the organization have redefined themselves in terms of the organization and therefore as essentially identical. It must be (b) powerful - in the sense that the individuals, as organized, are rational, know what they are doing, and are competent to do what they are doing and in control of the situation. This would be a presupposition of the possibility of the organization being immortal and therefore providing immortality for those individuals redefined in terms of it. And (c), it must be free of anxiety at the level of identity. That is to say, the individuals involved would have to be conceived as performing their organizational roles, not out of a feeling of obligation or compulsion, so as to avoid internal or external rejection, but out of desire or self-expression - not out of lack, but out of plenitude. This would be equivalent of specifying that the two mentioned causes of anxiety, individuality and mortality, have been overcome.

Various elements of these contens of the organization ideal have been promulgated by normative organization theorists such as the human relations school (e.g. Mayo, 1933), the industrial humanists (e.g. Argyris, 1964), and students of bureaucracy (e.g. Weber, 1947).

Relationship of the Individual to the Organization Ideal

As we saw before, humans never reach the ego ideal. That would imply immortality. This is so for the organization ideal as well. Organizations never reach the organization ideal. That would imply frictionless interaction among totally competent, perfectly rational individuals acting purely out of desire. It would imply an organization not only in perfect coexistence with its environment, but assured of the permanent continuity of this coexistence. This would imply that the organization would be in total permanent control of its environment. This is so unlikely that we can only believe it to be possible because we need to believe it.

Committed organizational participants, who require that the organization specify an identity for them, are precisely those who have the need to believe this. They are thus likely to feel that deviations from the organization ideal are the result of the fact that it is they who do not fulfil the conditions of their identity. The resultant feeling therefore must be one of personal responsibility for failure - the anxiety experienced as personal shortcoming, or shame.

Baum (1983) has pointed out the pervasiveness of the feeling of shame among organizational participants. He has observed that superiors can invoke shame among their subordinates simply by doing their job. This brings us to another point regarding the relationship of individuals to the organization ideal. It is related to the necessity of defending the illusion of the organization ideal from being revealed as an illusion, in order to maintain the ontological function. This implies that while committed organizational participants believe that their lapse from the organizational ideal is a failure on their own part, they may believe that others fulfill the organization ideal.

An important feature of organizational phenomenology in this connection is the experience of hierarchy (Schwartz, 1983, 1987a, 1987b). It is possible to reconcile individual failure, and even the failure of one's associates to measure up to the organization ideal, with maintenence of belief in the organization ideal through the belief that, at higher levels of the organization, people do approach the organization ideal. Indeed, one may go so far as to say that a large part of organizational dramaturgy is devoted to the enactment of the presumed competence and goodness of organizational superiors (Klein and Ritti, 1984). This point obviously relates as well to the motivation to proceed "up the organizational ladder", as the organizationally defined path to the ego ideal.

Defense of Identity through Defense of the Organization Ideal

To the extent that the individual is committed, derives his/her identity from the ontological process, that identity is put into question by threats to the organization's existence. Indeed, one can go even farther than this and say that, to the extent that the individual's identity is an organizational identity, threats to the organization are experienced as threats to the individual. Thus, defense of the organization becomes self-defense. Moreover, since the organization ideal is an ideal, threats to the organization are perceived as having a hostile colloration, as aggression, as bad. Defense of the organization may be experienced as a righteous and virtuous action, therefore, regardless of the light in which such action may be seen by the organization's environment - which is seen, after all, as the source of the aggression. Finally, recalling that the organization is seen as the organization ideal, we may note that it is not only real threats to the organization that are seen as reprehensible acts of aggression. It can even be mere threats to the image of the organization as perfect. Thus, in a similar fashion, "slander against the State" is considered a crime in the Soviet Union.

Explaining Anti-social Actions of Committed Participants

Putting these three elements together gives us an adequate theoretical base for understanding how committed organizational participants can engage in illegal and anti-social acts.

First, and most obvious, we may observe how the interaction of belief in the ideal character of the organization with feelings fo shame over one's own failure to fulfil the organization ideal, can lead to the sort of malignant obedience to authority investigated by Milgram (1963). Feelings of shame over failing to meet the ego ideal lead to a moral delegitimation of the self and its natural responses. One is, after all, not what one is supposed to be, and therefore one's spontaneous responses should not be taken as the determinants of one's action. On top of that, higher authority is what it is supposed to be, and therefore its directives are experienced as moral enhanced, and more credible as moral directives, than the individual's own moral feelings. But while this process surely explains some anti-social activity on the part of committed participants, it does not explain all of it. Specifically, it does not explain the actions of those who gave the orders and, generally, it does not explain self-directed anti-social action, a class which probably includes the retouching of photographs described in the first paragraph.

The key to the understanding of self-directed anti-social actions lies in the phenomenology of the individual who experiences threat to the organization as threat to his/her own identity. The point here is that, since individuals never reach the ego ideal, identity is always in question: and since the organization itself falls short of the organization ideal, in the sense of being less in control of its circumstances than its own mythology requires, the precarious conditions that all organizations face all the time may be interpreted as the result of unfair, hostile and aggressive acts on the part of outside forces - who must be playing unfairly, after all, since the organization is the organization ideal and is therefore doing everything properly and correctly. Under the circumstances the committed individual may feel that the moral response is one of hostility and aggression.

In order to get a more rounded perspective on what this anti-social action amounts to, it may be useful to consider the relationship between the organization and its environment. The organization serves, through the committed individual's belief in the organization ideal, an immortality function for the individual (Schwartz, 1985). It is, in effect, an instrument for the denial of the individual's finitude. But in order to fulfil this function, it must itself be considered to be immortal. As we have seen, the individual denies his or her mortality by defining him or herself as part of an organization that is conceived to be in perfect, permanent control of its environment. But organizations are subject to the same question of their identity as individuals are. They are never perfectly in control of their environments. Nor, it is important to note, should they be.

The point is, that from a systems perspective, the environment should be in control of the organization. The environment is, after all, where everyone who is not a committed organizational participant exists and has such identity as they can manage to have. From the point of view of the environment, the organization is a source of goods and/or services. It is an exchange for the supply of these goods and/or services that the environment provides resources, its own resources, that permit the organization to continue. When the organization fails to provide such goods and/or services as the environment deems sufficient to balance its investment of resources, the environment responds by withholding resources and thereby threatens the survival of the organization. What's wrong with that?

When work is viewed as one side of an exchange relationship between producer and consumer, it always makes sense to ask, in evaluating an organization, "What is it good for?" What does the organization do for its environment that makes it worthwhile for the environment to keep it in existence at a cost to itself? But this is not a question that is asked by committed organizational participants. For them, the criterion of worth is not defined by the environment but by the organization. Indeed, the criterion of worth is the organization ideal.

Thus, what appear from an extra-organizational perspective to be legitimate demands that the environment places on the organization, appear from the standpoint of the committed participant to be illegitimate, hostile and aggressive challenges to the organization's and the individual's existence.

When we referred before to the need of the committed participant to believe that the organization controls its environment we were putting the matter too mildly. What we can see now is that the committed participants cannot tolerate the organization having an independent environment at all. From this individual's standpoint, the environment is ontologically linked to the organization, in that its meaning is a function of the organization's needs and agenda. Thus, rather than the organization existing and justifying itself by fulfilling needs of the environment, the environment is thought to exist in order to admire and attend to the organization.

Earlier, we saw that the ego ideal symbolizes the return to narcissism. Now we can see how the organization ideal does so as well. Only now it is the organization that is narcissistic, and just as the narcissistic child expects the world to revolve around it, so the organizationally committed individual expects the world to revolve around the organization, conceived as the organization ideal. Moreover, just as the infant responds with rage when the world does not respond to its whims, so the committed participant may respond with self-righteous, hostile, aggressive, and even criminal activity when the world does not respond to whims of the organization.

Thus, what we see is that anti-social actions, from the standpoint of the broader social world, are by no means to be regarded as an aberration from normal organizational activity on the part of organizationally committed participants. On the contrary, they appear to be a natural concommitant of organizational commitment itself. "Evil", Hobbes said, "is a robust child" (cited in Becker, 1975). We might add, and for the very same reason, that it can also be a robust organization.

Organizational Commitment and Anti-social Socialization

The observation that anti-social organizational behaviour is a natural concommitant of organizational commitment, which itself would be expected to be related to organizational effectiveness and perhaps social usefullness makes it important for us to consider the question of the circumstances under which such behaviour might take place. While this is properly a question for further research, it does seem possible to use previous work on organizational commitment and socialization as providing as basis for informed speculation and for establishing possible directions for research.

For present purposes I shall restrict myself to a previously mentioned work by Schein (1983/1968) which I think provides some very interesting clues. Schein says:

> One mechanism (for building commitment) is to invest much effort and time in the new member and thereby build up expectations of being repaid by loyalty, hard work and rapid learning. Another mechanism is to get the new member to make a series of small behavioural commitments which can only be justified by him through the acceptance and incorporation of company values. He then becomes the agent of his own socialization. Both mechanisms involve the subtle manipulation of guilt. (Schein, 1983/1968, p. 195).

Going beyond the case of the new recruit to the general case of the organization participant who has been selected for special treatment, and putting this matter in terms of the ego ideal, it seems to me this passage is suggesting that selected participants will most strongly take the organization ideal as their ego ideal when (1) the organization succeeds in presenting itself as an organization ideal, (2) progress toward this organization ideal seems probable for the individual in question, and (3) other possibilities for the ego ideal have been eliminated. It further suggests that guilt is involved both in the attraction toward the organization ideal and in the elimination of alternatives. The influence of guilt (or shame, as we shall see) may provide a key to the whole process.

Take the guilt involved in the presentation and accessibility of the organization ideal. The organization lavishes resources on the participant, indicating to the participant that if he or she takes the organization as an organization ideal, the hierarchical route to that ideal is open to him or her. The participant, if he or she is to think him or herself worthy of these resources and of the promise of more to come, "must repay the company with loyalty and hard work. He would feel guilty if he did not".

The crucial question to ask at this point is, where do these resources really come from? The answer can only be that they come from the environment. Proximal control over them may rest with the organization, to be sure. But ultimately, of course, they must originate outside the organization. The organization can be no more than a steward for these resources. Accordingly, such a relationship of guilt as may exist would have to be caused by an unbalanced exchange relationship between the participant and the environment, the producer and the consumer. Thus, it appears that the first step in process through which organizational commitment comes to develop anti-social potentialities is through an obscuring, on the part of the organization, of the source of the resources it employs.

We can see this obscuration in Schein's observation that the organization builds up "expectations of being repaid by loyalty, hard work, and rapid learning". We can see where hard work and rapid learning go into balancing the exchange relationship between participant and environment, but loyalty to the organization? The point to be noted here is that, in the most fundamental sense, with regard to the exchange relationship of work, the organization is not a party in the transaction. The organization, strictly speaking, is simply a patterning of this very complex relationship. This is at least one meaning that can be given to Karl Weick's (1969) observation that the organization does not exist, but only the process of organizing. Thus, bringing the organization in as the main party in the transaction is already an act of obscuration.

How is this obscuration possible? I suggest that it becomes possible through the same process in which the organization comes to present itself as an organization ideal. The organization, as a process, once had a positive effect on its environment; and the environment, eager to have the relationship continue, bestowed upon the process an attribution identity, of causal centrality, and entrusted the constructed entity with the resources which it now commands. Thus, the environment relinquished proximal control over these resources out of the very admiration and idealization of the organization which make it attractive to the individual rising in its ranks.

But there is more involved than this. By asserting its control over the participant's guilt, the organization asserts its right to end it and asserts that it, itself, is free of it: and along with that, is free of the limitation and finitude that the phenomenology of guilt contains. In other words, it presents itself as being beyond, as transcendence of, guilt, finitude and limitation - as the solution to the problem of identity, the return to narcissism, the ego ideal in organized form, the organization ideal.

Moreover, by offering to absolve the participant of guilt in exchange for loyalty, the organization creates a self-fulfilling proposition. For loyalty, after all, is the acceptance of the organization as one's ego ideal, by which act one does, after all, believe that one is getting away from one's finitude, limitation and guilt - in the terms used earlier, one creates for oneself an identity. Thus, the commission of the psychic act of organizational loyalty is the very self-deception, the obscuration, which, from one's own point of view, gives oneself identity, gives the organization life, and motivates one to entice others, both within the organization and outside it, to do the same.

Now take the technique of getting behavioural commitments. One example Schein uses is the Communist brainwashing practice of forcing a public confession from a prisoner. Another is the act of enticing a rebellious individual to accept a promotion. In both cases, what we see is a behaviour that invokes shame among the individual's prior reference group, as a violation of its own ego ideal - a shame which can only be avoided by rejecting the previous reference group as a source of potential admiration, restricting oneself to the organization ideal, and limiting the circle of one's identifications to those who also have taken the organization ideal as their ego ideal. Then, what would otherwise be seen as shameful actions come to be viewed as signs of commitment and highly valued. This has the effect of refreezing the participant's identity into the organization's meaning system and, effectively, of isolating that meaning system from its environment.

Given that actions, no matter how shameful they look to the environment, may be looked upon as worthwhile within the organization; and given that by presenting itself as an organization ideal the organization obscures the moral relationship that exists between participant and environment, it is clear that anything has become possible. When we repeat the point made earlier, that identity so defined is threatened by the very existence of an independent environment, it appears that it is only circumstances that prevent the possible from becoming probable.

Conclusion

These last considerations show how the potentiality for anti-social actions is built right into the process of the socialization for organizational commitment. They also show how it is precisely those organizations which had, at one time, a favourable response from their environments that are most likely to build up the sort of commitment that may lead to anti-social actions when the favour with which the organization is held begins to slip. This second point has to be a cause for pessimism, since it implies both that (1) nothing is stable about the kind of identity which commitment to an "excellent" (Peters and Waterman, 1982) organization offers, and that (2) there is no way of dealing with this problem in a programmatic, institutional fashion, since any institution which was successful in dealing with it would itself be subject to the process of degeneration which has been suggested.

Moreover, there is no cause for optimism in the idea that the solitary individual may be able to withstand the organization's blandishments and maintain a strong moral sense. For while some rare individuals will do so , many will not. It is, of course, the organization that selects those individuals upon whom it will shower resources and raise to positions of power, expecting commitment in return. Then the solitary individual becomes a deviate, and there is no necessity in this work to repeat what we know about how groups deal with deviates. Look, at what happened to Karen Silkwood.

All in all, there is not much cause for optimism in any of the considerations adduced in this paper. But, then, it is the demand that all of our stories have the happy endings that lead to these dynamics in the first place.

REFERENCES

ARGYRIS, C. Integrating the individual and the organization. New York: Wiley, 1964.

BECKER, E. Escape from evil. New York: Free Press, 1975.

BAUM, H.S. Autonomy, shame and doubt: Power in the bureaucratic lives of planners. Administration and Society, 15(2), 1983, 147-184.

CHASSEGUET-SMIRGEL, J. The ego ideal: A psychoanalytic essay on the malady of the ideal. New York: Norton, 1985.
FREUD, S. Group psychology and the analysis of the ego. Standard edition, Volume 18. London: Hogarth, 1955. (Originally published, 1921.)
FREUD, S. On narcissism: An introduction. Standard edition, Volume 14. London: Hogarth, 1957. (Originally published, 1914.)
KATZ, D., & KAHN, R.L. The Social Psychology of Organizations. New York: Wiley, 1966.
KLEIN, M. Contributions to psychoanalysis. London: Hogarth, 1948.
KLEIN, S.M., & RITTI, R.R. Understanding organizational behavior (Second edition). Boston: Kent, 1984.
LICHTENSTEIN, H. The dilemma of human identity. New York: Aronson, 1977.
MAYO, G.E. The human problems of an industrial civilization. New York: Macmillan, 1933.
MILGRAM, S. Behavioural study of obedience. Journal of Abnormal and Social Psychology, 67, 1963, 371-378.
MOWDAY, R.T., LYMAN W.P., & STEERS R.M. Employee-organization linkages. New York: Academic Press, 1982.
PETERS, T.J., & WATERMAN, R.H. In search of excellence: Lessons from American's best-run companies. New York: Harper and Row, 1982.
SCHEIN, E.H. Organizational socialization and the profession of management. In Psychological foundations of organizational behavior (Second edition), Barry M. Staw (ed.). Glenview, Ill.: Scott, Foresman, 1983, 191-201 (Originally published, 1968.)
SCHWARTZ, H.S. Maslow and the hierarchical enactment of organizational reality. Human Relations, 36(10), 1983, 933-956.
SCHWARTZ, H.S. The usefulness of myth and the myth of usefulness: A dilemma for the applied organizational scientist. Journal of Management, 11(1), 1985, 31-42.
SCHWARTZ, H.S. Rousseau's Discourse on Inequality revisited: psychology of work at the public-esteem stage of Maslow's hierarchy. International Journal of Management (forthcoming), 1987a.
SCHWARTZ, H.S. On the psychodynamics of organizational totalitarianism. Journal of Management (forthcoming), 1987b.
WEBER, M. The theory of social and economic organization (edited by Talcott Parsons). New York: Free Press, 1947.
WEICK, K.E. The social psychology of organizing. Reading, Mass.: Addison-Wesley, 1969.

CHASSEGUET-SMIRGEL, J.: The ego ideal: A psychoanalytic essay on the malady of the ideal. New York: Norton, 1985.

[illegible]

[illegible]

KATZ, D. & KAHN, R. L.: The social psychology of organizations. New York: Wiley, 1966.

KLEIN, M.: Contributions to psychoanalysis. London: Hogarth, 1948.

[illegible]

[illegible]

[illegible]

[illegible]

[illegible]

Narcissism Project and Corporate Decay: The Case of General Motors

Howard S. Schwartz

INTRODUCTION

When I left graduate school and began teaching organizational behavior courses, I was struck by the irrelevance of what I had learned to the actual organizational experience of my students. My students experienced and understood organizational life as a kind of "vanity fair," in which individuals who were interested in "getting ahead" could do so by playing to the vanity of their superiors. One needed to do this in two respects. One needed to flatter the superior as an individual and as an occupant of the superior role. This latter process tended to trail off into an adulation of the organization in general.

Work either fit into this process of adulation, in which case it made sense; or it did not, in which case it did not make sense. Work which did not make sense in this way, my students felt, was best left to the suckers who hadn't figured out yet how to get ahead and who deserved whatever torment this system led them to inherit. If, through this process, important, valid information was lost to the system by being withheld or simply unappreciated, that was not their concern. Through luck or guile, the consequences would, or could be made to, occur on somebody else's watch.

At first glance, my students' attitude looked to me like cynicism. But closer analysis suggested that, although they had a great deal of cynicism in them, they were not simply being cynical, for they believed in the righteousness of what they were doing.

For them, getting ahead was a moral imperative, which justified any means necessary for its accomplishment. But more than this, the system itself which called upon subordinates to idealize it was held morally sacrosanct. A person who refused to go along with the system was seen as not only stupid and naive, but as morally inferior. And this was so even if the individual in question was offering a point of view that was essential for the organization to do its work effectively and efficiently.

It thus seemed to me that, for my students, the organization's

---

Reprinted by permission of New York University Press from Howard Schwartz, Narcissistic Process and Corporate Decay: The Theory of the Organization Ideal (New York: New York University Press, 1990).

processes were held to define moral value. As defined by its processes, the organization seemed to exist in a moral world of its own, which served to justify anything done on its behalf, and which did not require justification on any grounds outside of itself. This view was inconsistent with a view of the organization as an instrument to do work. For my students, the organization did not exist in order to do work; it did work in order to exist.

Yet even while holding this point of view, many of my students did not appear to have a deep loyalty to the organizations which they so supported. On the contrary, for the most part they were willing to change organizations with no regrets or guilt. Their loyalty, if that is what it was, seemed to be to an abstract idea of organization, an idea of the organization as a vehicle for the revelation of their own grandiosity. Ultimately, therefore, their loyalty appeared to be directed at themselves.

Over time, trying to be a good empiricist, I came to take their stories about organizational life increasingly seriously. I made the assumption that organizational life was just what my students, whom I came to consider my research subjects, and sometimes informants, appeared to be living. Relegating what I had learned in graduate school to the status of a fantasy, I tried to fashion a theoretical conception that would explain this organizational reality. Following Shorris (1981), I called the syndrome "organizational totalitarianism" (Schwartz, 1987a).

I first understood organizational totalitarianism in moral terms, in terms of the psychological damage done to the individuals involved (Schwartz, 1987a). But as time went by it became more and more clear to me that the processes I was coming to understand must have practical consequences as well - consequences for the effective functioning, the efficiency, the profitability, the competitiveness of organizations. In a word, it did not seem to me that organizations as I understood them could possibly be successful even in terms of the narrowest economic criteria, without regard to the moral costs involved. So, when American industry seemed to be incapable of competing with foreign enterprises, I did not find myself at all surprised.

Getting beyond my students' accounts to gain evidence of the systemic effects of the process, however, proved to be a problem. There is a kind of "uncertainty principle" that applies here. Organizational participants who are in a position to be able to describe these systemic effects have given up the moral autonomy that would have enabled them to perceive them. Participants who insist on retaining their moral autonomy are typically excluded from important positions in the system precisely because of that insistence. Thus, the closer one is to the data, the less likely one is to be able to see it.

Accordingly, in the present paper I am going to rely heavily on one of the very few accounts that I know of by a highly positioned insider who became alienated from the system and reported on its processes to the outside. This is a book by John Z. De Lorean, co-written by J. Patrick Wright and published by the latter under his own name, called "On A Clear Day You Can See General Motors" (1979). There are two problems with using De Lorean's testimony, arising primarily from his subsequent problems with the law and from the apparent mismanagement of his own car company. Fortunately, therefore, there is a more recent account of GM by Maryann Keller (1989), which bears none of his taint. I will be using her work to lend secondary support to my case.

An independent source for a description and explanation of the process of decay is a remarkable book by Robert Jackall called "Moral Mazes: The World of Corporate Managers" (1988). Unfortunately, I came upon this book too late to integrate it into the present paper. Jackall's approach is sociological, and takes for granted that "striving for success ... is a moral imperative in American society" (p.43). My concern is to reveal the psychodynamics of this striving and to show how decay follows from these psychodynamics. Aside from that, and from my increased emphasis on the loss of reality that follows from this, I see our approaches as being strikingly complementary. I might add that the high degree of descriptive and explanatory agreement between these two entirely independent works represents a satisfying level of mutual confirmation and cross-validation.

ORGANIZATIONAL TOTALITARIANISM AND THE THEORY OF THE ORGANIZATION IDEAL

The theory I shall use to discuss organizational totalitarianism begins with the premise that, for people like my students, the idea of the organization represents an ego ideal - a symbol of the person one ought to become such that, if one were to become that person, one would again be the center of a loving world as one experienced oneself as a child. The ego ideal represents a return to narcissism (Freud, 1955, 1957; Chasseguet-Smirgel, 1985). It represents an end to the anxiety that entered our lives when we experienced ourselves as separate from our apparently all-powerful mothers.

With regard to organizations, this means that individuals redefine themselves as part of an organization, conceived of as perfect. Thus, the image of such an organization is one in which members are perfectly integrated into a collectivity which is perfectly adapted to its environment. An image of an organization serving as an ego ideal may be called an "organization ideal" (Schwartz, 1987a,b,c). The organization ideal, thus, represents a project for the return to narcissism.

The problem with the organization ideal, like any ego ideal, is that it can never be attained. It represents a denial of our separation, finitude, vulnerability and mortality; but these remain with us by virtue of our existence as concrete individual human beings (Becker, 1973; Chasseguet-Smirgel, 1985; Schwartz, 1987b).

Given the importance of maintaining belief in the possibility of attaining the ego ideal, organizations often attempt to generate a way of preserving the illusion of the organization ideal in the face of the failure of the organization to exemplify it. The attempt to manage an organization by imposing this illusion is what I call "organizational totalitarianism."

Organizations attempt this imposition in a number of ways. As Klein and Ritti (1984) observe, they give and withhold information to create a myth of the organization as more effective than it really is. They impose patterns of speech and behavior on participants that make them seem more integrated than they really are. They promote the attribution that their problems are due to forces which do not belong in the world, which is to say to "bad" forces. And they generate an image of a gradient of Being, an "ontological differentiation," in the organization (Schwartz, 1987a,b,c; also see Sievers, 1987,and Schwartz, 1987d) which idealizes the higher figures in the organization (Klein and Ritti, 1984, p.170-172) as individuals who have fulfilled the project of the return to narcissism and become centers of a loving world. This provides the drive to climb the hierarchy that my students experience as the central spirit in their moral world (Schwartz,1987a). Moreover it delegitimates those who are farther down (Sennett and Cobb, 1973). This makes it possible for organizations to maintain the idea of the perfection of the organization's core and blame its imperfections on peripheral elements.

ORGANIZATIONAL DECAY

The problem is that such symbolic manipulation places falsehood right at the core of organizational functioning and therefore cannot help but lead to a loss of rationality. For the return to narcissism is impossible, short of psychosis (Chasseguet-Smirgel, 1985), and therefore organizational totalitarianism means the superimposition of a psychosis upon organizational functioning. Ultimately, whatever the gains in motivation, such a loss of rationality leads to generalized and systemic organizational ineffectiveness.

Moreover, I suggest that this condition of generalized and systemic ineffectiveness has a unity to it, and therefore represents something like an organizational disease. I would like to give it the name "organizational decay," with the intention being to convey the impression of an internal process of rot, not occasioned by outside forces; and with the intention as well to give the impression of a holistic process, not taking place in isolated parts of the organization but typically and increasingly sapping the vitality of the organization as a whole. This decay eventually may manifest itself in any of a number of ways. I shall discuss a few of them, relying on De Lorean's and Keller's books about General Motors to provide illustrations.

SOME CAUSES OF DECAY

Commitment to Bad Decisions

Perhaps the most obvious symptom of organizational decay is the commitment to bad decisions. Staw (1980) has noted that the tendency to justify past actions can be a powerful motivation behind organizational behavior and can often run counter to rationality. As he notes, the justification process leads to escalating commitment. When mistaken actions cannot be seen as mistaken actions, the principle on which they are based is not seen as being mistaken. Worse yet, our feeling that it is a valid principle becomes enhanced through our need to defend our decision and subsequent decisions made on the basis of it.

This process must be especially lethal in the case of the totalitarian organization, where the idea of the perfection of the organization provides the organization's very motivational base. Here, the assumption of the identity of the individual decision maker and his or her organizational role turns the tendency to justify past actions from a defensive tendency on the part of individuals to a core organizational process - a central element of the organization's culture.

The case of the Corvair illustrates the process of commitment to bad decisions. Modeled after the Porsche, the Corvair was powered by a rear engine and had an independent, swing-axle suspension system.

According to De Lorean, any car so powered and so suspended is going to have serious problems - problems which were well known and documented by GM's engineering staff long before the Corvair was offered for sale. Engineers put up a desperate fight against the design but:

> ...Management ... told dissenters in effect to "stop these objections. Get on the team, or you can find someplace else to work." The ill fated Corvair was launched in the fall of 1959 (p.66).

Despite the fact that the Corvair demonstrated itself to be unsafe almost immediately, and despite the fact that a stabilizer bar costing only $15 a car would have provided a solution, GM did not correct the problem until the release of the 1964 models, by which time numerous lives had been lost and millions had been spent in legal expenses.

Advancement of Participants Who Detach Themselves from Reality and Discouragement of Reality-oriented Participants Who are Committed to Their Work

When core organizational process becomes the dramatization of the organization and its high officials as ideal, the evaluation of individuals for promotion and even for continued inclusion comes to be made on the basis of how much they contribute to this dramatization. This means that, increasingly, promotion criteria shift from achievement and competence to ideology and politics. (1)

Thus De Lorean says that wether or not someone was promoted often depended on something other than competence:

> That something different was a very subjective criterion which encompassed style, appearance, personality and, most importantly, personal loyalty to the man (or men) who was the promoter, and to the system which brought this all about. There were rules of this fraternity of management at GM. Those pledges willing to obey the rules were promoted. In the vernacular, they were the company's "team players". Those who didn't fit into the mold of a manager, who didn't adhere to the rules because they thought they were silly, generally weren't promoted. "He's not a team player," was the frequent, and many times only, objection to an executive in line for promotion. It didn't mean he was doing a poor job. It meant he didn't fit neatly into a stereotype of style, appearance and

> manner. He didn't display blind loyalty to the system of management, to the man or men doing the promoting. He rocked the boat. He took unpopular stands on products or policy which contradicted the prevailing attitude of top management.(p.40)

Keller (1989) adumbrates this point in a number of places, for example this about recently retired chairman Roger Smith:

> For thirty-one years, Smith moved up through the ranks of GM as the consummate corporate player - the GM culture coursed in his veins. Admiration for and loyalty to the organization was at the core of his being. He was one of a new breed of corporate politicians whose success depended on their ease in wearing the corporate mantle. Translated, that meant, "Above all, be loyal to your superior's agenda." (p.66)

One result of this will be that those individuals who are retained and promoted will be those who will know very well how things are supposed to look, according to the viewpoint of the dominant coalition, but who will know less and less about reality insofar as it conflicts with, or simply is independent of, this viewpoint. The problem is, of course, that since no organization is, or can be, the organization ideal, this means that those individuals who are retained and promoted will be those who can cut themselves loose from discrepant reality.

Another result of this sort of selection must be that realistic and concerned persons must lose the belief that the organization's real purpose is productive work and come to the conclusion that its real purpose is self-promotion. They then are likely to see their work as being alien to the purposes of the organization and must find doing good work increasingly depressing and useless.

De Lorean gives this example of the clash between the incompetent who have been promoted and their competent but discouraged subordinates:

> Increasingly, group and upper managers seemed to look upon their jobs in such narrow terms that it was impossible to competently direct broad corporate policy. Often misplaced, unprepared or simply undertalented, these executives filled their days and our committee meetings with minutiae. After one particularly frustrating meeting of the Administrative Committee, John Beltz and

> I were picking up our notes when he looked down at the far end of the conference table at the corporate management and said to me, I wouldn't let one of those guys run a gas station for me." It was a bitter and sad indictment of our top management by one of the then young, truly bright lights of General Motors management. (p.256)

A third effect, made obvious by this point, is that higher management is effectively isolated from criticism (2), or even serious discussion, of its thought and actions.

De Lorean gives this account:

> Original ideas were often sacrificed in deference to what the boss wanted. Committee meetings no longer were forums for open discourse, but rather either soliloquies by the top man, or conversations between a few top men with the rest of the meeting looking on. In Fourteenth Floor meetings, often only three people, Cole, Gerstenberg, and Murphy would have anything substantial to say, even though there were 14 or 15 executives present. The rest of the team would remain silent, speaking only when spoken to. When they did offer a comment, in many cases it was just to paraphrase what had already been said by one of the top guys. (47)

Indeed, as organizational promotion and retention criteria shift toward the dramatization of the perfection of the organization, this shapes the very job of the subordinate into what Janis (1972) calls "mindguarding" - the suppression of criticism.

Keller also comments on the conflict between what one needs to do to get promoted and the quality of one's work:

> One retired executive rails against a system that creates vertical thinkers and cautious leaders. "The whole system stinks once you're in it. You continue to want to make vertical decisions: "What is it that I should decide that will be good for me. Never make a horizontal decision based on what is good for the company. I want to get promoted." So you get promoted because you are sponsored by someone; you get promoted before they catch up with you. I can go through a litany of those clowns. They go from this plant to that complex and then, all of a sudden, they've got plaques all over the walls that say how great

> they've done - but the plant's falling apart and the division's falling apart." (p.34)

The Creation of the Organizational Jungle

The more successful the organization is at projecting the image of itself as the organization ideal, the more deeply must committed participants experience anxiety. For the image projected, the image of the individual as perfectly a part of the perfect organization, is only an image; and the more perfect it is, the more acute the discrepancy between the role and the role player. Given the importance of the organization ideal in the individual's self-concept, some way must be found in which the individual can reconcile the discrepancy between the centrality in a loving world he or she is supposed to be experiencing and the wretchedness he or she in fact feels. As we have seen above, the typical way is to attempt to deepen the identity of self and organization by rising in the organization's hierarchy and by fighting off what are perceived as threats to the organizational identity one has attained - perceived threats which are often projections of one's own self-doubts.

The result of this is that individuals become obsessed with organizational rank. They become compelled to beat down anyone who threatens or competes with them in their pursuit of higher rank or who is perceived as threatening the rank they have already acquired. Thus, ironically, behind the display of the organization ideal, of everyone working together to realize shared values, the real motivational process becomes a Hobbesian battle of narcissism project against narcissism project. (3) The consequences of this for coordination, cooperation, and motivation are clear enough. De Lorean says:

> Once in a position of power, a manager who was promoted by the system is insecure because, consciously or not, he knows that it was something other than his ability to manage and his knowledge of the business that put him in his position.... He thus looks for methods and defense mechanisms toward off threats to his power. (p.49)

Isolation of Management and Rupture of Communications

A related problem is that the greater the success of the totalitarian manager, the more the manager is isolated from his or her subordinates. The world that the subordinates live in is the world of the organization ideal as created by the totalitarian manager. The world that the totalitarian manager lives in is the world of the construction of the image of the organization ideal. These two worlds are incommensurable and it cannot help but happen that communication and trust must break down between them. For communication and trust mean two different things to these groups. Indeed, for totalitarian management, communication to subordinates is not communication at all - it is deception. (4)

In this fashion, the organization comes to be stratified in an insider/outsider dimension that has been likened to the structure of an onion (Shorris, 1981; Arendt, 1966) and which serves the same function as party membership in the totalitarian state. This must make a mockery of all attempts to break down status barriers that stand in the way of effective communication - as appears to be the idea behind various "quality of working life" efforts.

Development of Hostile Orientation Toward the Environment

If the totalitarian manager is successful, as we have seen, organizational participants take the organization as an organization ideal. It must follow, in their thinking, that such an organization will be successful in its dealings with the world. This poses a difficulty of interpretation for the necessarily problematic relationships between the organization and its environment.

Thus, in the nature of things (Katz and Kahn, 1966) the environment places constant demands on the organization. Failure to meet them will result in the organization's death. But from the standpoint of the totalitarian manager committed to portraying the organization as the organization ideal, this sort of reasoning cannot be acknowledged. From this point of view it is the organization that is the criterion of worth. The environment is not conceived of as existing as an independent environment at all; it exists only in order to support the organization. From this standpoint the demands of the environment must be presented as hostile actions on the part of bad external forces - hostile actions to which a legitimate response is equally hostile action.

The General Motors Corporation, in response to Ralph Nader's (1965) book about the Corvair, "Unsafe At Any Speed", hired private detectives to find ways to discredit him. Sending private detectives to find out the dirty details of his private life suggests something about their attitude toward him. It suggests that they expected to find something to show that he was a bad person. He had to be a bad person: he had attacked GM, hadn't he?

Again:

> Criticism from the outside is generally viewed as ill-informed. General Motors management thinks what it is doing is right, because it is GM that is doing it and the outside world is wrong. It is always "they" versus "us." (p.257)

And when Peter Drucker, wrote "The Concept of a Corporation" (1946), a work which was generally regarded as decidedly pro-business and pro-GM, "he was resoundingly criticized within the company for daring to criticize the organization of the corporation." (p.258)

Thus, the picture of the organization as organization ideal leads to an orientation toward the world that can best be described as paranoid. It is clear enough that such a conception must degrade the relationships with the environment that ultimately the organization requires for its survival.

The Transposition of Work and Ritual

When work, the productive process, becomes display, its meaning becomes lost. Its performance as part of the organizational drama becomes the only meaning that it has. Accordingly, the parts it plays in the organization's transactions with the world become irrelevant. When this happens, it loses its adaptive function and becomes mere ritual.

At the same time, those rituals which serve to express the individual's identification with the organization ideal, especially those connected with rank, come to be infused with significance for the individual. They become sacred. Thus, reality and appearance, signified and signifier, trade places. The energy that once went into the production of goods and services of value to others is channelled into the dramatization of a narcissistic fantasy in which the organization's environment is merely a stage setting.

Consider how this shows up in the matter of dress. One can easily make a case that patterns of dress among organizational participants often have some functionality. But when the issue comes to be invested with great meaning, one must suspect that ritual has supplanted function. Thus, De Lorean describes how half of his first meeting as a GM employee was taken up in a discussion of how a vice-president had been sent home for wearing a brown suit. (p.40)

The dynamics of the ways in which ritual comes to assume the importance work should have helps to explain the dynamics of the ritualization of work. For the willingness to allow one's behavior to be determined by meaningless rituals comes to be justified by an idealization of the organization that elevates its customs above, and discredits, one's values - one's sense of what is important. This willingness to subordinate and delegitimate, in a word to repress, one's own sense of what is important, even about matters that should be within the competence of anyone's judgement, must have its consequences magnified when the matters in question become more abstruse and difficult to make judgments about, as is the case with real executive work. Then the repression of one's values deprives one of any basis for making such judgments, and leads naturally to a superimposition of the rituals with which one is familiar, even where, patently, they do not belong.

Thus, De Lorean recalls that when he was elevated to the Fourteenth Floor, GM's executive suite, as group executive in charge of the domestic Car and Truck Group:

> ...I saw that the job... often consisted only of ... little, stupid, make-work kinds of assignments, things which I thought should have been decided further down the line. Some of these things, which had little or no impact on the business, were an insult to a person's intelligence.... As I recall, [for example, my boss] asked me to catalogue service parts numbers and to prepare reports on the size of parts inventories (p.26-27)

De Lorean, feeling that a person at his high level should be involved in planning, rather than in trivia, set up a meeting with Vice-Chairman Thomas Murphy to straighten out his job assignment. But Murphy found nothing peculiar, and:

> I suddenly realized that what I felt was a weakness of life on the Fourteenth Floor, he and others thought was "business as usual." They were quite happy to let their jobs drag them from one place to the next, trying to solve problems as they came up, but not getting into the kind of long-range planning that Fourteenth Floor executives were supposed to be doing.

Loss of Creativity

The delegitimation of one's sense of what is important gives rise to a special case of the ritualization of work - the loss of creativity. Thus,

Schein (1983) describes the condition of "conformity" which follows from an insistence by the organization that all of its norms be accepted as being equally important. Under that condition, the individual

> ... can tune in so completely on what he sees to be the way others are handling themselves that he becomes a carbon-copy and sometimes a caricature of them.

And he notes:

> ... The conforming individual curbs his creativity and thereby moves the organization toward a sterile form of bureaucracy. (p. 197)

Maslow (1970) gives us insight into the psychodynamics of this when he observes that creativity is characteristic of both ends of the continuum of personality development, but not of the stages in the middle (pp.170-1). Creativity, this suggests, is a function of spontaneity, a function of taking seriously our actual affects and interacting in the world in consideration of our spontaneous feelings. But as the self comes to be dominated by a concern for how things appear to others, which is characteristic of the middle stages of personality development (Schwartz, 1983), creativity disappears as a mode of interacting with the world. As the organization requires that the individual subordinate his or her spontaneous perception to an uncritical acceptance of the ideal character of the organization, it thus determines that the affective basis of creativity will be repressed.

The lack of creativity, since it is a lack of something, cannot be positively demonstrated. As an experience, it makes itself known as a feeling of missing something different that has not occurred, even though one does not know what the different element would have been. Thus, De Lorean found himself introducing a "new" crop of Chevrolets that were not really new at all:

> "This whole show is nothing but a replay of last year's show, and the year before that and the year before that. The speech I just gave was the same speech I gave last year, written by the same guy in public relations about the same superficial product improvements as previous years.... Almost nothing has changed.... there was nothing new and revolutionary in car development and there hadn't been for years." (pp.60-1)

In benign times, one may experience boredom: the consciousness of a sameness, a lack of originality. When circumstances are harsh, partly as a result of the lack of creativity that the organization needed if it was to have adapted, one may simply experience the intractability of the situation. Adding up the figures in the usual way simply shows one, again and again, how hopeless the situation is. One may then experience the loss of creativity as a wish for a savior who will make the organization's problems disappear.

In the hard times, I suspect, one rarely comes to recognize that the ideas that the organization needed in order to have avoided its present hopeless state may have been upon the scene a long time ago. But the individuals who had them might have been passed over for promotion because they were not "team players," or perhaps they were made to feel uncomfortable because they did not fit it in, or maybe they were scapegoated whenever the organization needed a victim. Indeed, ironically, the very ideas that were needed might have been laughed at or ignored because they were not "the way we do things around here."

Dominance of the Financial Staff

Another hypothesis may be used to account for the emergent dominance of the financial function of the corporation that De Lorean finds in General Motors and that others, for example Halberstam (1986) have partly blamed for the decline of American industry.

As envisioned by Alfred P. Sloan, the financial function and the operations side of the corporation were both supposed to be represented strongly at the top level of the corporation. But, as De Lorean notes, over time, and specifically through the rise of Frederick Donner, the financial side came to dominate the corporation. Why?

I propose that finance, rather than operations, offers the greater narcissistic possibilities. As Nader and Taylor (1986) note, operations, the productive process, tends to temper grandiosity. The recalcitrance of matter, so to speak, exerts a humbling influence. Not so with finance. I suggest that the financial world-view can be understood as a kind of latter-day Pythagoreanism in which the world is seen as mere instantiation of number, and as imposing no bounds on the imagination's flights. Everything seems possible as long as the numbers can be made to work, and the one who can make them work can take this as a sign of omnipotence. When the matter comes to competitive elevation of the organization ideal, who can do it better, who can represent it better, than the officer whose bonds to earthly substance are the lightest. Who better than the specialist in finance?

Keller's analysis is similar:

> The tyranny of the number crunchers has evolved, to a great extent, from GM's reluctance to hear bad news about itself. If the finance guys can present the right numbers, everyone breathes a sigh of relief, and the finance people look like heroes. There's no incentive for executives in finance positions to give bad news; the more facile they can be with numbers, the higher their fortunes rise. (pp.27-28)

Cynicism and Corruption or Self-Deception and the Narcissistic Loss of Reality

Referring to the ways people are related to their own presentations, Goffman (1959, 17-18) notes that one can either be taken in by one's own performance or not taken in by it, using it only "to guide the conviction of his audience ... as a means to other ends." In the latter case we refer to the individual as a cynic. Such persons disassociate themselves from discrepant information consciously and through deception. In the former case, the individual "comes to be performer and observer of the same show." Goffman adds:

> It will have been necessary for the individual in his performing capacity to conceal from himself in his audience capacity the discreditable facts that he has had to learn about the performance; in everyday terms, there will be things he knows, or has known, that he will not be able to tell himself. (p.81)

Goffman notes that these persons cut themselves loose from discrepant information through repression and disassociation, a point which corresponds perfectly with psychoanalytic theory concerning the maintenance of the ego ideal.

We may refer to such individuals as self-deceptive. Thus, in the totalitarian organization, no matter what its espoused values, promotion and even continued inclusion will tend to go to deceptive cynics whose moral involvement in their organizational activity is attenuated, or to self-deceptive persons whose involvement in reality is attenuated.

Of the two, it is difficult to say which is to be preferred. Cynics at least know what is going on around them; and if their moral involvement in their organizational role is attenuated, that does not seem inappropriate in an organization as deceptive as one which is managed by totalitarian means. Indeed, in organizations which have seriously degenerated as a result of these processes, it is often only the cynics who can get anything done at all.

Nonetheless, there is no doubt that cynicism tends toward corruption. Corruption does not play a major role in De Lorean's picture of General Motors, but he does note its presence (p.83).

Our analysis leads us to suspect that, as time goes by, if GM continues to deteriorate, it will become increasingly difficult for even minimally functioning individuals to idealize it. Then, corruption will increasingly become a problem.

For the present, I think the more serious problem comes in with those who deceive themselves and distance themselves from reality. For as the processes I have described operate, and as the organization degenerates accordingly, it becomes increasingly difficult to see it as the ideal, and individuals who are able to do so must become increasingly self-deceptive. A point must come when such individuals may not be said to be psychologically living in the same world that the real organization is in. What makes this even worse is that, since this capacity for self-deception is an important advantage in the race for promotion, the total disassociation of the individual from organizational reality is likely to be correlated with the individual's position in the hierarchy. Then the most important processes within the organization come to be under the authority of people who are not operating in the real world as far as the organization's requirements are concerned.

Keller hints at this:

> During the 1970's, a writer for Fortune magazine set out on a quest for dissenting views at General Motors, and found it hard "to find a top executive at GM who does not evidence enthusiasm for what he or the company is doing." One view might hold that GM had achieved a state of management consensus that would be the envy of any company. But more likely, the lack of dissension was motivated by self-interest. It was managerial suicide to be the person who got labeled a naysayer. There was also an element of denial; in the same way that children of alcoholics often refuse to accept their parents' addiction, GM employees refused to admit the truth about their corporate parent. They didn't want to believe.(pp. 65-66)

Overcentralization

The narcissistic loss of reality among those at the top of the corporation may be a major cause of overcentralization of operational decision making. De Lorean found this overcentralization to characterize General Motors, and with it the tendency to provide simplistic answers to complex questions. The idea that, having risen to the top of the corporation, individuals would hold themselves as bearing all of its knowledge and virtues follows immediately from what we have been saying.

From this would follow the tendency of top management to believe themselves more capable than anyone else of providing answers to any questions that arise. Having no command of specific details beyond those in their imaginations, the answers which they give, and which would come to bind the rest of the corporation, would necessarily be simplistic and inappropriate. Moreover, as the decay process continues, and as the competence of top management declines accordingly, both their tendency to impose simple answers to complex problems, and the specific inadequacy even of the simplistic answers they propose, would tend to increase. Moreover, the capacity of the system to correct itself would tend to decrease, since the increasing power of the higher echelons of the corporation, and their increasing narcissism, would tend toward an attribution of blame to the lower levels of the organization. This would delegitimate those whose judgement would be necessary to reverse the decay process.

De Lorean and Keller provide a number of examples of this. This one, from De Lorean, will serve our purpose:

> ... the corporate program for maximum standardization of parts across product lines was a knee-jerk cost-cutting reaction to the incredible proliferation of models, engines and parts which took place in the uncontrolled and unplanned boom of the 1960's. However, the program was not intelligently thought out. It was not thoroughly analyzed for its actual effect on the company. On paper the concept looked good and seemed like a sure way to save money. In reality it wasted money. The car divisions rebelled at various stages of the standardization program. Their cries were unanswered. When Chevrolet rebelled against using the new corporate U-joint... Keyes told me, "Use the corporate one or I'll get someone in Chevy who will."
>
> We used it, at an investment of about $16 million in tooling, and our costs rose $1.40 per car. In addition, the

> corporate design failed in use and Chevy paid out about $5 million extra in warranty claims.
> Instead of saving money, the standardization program at GM wound up costing the corporation about $300 million extra per year....
> The last straw came in 1972, however, when management asked us: "Why is the cost of building a Chevrolet $70 closer to Oldsmobile today than it was in 1964?" The question from the top was offered in the usual "you aren't doing your job" manner. The irony was incredible. (p.252-3)

AN OVERVIEW

Before concluding this discussion of the practical consequences of totalitarian management, it is worthwhile to note a characteristic that the consequences mentioned have in common: they are all cumulative and interactive with each other. They all tend to build within the system and, interacting with each other, take over the system bit by bit. This is the way in which the ineffectiveness characteristic of the decadent organization becomes systemic and generalized. Thus, for example, the accumulation of bad decisions taken within the system suggests that those who manifest belief in it as an organization ideal must increasingly be self-deceptive or cynical, which in turn decreases the retention of realism and concern for work, which leads to a further increase in bad decisions, further degradation of the relationship with the environment, and so on.

The result of this is that the rate of decay will tend to accelerate. On the basis of this the fact that GM's market share took six years to decline from 46% to 41%, but only three more years to go to 35% (Ingrassia and White, 1989), comes to make a certain chilling sense.

CONCLUSION: ON AVERTING ORGANIZATIONAL DECAY

There is no doubt that fantasy plays an important part in our mental lives. To say this one does not need either to approve of fantasy or to regret its inroads into the psyche. Fantasy simply is. So it is with the ego ideal, which is a particularly central fantasy in our lives.

But the same cannot be said for organizational totalitarianism and organizational decay. These are not either necessary or inevitable features of organizational life. They become features of organizational life when the desire to be the center of a loving world becomes a demand and when the power is available to turn this demand into a program of action.

What this suggests is that (1) organizational totalitarianism and organizational decay, which first appeared to us as systemic problems that concern the organization are at their root existential, moral, even spiritual problems which concern the individual; and (2) these problems at the individual level become systemic problems for the organization when organizational power is used to effect this transformation.

Putting the matter this way enables us to perceive a continuity between our analysis of organizational decay, on one hand; and the Greek conception of tragedy, on the other. What we see in both cases is the horror that comes from the claims of powerful mortals to be more than mortal. The Greeks called this "hubris" and they knew that the gods, whom we might refer to as reality, do not stand for it. They demand humility.

NOTES

(1) Note the connection here with the findings of Luthans, Hodgetts, and Rosenkrantz (1988) on the unrelatedness of competence and organizational success. From the point of view of the theory of organizational decay, the further intriguing possibility presents itself that these researchers have managed to capture only a phase of the decay process. On the basis of the considerations adduced here, one would expect to find that as the organization decayed further, the correlation between competence and organizational success would become negative. In organizations of this sort, bad managements drives out good.

(2) It is interesting to note that the isolation of management from criticism takes place outside of the corporation as well. Thus, in the 28 August 1989 issue of Fortune magazine, an article by Julie Connelly called "The CEO's Second Wife" details what happens to the first:

> As their husband rise in the corporation, first wives may become convinced that power is corrupting the presumably wholesome lads they married. "They become self-appointed critics and consciences," says Manhattan psychiatrists Clifford Sager, who specializes in marital therapy. "They try to cut their husbands down to size." (p.55)

(3) The contrast between the benign world of the role performance and the malevolent world of the performers is illustrated in Terkel's (1974) interview with Larry Ross, a former president of a conglomerate. Thus:

> You walk down the corridor and everybody bows and says, "Good morning, Mr. Ross. How are you today?" As you go up the line, the executives will say, "How is Mr. Ross?" Until you get to the higher

> executives. They'll say, "How is Nancy?" Here you socialize, you know each other. Everbody plays the game. (p.411)

But:

> As he struggles in this jungle, every position he's in, he's terribly lonely. He can't confide and talk to the man he's working for. To give vent to his feelings, his fears and his insecurities he'd expose himself. This goes all the way up the line until he gets to be president. The president really doesn't have anybody to talk to, because the vice presidents are waiting for him to die or make a mistake and get knocked off so they can get his job. (p.408)

(4) Actually, what we have here is a form of "retreat from language" of the type that concerned John R. Searle (1969, p.198) when he wrote:

> The retreat from the committed use of words ultimately must involve a retreat from language itself, for speaking a language... consists of performing speech acts according to rules, and there is no separating those speech acts of them. (Cited in Hummel, 1987)

Also see Hummel's interesting discussion of the separation of language from meaning in bureaucracy.

REFERENCES

ARENDT, H. The Origins of Totalitarianism. New York: Harcourt, Brace and World, 1966.

ARGYRIS, C., & SCHON, D.A. Theory in Practice. San Francisco: Jossey-Bass, 1974.

BECKER, E. The Denial of Death. New York: Free Press, 1973.

BURNS, J.M. Leadership. New York: Harper and Row, 1973.

CHASSEGUET-SMIRGEL, J. The Ego Ideal: A Psychoanalytic Essay on the Malady of the Ideal. (First American edition, P. Barrows, translator) New York: Norton, 1985.

CHASSEGUET-SMIRGEL, J. Sexuality and Mind: The Role of the Father and the Mother in the Psyche. New York: New York University Press, 1986.

FREUD, S. Group Psychology and the Analysis of the Ego. (StandardEdition, Volume 18) London: Hogarth, 1955a.

FREUD, S. On Narcissism: An Introduction. (Standard Edition, Volume 14) London: Hogarth, 1957.

GOFFMAN, E. The Presentation of Self in Everyday Life. New York: Doubleday Anchor, 1959.

HALBERSTAM, D. The Reckoning. New York: William Morrow, 1986.

HUMMEL, R.P. The Bureaucratic Experience. (Third Edition) New York: St. Martin's Press, 1987.

INGRASSIA, P., & WHITE, J.B. Losing the Race: With Its Market Share Sliding, GM Scrambles to Avoid a Calamity. Wall Street Journal, December 14, 1989, 1.

KATZ, D., & KAHN, R.L. The Social Psychology of Organizations. New York: Wiley, 1966.

KELLER, M. Rude Awakening: The Rise, Fall, and Struggle for Recovery of General Motors. New York: William Morrow, 1989.

KLEIN, S.M., & RITTI, R.R. Understanding Organizational Behavior. (Second Edition) Boston: Kent, 1984.

LUTHANS, F., HODGETTS, R.M., & ROSENKRANTZ, S.A. Real Managers. Cambridge, MA: Ballinger, 1988.

MASLOW, A.H. Motivation and Personality. (Second Edition) New York: Harper and Row, 1970.

NADER, R. Unsafe At Any Speed. New York: Grossman, 1965.

NADER, R., & TAYLOR, W. The Big Boys: Power and Position in American Business. New York: Pantheon, 1986.

SCHEIN, E.H. Organizational Socalization and the Profession of Management. In: Psychological Fundations of Organizational Behavior. Second Edition, edited by B.M. Staw. Glenview, Ill.: Scott, Foresman,.

SCHWARTZ, H.S. Maslow and the Hierarchical Enactment of Organizational Reality. Human Relations, 36 (10), 1983.

SCHWARTZ, H.S. On the Psychodynamics of Organizational Totalitarianism. Journal of Management, 13 (1), 1987a, 38-51.

SCHWARTZ, H.S. Antisocial Actions of Committed Organizatinal Participants: An Existential Psychoanalytic Perspective. Organization Studies, 8 (4), 1987b, 327-340.

SCHWARTZ, H.S. On the Psychodynamics of Organizational Disaster: The Case of the Space Shuttle Challenger. The Columbia Journal of World Business, XXII (1), 1987c, 59-67.

SCHWARTZ, H.S. Rousseau's Discourse on Inequality Revisited: Psychology of Work at the Public Esteem Stage of Maslow's Hierarchy. International Journal of Management, 4 (2), 1987d, 180-193.

SCHWARTZ, H.S. The Symbol of the Space Shuttle and the Degeneration of the American Dream. Journal of Organizational Change Management, 1 (2), 1988, 5-20.

SEARLE, J.P. Speech Acts: An Essay in the Philosophy of Language. London: Cambridge University Press, 1969.

SENNETT, R. & COBB, J. The Hidden Injuries of Class. New York: Vintage, 1973.

SHORRIS, E. The Oppressed Middle: Politics of Middle Management/Scenes from Corporate Life. Garden City, New York: Anchor Press/Doubleday, 1981.

SIEVERS, B. Beyond the Surrogate of Motivation. Organization Studies, 7 (4), 1986, 335-351.

STAW, B.M. Rationality and Justification in Organization Life. In B.M. Staw & L.L. Cummings (Eds.), Research in Organizational Behavior Vol. 2, 45-80. Greenwich, CT: JAI Press, 1980.

WRIGHT, J. P. On a Clear Day You Can See General Motors: John Z. De Lorean's Look Inside the Automotive Giant. New York: Avon, 1979.

Adapting to Doom: The Group Psychology of an Organization Threatened with Cultural Extinction

Howard F. Stein

> In order to be accepted in a culture one must accept or adopt an uncritical attitude toward its customs and its fears. ... A consequence of this is unthinking acquiescence and extinction of all possibility of solving the underlying problem. - Jules Henry (1963, p.122)

Introduction

This paper illustrates the role of unconscious activities in organizations and cultures. Through a case study, it describes the interplay between organizational fantasies and organizational realities in the political life of a medical corporation. This case study is of the decline of a corporate group that has been slowly allowed by its parent company to atrophy, and of the relationship between the subsidiary, which I shall call Managed Care Affiliate (MCA), and its corporate headquarters. It explores the dynamics of grief-work and of impediments to it posed by a sense of catastrophe. In this paper, I also explore my evolving role as an organizational consultant seeking to help - albeit in a limited way - the subsidiary, MCA, through its protracted uncertainty, rage, and grief. At the descriptive level, the case study interweaves two stories: (1) the story of an organization whose members are haunted by a sense of doom, and (2) the narrative of my role as organizational consultant, a role which both gave me access to the organizational narrative, and provided conflicting expectations for my interventions on behalf of MCA.

At one level, this is a case study in cumulatively traumatic culture (e.g., organizational) change. At another level, it is a contribution to: (a) the theory of culture and organizational identity; (b) the study of organizational/cultural decline and grief-work; (c) the study of the relationship between individual and group; (d) the study of the relationship between organizational fantasies and realities; (e) the analysis of the process of adaptation to the social environment; (f) the study of inter-group "transference" (e.g., projection, externalization), and its relationship to group images and their consequences; and (g) the literature on consultant roles, including the role of corporate consultant as transference object, and the opportunities and limitations

Reprinted, by permission of publisher, from Political Psychology, Vol. 11, No. 1, 1990. Office of Rights/Permissions, Plenum Publishing Corporation, New York.

of such roles. This paper attempts to address a central theoretical issue in all social/behavioral sciences: How does the researcher/scholar avoid reifying social units or organizations (ethnic groups, corporations, nations, political parties) while at the same time doing justice to informants' or participants' own felt and constructed worlds? How does one clarify reality within worlds in which social units are invariably metaphorically experienced as images of living organisms, biological bodies, or supernaturally created entities?

At the outset I wish to identify my roles in the main office and its subsidiaries, and to explain my choice of this case study. Both in the main office and in its branches I am employed principally as a behavioral science trainer in communication theory and skills. My official function is to offer seminars and workshops to physicians and clinical administrators on physician-patient-family-staff relationships, corporation-community networking, and cultural and religious factors in clinical practice. I actively involve community/service agencies and businesses in these training programs, including ethnographic visits to occupational sites from which some of the patients are drawn. Among my more informal roles, I also do individual and group counseling of executives, managers, and staff at all facilities. The official title of my role in the subsidiaries is "consultant."

Because of the rigidly hierarchical structure, role compartmentalization, and status distinctions at the home office, my roles there are more circumscribed and my authority more limited, than in the smaller subsidiary companies. In the smaller, largely rural, companies people learn multiple roles beyond their "job description" on paper, in order to be able to fill in for one another and keep the organization functioning. Initially, my role in all these sites was defined as consultant to the manager trainees and to the manager-development program. That is, I expected to limit my interaction mostly to the physician and administrator trainees.

Quickly in the subsidiary organizations, partly due to my "systems" or "contextualist" orientation, and partly due to the greater role latitude and autonomy allowed me, I began to include executives, mid-level managers, trainees, and medical and non-medical staff in my "round" of activities, in conferences, and in group problem-identification and problem-solving sessions. Often many of the problems the trainees were having with patients or families were exacerbated by conflicts between clinical service and administration or business sectors, between expectations of the laboratory and the nursing staff, between the medical and the administrative executives, and so forth. Analogous to clinical work with families in which an "identified patient" bears the symptoms for the family, I found it advantageous to involve - at first informally, unofficially - personnel of the subsidiaries whom I had not been officially hired to train or consult. Over the years, these informal roles grew into shared expectations (although nothing had changed on paper).

There has thus been an evolution from formal roles to those which include but transcend them: these might be called informal but not tacit. I am regularly enlisted by upper management at these subsidiaries to address company-wide issues of "communication" and morale. Mobility in the organization gives me a sense of the larger context of problems, the focus of which might be patient behavior, payment/ collections problems, or community relations. It is also a role that is regularly utilized by company members at the subsidiaries: for example, I am commonly asked to function informally as facilitator of communication between quarreling units, or as a mediator who brings key group issues to the attention of upper management (permitting group members to save face while assuring that the issue is addressed). I have on occasion been humorously labeled "the Henry Kissinger of MCA." It was in this expanded role that I gradually became aware of the chronic, widespread apprehension in MCA that it was targeted for extinction by the home office.

Over the last several years, I noticed from my seminars and workshops, and from individual supervision of trainees and consultation with managers, that they were much less interested in and capable of devoting concentrated attention on problem patients or problem families. I gradually concluded, and corroborated from work throughout MCA, that preoccupation with the apprehension of doom and with "survival" made all but the most routine clinical and educational activities of lower priority than in previous years - and this with some of the same managers and staff who had been ardently devoted to psychosocial and community issues. From cues such as demoralization, greater infighting, and diminished empathy toward patients, I began to pay greater attention to and inquire into (both in the subsidiaries and in the home office) the reality of the threat and the fantasies associated with their growing sense of fatalism.

As is true for many of my earlier studies in medical culture and in physician-patient relationships (Stein, 1985c, 1986b, 1988; Stein & Apprey, 1985), I did not initially set out to conduct a study of this medical corporation. Rather, the "case" took shape during the course of my regular work as an applied anthropologist in this corporation's home office and regional subsidiaries. During the course of ordinary clinical seminars and workshops, and during informal hallway conversations, I began to notice - or to think I was noticing - the emergence of certain new patterns. Using such techniques or tools as participant observation, open-ended interviews, and naturalistic observation, I conducted ethnographic fieldwork in the course of doing my job. I began to keep detailed notes, both to document and make sense of the "pattern" I thought I was discerning, and to provide additional observational data to test and revise earlier impressions.

In the earliest years as consultant to these often rural subsidiaries, I was viewed with suspicion variously as a "Yankee" (in the southern Great Plains, with heavy influence from the old South), as a "spy" for the home office, and as an "unknown quantity." After several years of cultural "probationary" time, I was accepted as one of "us" (at MCA), while my ties to "them" (headquarters) were acknowledged but without contamination by the insider/outsider dichotomy. MCA personnel came to realize that I had their welfare at heart. At the beginning of this phase, the group transference toward me shifted affective poles: from distrusted stranger who must prove himself and his loyalty, to ally, informer on the secret deliberations of executives hundreds of miles away, and one who might even be a rescuer.

As the years of collaboration continued, these idealizations diminished, giving way to more realistic perceptions of co-worker and friend. With each new visit I made, personnel would invariably inquire whether I had any new information from headquarters - with which they might better divine their future. Although this role of newsbearer has continued, MCA members have become increasingly realistic as to the limits of my omniscience. For one matter, I am not a member of executive councils at the home office, and am thus not privy first-hand to high-level corporate decision-making (including budget). Most recently, my ascribed role at MCA has been defined in terms of such epithets as "the listener," "our shrink," and - during the course of a three-hour marathon with one manager - as "our toilet paper, who takes us as we are."

Chronic role confusion and role limitation have not been unique to me. The mystification of corporate agendas and policies by the new Chief Executive Officer (CEO) at headquarters, his abrupt policy and priority shifts, and his inability to delegate authority or to share fiscal information, have engendered role confusion among many at all levels in the central office and subsidiaries. In my roles both at the home office and the subsidiaries, I have strived to serve as an advocate for psychosocially informed medical training and medical care, and as an advocate for group morale founded on reality acceptance and on a concern and respect for one another's welfare. I attempted to help the members of the subsidiary acknowledge perceptions and feelings they were dreading, while at the same time I attempted (informally) to document to the corporate executives at headquarters the consequences of actions and policies that they would not openly acknowledge. My written documentation and privately spoken expressions of concern to executives at the home office were characteristically met with reassurances that their "flagship" affiliate continued to have their unwavering support - or with discounting, incredulous smiles. Still, I staunchly advocated that executives from the home office and MCA make more frequent contact through visits, telephone, or letter. In sum, my advocacy was less for one "side" than it was for greater reality testing on the part of both.

The material discussed in the case was collected from such regular (weekly, fortnightly, monthly, quarterly) corporate activities as staff and managerial meetings (I was not privy to meetings of the highest executives in the corporate headquarters); clinical case conferences, division meetings (nurses, managers and trainees, business office); marketing meetings; and numerous individual consultations with various organizational members over six years. The case study is distilled from field notes. The case is discussed as an example of a widespread, if not universal, psychological process. Moreover, although the organizational group to be discussed has been in existence only 15 years, its dynamics in the face of continuous threats to its existence will be shown to be the same as those of anthropological tribes, ethnic cultures, factory towns, and intergenerational neighborhoods that have existed for decades if not for centuries.

Setting the Context for the Study

The medical corporation under consideration in this discussion, together with its regional subsidiaries, can be characterized as a bureaucracy both in the social structural sense and in the experience of authority. Baum, for instance, recently wrote of bureaucracies as

> hierarchical organizations in which authority is centralized and responsibility is diffused. ... The authority who assigns, variously controls, and evaluates a subordinate usually is relatively distant, relatively anonymous, and more or less autonomous. This situation of being controlled by someone powerful but poorly visible - a situation not unique to bureaucracy - encourages subordinates to fill in reassuring details by transferring past assumptions about authority to contemporary authority. Some of these transferred assumptions, deriving from infantile and childhood experiences, make bureaucratic authority seem larger, more powerful, and

> more punitive. ... [W]orkers may respond to organizational authority associated with earlier images of the superego and ego-ideal. (1986, pp.159-160)

The dynamic identified by Baum will be shown to apply not only to individuals within an organization, but to subsidiary organizations - subunits - of a superordinate corporation, units with which workers (members) have identified themselves culturally as an "us" who possess a shared fate.

Moreover, what Volkan (1980) writes of narcissistic leadership will be shown to characterize the leadership ambience at the home office in the case below:

> Clinging to the illusion of being powerful among others, some narcissistic people ambitiously seek the leadership of groups, organizations, or even nations. In their relentless search for power they use other people, discarding them without compunction whenever it seems advantageous. The success of such a person bent on leadership is obviously contingent on many variables, some of which may depend more on the psychology of the group itself than on his own. For example, a group may have undergone humiliation and defeat and be impelled on this account to seek a glorified leader who will lift them up. (1980, p.136).

He later identifies "the 'fit' between an individual's grandiose ambition and his potential followers' need" (1980, p.138), specifically the leader's need for power (together with his aura of power) and the group's sense of powerlessness and vulnerability (pp. 139-141).

In their psychobiography of Atatürk, founder of modern Turkey, Volkan and Itzkowitz (1984) offer a distinction in the dynamics of leadership that is especially germane to the dynamics of the relationship between MCA and its corporate headquarters. Writing of narcissism and leadership, they propose that

> Narcissistic leaders can be divided into two general categories. One is the destructive leader who attempts to protect the cohesion of his grandiose self chiefly by devaluing others in order to feel superior. The destructive narcissistic leader poses a considerable danger. History shows that an excessive need to devalue a group often leads to the destruction of that group. For the destructive leader the devalued persons or groups become targets for

> the externalization of his split and devalued self and object images, and those people and groups have to be suppressed.
> The other type of narcissistic leader is reparative, and Atatürk is representative of this category. The reparative leader wants adoration from his "valued" followers and may attempt to uplift them in order to build his support on as impressively high a level as possible. The followers are idealized so that their mental representations can be fused into the grandiose self of the leader, making the cohesiveness of his inner world more stable.
> In some respects the distinction between the reparative and destructive grandiose leaders is artificial, since one may turn into the other under certain circumstances. (Volkan and Itzkowitz, 1984, p.358)

In a bibliographic essay on "crisis cults," La Barre writes that

> Simple theories of stress fail to predict anything about the quality of the response. It is not stress [the external stimulus or challenge] *as such but the psychic style of reaction to it that is important*. ... Simple stress theory as a single cause cannot predict the nature of the response also because it concentrates too largely on "outer" realities ... (1971, p.23, emphasis in original).

In the case to be discussed, I shall argue that the group's anxiety over the future of their organization was followed by regression, by the release of aggression that was alternately outwardly and inwardly directed, and by projection leading in turn to the condensation of projective contents with apperceived reality, and thus to the diminution of "reality" testing. The case is interpreted as an example of the process of complicated mourning in bureaucratic cultures.

Freud (1917), Pollock (1961), Volkan (1979, 1981), Mitscherlich & Mitscherlich (1975), and the Group for the Advancement of Psychiatry (GAP, 1987) have explored the vicissitudes of complex mourning for individuals, families, groups, and cultures. Owen (1986, 1987) and Stein (1986a, 1988) have argued that whole organizational groups need to work through the difficult process of grieving if a new organization is to emerge. In the case to be described, I shall offer an interpretation that the reaction within the subsidiary corporation is not altogether accounted for by labeling it as "victim" and its parent company as "oppressor." I shall instead suggest that there is evidence of a tacit collusion between inner and outer realms.

One who looks at the social history of the United States since the late 1970s and early 1980s is struck by the belligerent atmosphere of competitivism, commercialism, corporate groupism, rampant survivalism - in short, the renewal of a "live and let die" social Darwinism (Stein, 1982a-c, 1985b). Catastrophism - from the religious to the ecological -- pervades ideologies of the inner as well as the outer environment. One reads almost daily of "hostile takeovers" of one corporation by another, of numerous mergers, of the insatiably large engulfing and devouring the vulnerably small. Bank failures and closings, farm foreclosures, the virtual disappearance of the once proud and productive "Steel Valleys" of the upper Midwest and the Northeast, and the replacement of solo and group medical practices by corporate outpatient and hospital conglomerates - these are but several instances of society-wide rapid transitions and losses of identity (Stein, 1985b).

During the 1960s and 1970s, large scale American urban redevelopment and relocation disrupted networks of meaning, information, succor, and mutual assistance, and inspired terror in many ethnic populations for whom home and neighborhood were experienced as coextensive with the world (Stein, 1980). On a large time scale, Fry (1970) and Shkilnyk (1985) have described societal disintegration and rampant self-destructiveness among Native North Americans experiencing rapid acculturation. Common Native American responses include emotional numbness, indifference, listlessness, passivity, disorientation to time and space, alcoholism and other substance abuse, random aggression - in short, what Jilek (1974) terms "anomic depression" (see also Jilek-Aall, 1986).

From two decades of intermittent ethnographic field work in the McKeesport area of the Monongahela "Steel Valley," principally among Slavic-American steel-worker families (Stein, 1980; Stein & Hill, 1979), I have witnessed once bustling mill towns become virtual ghost towns in which only the demoralized, the retired and those unable to move are trapped. During twice-annual visits to the Pittsburgh-McKeesport region, I have seen and read (in local newspapers) the same scenarios played and replayed. For instance, officials of USX (formerly United States Steel) urge greater economic realism on the part of devastated communities, admonishing them to relinquish their understandable but pathetic symbolic attachments to the steel mills (e.g., the "Dorothy Six" blast furnace at the former Duquesne Works). On the other hand, many newspaper editors urge greater regionalism and less localism in spirit, and press for a more cosmopolitan spirit of development (for example, thinking more of the greater Pittsburgh development than of micro developments in individual towns along the Three Rivers). At the same time, many townsfolk are members of multi-generation families for whom mill-church-tavern-market were The World, and not merely "a job," for whom symbols are never "merely" symbols.

Such attitudes as cosmopolitanism, parochialism, localism, tenacity against change, and tenacity for change, are all highly emotionally charged, symbolic operations. Not only in "Steel Valleys," but in all organizational policy development and planned change, it behooves us to understand the dynamics of those who have "everything to lose" and those who have "nothing to lose" (see Grieco 1988, on organizational culture and conflict). For the former, the boundary of the self is not the skin but the multi-generational way of life of which mill and town are living symbol: the "death" of that way of life is the same as for one's sense of self to die, for historical continuity to be forever severed. For the latter, the boundary of the self lies in the new future that differs entirely from the past, involving a new social epidermis - consisting, say, of a wider geographic compass of identity (Stein 1987a) and a new vehicle for a proud economic identity ("clean" informatics, telecommunications, banking, rather than "dirty" coal and steel).

It is perhaps ironic that both extremes - those who cling to their past and those who fling it from themselves - are dealing with grief in ways that avoid its pain and inner growth. Those who cling tenaciously to the mill-town past, who even hope for the resurrection of the steel-making way of life, avoid grieving by insisting that the old way is not really, or not necessarily gone: either by sheer denial, by angry, aggressive protests against corporate executives, or by a numbed, chronically depressed attempt to live life as usual amid the decay. Those who attempt to cast the past from their view, to efface it from memory and landscape, often seem to evince a kind of manic denial, a restless need to do and to change the outside so as to avoid feeling the loss and pain inside. Sadly, what is most needed by all participants to the calamity does not occur: that is, a public acknowledgment of the profound extent and depth of the change, and a public grieving on the part of all "interest groups," so that the past can be collectively worked through and only then relinquished.

As a result, organizational retrenchment, regression, and factional splitting (e.g., between the "progressives" and the "conservatives") occurs. Far from the wounds healing, they become more gaping, even as business ostensibly flourishes in some sectors. When an individual or group cannot bid farewell to an era, when it is either clutched as if it were life itself or flung as if it were death itself, organizational renewal is aborted (see Owen, 1986, 1987). All sides invariably become stuck perceiving another side as "betrayer" - of progress, of change, of the once solid and good way of life.

What Kohut (1972) described as "chronic narcissistic rage" assures that constant battle prevents deep bereavement. Neither flight into the past nor flight from the past permit an organization, a community, a culture, or a region to grieve what has been irrevocably lost. Moreover, attenuation of ties to the past becomes all the more unbearable when some external force is perceived as assaulting, if not severing those ties. In a number of studies (Stein, 1984, 1985a, 1987a; Stein & Niederland, 1989), I have discussed individuals' and groups' representation of themselves and their identities in terms of place and space. Under the rubric of "psychogeography" I have described how developmental issues over separation and individuation become symbolized in terms of the fusion of self-boundaries with the spatial boundaries of culture, workplace, and social organization.

Case Example: "How Long Can We Circle the Wagons?"

The case is an account of MCA, one of several subsidiaries of a medical corporation whose headquarters is located in the Great Plains of the United States. The corporate headquarters and its several regional subsidiaries are in the business of providing all areas of "patient care": clinical and preventive; hospital (inpatient) and clinic (outpatient); geriatric, family, adolescent and pediatric medicine; wellness programs for the healthy; rehabilitation programs; screening, referral and consultation. In the corporate headquarters, major programs, together with funding, are devoted to projections of future health trends, efforts to capture the market, the development of health policy statements, the design of medical practices based on cost containment and increased profit, and the development and implementation of clinical decision trees based upon probabilistic analysis.

The board of directors of the main office recommended, and the shareholders overwhelmingly approved, the hiring of a new corporate CEO in the early 1980s, a time during which a new national consensus over cost-containment, corporate competitiveness, and national social Darwinism was congealing. It was a time when corporate medicine became more explicitly profit-oriented and much less avowedly service-oriented. Kormos (1984) has labeled the era as the "industrialization of medicine." The new CEO, in tune with this emergent ethos, was seen by the board of directors who hired him as a "visionary" with a "grand vision of the future," a person who "flew high above everyone's heads, in the clouds, looking for megatrends of the future to capture the medical market." Many viewed him as a person who could rescue the company from its poor self-image and from its poor reputation among other corporations. He had been chosen among the applicants because he showed the most promise of expanding the company into greater profit, visibility, stature, and power in corporate medicine. He was hired with the understanding that he would increase the space, the local and regional influence, and the income of the company. From the outset, he invested corporate money and personnel time heavily in a proliferation of building plans and models, and architectural drafts, and in high technology acquisition involving multiple computer systems, with a series of disappointing results.

Soon after the installation of the new CEO and his staff, proposals, policies and practices all reflected a new set of polarities: among them, the corporate center versus the periphery (e.g., subsidiary companies); urban (or metropolitan) versus rural (where the subsidiaries were mostly located); income generation and cost containment versus service; medicine-as-product-line versus medicine-as-skill-and-service, which in turn generates a livelihood; the new executives and managers versus the old ones ("young blood" versus "old blood"); centralized authority versus local autonomy; high technology versus personal medicine. Certain metaphors or images of medicine favored by the CEO were: "the automated physician" (emphasis on high-technology-mediated, depersonalized care), medical practice as a "product line" and the physician as a "product line manager"; patient care as "managed care" given by "producers" of health care to "consumers" of health care; "the bottom line" as "cost containment" through "managed care systems." Within these perspectives, the rural subsidiary organization, MCA, was devalued, despite the fact that it continued to be a reliably high-income generator utilizing the old ways of a family-service-oriented, moderately low-tech, and hands-on approach to patient care.

For the first several years, the new leader at headquarters, unable to delegate responsibility and authority, repeatedly intruded into groups and projects he had assigned. He insisted on total control of the company's finances; he shared financial and development information only with a small inner circle. Although he frequently espoused an "open door policy" for any one to "drop in for a visit," in fact he was often out of town on business visits, or when he was in his office, layers of offices and secretaries served as blockades that intervened between himself and others. Eventually, the door to his office was completely closed.

During these early years, his executives, managers, trainers, and staff as a rule rationalized the already demoralizing situation and generously gave him the benefit of the doubt. "He needs to be up there [in the clouds] to see the big picture. He doesn't have time for us down on earth. But he has us at heart. It'll all pan out in the end. We just have to give him the time and the space he needs." His distance and personal aloofness inspired wonder and awe, as if he possessed some magical prescience and omnipotence. For the first several years, numerous displays of arrogance, his humiliation of managers, his driving off of junior executives and staff, his secrecy of decision-making and fiscal management, his aloofness and unavailability - all of these were excused and rationalized in his behalf by corporate members who had merged his vision with their future, and who had hitched their dependency to his often elusive wagon. When he would find the current of the future, while testing the high winds, the expectation remained that he would make his corporation wealthy, famous and powerful.

In exchange for the promised future of wealth and renown, he asked for commitment and for the unquestioning loyalty of his "team players" - a term merging their interest and fate with his, and one which he and others in the upper corporate would frequently invoke when subordinates began to deviate or rebel. (The accusation that "You're not a team player" was among the worst fates that could befall a corporate manager.) The CEO asked them to wait; eagerly anticipating the eventual payoff of the "vision," they were willing to wait.

A large turnover of junior executives and mid-level managers occurred with the installation of the new CEO. This was quickly justified by a polarization in which the old-timers were viewed as inadequate if not bad, and those brought in by the new CEO were admired as fresh and new. By contrast, MCA continued to be run by the "old guard." When many of the "new blood" at the corporate headquarters began to leave as well, this was further rationalized in terms of their having been poor "team players." For several years, many members of the corporation did their utmost to maintain their idealization of their "visionary" leader, upon whom they had become increasingly dependent. After several years, many, however, began to realize that his aggrandizement was purchased at their expense, that it was he who was not being a "team player."

After the transition in leadership at the corporate headquarters, numerous small events set the stage for an atmosphere of doom within MCA. Representatives of the subsidiary were often overlooked for notification of scheduling for such various corporation-wide meetings as marketing sessions, strategic planning, and the development of philosophy, policy and goals. Input from MCA members was rarely solicited about decisions that affected their company's internal functioning. Spontaneous visits to MCA by home office executives, and telephone calls from them, markedly diminished. Those few personnel from the home office who regularly consulted with, gave seminars at, or did trouble-shooting for MCA found that executives in the home office consistently "forgot" to credit this time spent, tending to define 100% time only in terms of that spent at the home office. In short, MCA personnel felt that they had gradually become the consistent target of discounting, or of "death wishes" on the part of the larger corporation.

Most recently, over a period of several years, MCA has seen an outflow and depletion of virtually all of those precious commodities necessary for its survival. Through the gradual centralization of decision-making and financial management, a sense of local autonomy about MCA's activities and about its fate has attenuated and been virtually lost. All important medical, administrative, and financial information about the organization has been computerized for management from the main office. Promotions in rank or replacement of vacant positions became notably rarer and slower at the MCA office than at the main office. Rewards for job performance were likewise far less frequent from the home office for MCA employees. Some years ago, not only did the CEO from the home office forget to bring plaques for an award ceremony to MCA, but some months later, on a visit to MCA, the COO (Chief Operating Officer) likewise forgot to bring the awards plaques for presentation. MCA has consistently been asked to make layoffs, cutbacks, and to endure hardships that the main office has not sustained for itself. The chronic experience of unequal sacrifices has made MCA suspect that the home office was growing and thriving at the expense of the affiliate.

Prestige has likewise diminished in MCA, both in the eyes of local/regional supporters and vendors, and in the eyes of the main office. In most recent years, local businesses, health agencies, and the local medical community, who have long enthusiastically supported MCA, have begun to wonder about whether MCA will survive. They wonder whether the main office is really behind its local affiliate and have begun to question whether the main office would honor MCA's commitments. With local confidence in MCA's future undermined, many businesses and health agencies have adopted a "wait and see" attitude. Similarly, fewer managers have applied to train at MCA, applicants having heard "via the grapevine" that MCA might not be long-lived and that the main office has been in keen competition with MCA. Thus, with the decline in prestige, the credibility of MCA has begun to decline both in the local organizational community and within the applicant pool which MCA counts on for its record of success and excellence.

This progression of events was experienced by MCA personnel as keenly felt, unrelenting death wishes from and abandonment by the home office. MCA's initial persistent response was the even more unrelenting pursuit of excellence and success, to prove to themselves and to others that they were indeed doing their job - unsurpassed by any. Yet, as Abse writes, "The very thought of having to justify one's existence is already expressive of a doubt about the right to be in the world" (1988, p.90). The CEO of MCA said to me with exasperation a few years ago: "We do the job we're supposed to do, and we're punished rather than rewarded for our accomplishments. What do they want of us?" The simple, frightening - and intolerable - answer, one that could only be voiced in gesture rather than in word was, disappearance. Both the main office and MCA acted as if extinction were the central agenda, to which MCA responded (for the most part) by striving all the more to demonstrate its quality, if not indispensability. Yet MCA could not perceive and accept that "doing better" could not save it from dissolution.

During the most recent years of which I have served as a consultant (as well as to some of its other affiliates and home office), MCA has been living with an unrelenting sense of threat to its existence. Because of the complex, ambiguous relationship it has had with the home office, it has been impossible for MCA's officers to determine how real the threat is. The 30-member medical affiliate has been acting for the past five years as if the threat to its existence were real, and as if annihilation were not only inevitable, but imminent. During this period, the central office has not effectively acted to deny or disprove this growing conviction. Through understanding both the home office and its subsidiary, MCA, and by knowing both the fantasy systems and realities of each, and their interaction, we can better comprehend and evaluate the intense subjective feelings (rage, grief, etc.) of MCA.

A recurrent theme or metaphor used at MCA over the years has been the frontier-image of "circling the wagons," a turning inward to protect the integrity of the organization. Feeling as if their very existence were under prolonged siege, members wondered how long the "encircled wagons" could survive. Moreover, the anger, resentment, rage, sense of chaos, and the like that they felt dare not be directed externally - to the main office or to vendors in the local community upon whom they also depended. Instead, they came to redirect these sentiments internally in the form of organizational infighting, schisms between sectors of the organization (care-giving, laboratory, business-administrative, public relations-marketing, etc.), increased incidence of MCA personnel illness and accidents, and widespread demoralization.

Ironically, in this corporation's history, MCA has been consistently regarded by the home office and by other admiring and envious subsidiaries as the "flagship" of the institution. Until recently, it had often been the case that the best of the applicant pool of medical and administrative personnel, managers and staff, and corporate trainees, selected MCA as their first choice in the organization in which to work. MCA has been envied as the most consistently productive, successful, and enjoyable worksite within the corporation. Since its inception fifteen years ago, its virtue has been its vice: envy and disparagement by other components of the organization have eaten away at MCA. MCA's successes become the home office's and other subsidiaries' failures; everything that MCA did well "made" the others look bad. At one home office executive meeting, at which recruitment of managers was discussed, an executive told a story about how he thought MCA succeeded in its recruitment: "They send one of their cute secretaries to take him [a management candidate] to a drive-in and give him a good time [the implication being that of sexual favors]. That's why they get them and we sometimes lose out."

It is unlikely that there has ever been an official written edict or explicit decision by headquarters to close MCA. Rather, members of MCA, and myself as well, have inferred and frequently reconfirmed this conclusion through acts of omission and commission by the upper management at the home office, through its euphemisms, metaphors and other turns of speech, and by its acts of mystification. Not so benign neglect has characterized much of the home office's practice toward MCA. Over a year ago, the headquarters published a lavish brochure describing and marketing all facets of their company - but omitting any mention of the MCA subsidiary, even though at a managers' meeting I had urged them to include MCA in the public relations brochure. The two most common responses I received from executives and managers at headquarters was that "We didn't have room" and "We forgot."

Furthermore, at corporation-wide workshops and managers' meetings (at which I am usually the only quasi-MCA spokesman present), I often have reminded the group of the fact of MCA's existence when input from, or program planning for, the entire corporate "family" (as many members call it) has been under consideration. Several mid-level managers and junior executives have approached me following the meeting and have said, some with embarrassment, "You know, it's easy to forget the MCA even exists, they're so far away, and you never see any of them down here." "Forgetting" has been frequently tantamount to the wish that MCA should disappear. Action at corporate headquarters often has seemed commensurate with the conclusion that this wish has been activated.

Themes of powerlessness, vulnerability and betrayal have pervaded MCA members' accounts of their recent history. Trying to plan for their future, they feel they have been given virtually no information, financial or moral support from the home office - support upon which strategically sound planning and emotionally sound anticipation can be based. The CEO of MCA recently said to me:

> I took it to heart when the chief at the main office said three Decembers ago that they were really hard up for money, and that we'd have to have some major cuts here at MCA. I'm willing to tighten the belt and share hard times all around. They said I'd need to let go of some people, and we couldn't fill several managers' and staff slots. I figured we'd all just have to put our shoulders to the wheel and work hard. During that time I was so concerned that I approached a number of community medical resources and vendors to see if we could fill the gaps that were going to be created by these losses. Then, as time went on, I saw the main office functioning as if money was available and flowing after all - but only for them. I saw new executives coming on board, new staff persons. I then felt embarrassed to have acted poor for my own people here at MCA and in the community. I felt like I'd lied to my own people and to the town that's dependent on our good faith. I feel hurt and somewhat betrayed, and foolish for having taken it all so seriously. A few months ago, several of my managers and staff threatened to quit. They don't want to go down with a sinking ship. Now, for the future, I'm determined just to submit requisitions and expect them to be processed and paid; I'm not going to hold back and keep tightening the belt when they're not doing the same down there on the red carpet.

For the past 4 years, many of the older members of MCA have felt as if they are living in the shadow of the folding, after the arrival of the new CEO at headquarters of another medical subsidiary of the corporation hundreds of miles away. The mysterious circumstances of its demise, its slow decline, the simultaneous withdrawal of community support and of support from corporate headquarters - these were frequently (and projectively) referred to as "The Handwriting on the Wall," portents of a fate that might or might not be fended off. The CEO of MCA, together with several managers and staff constantly attempted to assess the current status of their organization by calibrating it with the final years of their erstwhile "sibling" organization. Recently, the leader of MCA said to me, almost as if prophesying,

> Just you wait, we're being set up so that when our ship goes down, they'll (at the main office) be able to blame me for sinking, just like they hold Dr. X, the former CEO at Grainton, for their company biting the dust. They're sharpening their excuses, getting ready for the kill. I'm their scapegoat. You can be damned sure that they'll make it look like there's no blood on their hands. We're being set up for the sacrifice just like the hospital at Grainton was. Just you wait and see. I'll get the blame.

In most recent months, various MCA members would stop me in the hallways and begin to tell me about serious or terminal illnesses or deaths in their families. Although over the years I have consulted and counseled many MCA members on a wide range of professional and personal subjects, never before was there such a groundswell of thoughts on death. Our conversations would often drift onto the fate of MCA, suggesting to me that real as were these family events, they also served as displacements for the dread of MCA's organizational dissolution (cf. Yalom 1970, p.115) and loss of friendship networks and MCA identity.

The dispirited leader of MCA did his best to rally from time to time, and always vocalized mottos such as "Onward and upward," "Steadfast and determined," "Bowed but unbroken," "We'll make it." However, his actions - largely inactions to take advantage of the promised change of policy at the home office, together with his increasing absences and emotional unavailability (wishing to be spared further "bad news") - expressed the opposite. Junior executives, managers, physicians, and medical and administrative staff of MCA alike frequently told me they thought their leader depressed, that they had to assume increasingly large numbers of his decision-making functions, which he had tacitly ceded to them.

In the form of depressed leadership and group morale, the enemy was now as much within as without. Making MCA further a captive of its collective sense of doom was that both the home office - over a period of several years, during which the head of MCA had clearly and repeatedly announced his wish to retire and leave MCA in good hands - and local MCA junior executives did virtually nothing to secure a replacement and continuity of leadership. On several occasions, I spoke with senior executives of the home office, and I even wrote letters and memoranda to them as a subtle form of pressure ("documentation"), urging the central organization to assist in the transition, to make more frequent contact with MCA leadership, to show a greater interest in its future, etc.

Yet even when the home office executives would make a site visit and create a momentary stir of enthusiasm and hope, MCA leadership could rarely sustain the enthusiasm to try to save their organization. They immediately mistrusted the sincerity and follow-through of their visitors, and depressively fell back on the nostrum that the "Handwriting [was] on the Wall" long ago. Feeling tired, "burned out" after having led his organization for a decade through almost eight years of continuous corporate economic and political tumult, the CEO of MCA discounted the sincerity of the head of the home office to provide any help he could to turn things around. Taking little of the initiative, and giving few of the "pep talks" to his workers as he once did, his refrain became "Too little, too late." While not verbally giving up on MCA, and still wanting to have a successor take over "a ship in full sail," by his actions and inactions he hastened the very fate he feared. The motto "Too little, too late," externalized all responsibility for MCA onto the home office. "If they really mean business, they should come up here and talk with us. You know the old saying, 'Don't tell me, show me.' I'm waiting for them to show me their intentions." Feeling overwhelmingly discounted and demoralized, his increasing passivity and fatalism unwittingly played precisely into the hands of those executives at the home office who had been passive-aggressively undermining all of MCA's functions.

Having started out appearing to be and welcomed as, a "reparative" leader, the corporate CEO of headquarters came to be slowly, reluctantly recognized as a "destructive" one who not only directed group effort at defense against outer adversaries, but who targeted many within his company as well. I would characterize the head of MCA as more consistently of the "reparative" type. Further, their relationship, together with that of their respective organizations, can be identified as symmetrical (Bateson, 1972) in that the more the leader of MCA sought to mend or save his operation, the more the leader of the corporate office engaged in direct or indirect aggression towards the subsidiary group, and vice versa. In effect, each provoked an escalation of the more-of-the-same destruction/reparation dialectic in the other.

In most recent years, the head of MCA, unable to save his company by attracting new trainees, new staff, and a replacement for himself, has become increasingly albeit subtly destructive toward his unit.

Withdrawing from his formerly optimistic, encouraging style, he has become increasingly withdrawn, unavailable, and unwilling to make decisions that would involve confrontation with executives at the home office. Depressed - although avowedly never willing to give up - because of his chronic impotence as leader, he often seemed through his actions to have given up hope; he is biding his time for the final axe to fall. Feeling "tired," "burned out," "none of the earlier fire left," he has been unwilling to press his boss at the main office for the dramatic promises his boss had made many months earlier: that henceforth money would be no object, that they could have whatever they needed to recover.

His chief operations officer, in turn, long a conservative penny-pincher during the lean times, has continued to act in many respects as if the subsidiary were still in dire poverty. For instance, the physicians had requested new knee-length lab coats, because their old ones were becoming thin and frayed. No sooner had the new ones, ordered by the COO, arrived, than several of the physicians bitterly ridiculed them as "pillow covers, they're so thin; you can tell how cheap they were. That's how much we're worth." Out of protest, several physicians refused to wear the new ones.

At all levels of the organization, day-to-day work continues in perfunctory performance. Partly through identification with the depressed leader, many if not most members of MCA have given up on themselves as an organization; they have given up that sense of "we-ness" that is too painful to try to preserve if not reconstruct. If the demise of MCA becomes a fulfillment of the tacit wishes of the home office, it will for many of MCA managers, trainees and staff be a self-fulfilling prophecy, one in which they have unwittingly colluded.

Discussion: Organizational Effects of Adaptation to Doom

The organizational effects of adaptation to the sense of doom in the above case example were numerous, pervasive, and have become indelible:

(1) increased infighting and factionalism;

(2) increased discrepancy between the group's self-expectation to perform at 100% efficiency and responsibility and their inability to fulfill their expectations due to absence of sufficient personnel and financial support;

(3) episodes of group despondency, apprehension, self-blame, helplessness-hopelessness, resignation, outrage;

(4) rallying periods of resolve, hope through the infusion of "new blood" (e.g., new junior executives, successful marketing, annual new groups of medical managerial trainees);

(5) constant "patching things up," as with a trowel and plaster, while feeling pulled apart and falling apart (e.g., continuous negotiation with local and regional subcontractors and vendors for new corporate outlets and community support to shore up what has been lost from the main office);

(6) sense of abandonment, conviction that MCA is victim of an outside plot, belief that annihilation is only a matter of time, that their fate is out of their hands, that the main office has no place for MCA in its future but is not telling them;

(7) decrease of reality testing and concomitant regression;

(8) the discreet search for outside jobs by apprehensive executives, managers, salespeople and staff, to "jump ship before it sinks";

(9) sense of impotence on the part of MCA leadership;

(10) the merger of feared destruction with group self-destructive behavior by members of MCA; and finally

(11) the proliferation of and vulnerability to rumors about firings, resignations, omens, together with a magical "watching for signs" in facial expressions and attitudes of MCA leaders and/or home office management personnel.

The concept of projective identification (Klein, 1946, 1955) is a useful interpretive tool in understanding MCA as a shared representational system (possessing self and object attributes), and in understanding the relationship between MCA and its home office both as realities and as objects of unconscious fantasy. In terms of the principle of multiple function, it serves simultaneously as a defense, as an unconscious phantasy, as a mode of communication and as the vehicle for a wish (Apprey, 1986, pp.115-116). Meltzer, discussing the motives underlying projective identification, lists among the most powerful: "intolerance of separation; omnipotent control; envy; jealousy; deficiency of trust; excessive persecutory anxiety" (1967, pp14). Over time, MCA and its home office became bound by a fateful "symbiosis" of projective identification in addition to their real-world economic, political, ideological and training functions. Each came to embody or mirror the "worst" features of itself - with which battle was engaged with the "external"(-ized) enemy.

Ironically, many of the widespread dysphoric feelings within the main office of the medical corporation - aimlessness, leadership's distance from the daily affairs of the members, lack of clear roles and expectations, demoralization due to unacknowledged members' contributions, fear of abandonment, and spasms of accountability for problems beyond any individual's control - are those which were induced in the MCA affiliate office. Stated technically, mechanisms of defense such as displacement, projection, projective identification, splitting, isolation, and the like that are familiar in individual psychology can be used in regulating group cohesiveness, identity, aggressive and sexual impulses, "status anxiety," (De Vos 1966) and so on. Families , corporations, whole societies, and international (-group) relations can be, at least in part, governed by an affectively and fantasy-based division of labor (Stein, 1986a). Roles can be based on the complementarity of induction and embodiment of dysphoric if not catastrophic feelings, fantasies, and wishes (Devereux, 1980). In the case under discussion, the sense of integrity and safety within the home office was in part purchased by depositing the parallel sense of disorganization and danger in MCA - in fact, by inducing endangerment in MCA. Through MCA, the home office could dissociate itself from dysphoric feelings while "managing" them in a subsidiary that is at once a "part of" itself yet "apart from" it (Stein, 1987a).

Further, the home office experienced considerable ambiguity over its ideal professional identity, that is, regarding its medical care-giving and training vs. profit-making and hierarchy-maintaining roles. I suggest that MCA became a Bion-type of "container" (1963) for the devalued aspects of the home office, attributes that were nevertheless still touted as its official ideals: i.e., emphasis on continuity of physician-patient relationships, consumer-oriented medical practice, "consumer-friendly" medical products, contextually based medical and business relationships rather than financially and technologically dictated corporate values (see Stein & Hill, 1988). Over the years, a recurrent, even fixed, set of value priorities and stereotypes came to govern the mutual perceptions of MCA and the home office, and to regulate their interactions. The most salient of these are as follows: rural/urban, low tech/high tech, personal medicine/"electric" physician, informal/formal, input from all levels in decision-making/hierarchical (top-down) decision-making, interpersonal relations/"the bottom line," excellence in task performance/ appearance-image-marketing-public relations, service to vendors/ product line management. Klein (1946, 1955), Jaques (1955), Zinner and Shapiro (1972), Kets de Vries (1984) and Stein (1986a) have discussed in detail the operation of projective identification in cementing and stabilizing intrapsychic, interpersonal, familial, organizational and intercultural relationships. Likewise, this mental mechanism was a powerful force in perpetuating the relations - and the internal mental representations - between MCA and its home office (see also Apprey, 1986). For an extensive literature review on the subject of organizational dynamics, role formation, and the operation of various defense mechanisms, see Diamond and Allcorn (1986).

Over the years, the psychological foundation or unconscious position of MCA gradually shifted from what Bion (1959) called the basic assumption of "dependency" (i.e., the sense of "belongingness", if not oneness with the group, the sense that the leader[s] or that the group itself will fulfill succorance and nurturance wishes) to the basic assumption called "fight/ flight" (i.e., heightened vigilance, the sense of imminent danger, alternating readiness to attack or to withdraw, heightening of aggressive impulses). Interestingly, Bion's third basic assumption, called "pairing" (wherein the group hopes for rebirth via a redeemer who is a product of the fantasized pairing of two group members, or from external parent-figures), only intermittently and briefly appears, as does the hope for new, young, permanent leadership.

Organizational Crisis and Regression

Over 3 decades ago, George Devereux (1955) formulated a group or cultural psychology of crisis, one which I suggest is apt for the MCA episode under discussion.

> A crisis comes into being through the following process: In a situation of stress, which elicits *fear*, time-tested and traditional mechanisms of orientation and of action no longer produce the expected results. This leads to a schizophrenia-like disorientation and to catastrophic behavior. *Fear*, which is an objective appraisal of the magnitude of a real danger, is replaced by *anxiety*, which is a sense of the inadequacy of one's resources in the face of stress. Since anxiety is harder to endure than fear, society rapidly becomes more preoccupied with alleviating its state of anxiety than its fear, and practically ceases to do anything about the danger which elicited fear in the first place. Figuratively speaking, a society in crisis clamors for "cultural bromides" rather than for tools and weapons. This means that an autistically evolved intrapsychic *"threat"* replaces the objective *"danger,"* ,and comes to occupy the center of the psychological field. Society then attempts to bring into being in reality - to "materialize" - precisely the kind of objective *danger* which corresponds to the initially intrapsychic *threat*. ... From then on society fights the phantoms - the Frankenstein's monsters - which, in compliance with its needs to project its intrapsychic *threats* into the outer world it brought into being, and therefore ceases to fight the initial, objectively real, *danger*.

> In brief, crisis behavior is characterized by the presence of self-defeating mechanisms, leading to a downward spiraling, ever expanding, vicious circle, where the very attempts to cope with the problem on hand only exacerbate the stress and create new difficulties. (1955, p.147, emphasis in original)

In the face of chronic uncertainty over the future and continuity of MCA, what little information MCA managers received was quickly magnified into the most cataclysmic rumor, fueling the flames of doom that were already quite real enough. A plausible interpretation is that unconscious aggression was simultaneously projected onto the menacing outer world and was condensed with it, and within MCA it was projected from one member onto another, one work unit onto another, and combatted there through endless factionalism and infighting (e.g., health care versus administration, intramural versus extramural, training versus medical service units).

To reduce the intolerable feelings of passivity and vulnerability, many MCA members "identified with the aggressor," and further defended themselves against the intolerable anxiety by fighting enemies now embodied in the form of co-workers. While the main office and the local/regional community were silent targets of MCA projections, the only actual fighting that MCA members could allow to occur was between themselves. Thus, virtually irrespective of the main office's actual deeds and intentions, MCA members began to create their own self-fulfilling prophecy through unwitting collusion with the home office. Although MCA members became increasingly suspicious of the enemy within and the enemy without, it was only against the former that actual rage was directed, expressed and discharged.

Many of the junior executives, managers, practitioners, marketing specialists, and staff - especially those who rely more on environmental cues than upon inner directedness - perceive the CEO at MCA as having given up, as just biding his time before eventual retirement, as incapable of saving them or their corporation. Many quarrel with one another over prerogative, "turf" and responsibility, whereas before such issues were regarded as "petty." In the past, personal feuds were more successfully subordinated to the group mission. While members of the entire hierarchy attempt to "do their jobs" at "business as usual," everyone has acknowledged that "the old spirit is gone" - even as various executives try valiantly to rekindle it at weekly and monthly organizational meetings. It is as though at this point, they feel that MCA's fate is too far sealed, and too much out of their hands, for them to try to "rally around the flag" again. MCA now lives under the shadow of imminent death, never knowing when it will happen, but waiting for the lethal shot to be fired and fully expecting that it will. Perception of the outer world and fantasies dominating the inner world have become increasingly difficult to distinguish.

The past several years' history of MCA has been collectively traumatic in the sense hauntingly described by Kai T. Erikson in his study of the 1972 Buffalo Creek (West Virginia) disaster, in which the floodwaters from a burst dam inundated communities along the creek's path:

> By collective trauma, I mean a blow to the tissues of social life that damages the bonds linking people together and impairs the prevailing sense of communality. The collective trauma works its way slowly and even insidiously into the awareness of those who suffer from it; thus it does not have the quality of suddenness usually associated with the word "trauma." It is, however, a form of shock - a gradual realization that the community no longer exists as a source of nurturance and that a part of the self has disappeared. "I" continue to exist, although damaged and maybe even permanently changed. "You" continue to exist, although distant and hard to relate to. But "we" no longer exist as a connected pair or as linked cells in a larger communal body. (1976, p.302)

At MCA there occurred no single event so cataclysmic as a flood. Rather, the "collective trauma" has consisted of the slowly and subtly encroaching dysphoric sense of futurelessness for that "we-ness" in which many managers, trainees and staff had invested their very selves (not only their incomes).

In analysis of this kind, whether of whole cultures (ethnic, tribal, national) or organizational cultures, it is easy to slip into reifications as if a group were a self-standing entity, homogeneous, a living organism rather than an association of individual people. Many anthropologists and sociologists also must deal with their informants' own characterizations of their group or society as an immortal, ontological, if not supernaturally created entity. Yet, according to the model of methodological individualism (e.g., La Barre, 1972; Bion, 1959), groups do not exist apart from the people - and their motivations - who constitute and "belong to" them. That is, groups do not have independent motives of their own, although motives and characters may be ascribed to, projected or externalized upon, the group, resulting in reification for purposes of defense. All organizations and cultures are the creations and recreations of those who experience themselves as belonging to and loyal to "them" (Berger & Luckman, 1966).

Thus, while in one sense reification is inaccurate, in another sense it is necessary for us to assess its mental function for group members (see Shapiro, 1989, for a discussion of reification of the social group as a denial of death). In groups, mental operations differ from those of dyads or lone individuals, e.g., in groups there is greater proneness to regression, to the eruption of primary-process thinking and to action governed by it (cf. Alford, 1988, p.579). Through the oscillation of projection and introjection (and identification), the image of the group as the outer social epidermis of the self, the protective outpost or border for security operations, is reincorporated into the self. The group imago, so to speak, becomes an idealized object, the representation of which is then taken back into the self. Volkan says of the leader that "the identification with idealized external object creates an illusion that supports its [the self's] cohesiveness and stability" (1980, pp.138-139). I would slightly rephrase the sentence to read, with respect to groups, that the identification with idealized, mutually shared externalized objects creates an illusion that supports group members' cohesiveness and stability. Representations of groups, corporations, cultures often play the shared fantasized roles of external outposts of the self and one's defensive organization. They are the mental castle walls and moats, so to speak, that people use to give themselves boundary and distinctiveness, pride and uniqueness, separation and enclosure. These are a distal safeguard for what and who are contained within.

Discussing what binds people (in)to a group, Alford (1988) first quotes Freud (1921, p.48) who defined a group as "a number of individuals who have put one and the same object in the place of their ego ideal and have consequently identified themselves with one another in their egos." Alford continues with a succinct discussion of the leader and the group "itself" as representation:

> It is apparent that what binds the group is not love (at least not love for one another, object love), but narcissism. Individuals identify with one another; they feel bound to one another in some way, because they share a common ego ideal, represented by the leader. It is because of the shared common ego ideal that the group is bound together by narcissistic ties, understood as a self-love that extends to others because - and only because - they are like ourselves. It is also apparent that it is not an illicit abstraction, a reification, to speak of a group ego and group ego ideal. Both exist, in the form of attitudes and

> emotions directed by individuals toward the leader (who embodies the group ego ideal), and other group members (who together embody the group ego). (1988, p.579)

In the case discussed above, it was argued that such defenses as identification and externalization lead to the reification of the institution and to a merger of one's fate with that of the corporation (see also Diamond, 1984, 1988; Diamond & Allcorn, 1987). Moreover, I suggest that when the ability of the group to accomplish its missions and reach its goals is impeded by a threat to the very existence of the group, self-esteem will be undermined and various emergency maneuvers to restore it will be undertaken.

Intervention and Its Limitation

My roles as behavioral scientist/consultant/facilitator have been complex, and often ambiguous, throughout this case. My central informal role came to be what Rhodes (1986) has called an "institutional analyst," one whose task is to understand and emotionally encompass an entire institution and thereby to help the organization understand and help itself (see also Stein, 1987b). Although at the main office and in the other branches I am able to move freely among workers and middle-management personnel, I have been unsuccessful in my efforts to effect change by conveying to upper-management at the home office (whether through memoranda or through meetings with corporate vice presidents and treasurers) the sense of chronic urgency felt by MCA. As a result, there is little communication between upper-management at the home office and MCA, leaving a void filled at MCA by greater persecutory anxiety. In our role negotiation over the years, MCA members have relinquished their initial hope that I would be able to intercede for them at the home office and thus be able to "fix things." If I could not accomplish these wished-for things, what then could I do?

From individual counseling sessions, to executive and managers' meetings, to monthly meetings attended by all MCA personnel, my function became to listen, to help them and allow them to tell their stories, to help them understand the meaning of their stories, to help them - insofar as it was possible for me to do so - to compare their stories with the realities or official stories available to me from the home office, to help them to listen to each other with less condemnation and greater attentiveness and compassion, and through these, to help empower them to do whatever problem-solving and decision-making that was within their compass. In my rescue-fantasy, I had once wished to be able to "sound the alarm" or "blow the whistle" at the main office or even outside the organization.

However, neither alarm nor whistle were audible at the top levels of the organization and even outside it. The fate of MCA, and of its members' mental and physical health, thus rested entirely with themselves. Our individual and group discussions gradually helped to diminish their projections and projective identifications into one another, to decrease the infighting, to increase group morale and productivity, by helping them to have the courage to look at reality as directly as they could bear.

They often vacillated as a group between what Melanie Klein (1946) called the "schizoid-paranoid position" (of mistrust, mutual suspicion, recrimination, withdrawal, etc.) and the "depressive position" (sadness, wish to make reparation to the one who has been hurt), and both individual and group sessions helped diminish the persecutory anxiety and retaliation within MCA. Often taking flight from grieving by fighting, they courageously came to face their predicament over time as a group. One of my evolving roles within MCA was that of mediator, one who was given access to the stories and accounts of the various sub-groups (as well as of individuals within them), and who helped these warring factions to listen to one another, to try to understand the other's position. Thus I functioned not only as a welcome ear to their plight, but as a bridge initially between adversaries, and eventually as a facilitator of direct communication between them (see also Stein, 1987b).

During one meeting of the entire MCA corporate group, members of various units were hurling accusations against each other about how they made their own work difficult to accomplish. Short-handed, one work unit asked a second group to take care of obtaining business codes and signatures on requisitions and accused them of refusing to honor the simple request. The second group fired back that they were overworked and did not have the time or the authorization to do this additional paperwork. And besides, it was not their job to do other people's tasks. Yet another group of managers complained that community liaisons and public relations people were spending too much time outside the MCA offices when they were needed to coordinate efforts inside.

As the acrimony escalated during the meeting, I raised my hand and was recognized by the chief non medical administrator. I briefly said (roughly) as follows:

> These are terrible times for us all. We all feel bad that we cannot do better at our jobs and for MCA. People are doing their best. I think that everyone believes that. Don't point fingers because no one isn't giving 100 percent. It's

> difficult to prioritize values when we're so short-staffed yet have a full complement of physicians, executives and managers who are all trying to do their jobs and get their work done. They're supposed to be in the office, out in the community and traveling all over the region at the same time. Everybody is busy. In order to keep MCA afloat, at least as I understand it, we don't have the luxury of stopping doing such and such, or cutting back on something else. Everybody here knows we're walking a tight wire. Maybe if we can all realize that we can't prioritize our values at least for a long while, and if we accept that we can't live up to our goal of efficiency for a while, we will not be so hard on ourselves and on other co-workers who are trying as hard as we are.

Several members of the group, hitherto having verbally attacked others and having fended off others' criticisms, had tears in their eyes. The group, I believe, felt listened to, heard, and acknowledged rather than punished. The "solution" that there were numerous problems that could not be solved under the present circumstances was received as a relief to all. They no longer felt "bad" and accused as the source of their problems. The remainder of the meeting proceeded in a respectful, accepting, even warm tone.

Neither this meeting, nor other similar individual or group meetings, resolved matters once and for all. Indeed, one of my main points in the meeting was that disruptive, dysphoric, catastrophic feelings were inevitable for anyone who elected to continue business as usual in the present situation, and for whom the people and culture of MCA meant something more than "just a paycheck." My task went beyond "normalizing" the disturbing feelings and premonitions felt by the group: Rather, I consistently acknowledged and interpreted that which we all feared to acknowledge. Many in MCA came to realize that an instant solution was impossible. Labeling me as "the listener," and identifying with that function with which they had imbued me, they partly began to listen to each other.

In a recent paper on "The Ego and the Mechanism of Adaptation," Paul Parin writes that

> As the identification with the role is the chief instrument of the adjustment of the adult to social demands and compulsions, so the analysis of these identifications (whether exchangeable and short-lived or lasting) is an irreplaceable instrument of emancipation. In other words: The person is not master of his own home. The analysis

> must make him aware not only of these forces from his repressed material to which he is subject, but also of the powers of his environment that automatically dominate him because his ego, mostly unconsciously and through diverse role models, has identified with them. (1987, p.116)

In the context of Parin's argument, at MCA I have been trying to interrupt and interpret their automatic adaptive responses that lead to identification with their environment, i.e., with the role they are expected to play vis-a-vis the central office. For example, I speculated aloud whether much of the numbness, infighting, internal scapegoating, apathy, "waiting for the axe to fall," passivity (and its manic opposite, frantic activity to "save the ship") might express an identification with the role of the dead or doomed as well as identification with the aggressor. Such interpretation has often be welcomed as liberating, sense-making, and has led to a more realistic appraisal of both the internal MCA and external (home office, local community, etc.) situation.

MCA personnel come to understand that they are acting as if they are supposed to be dead, or at least in the process of dying and eventually disappearing. In separating - albeit incompletely and impermanently - their individual and collective "self" representation from the home office as an "object" representation, they are able to exercise greater choice about their future. In the least, they are not as ready to become accomplices in their own destruction.

Most recently, at a regular monthly managers' meeting, the full force of MCA's jeopardy was suddenly realized. Managerial trainees, mid-level managers, and upper-level administrative division heads usually participate in these meetings. On this occasion, both the subsidiary's CEO and the COO were absent. No one seemed to know where the CEO was, and vicious humor about the COO circulated through the group. One item on the agenda was recruitment of trainees and managers. The group of current trainees noted that there was little interest in transferring to MCA among junior trainees at the home office. One member of the MCA group had recently announced that he was transferring back to the home office. At headquarters, a junior manager who earlier had planned to complete his training at MCA had expressed to MCA trainees serious second thoughts about relocating to MCA at all: he feared that there would be far too much work to do among the diminishing managers and trainees at MCA.

There was much talk about continuous "bad news," and the repeated reiteration that "We don't want to talk about bad news." But then soon afterwards: "What if there's only three of us here next year? It's not all our responsibility to recruit. ...It hasn't hit us, that if we don't beat the bushes we won't have jobs. The CEO's gotten so passive, and the COO's so stubborn and so afraid to spend any money that our hands are tied when we try to make changes. How do we counter that apathy?" The group then divided up the labor of approaching potential recruits in various states: each trainee would take one state and contact the appropriate institutions in it. "How do we break the ice in these places?" one manager asked. Another said with resentment: "MCA has never been actively promoted by our CEO, the COO, or the other top management. I don't know where to go, who to talk to. We've been resting on our reputation."

The previous several weeks at MCA had been characterized by frenetic activity (recruitment, business-as-usual). Many MCA members recited in the halls the words of a popular song, "Don't worry, be happy," in a stereotypic, ritualistic manner. By the time of the managers' meeting, what could be seen as the "manic defense" had all but collapsed. Despair was everywhere felt and fought.

I keenly identified with and felt the managers' frustration, their sense of impasse, yet their need to do something quickly. I shared with them my fantasy of their being the "kids" in a family of alcoholic parents, or where parents had emotionally abandoned them, leaving the children to fend for themselves. I urged them to try to remember that the "kids" cannot be the "parents," much as the group of managers would like to try to help one another, if not to salvage MCA from annihilation. I interpreted the manic plans as attempts to escape the profound depression and despair that had come to the surface. Many members of the group nodded their heads in assent; they felt understood rather than criticized for not being "good enough" kids. They concluded that the apathetic, resigned attitude of "I don't care" is the major problem at MCA, that they would do their best but also realize that there were limits to their authority and power. They resolved to try to help the survival of MCA, but with their eyes open to reality-testing of actual opportunities and limitations. They became appropriately (in my view) depressed rather than continuing their manic flight into action and ritualized optimism.

On a technical note, during this emotionally pivotal meeting, I imagined for a time that I was functioning as a play therapist (in the Melanie Klein tradition). I was witnessing both the process of play and the crucial play disruption that signals underlying anxiety. The moment of "disruption" occurred as the group realized with dread and despair that their frenetic activity might be to no avail, that they could not accomplish their heroic rescue alone. This feeling triggered in me the concomitant feeling of abandonment anxiety, which in turn I interpreted to the group.

Some four hours later, the group of medical managers and trainees attended a seminar/workshop on death-and-dying and hospices (organizations that works with the terminally ill, and prepare the patient and the family emotionally for the death). The conference had been scheduled months in advance, as had a guest speaker for the occasion. As I later discussed with several group members after the guest presenter had left, the conference was deeply upsetting and uncannily "too close to home" emotionally for the participants of MCA. The topics presented included the following: patients' and families' need to finish, to bring closure to, their lives prior to death; the patient's being sent home to die, and the family's and the physician's inability to truly "hear" that (i.e., denial); the family's oscillation in and out of denial; the frequent conflict between the patient's need and wish to die and the family's and physician's need and wish for a cure and for a fight to the end; physicians' feelings of helplessness in the face of issues of mortality and their wish to counter these feelings by "doing something"; the emotional reactions evoked in health care workers by the proximity to death and by the passive (as contrasted to the biomedically orthodox "aggressive") approach to death; and the issue of whether to make time-predictions as to how much time the patient has left to live.

Throughout the conference, the usually attentive and respectful participants made numerous sardonic outbursts. One protested, "I don't want to die"; another declared, "I'm not going to die." During a discussion of the use of butter suppositories, with ground-up medication, for patients who no longer can take medicine orally, one trainee snapped, "Parkay the rectum" (Parkay being a brand of margarine), this phrase being followed by raucous laughter in the group. The participants went through a miming and exclaiming of "Shake the patient!" One manager proposed that, if the patient lived longer than the six-month limit set by hospice, the physician should tell the patient, "You're going to die" (spoken as a command). Many members of the group erupted into laughter after this brief role-playing. During the discussion of prediction of death, a manager cracked the joke, "It's OK to be dead wrong in hospice!"

I felt that it would have been inappropriate to bring up internal group issues while the guest was present, so afterwards I discussed the group dynamics with several manager/trainee participants and with the chief trainee. They unanimously reported that they, or others, had been "flaky" and "definitely not in the mood to hear this." The topic had coincided with their worst fears about the group itself and its future. I would interpret this to mean that since they had identified their very selves and futures with MCA (that is, its representation or inner image), the discussion of a patient's death became linked to the repugnant idea of their own death via the death of MCA. Although the group's manic denial had earlier lifted somewhat (and only momentarily), the group was not emotionally prepared to consider the possibility of grieving for their organization.

They had translated (emotionally transferred) the hospice issue of death-and-dying onto the dying and death of MCA. Earlier that day, the "mortality" of MCA had dawned on them. They acknowledged that they were not ready to go further with those disturbing feelings. Stated differently: they emotionally knew where they were not yet prepared to go. At the same time, they knew that I was available to listen and help them "process" their feelings and perceptions about the complex relationships between themselves as individuals, as members of MCA, and MCA's relationship to the home organization. I thus both interpreted the resistance and acknowledged that they still might need it.

Over time, the group became more often resilient and rallying than regressed. That the episodes of rallying attested to genuine creativity, productivity, and even intimacy rather than to a "manic denial" of reality is suggested by the greater degree to which MCA members verbalized to one another (as well as to me) and expressed their feelings about living with a foreshortened sense of time. What could not be changed at least could be openly acknowledged: the taboo that had kept the dread shrouded in secrecy had been lifted. MCA managers, trainees and staff began to talk openly about group-death, of the possible limits to, if not futility of, their still valiant efforts.

Several members expressed sadness over the recent loss of one manager-trainee who had returned to the home office. Others voiced resentment that he had "abandoned" them, thereby creating more work for those who remained. One manager even angrily demanded that the "defector" be required to commute periodically to MCA and bear the burden of his own work-load (i.e., acknowledging but attempting to undo the traumatic loss, symbol and harbinger of even more ominous losses).

An executive secretary openly talked with me about feeling "dead." She continued, using the metaphor of violent weather:

> It's like we're in the eye of a tornado - or, you know what I mean, - in the eye of a hurricane, not knowing whether we're going to be hit and blown away or whether it will go

> around us. It's really hit us lately, that we could be gone this time next year, that we might not have our jobs then. We try not to think about it, but it's there. We try extra hard at our jobs.

Using poignant medical metaphors, one physician-manager said with quiet foreboding: "The pulse is weak," and later wondered aloud in the group: "Is it time for DNR?" (i.e., a "Do Not Resuscitate" order often used with terminally ill patients).

The inability to plan for longer than a several-month stretch, or, differently stated, short-term planning rather than the customary long-term planning, became more openly accepted. That MCA could dissolve within six months or a year was still profoundly distressing to all its members. However, they now showed greater resolve and commitment to "give it their all" for as much time as there remained. Genuine sadness - rather than the erstwhile frenetic activity to seal over the unspeakable dread - began to show. There was a sense among MCA employees that they had somehow managed to take at least part of their fate into their own hands.

Conclusions

The contribution of unconscious dynamics to human social organization was studied through a case example. The group psychology of an organizational culture (MCA) gripped by a sense of imminent destruction was described and interpreted. The oppressive sense of foreboding among MCA members was shown to be inseparable from an interplay of (1) real probable organizational demise; (2) central office's (at least many of its highest executives') conscious and unconscious fantasies about MCA and themselves; (3) MCA members' own fantasies about chronically and increasingly ambiguous circumstances, about their own depressed leadership, and about their home office after a phase of dramatic transitions there; and (4) the dynamics and history of political succession (leadership) in both the home office and the subsidiary company. The paucity of contact between MCA and its distant home office, together with the type or character of the contact when it did occur, amplified both groups' fantasy systems and defensive organization.

The case was placed in the larger context of widespread closures, mergers, rapid culture change, and catastrophism. My multiple roles (and role ambiguity) as participant observer, consultant, counselor and facilitator simultaneously gave me access to many facets of the unfolding institutional narrative, permitted a degree of psychological intervention, and limited my ability to affect structural change within the larger organizational environment that underlay the apprehension of doom.

It is hoped that this study will stimulate further research and consultation in other organizational cultures, and in larger ethnic or national groups, wedged in uncertainty over their futures if not oppressed by a sense of disappearance as a group. The dynamics of grief-work over the anticipated and actual loss of culture remain a still little-explored frontier in human development, in the psychology of groups, and in applied behavioral science. Finally, in examining the role of unconscious processes in bureaucratic organizations, this paper has contributed toward building a conceptual bridge between individual, group, organizational and cultural psychology.

REFERENCES

ABSE, D.W. Kriegman's "nonentitlement" and Ibsen's Rosmersholm. In: V.D. Volkan, & T.C. Rodgers (Eds.), Attitudes of Entitlement: Theoretical and Clinical Issues. Charlottesville, VA: University Press of Virginia, 1988, 79-92.

ALFORD, C.F. Mastery and retreat: Psychological sources of the appeal of Ronald Reagan. Political Psychology, 9(4), 1988, 571-589.

APPREY, M. Discussion: A prefatory note on motives and projective identification. International Journal of Psychoanalytic Psychotherapy, 11, 1986, 111-116.

BATESON, G. Steps to an Ecology of Mind. San Francisco, CA: Chandler, 1972.

BAUM, H.S. Response to commentary by Cynthia McSwain. Political Psychology, 7(1), 1986, 159-162.

BERGER, P., & LUCKMAN, T. Social Construction of Reality: A Treatise in the Society of Knowledge. New York: Doubleday, 1966.

BION, W.R. Experiences in groups. New York: Basic Books, 1959.

BION, W.R. Elements of Psycho-Analysis. New York: Basic Books, 1963.

DEVEREUX, G. Charismatic leadership and crisis. Psychoanalysis and the Social Sciences, 4, 1955, 145-157.

DEVEREUX, G. Basic Problems of Ethnopsychiatry. B.M. Gulati & G. Devereux (Trans.). Chicago: The University of Chicago Press, 1980.

DE VOS, G. Toward a cross-cultural psychology of caste behavior. In: G. De Vos & H. Wagatsuma (Eds.), Japan's Invisible Race. Berkeley and Los Angeles: University of California Press, 1966, 377ff.

DIAMOND, M.A. Bureaucracy as externalized self-system: A view from the psychological interior. Administration Society, 16(2), 1984, 195-214.

DIAMOND, M.A. Organizational identity: A psychoanalytic exploration of organizational meaning. Administration Society, 20(2), 1988, 166-190.

DIAMOND, M.A., & ALLCORN, S. Role formation as defensive activity in bureaucratic organizations. Political Psychology, 7(4), 1986, 709-732.

DIAMOND, M.A., & ALLCORN, S. (1987). The psychodynamics of regression in work groups. Human Relations, 40(8), 1987, 525-543.

ERIKSON, K.T. Loss of communality at Buffalo Creek. American Journal of Psychiatry, 133(3), 1976, 302-305.

FREUD, S. Mourning and melancholia. In: J. Strachey (Trans.). The Standard Edition of the Complete Psychological Works of Sigmund Freud, Vol.14, 1917. London: Hogarth Press, 1957, 239-250.

FREUD, S. Group Psychology and the Analysis of the Ego, J. Strachey. (Trans.), 1921. New York: Norton, 1959.

FRY, A. How a People Die. Toronto: Doubleday, 1970.

GAP. Us and them: The Psychology of Ethnonationalism. Report 123 of the Committee on International Relations, Group for the Advancement of Psychiatry (co-authored by H.F. Stein). New York: Brunner/Mazel, 1987.

GRIECO, M.S. Birth-marked? A critical view on analyzing organizational culture. Human Organization, 47(1), 1988, 84-87.

HENRY, J. Culture Against Man. New York: Random House, 1963.

JAQUES, E. Social systems as a defence against persecutory and depressive anxiety. In: M. Klein, P. Heimann, R. Money-Kyrle (Eds.), New Directions in Psycho-Analysis: The Significance of Infant Conflict in the Pattern of Adult Behavior. New York: Basic Books, 1955, 478-498.

JILEK, W.G. Salish Indian Mental Health and Culture Change. Toronto: Holt, Rinehart & Winston, 1974.

JILEK-AALL, L. Review of A.M. Shkilnyk's A Poison Stronger Than Love: The Destruction of an Ojibwa Community. Transcultural Psychiatric Research Review, 23, 1986, 241-244.

KETS DE VRIES, M.F.R. The Irrational Executive: Psychoanalytic Studies in Management. New York: International Universities Press, 1984.

KLEIN, M. Notes on some schizoid mechanisms. International Journal of Psycho-Analysis, 27, 1946, 99-110.

KLEIN, M. On identification. In M. Klein, P. Heimann, & R. Money-Kyrle (Eds.), New Directions in Psychoanalysis. New York: Basic Books, 1955, 309-345.

KOHUT, H. Thoughts on narcissism and narcissistic rage. The Psychoanalytic Study of the Child, Vol. 27. New York: Quadrangle/The New York Times Press, 1972, 360-400.

KORMOS, H.R. The industrialization of medicine. In J.L. Ruffini (Ed.), Advances in Medical Social Science, Vol. 2. New York: Gordon and Breach Science Publishers, 1984, 323-339.

LA BARRE, W. Materials for a history of studies of crisis cults: A bibliographic essay. Current Anthropology, 12(1), 1971, 3-44.

LA BARRE, W. The Ghost Dance: The Origins of Religion. New York: Dell, 1972.

MELTZER, D. The Psycho-Analytical Process. London: Heineman Medical Books, 1967.

MITSCHERLICH, A., & MITSCHERLICH, M. The Inability to Mourn: Principles of Collective Behavior. New York: Grove Press, 1975.

OWEN, H. Griefwork in organizations. The Foresight Journal, 1(1), 1986, 1-13.

OWEN, H. Spirit: Transformation and Development in Organizations. Potomac, Maryland: Abbott Publishing, 1987.

PARIN, P. The ego and the mechanism of adaptation. In: L.B. Boyer, & S. Grolnick (Eds.), The Psychoanalytic Study of Society, Vol. 12. Hillsdale, New Jersey: The Analytic Press, 1987, 97-130.

POLLOCK, G.H. Mourning and adaptation. Internal Journal of Psychoanalysis, 42, 1961, 341-461.

RHODES, L.A. The anthropologist as institutional analyst. Ethos, 14(2), 1986, 204-217.

SHAPIRO, W. Thanatophobic man. Anthropology Today, 5(2), 1989, 11-14.

SHKILNYK, A.M. A Poison Stronger Than Love: The Destruction of an Ojibwa Community. New Haven: Yale University Press, 1985.

STEIN, H.F. An Ethno-Historic Study of Slovak-American Identity. New York: Arno Press/New York Times Press, 1980.

STEIN, H.F. "Health" and "wellness" as euphemism: The cultural context of insidious draconian health policy. Continuing Education for the Family Physician, 16(3), 1982a, 33-44.

STEIN, H.F. Neo-Darwinism and survival through fitness. The Journal of Psychohistory, 10(2), 1982b, 163-187.

STEIN, H.F. Wellness as illusion. Delaware Medical Journal, 54(11), 1982c, 637-641.

STEIN, H.F. The scope of psycho-geography: The psychoanalytic study of spatial representation. The Journal of Psychoanalytic Anthropology, 7(1), 1984, 23-73.

STEIN, H.F. Culture change, symbolic object loss, and restitutional process. Psychoanalysis and Contemporary Thought, 8(3), 1985a, 301-332.

STEIN, H.F. The Psychoanthropology of American Culture. New York: The Psychohistory Press, 1985b.

STEIN, H.F. The Psychodynamics of Medical Practice: Unconscious Factors in Patient Care. Berkeley, Los Angeles, CA: University of California Press, 1985c.

STEIN, H.F. Social role and unconscious complementarity. The Journal of Psychoanalytic Anthropology, 9(3), 1986a, 235-268.

STEIN, H.F. Unconscious factors in organizational decision-making: A case study from medicine. Organization Development Journal, 4(2), 1986b, 21-24.

STEIN, H.F. Developmental Time, Cultural Space: Studies in Psychogeography. Norman, OK: University of Oklahoma Press, 1987a.

STEIN, H.F. Encompassing systems: Implications for citizen diplomacy. Journal of Humanistic Psychology, 27(3), 1987b, 364-384.

STEIN, H.F. Aggression, grief-work, and organizational development: Theory and case example. Organization Development Journal, 6(1), 1988, 22-28.

STEIN, H.F., & APPREY, M. Context and Dynamics in Clinical Knowledge, Vol. 1 of the Monograph Series in Ethnicity, Medicine, and Psychoanalysis. Charlottesville, VA: University Press of Virginia, 1985.

STEIN, H.F., & HILL, R.F. Adaptive modalities among Slovak- and Polish-Americans: Some issues in cultural continuity and change. Anthropology, 3(1-2), 1979, 95-107.

STEIN, H.F., & HILL, R.F. The dogma of technology. In: L.B. Boyer, & S. Grolnick (Eds.), The Psychoanalytic Study of Society, Vol. 13. Hillsdale, New Jersey: The Analytic Press, 1988, 149-179.

STEIN, H.F., & NIEDERLAND W.G. (Eds.) Maps from the Mind: Readings in Psychogeography. Norman, OK: The University of Oklahoma Press, 1989.

VOLKAN, V.D. Cyprus - War and adaptation. Charlottesville: University Press of Virginia, 1979.

VOLKAN, V.D. Narcissistic personality organization and "reparative" leadership. The International Journal of Group Psychotherapy, 30(2), 1980, 131-152.

VOLKAN, V.D. Linking Objects and Linking Phenomena: A Study of the Forms, Symptoms, Metapsychology, and Therapy of Complicated Mourning. New York: International Universities Press, 1981.

VOLKAN, V.D., & ITZKOWITZ, N. The Immortal Atatürk: A Psychobiography. Chicago: University of Chicago Press, 1984.

YALOM, I. The Theory and Practice of Group Psychotherapy. New York: Basic Books, 1970.

ZINNER, J., & SHAPIRO, R. Projective identification as a mode of perception and behavior in families of adolescents. International Journal of Psychoanalysis, 53, 1972, 523-530.

Power and Politics in Organizations: Pragmatics and Pathologies*

Abraham Zaleznik

I must confess to a certain trepidation as I undertake the presentation of this paper. The cause of my unease is the title of this symposium, although I am prepared to entertain the possibility that I am reading ominous interpretations into the title not in the minds of the organizers of this symposium.

The word "empowerment" juxtaposed with "the abuses of power" suggests certain interests in ideology that however well intentioned, serve to obfuscate the subject of power if not to orient our thinking toward the belief that power is bad and that if one has it, whatever the "it" is, one should redistribute power to those who have less. It is as though the evil effects of power reside in its hierarchical form. Some have more and some have less. This pyramid creates the evil conditions of power and in remedying the inequalities of power, we will have gone a long way towards removing its noxious features.

Of course, there are abuses of power. As we approach the end of the twentieth century, we devoutly hope that mankind has learned some enduring lessons about violence, scapegoating, hatred, and sadism, which manifest themselves in their individual and collective forms as abuses of power. More specifically, these abuses become apparent when a dictator succeeds in gathering all the workable power in his hands.

An audience such as this needs no reminder that power in the hands of sick individuals produces human suffering. But it is seldom raw power that produces the tyranny. It is power as it is rationalized, couched in ideologies, and institutionalized that ultimately produces affliction. Hannah Arendt understood clearly the effects of institutionalization coupled with ideology when she coined the term "the banality of evil"[1] to describe how ordinary people, who undoubtedly would have been certified as sane and possibly even free of significant neurotic tendencies, embraced organized hatred and murder and applied the rational principles of efficient management to carry out the aims of Naziism in its program of genocide to destroy the Jews of Europe and Judaism as a religion. Indeed, I am convinced that political activism along with the internalization of an ideology are

---

[1] ARENDT Hannah. A Report on the Banality of Evil: Eichmann in Jerusalem. New York, NY: Penguin Books, 1977.

sure fire cures for depression and many other symptoms of psychological disturbançes. The mechanism for the cure lies in the individual acquiring self esteem through membership and the gains of institutional narcissism, a theme I want to return to later in this paper.

If you believe that the banality of evil resides purely in the content of an ideology, I would urge you to examine this belief with care. Some would argue that the form by which the individual attaches himself to an ideology is the root of the problem of why power goes awry. In a book that deserves a wider reading than it has received, Robert Waelder states that "power is necessary not because men are evil or lacking in love, but because they differ in their thinking; the struggle between conflicting altruisms has often been fiercer than that between conflicting egoisms".[2]

Opposed to ideology as an organizing principle in thought and action is pragmatism. In this connection, I commend to your attention the careful reading of the British philosopher and historian, Isaiah Berlin, who in tracing his own intellectual development discovered the ways of the pragmatist. Deeply suspicious of ideologies, Berlin weighed in for the partial solutions to human problems rather than the encompassing solutions incorporated in utopias, the counterpart of ideology. In quoting the philosopher Emmanuel Kant, who stated, "No straight thing was ever built from the crooked timber of humanity",[3] Berlin instructs us not to expect perfection either in institutions or in individuals as they go about conducting the transactions of everyday life. Berlin unabashedly describes the enormous impact on his intellectual development of the writings of Macchiavelli, who in "The Prince", explicates situational thinking as the cornerstone of pragmatics. Careful observation and the unwillingness to allow the best to interfere with the good solution is the hallmark of Macchiavelli's thought, which subtly uses advice to powerholders as a conduit for description, how the world is and not necessarily how it should be.

The British historian, Lord Acton, poses a challenge for this symposium, as with all inquiries into power, whether done under the umbrella of political theory, sociology, psychology, or psychoanalysis. Acton's axiom of power, and I am certain you are familiar with it, states that "power tends to corrupt; absolute power corrupts absolutely". This axiom leaves open for question the sources

---

2 WAELDER, Robert. Progress and Revolution, A Study of the Issues of Our Age. New York, NY: International Universities Press, 1967, p. 139.

3 BERLIN, Isaiah. The Crooked Timber of Humanity: Chapters in the History of Ideas. New York, NY: Alfred Knopf, Inc.,1990.

of the corrupting influences of power. Is it inherent in individual psychology, postulating a class of appetites which, unlike sex, thirst, and hunger, have no satiation level? If this be true, then we would be up against the problem of explaining why for some powerholders there is no corruption. Any of us can cite numerous examples of powerholders who far from acting as though they cannot get enough power feel little concern about how much power they have and considerable concern for using wisely the power they do have. We can easily name leaders who upon acquiring power retain their good sense, their understanding of the human condition, and their compassion for the plight of mankind. The example that immediately comes to my mind is President Harry S. Truman.

The world expected little from this man from Missouri when he was thrust into office upon the death of the charismatic President Franklin Delano Roosevelt. But the world received a great deal from this self-effacing individual. The litany of accomplishments is long, including the Marshall Plan for the postwar reconstruction of Europe, and the foundations of policy that helped bring about the dissolution of the Soviet Union, and the introduction of democracy and free markets to the Republics called the Commonwealth of Independent States.

The closest one can come to observing corruption of power during Truman's administration seems connected to his loyalty to his cronies. He loved to play poker with his friends and readily excused their modest transgressions. Compared to Watergate and the Iran-Contra scandals, President Truman's infractions, such as they were, and I cannot remember what they were, make him look like a Boy Scout. And to emphasize that he retained his humanity despite the awesomeness of the power he wielded as President of the United States, recall his blast at the music critic who panned his daughter Margaret's concert singing. I understand that she abandoned this career to become an accomplished writer and novelist, specializing, I believe, in mystery stories. These reflections on President Truman and his uses of power take into account the fact that he authorized the atomic bombing of Hiroshima and Nagasaki as a means of bringing the Pacific war to a close without a bloody invasion of the Japanese Islands.

For those intrigued with the pragmatics of power and power relations in formal organizations, the issues appear infinitely complex and least capable of solution by resort to some ideology. From my experience in business organizations, it seems abundantly clear that attempts to empower workers in the name of one ideology or another, and attempts to democratize the workplace, to flatten if not to eliminate hierarchy in order to reduce the differentials of power between the top and the bottom of the pyramid, all have failed. These experiments fell by the wayside, including the recent innovation at Volvo, the Swedish automaker, to place controls of work in the hands of the workers and away from the specialists in industrial engineering and from factory supervisors.

The reason these experiments are abandoned is because they do not address the realities of productivity. From the standpoint of the workers' contribution to productivity, the major variables are technological. If powerholders do their job properly, such as accentuating capital investment in plant and equipment, they will present a rational face to the realities of meeting competition. When ideology is the substitute for attention to the logics of the marketplace and the factory, those with relatively little power soon recognize that magical thinking has overtaken rationality. Process dominates substance and organizational stasis sets in. In the end, all members of an organization should be able to rely on the capacities of powerholders to make the right choices in solving the substantive problems that affect the survival of the organization. If we need a case study to test the validity of these ideas, the automobile industry provides a marvelous example, along with many other corporations in the electronics, machine tool, steel, and transportation industries. These industries lost market share, which in human terms means the loss of jobs, primarily to the Japanese, but also to other Asian nations such as Korea and to European corporations. It is a long and complicated story to relate why this devastating deindustrialization of America occurred, but suffice it to say that a large portion of the responsibility falls upon the shoulders of the corporate and union executives in power during this period of demise.

The basic inequality in organization, ultimately leading to real inequities resulting from the distribution of power, is the lack of proportionality between power and the consequences that follow the uses of power. Leo Tolstoy reflected elegantly on this disproportion in his afterword to "War and Peace". Society consist of the few and the many. According to Tolstoy, the few operate on the delusion that their decisions make history, while the many suffer the real consequences of the directives leaders issue. One wishes it were possible to cure this problem, but there is no way I know of to redress this inequity except to hold leaders to a higher standard of competence than we have been willing to uphold. It is nothing short of ludicrous to expect that the cure lies in a massive redistribution of power so that the many control the policies that the few could initiate. The impact of making the right substantive decisions should be in direct proportion to the power an individual holds in an organization. This proportionality, along with accountability, represents the primacy of reality over fantasy that is essential to the prosperity of an organization and its constituents. Please remember as we discuss the esoterics of power and empowerment that we are talking about people making their living, carrying out their responsibilities as adults, caring for their children, and somehow retaining their dignity and self esteem in a world, despite its apparent abundance, is harsh and demanding, especially in judging our ability to confront reality.

In case you are wondering when I intend to consider specifically the psychoanalytic study of power in organizations, you may breathe a sigh of relief. The concept of reality reminds us of Freud's two principles of mental function. The first he called the pleasure principle and the second the reality principle. Among his applications of these two principles of mental function, he traced the fate of both in human development, which is a transition from utter dependency to its reversal: the capability attributed to the ego that makes an adult a fit person upon whom others can depend.

David Rappaport traced the changing conceptions of reality in psychoanalytic theory. Beginning with defense and proceeding to adaptation, reality as objectively conceived and subjectively structured, plays an essential part in the individual's self esteem and self respect.[4] Although hints abound in the literature of a larger perspective, conceptions of reality are microscopic, focusing as they do on objects and the family. The conceptions of reality that are central to questions of power require a close examination of markets and of large scale organizations, the institutional side of reality. In my view, enlarging our focus does not entail major revisions in psychoanalytic theory, simply because the dynamism of institutions, so far as it influences individuals, lies in the well known capacities for identification, internalization, and idealization. Initially viewed as defenses, these ego capacities become significant in the ways of adaptation in which the mutual influence of individual and organization proceeds. In structural terms, this mutual influence is extremely important in reinforcing certain tendencies in superego formation, and preempts certain psychic processes in narcissism and self esteem. And, it is through these processes that power transactions occur.

Before inquiring further into the nature of reality as it bears on the problem of power, it is important for us to recognize that psychoanalytic theory has resisted the temptation to posit independent

---

4 RAPAPORT, David. The Structure of Psychoanalytic Theory. Psycho-logical Issues, Vol II, No. 2. New York, NY: International Universities Press, 1960, pp. 57-61.

motives such as one finds in academic psychology. While there are many practical reasons for delineating a plethora of motives, psychoanalysis would have lost its ability to deal with pathology in individuals as well as groups from dynamic, developmental, economic, and structural points of view had it focused on single motives. But this aspect of power in psychoanalytic theory had best be left for another symposium.

Because of its concerns with how and why people fall ill, psychoanalysis of necessity has had to limit its inquiry into reality. From my perspective, the study of power requires an expanded perspective on reality, which I shall outline briefly. The place to begin is with economic theory, and here I am not referring to the economics of drives and drive derivatives. I have no intention of conducting a minicourse in economic theory (not that I am necessarily your best source on this subject) but I do need to point out that in its concerns with value, economic theory stares reality in the face in its discourses on markets.

Markets are impersonal, which makes them at once interesting phenomena because alongside the inexorable quality of market forces, there appears ample room for the play of fantasy in the service of individual ego and the collectives we call corporations. The purest example of an impersonal market is in commodities such as wheat. Within fairly narrow limits, one farmer's wheat is just like another's and neither seller nor buyer exist as subject or object. Whatever transactions occur depend not at all on what we consider a relationship. Prices result from the interplay of supply and demand. The seller has no human concerns for the buyer, just as the buyer could care less about the well being of the seller.

This view of the impersonal market, in which individuals have little, if any, power is the classical position in economic theory. One of the major transitions in history is the alteration of consciousness that derived from modernization. Very bright and energetic people acted on the realization that it may be possible to influence markets to great advantage over one's competitors. Within the narrow limits I referred to earlier, the farmer's wheat is undifferentiatable. But as one moves along the path toward the consumer, it may be possible to differentiate products, and to influence the consumer into an awareness that products are not all alike. Thus, a consumer will enter a supermarket, itself a remarkable product of applying the reality principle to everyday life, and look for King Arthur flour, having the conviction that paying a few pennies more will be rewarded with a superior product. Indeed, it has become every commodity producer's dream to invent a differentiated product, one that will generate consumer interest, loyalty, the intent to buy that, and only that product. Many try, but few succeed, which reflects the stubbornness of market phenomena.

I am sure all of you have seen the advertisements of Frank Perdue as he tells you earnestly that "it takes a tough man to make a tender chicken". Who would ever dream that it would be possible to differentiate in the minds of consumers one chicken from another? Evidently, Frank Perdue did dream such a dream and owes his success not only to his product, but also to his marketing techniques not the least of which is his ability to look like a chicken as he appears on television spots. I often wonder if he got the idea for his ads from the hilarious and touching film "Bread and Chocolate".

Modern conceptions of marketing carry the idea of influencing the market beyond the simple conception of product differentiation. Whoever the gifted marketers are, they become keen students of the pleasure principle, the interplay of fantasy and reality, as they discover that they have it within their power to amplify the pleasure principle by influencing people to act like consumers. Thus, a walk through a supermarket, a discount department store such as Walmart's, an electronics store such as Circuit City will soon convince us that the pleasure principle finds its end points in many locations and in many of the daily actions of ordinary people. These actions are called "shopping", which finds it ultimate expression in the slogan, "shop until you drop" .

Now one might well argue that the "marketing orientation", to use Eric Fromm's characterization, is evil, reflecting greed, false values, deceptiveness, and a cultural condition inferior to the "production orientation". One might also attribute to it the burgeoning consumer debt, with its ominous implications of a nation whistling its way along the path to bankruptcy. Comparisons of Japan and the United States seldom fail to point out that the Japanese people save about 20% of personal income while the American people save about 2%, casting serious questions on our ability to create capital to sustain a much needed rate of investment in plant and equipment. While reflecting on the so-called evils of consumerism, imagine you are telling the citizens of Russia, the Ukraine, and the other Republics in the newly formed Commonwealth of Independent States, of the dangers that lie ahead as they seek to raise their standard of living. I guarantee that your message will fall on deaf ears, and should these citizens hear you, they will be tempted to respond with a punch in the nose, particularly if you ply them with this version of the truth while they stand on long lines in the bitter cold waiting to buy pitifully scarce rations of bread and meat.

In tracing the course of this change in consciousness, in which the posture toward markets changed from passive to active, we can find a plethora of examples in the development of the modern corporation where the uses of power were directly linked to the acting out of neurotic conflict on the part of dominant power figures. And we owe much in our understanding of this linkage to the pioneer political scientist, Harold Lasswell, who following his studies in psychoanalysis, presented his findings in his 1930 book entitled "Psychopathology and Politics".[5]

Lasswell introduced the idea that private conflicts can be displaced on to public issues. While he was concerned directly with government officials and politicians, his hypothesis on displacement goes a long way in explaining the behavior of great business leaders, usually men of great vision, if not of single-minded purpose, who out of unconscious conflict were driven to transform the world. Tracing this conflict leads us into the desperate need to rewrite personal history, to right the wrongs of real or imagined deprivations, to restore a past that may never have existed, and to seek restitution for perceived personal injuries in fateful attachment to parents.

The study of such great men and women, while familiar to us from our observations behind the couch, never ceases to amaze in the quality of the narratives that led these gifted individuals into history. In the business world, the names of Henry Ford, Frederick Winslow Taylor, Andrew Carnegie, Alfred Sloan loom large while in more recent times the names of Thomas Watson, father and son, as well as Sam Walton, Edwin Land, William Gates, and a myriad of other leaders, remain imprinted on the American and world economies. In each case, the story to be told is not too far from the plots laid out in Harold Lasswell's fruitful hypothesis.

One of the intriguing aspects of these narratives is the unwillingness of these gifted and troubled men to relinquish the past even as they transformed the present and prepared a future that so deeply affected the modern consciousness that few would have believed possible in their lifetime. This unwillingness, or failure of insight, led in so many cases to the familiar patterns of grandiosity, megalomania, and manic activity as a defense against depression, causing in so many cases near ruin of the great works they had wrought. I do not know if the legendary financier, André Meyer, of the investment banking firm Lazard Freres had these case studies in mind when he replied to the question, "What is finance", with the retort "5% arithmetic and 95%

[5] LASSWELL, Harold. Psychopathology and Politics. New York, NY: The Viking Press, 1960.

psychoanalysis". But surely he was reflecting on the peculiar interplay of fantasy and reality as it affects business decisions on both personal and corporate levels.

As a footnote to this tribute to Harold Lasswell in his explication of the connection between psychopathology and politics, he took an interesting turn in his approach to power. As with Lord Acton, Lasswell became suspicious, (obsessed may be too strong a word) about the inherent threats of power in the hands of individuals. So he stopped examining the psychology of powerholders and turned his attention to the normative question, "How should society go about taming power". As a result, he could not go beyond Alfred Adler's simple formulation on power as a compensatory motive to explore, for example, the deeper issues of the forms and vicissitudes of psychopathology in institutional and corporate relations. As is almost predictable, the turn away from observation and understanding to the preoccupation with normative issues led to flirtation with ideology and institutional controls to overcome what for him became the almost inevitable abuses of power. In short, powerholders are not to be trusted, a doctrine while finding much support in history fails in its grasp of the nature of power, of politics in organizations, and of more importance to this audience, of the nuances of pathology in organizations.

While for me it is still an open question as to why changes occur in the types of illnesses patients present in our offices, I am somewhat more confident in the knowledge that significant changes have occurred in the types of pathologies displayed in corporations. To me the issue of the displacement of private conflict on to public issues must take a back seat to a phenomenon what despite the hints in Freud and the later literature on adaptation, narcissism, and the superego, is the current challenge to our understanding of power and politics in the commonalities of corporate life.

As I suggested at the start of my paper, individuals who would be certified as normal and even free of serious neurotic disturbances, in their institutional relations act in ways to assure the maladaptiveness of the organizations they represent. Indeed, as I shall try to show in the time remaining to me, the conditions of their continued normality lie in the perpetuation of the sources of their self esteem.

There are narcissistic gains in the attachment of individual to organization that go beyond the conventional rewards of money and power. These gains include identity, the amplification of ego interests, and a degree of self esteem that wraps the individual in a protective cocoon nowhere adequately comprehended in the concept of defense.

To defend against unconscious conflict safeguards self esteem. But the ravages of unconscious conflict must be placed alongside the vulnerability to narcissistic injuries to which individuals are at risk in the marketplace of organizational politics. For alongside the external markets to which economists have long displayed their interest, a market exists inside organizations dealing in the currency of power and ultimately the currency of self esteem. This market defines who is and is not a player, someone to be acknowledged on the fast track, upwardly mobile and willing to engage in the transactions that we come to recognize as organizational politics. These transactions can be as simple as being able to handle oneself in the interminable number of meetings in which the players play. Imagine yourself going into a meeting to discuss an important problem such as how to develop the product line in order to protect and enhance market share. Suppose you do not understand the local mores and begin to commit gaffes such as sitting in the "wrong" place, not knowing when it is your turn to speak, and more subtly, not knowing the forms for showing aggression, or the proper method of responding to aggression. This knowledge, which is partially hidden in the culture, is often called "local" knowledge and if you are interested in pursuing the nature of this knowledge, I have no better suggestion than to read in the works of Erving Goffman, a social psychologist who took an interest in the microcosmic side of community and organizational life. His first book is called "The Presentation of Self in Everyday Life".[6] We would have little difficulty in imagining how he derived his title. The important point I want to make is that despite Goffman's far removed interest in the dynamic unconscious, the examination of forms and methods of communication in everyday life instructs us as psychoanalysts on the varied and layered mental images that support the individual's narcissistic attachment to organizations.

These forms and methods of daily communication, both verbal and nonverbal, belong to the range of questions Heinz Hartmann raises in his broadening of ego psychology.[7] The term power does not appear in the index to "Ego Psychology and the Problem of Adaptation". Neither do the terms mastery and actualization. Action does appear prominently in the discussion of the ego, along with will, which according to Hartmann is regulated to a considerable degree by the external world.[8] The coda, or decision rules, which once learned regulate social behavior, are largely preconscious automatisms.

---

[6] GOFFMAN, Erving. The Presentation of Self in Everyday Life. Garden City, NY: Doubleday (Anchor Books), 1959.

[7] HARTMANN, Heinz. Ego Psychology and the Problem of Adaption. New York, NY: International Universities Press, 1958.

[8] Ibid, p. 74.

Hartmann quotes Freud's comments in "Wit and Its Relation to the Unconscious" that these preconscious automatisms require little psychic energy to sustain them.[9] Rather than simply accepting this comment, it is worth investigating the degree of mental energy absorbed in utilizing these automatisms.

Membership in institutions, whether in the form of corporations or the aggregations known as professions, seem to require skillful use of these automatisms in the flow of activity. As I said earlier, the failure to learn the coda and to incorporate the requisite behavior as part of the preconscious automatisms will limit if not destroy an individual's career. So, it is little wonder that in preparation for the professions attention is given to learning and incorporating what will become automatisms. In business they are called social skills.

Whatever their neuroses individuals seem remarkably swift in learning social skills as the route to adaptation to organizations. But in the process of adaptation, these same individuals become less fit for exercising leadership, if you care to define leadership as the mobilization and use of power to maximize the achievement of purposes. They may mobilize power, but fall short in defining the best uses of this power. In other words there are two standards against which to judge adaptation. The first is the standard established within the internal market place of the organization. The second standard is the market place of "the real world", indeed the only market place that counts over the long run. Pick up your daily newspaper and you will not fail to read of once great institutions enduring wrenching changes in attempts to make up for the time lost while those who "belonged" enjoyed the narcissistic advantage of their membership. As I said earlier, the economics of the real market place are relentless in their evaluations, taking into consideration the time it takes for reality to catch up with the inner fantasies associated with narcissistic advantage. I will not bore you with the list of great corporations, such as General Motors and IBM, undergoing vast internal changes as a result of their delayed reactions to economic threats. But one anecdote will make the point. An economist friend of my vintage told me that his grandfather had advised him to save his money and invest in the Pennsylvania Railroad and United States Steel Corporation with the assurance that, if he followed his grandfather's advice, he would have no economic worries as an adult. Fortunately, my economist friend maintained his affection for his grandfather, while ignoring the well intentioned advice.

---

9 Ibid, p. 89.

Allow me to step back for a moment to recall an interesting experience I had at 15 Commonwealth Avenue a number of years ago. I heard a paper entitled, "The Normal Personality in Our Culture and the Nobel Prize Complex".[10] The late Dr. Helen Tartakoff presented this paper as the culmination of considerable observation of young and gifted patients. I presented one such patient to Dr. Tartakoff, who took over the supervision of my first control case upon the death of Dr. Joseph J. Michaels. In addition, similar cases appeared in our Group Control and Clinical Seminars, so that the theme of the so-called normal personality was very much in the forefront, especially in the light of heightened interest in narcissism and the disorders that accompany grandiose self images.

The "normal personality of our culture" Dr. Tartakoff describes in her paper, are especially gifted individuals, frequently in the sciences (hence the attention to the wish to win a Nobel Prize), but also well represented in the professions. These ambitious individuals present themselves for treatment sometimes because their careers are foundering, but also because their love life fails. Standing alongside their ambition to win a Nobel Prize these patients sustain an idealized image of falling in love. For the male, this idealized image is easily representable. She is young, has a slim body, long blonde hair, and, is breathtakingly beautiful. Unlike many idealized images, this one seems to exist in the real world. Our patients are adept at finding her, charming her, and falling in love to begin a tempestuous and ultimately failed relationship. On the side of work and career, as you can imagine, it is no small achievement to win a prize, let alone a Nobel, which rather than being the real goal stands metaphorically for singular achievement. The net effect of this overpowering ambition is depression, a sense of emptiness, and fits of rage. I remember one of my patients, a very talented business man, who periodically raced his car on city streets. When the police stopped him, he became enraged at the policeman, falling only slightly short of physical violence. The fact that he did not end up in jail testifies to his gifts of adaptation: he was adept at getting out of the trouble he got himself into in the first place.

Underlying this description of the normal personality (that is, the personality whose mental equilibrium depends upon adapting to his environment) is a remarkably consistent personal history. It appears as though these young patients had entered into a compact

---

[10] TARTAKOFF, Helen. The Normal Personality in Our Culture and the Nobel Prize Complex. In R. M. Lowenstein, L. M. Newman, M. Schur, et al, eds., Psychoanalysis: A General Psychology, Essays in Honor of Heinz Hartmann. New York, NY: International Universities Press, 1966.

(unconscious, of course) with a parent, usually their mother in which great achievement, and nothing less, awaits them as a promise and a personal commitment. Nothing less than a Nobel Prize, either actually or metaphorically, will satisfy just as the search for the perfect lover focuses their object relationships. Naturally, the repressed rage at this figure who is at the other end of this compact, along with the difficulties reality presents in realizing their ambitions, and the disappointments in their choice of love objects, leads them to emptiness, depletion of the ego, finally propelling them after many set backs to seek treatment in psychoanalysis. I suppose that another way of describing these patients is to use the language of power, but I do not think such language will add much to our deliberations.

The plight of these gifted patients arises mainly from the depletion of their ego rather than excessive narcissism.[11] Evidence of grandiosity appears when the external world meets their expectations in job advancement and on those occasions when they find their ideal love object. Their so-called normality exists in an intense search in the external world for matchups with inner imagos, whether in work or in love, presenting some remarkably keen issues to challenge psychoanalytic theories of adaptation.

These individuals, who are chameleon-like in their ability to adapt, learn to become players in their professions and the organizations they enter. They are skillful in process and woefully weak in substance. Insofar as organizations cannot distinguish between process and substance, these individuals succeed, wend their way to the top of the hierarchy, and now sooner rather than later become identified with failed adaptation of the organization.

Bert Lance, the shrewd Georgia politician who served President Jimmy Carter as budget director and trusted aide, became famous for his statement about the pragmatics of organizational and governmental politics. He said, "When it ain't broke, don't fix it. The lessons of economics lead to a very different pragmatic. "When it ain't broke is the only time you can fix it." The individuals who can understand this reversal of Bert Lance's dictum have achieved autonomy of the ego from the organizations and professions in which they use their talents and acquire power. This autonomy of the ego is best expressed as being in, but never of, the institution.

---

11 FREUD, Sigmund. On Narcissism: An Introduction. The Standard Edition, Vol II. London, UK: The Hogarth Press, 1914, pp. 98-101.

NOTES

* Presented at the symposium on "Power: Empowerment and Abuse in Clinical Practice and Everyday Life" sponsored by the Boston Psychoanalytic Society and Institute, Inc. and held at MIT, Cambridge, MA, March 14 and 15, 1992.

The Roots of Applied Psychoanalysis to Management

Monika List

1. Introduction

Though there is today an enormous amount of literature concerning research work based on psychoanalytic knowledge in combination with management, I am afraid one might forget from where this interesting movement of psychoanalytic approach started. In the fifties some professors and their assistants founded a small group of common interest. It was Professor Abraham Zaleznik who from the very beginning on was one of the leading personalities who attributed important and interesting impulses. Later on he was one of the founders of "The International Society for the Psychoanalytic Study of Organizations". (1) "Human Dilemmas of Leadership" is the book, which introduced this totally new scientific development concerning leadership and organization. This important contribution of Zaleznik includes the very first ideas concerning the problem how to combine applied psychoanalysis and management discourse. (2) So he started the scientific discussion and his book was first of many publications to come.

Though there are many important publications of this concrete direction by other famous authors, this paper only wants to show that the intention of the above mentioned book is of enormous importance until today. (3) This article shows the essential intentions of the author, especially concerning authority and power in work relations and leadership and shall remember that they have proved as very valuable for the practical management. Zaleznik considered authority and power in organizations as central issue of his research work from the very beginning on. (4) This short comment can only be seen as a small part of Zaleznik's work, so it is left to the reader to convince himself that "Human Dilemmas of Leadership" is of actual importance when he is reading the book. (5)

2. Foundations

"Human Dilemmas of Leadership" appeared in a time, when the idea came up, that traditional theories and concepts were no more enough for the understanding of organizations and behavior of leaders. The consciousness was growing that fundamental psychological and behavioristic knowledges were necessary to understand interhuman communication in leadership and authority relations. Also it could no longer be denied that unconscious energies and motivations are playing an enormous role.

The author Abraham Zaleznik has proved with his work for the very first time that psychoanalytical thinking applied to management is not only possible but also of great advantage. When the book appeared Zaleznik already was a member at the faculty of the Harvard Graduate School of Business Administration for more than 12 years. His career was based on the research of human behavior in organizations. "Human Dilemmas of Leadership" sums up for the very first time his research work, his way of understanding problems and conflicts which might rise when individual responsibility in organizations is taken over.

Zaleznik (Zaleznik, 1975, p.25) is absolutely right to stress already at the beginning, that leading personnel is under the pressure of many expectations from internal management as well as from external groups of interests, such as the readiness for overtaking responsibility and risks and managing critical situations. These expectations include that leading personnel maintains its psychic and physic health and is able to control energy in a senseful way. Leaders need a steady readiness of activity, a positive narcissism and an ability of self control in order to maintain the position in leadership and management. This is why leaders have to be in the position to know their fears, doubts and insecurities in order to get along with them.

In this publication Zaleznik discusses not only problems of singular members of organizations at their place of work or in the framework of their career, he also deals with important questions of organization concerning aspects of power, authority, dependence or the choice of the correct leadership style. Using many examples he demonstrates possible conflict, which might come up when a career with much responsibility has started.

His theories and ways of thinking are proved by an enormous amount of clinical studies and research projects. He himself considers them not as a recipe for practical application but as his personal wish that the reader learns something about human behavior and his own unconscious wishes, tendencies and ways of behavior in order to know them and to change them. Zaleznik uses interviews with leaders, workers and officials in trade and industry to find something out about humanity in general and its experiences. His main point of interest is not only the organization with its common structure, it is more and more the individual with his wishes, tensions and conflicts. Main parts of the book result from research which Zaleznik did together with the research department of the Harvard Business School.

His conclusions are drawn from a psychological basis. I believe that his special merit can be seen in the application of theoretical and clinical concepts using psychoanalysis regarding to his research material. Professor Zaleznik absolved the Trainee Programm for non-medical applicants of the Boston Psychoanalytic Society and Institute and in the framework of his research work he was influenced by the psychoanalytical concept of Sigmund Freud. Psychoanalysis is a method which was founded and further on developed by Freud, first as a psychological theory and second as a method to cure neurotic disturbances. Freud's main issue was the reconstruction of traumatical events of his patients from the unconscious to the conscious. So he could gain a real inside into the psychic reasons of his patients' illness. He got to know that suppressed material can be found in symptoms such as Freudian mistakes, dreams, fears and nervous disturbances. (6) A psychoanalytic cure means that suppressed material, mainly based on events in the childhood, is brought back to the conscious in order to solve it with the help of transference. (Strotzka, 1982, p.43)

But psychoanalysis is not only a method of healing it is also a possibility for the interested layman to understand fundamentally his behavior, motivations and energies in the different dimensions of his life as a human being. It is sure that styling and maintenance of relations concerning work and authority are also based upon the personal development and experiences of the individual. A traumatized childhood leads to a life full of neurotic conflicts and to a different management of critical situations. Due to the way of his disturbance the person concerned chooses neurotic behavior and mechanisms which can be derived from his proper character. Though inheritated dispositions cannot be totally denied, it is sure that positive and negative influences are determining the development of a person mainly in the childhood but also later on. These influences are forming the personal character and the behavior later on. Of course they will influence the interhuman relations with colleagues, superiors and co-workers and might possibly deteriorate the relationships in work. It is easy to understand, that when unconscious material becomes conscious, personal behavior can be changed when the basic conflicts are discussed. After this process relationships of leaders and workers can be improved.

Knowing oneself is only an ability of few people, but it is necessary to lead other people in an efficient way without forgetting their personal development. It is a very difficult task to watch oneself personally in an objective way and to understand the own behavior in interhuman relations in order to change it if necessary, because the human being loves to deny weakness and conflicts of the own self and to make the environment responsible for them (mechanism of projection; see Freud A., 1984, p.36). When the person is older, the neurotic disturbances become more and more complicated because the neurotic behavior is trained for a long time. In this case a total change of the personal structure becomes very difficult.

Zaleznik wants to reach mainly those people who are engaged with human problems of different kind in organizations, especially persons in leading positions. These persons are mostly psychoanalytically untrained. This is why Zaleznik tried to make his opinions understandable to the layman. He managed in an impressive way the transference of knowledge as well as the understanding for thinking, feeling and acticity of the working person.

3. Problematic Aspects in Authority Relationships

Each member working in an organization hierarchy has to be able to manage differences in status and power. Everybody has at least one superior, maybe he is even responsible towards more than one. He also works together with subordinate colleagues whom he has to lead concerning their abilities and for whom he has to overtake responsibility. Due to these reasons Zaleznik shows the consequences of authority relations as origins of stress and he shows as well how stress can threaten the steady fight for individualism. (Zaleznik, 1975, p. 47)

3.1. Independence versus dependence

The historic roots of this conflict can be found in the experience of early childhood in family life. First there is a dependence from mother and father, later on from brothers and sisters. During the personal development a more or less independent position can be built up by friends who are not part of the family and by overtaking constantly increasing responsibilities.

Nevertheless it would be an error to believe that the foundation of partnerships and friendships outside of the family means that the process from dependence to independence has totally finished. The wish to be in dependent warmth and passive relations is never forgotten. If these unconscious wishes are denied they might come back in a disguised form (such as in depressions or psychosomatic diseases). (7)

Superiors and their co-workers have to be able to manage their authority relations in a way that they find a balance between the wish of independence versus the wish of dependence. This is a difficult task. A maintenance (which might be unconscious) of extreme positions or a constant change of the two positions can be of great damage for the person concerned and for the working relation.

3.2. The problem of rivalry

A clear responsibility can mean enormous stress for people with a tendency towards dependence. It is difficult for them to start initiatives and if such initiatives are important for the organization, they are considered as extremely endangering. It is logic, that in the contrary people who like independence are threatened by situations in which they lose control and responsibility. These are circumstances which lead to fights for power and intensive feelings of hostility.

Difficulties may come up especially then, when the superior and his subordinate are living together as rivals concerning authority relations. Both of them are concentrated on their authorities and show definite tendencies to start a fight for independence. Rivals who are under pressure of such authority relations do often have ambivalent ideas concerning authorities. (Zaleznik, 1975, p.51) On the outside they are playing an active and independent role; in the unconscious fears can be found which are based on doubts about the own independence and the ability to manage working and family relations. These basic and unconscious needs are fought down in form of response (Reaktionsbildung). Freud was the one who found out the meaning of response as a basic defense mechanism in the psychic household. The term of response is to be understood as a mechanism in which the real feeling is denied and the contrary feeling comes out (for example love is expressed instead of hatred; see Brenner, 1989, p.85). These people are dominated by an extreme difference between conscious wishes which are shown in reality and unconscious fantasies.

The contrary shows similar problems: the superior as well as his subordinate are showing a denying behavior. This means that each of them makes the other one responsible and does not need authority for himself. If two personalities of such a passive-dependent type meet in an authority relation, the working relation will be extremely endangered - it might even become impossible.

We can derive that problems in authority relations are often based on the individual development in the past, and not on the framework of organizations.

3.3. Forms of inner conflicts

In his oevre Zaleznik mentions two different forms of conflicts which can be found very often in management: status anxiety and competition anxiety. (Zaleznik, 1975, p.70)

If somebody starts to achieve some success and recognition in his work, he has to take into consideration that the relationships between his colleagues and himself will start to change. Friendships of yesterday turn into suspect and distance; the good relationships between colleagues are cooling down. This situation may be the beginning for status anxiety because the new leader is torn down between the reponsibility of his authority and the strong need to be liked. Respect on the one hand and friendship on the other hand may lead to an ambivalent inner conflict. If the leader does not see the difference, severe difficulties may come up. Fears of this kind may lead to a denying behavior concerning adequate authority (giving up the own status) and a much too friendly policy in order to be loved further on. For sure these measures have to fail because the leader will lose his ability of being active (total loss of authority). Such a situation is followed by aggressions, feelings of helplessness and a loss of energy as well as on the side of the superior as on the side of the subordinate.

A leader will be at least enfenced in his activities when he is afraid of aggression and relations. He does not dare to make his point of view absolutely clear because he is afraid of aggressions and he still takes other interests into consideration. Aggressions are always part of activities and do not imply hostility. A manager has to be in the position - due to his self-security - not only to tolerate aggressions but also to be able to let them out. This is one of the fundamental hypotheses for a constructive working climate.

Another source for inner conflicts is competition anxiety. A manager who cannot bear competition in his surroundings will not be successful. There are two forms of competition anxiety: fear of failure and fear of success. (Zaleznik, 1975, p.71)

Zaleznik thinks that the fear of failure is based on the missing of self-respect and identity. This is manifestated already in the childhood and can lead to the impossibility of using talents and gifts. The unconscious feeling that each activity will fail in the final analysis leads to the fact that people with this specific fear do give up even before they have started.

The contrary of the fear of failure is the fear of success. This fear is combined with the knowledge that a position can only be reached by displacing a competitor. This may lead to a feeling of guilt and the need to change decisions of the past. If these conflicts are strong enough, they can cause fears which hinder the activity in work.

This unconscious conflict can be seen in the following ways of behavior. A person works hard in order to gain a target but if the target is near enough, he is acting against himself because the unconscious feelings of guilt are winning deciding influence.

Zaleznik shows by these examples the following: self-confidence of leaders is important; they have to know their own inner conflicts (in order to avoid the mechanism of projection); they have to learn how to handle them in order that activities and decisions are in true relation with reality and that they are not the product of inner tensions. It is absolutely necessary to have a healthy feeling of identity and to know the own position and at least to have an idea about futurous decisions in order to be able to reach a constant behavior towards the environment. The last demand is extremely important because the change of behavior towards co-workers and subordinates may lead to insecurity.

4. The Dynamics of Equality

Combined with the problem of rivalry are the worries of the superior concerning equal treatment of subordinates. Many managers treat their co-workers in the most equal way possible because they want to avoid rivalry between them. This argument is not always right because in many cases rivalry is necessary in order to maintain better individual performance and personal happiness between those subordinates who are gratified due to their specific activities. This so-called equality leads to equal treatment but not to a realistic judgement. It does not care for the individualism of a specific person and also not for different capacities - these are both aspects which are important for the continued existence of an enterprise in the long run.

Which are the reasons which cause in managers such an obviously non-understandable behavior? This was the subject of Zaleznik's studies (Zaleznik 1975, p.119) and his conclusion was that exaggerated worries concerning equal treatment very often are the mirror of the managers own personal conflicts. Due to Zaleznik the explanation of this behavior can be found in the rivalry between brothers and sisters in early childhood. After the birth and in the first months of life the child is the main point in the life-saving relation with the mother. This idea can be destroyed very suddenly and unconveniently by the birth of another child and can provoke hostile aggressive energies towards the parents and especially towards the new brother or sister. Again, these feelings produce fears to lose parental love and protection. Those children who cannot tolerate this conflict react with a variety of changes in their behavior. The defense mechanism of response changes feelings of hostility and rivalry into love and respect such as it is wanted by the parents. Response is used as adequate defense mechanism against fear and it is always an energy for the development of social behavior in the community. If this changing affect is too sudden and too strong, it is possible that the person concerned is dominated by restrictive behavior and becomes intolerant towards aggressions and differences in opinions. Many grown-ups maintain this psychic position. Extreme cases become more and more passive and put themselves back in the process of work as well as in interhuman relations.

A short example by Zaleznik shall help to better understanding. He is characterizing a top-manager who felt intensive fury and fear when he was critiziced by others. These tensions of feelings could never be lived out such as it would have been possible in an energic discussion with the critizicer. The above mentioned person became silent and passive when the slightest criticism came up and answered with positive reactions and feelings instead of his inner fury. The incapacity to deal with his inner fury and to work it out in a constructive way had the origin in his fear concerning his own aggressions and those from other sides. He tried to cope the problem in hiding his inner feelings and showed contrary feelings and behaviors in the following way: instead of fury he showed friendly interest, instead of criticism admission. The result was that the inner conflict could not be solved and extreme tensions were provoked in this person.

Leaders who are afraid of rivalry between subordinates do not dare at all to praise singular co-workers which is independent of the exceptional activities of these persons in their work. If managers maintain this principle of equality it may be derived that similar problems of rivalry had to be overcome in the relation between parents and brothers and sisters in the early childhood. These feelings still seem to work until today. If big organizations do not accept the worth of individualism there is the danger that an enormous amount of creativity, initiative and activity will be lost.

5. The Dynamics of Subordinacy

Not only leaders but also their subordinates often integrate inner unconscious conflicts into the ways of their work and relations towards their superiors. Unconscious fantasies and wishes which derive from former steps of development may lead to an unrealistic behavior towards reality and may influence relationships in work. Ambivalent emotions towards superiors, exaggerated passivity, doubts about the own self and hidden aggressions may be extremely disturbing.

Zaleznik (Zaleznik, 1975, p.79) tries in his work to understand and develop the fundamental dynamics of submission from the psychoanalytical point of view. In the framework of his studies he found four different schemes of behavior in which the subordinate is showing an either active or passive behavior and is vice versa dedicated by a more or less strong need to dominate others or to be dominated by others. Due to these two dimensions he distinguishes the following four constellations of behavior:

5.1. The impulsive (dominating-active) subordinate

This personality tries to dominate the relation towards authorities by active means while fighting against them. Abolishing authority is the unconscious aim which means the unconscious wish to submiss the father of former times. This type is specific for persons who are not able to maintain a position because of lacking self-control and prefer to change whenever the fight against the superior (vice versa the father) becomes unbearable even only in fantasy.

If the needs for activity and protest are understood in a constructive way, such a person can be of great value for the success of a manager because his drives are consisting now of senseful criticism concerning upcoming problems. The limits between constructive activity and destructive revolution are expressed by the measure of self-control.

5.2. The compulsive (dominating-passive) subordinate

The compulsice subordinate is ensuring domination and power by passive means, i.e. by indirect and manipulative influencing. This type is characterized by a sensitive conscience and extreme feelings of guilt. These feelings are combined with the wish to dominate authorities. There is a strong relation between the ambivalent feelings, the doubts and a stubbornness in his behavior and the fight against these wishes by the strong desires of conscience. These wishes and feelings of guilt derive from former experiences and are most of the time unconscious. Zaleznik means that the central conflict of the compulsive subordinate derives primarily from this unadequate balance between wishes of being dependent or independent.

5.3. The masochistic (submissive-active) subordinate

Masochism is defined as the feeling of lust while suffering pain (8). Real sadistic masochism is a severe psychic illness which has to be treated, in a minor form it can be found in the character of many people. Due to unconscious motivations a masochistic subordinate tries to submiss himself concerning the domination of authorities. The research work of Zaleznik shows that a submission in his way is combined with the intention to provoke aggressions by the authority in order to protect himself against aggressive intentions of the own self. The person concerned is afraid of his own aggressions and the possibility that he might lose self-control if they become free. He is constantly hurting himself instead of hurting others as a form of self-protection.

This type is the subordinate who tends to accidents. Unallowed aggressions towards the authority are answered by feelings of guilt, which lead to self-punishing activities such as accidents. These activities are most of the time unconscious and the person concerned is considered as a victim of unhappy circumstances. He does not know consciously that he himself created these circumstances.

A more subtile form of masochism is to reduce the own value by non-production. The explanation for this phenomenon cannot be found in the non-existing abilities or activities of the person concerned. In reality he cannot take over responsibility and acceptance due to unconscious motivations. He tries to be followed up and to be ashamed by an aggressor who only exists in fantasy. All these proceedings are parts of the unconsciousness and stand for wishes of the early childhood.

5.4. The withdrawn (sumissive-passive) subordinate

This subordinate has lost his interest for the outer world and turned it into the inside. His emotions take place in fantasies, hidden to other people. The person concerned does only react, when his environment becomes active, he himself is quite passive and does not show any emotional reactions. This is submission, because the work itself is no more of any importance.

Zaleznik (Zaleznik, 1975, p.94) believes that such a retreat is caused mainly by a lack in belief in the environment which is seen as hostile and mean. These are impressions which were gained also in the unconscious of early childhood. Zaleznik could find out in many discussions that in these cases the father was seen as passive-drawn back, and the mother as cold and hostile which made it impossible to live aggressions through. Aggressions against oneself may lead to depression. A withdrawn subordinate can be successful in the work he is used to do but he does not do more which does not lead to positive work relations.

In the final analysis I would like to stress out that Zaleznik only showed the extreme forms in the description and interpretation of the four schemes of behavior. Though people in subordinate positions tend to these four forms, one cannot deny a certain form of flexibility which is derived from the personality, the age and many other facts.

Nevertheless his demonstration is an important point of view in order to understand working relations which are more or less bad. Whatever happened to a singular person in the past in reality or in fantasy, is the foundation for his behavior towards other people, in his own family or at his place of work.

6. Aspects of Solving Conflicts

Submission conflicts can be the result of immature patterns of behavior of subordinates as well as authorities. Each person has to learn how to distinguish his reactions and those of other persons, to take over responsibility, e.g. not to make somebody else guilty for a difficult position of the own self. In order to overtake responsibility for the own behavior, one has to know consciously whether and to which extent inner conflicts of previous developments are playing a role in the interhuman relations of today. In those cases in which the past has displaced reality, it will be the best idea to advise a therapy to the person concerned.

Zaleznik (Zaleznik, 1975, p.107) advises first of all that the superior should avoid a paralysing reciprocal behavior. This means to avoid a behavior, which a subordinate expects from his superior when he has a conflict. Somebody for example who submisses himself in a masochistic form, is expecting punishment and an aggressive-authoritarian behavior. If this vicious circle is interrupted by the superior, the conflict can be reduced but not yet solved and the subordinate has to ponder about his personal situation which means a first step into the direction of change of behavior.

Zaleznik does not at all advise, to discuss emotional reasons of conflicts directly with the persons concerned in order to lead to a change of behavior. Such a behavior will lead first of all to resistance and hostile feelings, which avoid the solution of conflicts. Sometimes the "policy of small steps" is of great value, which means that parts of solutions are found and not that the conflict itself is solved directly.

7. Conclusion

From this short part out of "Human Dilemmas of Leadership" can be derived: interhuman relations which are based on the past and come up again in the presence are of deciding importance for relationships in work. Colleagues and superiors replace very often family members and previous relations and experiences. This phenomenon is called "transference" and means that extensive feelings, wishes and fantasies from the past are playing an important role in the present situation. (Nagera, 1991, p.484) This transference can be noticed in many relations of grown-ups, it influences how relations are seen in general. Knowing the background intensive and displaced emotional reactions which could not be explained before, can now be seen as transference. Even sudden changes in interhuman relations and in the style of work can sometimes be explained that unconscious and suppressed conflicts come to the surface.

Zaleznik shows in his work, that human behavior can be complex and that even analytically trained observers can only guess individual conflicts and tensions which are not yet conscious for the person concerned but may be expressed in an analytical dialogue. The work of an analytically trained consultant is similar to the work of an analyst. He has to understand from where psychic conflicts derive when persons in organizations are concerned. Psychic conflicts are a mixture of drives, fears, feelings of guilt and defense and show themselves in the behavior of the individual. (9) Private and official relations may suffer when two different neurotic ways of behavior are meeting. This leads to unhappiness and tension of the persons concerned who are not able to change their ways of behavior and their feelings. Analytically trained consultants who know that such conflicts may disturb not only relations in work and leadership but also the whole organization, can help the persons concerned to win new aspects and be of great help for the whole organization. In the United States the number of consultants with a psychoanalytic training is growing because the management sees that too many aspects, which have been denied, have to be taken into consideration. Hopefully this development will also take place in Europe.

NOTES

(1) Members of this organization, which was founded at the beginning of the eighties are mainly engaged how to apply psychoanalytical and therapeutical knowledge in management. The results are presented each year in conferences.

(2) "Human Dilemmas of Leadership" (in german language: "Das menschliche Dilemma der Führung") was published first in 1966 by Harper & Row.

(3) Another important book is "The Exceptional Executive" of Harry Levinson.

(4) See Zaleznik, A. and Kets de Vries, M.: "Power and the Corporate Mind".

(5) The following remarks concern chapter 1, 2, 3, 4 and 5 of "Das menschliche Dilemma der Führung".

(6) The basic research work of Sigmund Freud can be found in Freud S.,"Vorlesungen zur Einführung in die Psychoanalyse. Neue Folgen der Vorlesungen zur Einführung in die Psychoanalyse".

(7) The knowledge that diseases of stomach and intestine are in close connection with unsolved conflicts of dependency is scientifically accepted. See Uexküll, p.512.

(8) See Nagera (p.91) for the definition of the concept of masochism.

(9) See Nagera (p.19) for the problematic aspects of psychic conflicts of drives.

References

BRENNER, C. Grundzüge der Psychoanalyse. Frankfurt: Fischer, 1989.

FREUD, A. Das Ich und die Abwehrmechanismen. Frankfurt: Fischer, 1989.

FREUD, S. Vorlesungen zur Einführung in die Psychoanalyse. Neue Folge der Vorlesungen zur Einführung in die Psychoanalyse. Studienausgabe, Band 1, Frankfurt: Fischer, 1982.

LEVINSON, H. The Exceptional Executive. Cambridge: Harvard University Press, 1968.

NAGERA, H. Psychoanalytische Grundbegriffe. Frankfurt: Fischer 1991.

STOTZKA, H. Psychotherapie und Tiefenpsychologie. Wien und New York: Springer, 1982.

UEXKÜLL, T. Psychosomatische Medizin. München - Wien - Baltimore: Urban & Schwarzenberg, 1990.

ZALEZNIK, A., & KETS DE VRIES, M. Power and the Corporate Mind. Boston: Houghton Mifflin Company, 1975.

ZALEZNIK A. Das menschliche Dilemma der Führung. Wiesbaden: Betriebswirtschaftlicher Verlag Dr. Th. Gabler, 1975.

Contributors

Seth Allcorn, Ph.D., is Associate Dean for Fiscal Affairs at the Stritch School of Medicine, Loyola University, Chicago.

Gilles Amado-Fischgrund, DEA de gestion, is Professor of the Département Management et Ressources Humaines, Groupe HEC, Jouy-en-Josas, France and a practicing psychoanalyst.

Howell Steven Baum, Ph.D., is Professor of Planning of the Department of Urban Studies and Planning, University of Maryland, College Park, Maryland.

Michael A. Diamond, Ph.D., is Professor of Public Administration and Chair at the College of Business and Public Administration, University of Missouri, Columbia.

Leopold W. Gruenfeld, Ph.D., is Professor of the Department of Organizational Behavior, Field of Psychology, Industrial and Labor Relations, Cornell University, New York.

Larry A. Hirschhorn, Ph.D., is a principal of the Wharton Center for Applied Research, Inc. in Philadelphia, an independent management consulting company.

Manfred Kets de Vries, Ph.D., is Professor of Organizational Behavior and Management Policy, McGill University, Montreal, Canada, and a practicing psychoanalyst. He holds the Raoul de Vitry d´Avaucourt Chair of Human Resource Management at the European Institute of Business Administration (INSEAD) in Fontainebleau, France.

James Krantz, Ph.D., is Senior Fellow of the Wharton School, Center for Human Resources, Philadelphia, and Adjunct Assistant Professor of the Department of Social and Organizational Psychology, Columbia University. He is a principal of the organization consulting firm of Gould Krantz White.

Jean-Paul Larçon, Doctorate, is Associate Professor, Management Policy Centre d'Enseignement Supérieur des Affaires, Jouy-en-Josas, France, and Director of the Centre d'Enseignement et de Recherches Appliquées de Management at CERAM.

Harry Levinson, Ph.D., is Clinical Professor Emeritus of the Department of Psychiatry, Harvard Medical School, and Chairman of the Levinson Institute, Cambridge, Massachusetts.

Monika List, Magister, is University Assistant in the Department Wirtschafts- und Verwaltungsführung sowie Wirtschaftspädagogik, Wirtschaftsuniversität Wien, Austria.

Roland Reitter, D.B.A., is Professor of the Department Strategie et Politique d'ènterprise, Groupe HEC, Jouy-en-Josas, France.

Howard S. Schwartz, Ph.D., is Professor of Organizational Behavior at the School of Business Administration, Oakland University, Rochester, Michigan.

Howard F. Stein, Ph.D., is Professor of the Department of Family Medicine at the College of Medicine, University of Oklahoma Health Sciences Center, Oklahoma City, and Adjunct Associate Professor of the Department of Social Sciences and Health Behavior, College of Public Health, Oklahoma City.

Abraham Zaleznik, Ph.D., is Konosuke Matsushita Professor of Leadership and Emeritus at the Harvard University Graduate School of Business Administration, Boston, Massachusetts. He is a practicing psychoanalyst.

MIX
Papier aus verantwortungsvollen Quellen
Paper from responsible sources
FSC® C105338

If you have any concerns about our products,
you can contact us on
ProductSafety@springernature.com

In case Publisher is established outside the EU,
the EU authorized representative is:
Springer Nature Customer Service Center GmbH
Europaplatz 3, 69115 Heidelberg, Germany

Printed by Libri Plureos GmbH
in Hamburg, Germany